PALESTINE
A GUIDE

BY MARIAM SHAHIN
PHOTOGRAPHY BY GEORGE AZAR

With contributions by:
Inea Bushnaq: poetry and folklore; Taufic Haddad: refugee camps, Tiberias, and Bisan; Norman Ali Khalaf; flora and fauna; Michel Moushabeck: fiction in translation and music; Christiane Dabdoub Nasser: culinary traditions; Haifa Shawwa-Masri: traditional dress and jewelry.

D0103103

Interlink Books

First published in 2006 by

INTERLINK BOOKS
An imprint of Interlink Publishing Group, Inc.
46 Crosby Street, Northampton, Massachusetts 01060
www.interlinkbooks.com

Library of Congress Cataloging-in-Publication Data
Palestine : a guide / by Mariam Shahin ; photography by
George Azar—1st American ed.
p. cm.
ISBN 1-56656-557-X (pbk.)
1. Palestinian Arabs—History. 2. Palestinian Arabs—
Israel—Social life and customs. 3. Palestinian Arabs—Gaza
Strip—Social life and customs. 4. Palestinian Arabs—West
Bank—Social life and customs. 5. Israel—Descriptions and
travel. 6. West Bank—Descriptions and travel. 7. Gaza
Strip—Description and travel.
8. Cookery, Middle Eastern. I. Title.
DS113.7.S525 2005
305.892'7405694—dc22   2004022156

Publisher/Editor: Michel Moushabeck
Editorial Director: Pamela Thompson
Art Director: Juliana Spear
Editorial Assistant: Hilary Plum

Printed and bound in China

To request our complete 40-page full-color catalog,
please call us toll free at **1-800-238-LINK,** visit our
website at **www.interlinkbooks.com**, or write to
Interlink Publishing
46 Crosby Street, Northampton, MA 01060
e-mail: info@interlinkbooks.com

To our families and teachers
who shared their memories of Palestine

To our children
so they will cherish our heritage

And to those who still cannot visit their homeland

Acknowledgments

This book is the work of many. We would first like to thank the following contributors and co-authors: Taufic Haddad, who wrote about all the refugee camps and Tiberias and Bisan; Inea Bushnaq, the author of the chapter on literature and folklore; Christiane Dabdoub Nasser, the author of the chapter and sidebars on culinary traditions; Haifa Shawwa-Masri, the author of the chapters on the traditional dress and jewelry; Norman Ali Khalaf, whose work made possible the section on flora and fauna; and PENGON (Palestinian Environmental NGOs Network), which compiled the information in the section on the Wall.

Furthermore, this work would not have been possible without Tahani Tahboub and Mike Smeir, our research assistants, senior consultant Khaled al-Nashef, Moin Saddeq, and Saleh Abdul Jawad.

The many Palestinian academics and institutes have considerably facilitated our research: the Institute of Jerusalem Studies, the Applied Research Institute Jerusalem (ARIJ), the Palestinian Academic Society for the Study of International Affairs (PASSIA), the Institute of Palestine Studies, *All That Remains*, edited by Walid al-Khalidi, and the considerable volume of work by geographer Shukri Arraf.

The Higher Council for Arab Tourism in Jerusalem kindly supported this endeavor. But the views expressed within this book do not necessarily reflect the official views or policies of this organization, nor do the boundaries and names shown on any map, or referred to within, imply endorsement by any official channel or institution.

Maps were kindly made available by PASSIA and Negotiations Support Unit (NSU).

Thanks to Widad Kawar, for sharing her vast collection of historic Palestinian dresses and jewelry, which she kindly allowed us to photograph for the traditional dress and jewelry chapters. Thanks to Hala Abu Zayyad and Nadia Odeh for modeling them.

So many others have helped along the way: Abdul Kareem Ataita, Raed al-Atharmeh, Waleed Ayyoub, Azzeh al-Azzeh and family, Heba and Mohammad Farsakh, Enzo Gazzella, the Jedda family, the Husam Khader family, Sani Meo and the team at *This Week in Palestine*, Wafa Obeidat and the Hebron municipality, Nidal Rafi and family, Eyad Serraj, Amin Tukan, Jasmin Zahran, Maa'rouf Zahran and the Qalqilia municipality, and the Municipality of Deir al Balah and the Municipality of Tulkarem.

Finally, a very special thanks go to Tim Rothermel, Mounir Kleibo, and Abeer Nusseibeh. Without them, and my parents, Majdi and Anneliese Shahin, this book would never have seen the light of day.

—*Mariam Shahin*

Introduction

I gaze upon the procession of ancient prophets
Climbing barefoot to Urashalem
And I ask, will there be a new prophet for this new time?

I gaze upon the Persians, the Romans, the Sumerians
And the new refugees...

I gaze upon the wind chasing the wind
So that it might find a home on the wind

—"I See My Ghost Coming from Afar," Mahmoud Darwish

Perhaps there is a no more appropriate way to be introduced to Palestine and its people than through the works of its poets. For the dispossessed of the 20th century, poetry, song, and lore have largely taken on the significance of modern national symbols such as flags, passports, and borders. In a world where all nations carry flags, Palestine's flagship is its poetry and its poets are its most revered ambassadors.

To pretend that coming to Palestine is like visiting any other place in the world undermines not only its extraordinary history and unique contribution to world civilization, but also belies its unbelievably bizarre state of being in the 21st century. Taking into account both of these facts, this book is a search for all things Palestinian—past and present—in historic Palestine.

A land of many narratives, Palestine is a Holy Land to Muslims, Christians, and Jews; the homeland of the Palestinian people; and for the last 2,000 years perhaps the world's most sought after sliver of real estate. In the 20th century most of Palestine was usurped into a nation-state created by primarily European Jews and known as modern Israel. Inside Israel today, Palestine lives under house arrest, its people under siege and their identity negated to the status of "native."

For some million Palestinians who have been allowed to become citizens of Israel, existence on their native soil has often come at the price of suppressing both their identity and forfeiting their right to live as equals with those that rule. For the almost 3 million Palestinians who live in a series of reservation-like cities and towns, known as the

The Dome of the Rock seen from al-Aqsa Mosque

West Bank and Gaza Strip, clinging to their identity and their land has given them the privilege of being at the center of the most debated international political issue for the last three decades. They have the international status of an "occupied" people.

Half of all Palestinians live in the diaspora. They either have the status of refugees in host states or are nominal citizens in over 100 countries worldwide. An internationally backed peace plan, the Oslo Accords, has given Palestinians limited self-rule in a few select locations.

To understand what Palestine is and who the Palestinians are—to consider not only the current political reality, but also the history, religion, literature, music, art, and the natural world—makes for an astonishing voyage. Starting with the towns of pre-history like Jericho, Gaza, Jerusalem, or Tiberias and moving to the more "modern" cities of Bethlehem, Nablus, Haifa, or Ramallah, a contemporary journey of this rich and colorful society includes both visible and invisible histories and untold narratives. Contemporary Palestine is an overlapping and interwoven mosaic that no archeologist can fully explain. Palestinian tour guides, forbidden from working for decades, are back at work with a vast array of traditional and alternative tour itineraries. Whatever their perspective, their first words will always be "*Ahlan wa sahlan fi filistine*"—Welcome to Palestine.

A Palestinian woman shows off her grapes near Hebron

PART ONE

Palestinian Life

1.

A Brief History of Palestine

Palestine always brought to my mind a vague suggestion of a country as large as the United States.

—The Innocents Abroad, *Mark Twain, 19th century*

Palestine, the land of many narratives, contrasts, layers, and textures, was always a small country, measuring no more than 34,000 square kilometers (21,250 sq mi), positioned between Europe, Africa, and Asia. While for most of the last 2,000 years it has been known as the Holy Land, its history and culture reach back long past monotheism to some of the earliest stages of the development of humankind.

Paleolithic and Neolithic Periods: 1,000,000–5000 BCE

The earliest human remains in the area, found south of Lake Tiberias, date to about 600,000 BCE and belonged to the Neanderthal group. The 1925 unearthing of the "Palestine Man" in the Zuttiyeh Cave in Wadi Al-Amud (near Safad) shed unprecedented light on human development in the area.

The Natufian Culture, from 12,500 to 10,200 BCE, was notable for its use of stone, wood, and animal bone tools. Found in the caves of Shuqba (Ramallah) and Wadi Khareitun (Bethlehem), the Natufians were hunters, fishers, and gatherers of cereals. They are believed to have settled even before agriculture was introduced. Early religion, which included the belief in an afterlife, played a great role in their lives. Remains of that era have been found at Tel Abu Hureura, Ein Mallaha, Beidha, and Jericho.

Al-Radwan Castle, Gaza

3

Agricultural communities were established in the Neolithic period from 10,000 to 5000 BCE by what remained of the Natufian communities. Both rounded and square dwellings made of mud bricks, as well as pottery shards and remains of woven fabrics from this time, have been discovered at Tel al-Sultan, Jericho.

Bronze Age: 3000–1200 BCE

In the run-up to the Bronze Age, the Chalcolithic period (or the Copper or Ghassoulian Age) from 4500 to 3000 BCE was marked by the use of copper and stone tools and a culture that originated in Syria and prospered and flourished along the Jericho/Dead Sea–Bir es-Saba–Gaza and Sinai route. New migrant groups to the region then formed part of an increasingly urban fabric and culture during the Early Bronze Age.

The independent Canaanite city-states of the early Bronze Age (3000–2200 BCE) were situated mostly in plains or coastal regions, surrounded by defensive walls built of mud brick and guarded by watchtowers. Most of the cities were surrounded by agricultural hamlets, which supplied their food needs.

Trade and diplomatic relations with Egypt and Syria were significant. A thus far inexplicable series of events (ca. 2300 BCE) destroyed parts of the Canaanite urban civilization and was followed by incursions into the country by nomads from the east of the Jordan river, most of whom settled in the hill country.

Remnants from the early Canaanite era were found mainly at sites in northern and central Palestine, Tel Megiddo (near Nazareth), Jericho, Tel al-Far'a (Gaza), Bisan and Ai (Deir Dibwan/Ramallah District), Tel an Nasbe (al-Bireh) and Al-Jib (Jerusalem).

During the Middle Bronze Age (2200–1550 BCE) the highly politicized culture in Canaan was influenced by Egypt, Mesopotamia, Phoenicia, and Syria and boasted diverse commercial ties and an agriculturally based economy.

People developed new pottery forms, cultivated grapes, and used bronze extensively. Burial customs seemed to be significantly influenced by a belief in the afterlife. The Phoenicians became partners in the dye and textile industry and were paramount in the export and popularization of much coveted purple textiles.

The period in the Late Bronze Age between 1450–1350 BCE is vividly illustrated by several hundred cuneiform documents known as the Amarna Letters. These documents describe political, commercial, and military events in Canaan, as depicted by ambassadors and Canaan proxy rulers to the Egyptians.

Roman statues in Caesarea

In about 1250 BCE, the arrival of the Philistines, Sea Peoples from the Aegean, and the migration into Canaan of the Hebrews, changed the landscape forever. Both groups are believed to have mingled with the local population, but only the former fully amalgamated, losing its separate identity over several generations.

Iron Age: 1200–330 BCE

Remains of pottery decorated with stylized birds discovered in Askalan, Isdud, Gath, Ekron, and Gaza were the first evidence of Philistine communities in Palestine. The commerce-minded Philistines introduced new ways to ferment wine, as well as tools and weapons and chariots made with iron. The Philistines, unlike their neighbors the Hebrews, consumed pork and did not circumcise their men.

Constant conflict with the Hebrews, who had settled inland and became a considerable force, created much destruction and havoc as kingdoms were established and destroyed. According to Hebrew teaching, the Jewish King Solomon (970–928 BCE) built a great temple at this time. Though archeologists have yet to verify the historic existence of this temple, many of the stories in the Bible come from this time.

Although Ekron was still considered a distinctly Philistine city, by the time the Assyrians ruled Palestine in 722 BCE, the Philistines had become part and parcel of the local population and the "kingdom of Israel" had been destroyed. But it was not until 586 BCE, when the Babylonians stormed the country with their largely Chaldean troops and carried off significant numbers of the population into slavery, that the distinctly Philistine character of the coastal cities ceased to exist.

Persian Rule: 539 BCE

During Persian rule most people in Palestine lived in the shadows of their foreign rulers, often serving as soldiers and lay people in the administration and tending to agriculture. Sabastiya (near Nablus) was the northernmost province of the Persian administration; its southern borders were drawn at Hebron.

Almost parallel to Persian rule, the Nabateans (400 BCE–160 CE), with their capital in Petra (Jordan), made inroads into southern Palestine and built a separate and flourishing civilization in the Negev.

Unlike the Babylonians, the Persians favored certain groups in society and granted Jews the right to build synagogues and temples.

Hellenistic Rule: 333 BCE

Alexander the Macedonian took Palestine in a bid to control the East–West trade routes and then enslaved most of the local population. During this era, extensive growth and development changed the landscape of the country, giving rise to urban planning and the establishment of impressively well built fortified cities. Hellenistic pottery flourished, absorbing the Philistine tradition. Trade and commerce grew, especially in the most Hellenized areas: Nablus (Sabastiya, Tel Balata and Jabal Jirzim), Jerusalem, Jaffa, Askalan, and Gaza.

Roman Rule: 63 BCE

Although General Pompeii arrived in 63 BCE, Roman rule did not really begin in earnest until Herod the Edumite was appointed king.

Under the Romans, urban planning grew to new heights. Cities were designed around two main streets (the Cardo from north to south and the Peladious from east to west) that intersected at the Forum, the center of the city. Sabastiye and Nablus are among the best examples of Roman cities in Palestine.

Connected through an extensive network of roads developed for military and economic purposes, the country was run like clockwork. Herodion (Tel al-Fureidis) to the south of Bethlehem, Herod's winter palace in Jericho (Tulul Abu al-Alayiq), and Caesarea Maritima (Caesarea) are among the most notable remnants of this era.

Nevertheless, the decentralization this growth demanded created instability, and by the time that Christ was born, Roman Palestine was in a state of disarray. Direct Roman rule was re-established and Christianity, along with freedom of expression, was oppressed. During this era, the country became known as Syria Palaestina. While most inhabitants became Romanized, others, especially Jews, found the rule of empire unbearable, and bloody revolts punctuated this period of history.

The Emperor Hadrian (132 CE) made Jerusalem into a Greco-Roman city, renaming it Aelia Capitalina and building temples to Jupiter. Meanwhile, Christianity was still practiced in secret and Tiberias became the seat of the exiled Jewish patriarchs. The Hellenization of Palestine continued under Septimius Severus (193–211 CE), and new cities were founded at Eleutheropolis (Beit Jibrin), Diospolis (Lydd), and Nicopolis (Emmaus).

Byzantine Rule: 330–640 CE

Although Christianity was born in Palestine, it was not until Emperor

Constantine I converted around 330 CE, that it became the country's official religion. The Church of the Holy Sepulcher was built after his mother, the Empress Helena, identified the spot she believed to be the site of Christ's death and crucifixion. During Constantine's reign the Church of the Nativity in Bethlehem and the Church of Ascension in Jerusalem were also constructed.

Thus Palestine became the world's greatest pilgrimage site. It became the center for ascetic life for men and women from all over the world, who came to the Palestinian wilderness to become hermits. Soon it was dotted with monasteries, many of which can still be visited today. They include St. George Monastery in Wadi al-Qilt, Deir Quruntul and Deir Hijle next to Jericho, and Deir Mar Saba and Deir Theodosius east of Bethlehem, as well as the remains of many others in the Negev and Gaza.

Constantine added the southern half of Arabia to the province of Palestine, naming it Palestine Tertia. At the end of the 4th century, Palestine was divided into three provinces: Palaestina Prima, with its capital at Caesarea; Palaestina Secunda, with its capital at Scythopolis (Bisan); and Salutaris, with its capital at Petra. Jerusalem became the spiritual capital of the Byzantine world.

In the meantime, in the year 352, a Jewish revolt against Byzantine/Roman rule at Tiberias and in other parts of the Galilee, was brutally suppressed. In 611 the Persian forces launched an invasion, capturing Jerusalem in 614. By most accounts they were destructive, safeguarding only the Church of Nativity in Bethlehem from their swords. The Byzantines briefly regained power in the ravaged land, only to concede it soon afterward to the newly converted Islamic tribes from the Arabian Peninsula.

Arab–Islamic Rule: 638

In 638 CE, Caliph Omar Ibn al-Khatab (634–44 CE) and Safforonius, the Byzantine governor of Jerusalem, signed *Al-Uhda al-'Omariyya*, an agreement that stipulated the rights and obligations of all non-Muslims in what had become Muslim Palestine.

In an unprecedented show of humility, Omar was the first conqueror of Jerusalem to enter the city on foot. Muslim rule came relatively easy, as the population had grown weary of an archaic Byzantine system. Palestine was proclaimed a blessed land in the Quran, the sacred book of Islam, and Jerusalem was home to the first *kiblah* toward which, until 623, Muslims turned in prayer. When visiting the Haram al-Sharif, Omar declared it a "sacred" place of prayer.

Al-Jazzar Mosque, Acre

In the registry of the Muslim Arabs who entered Palestine, the following cities accepted their rule: Jerusalem, Nablus, Jenin, Acre, Tiberias, Bisan, Caesarea, Lajjun, Lydd, Jaffa, Imwas, Beit Jibrin, Gaza, Rafah, Hebron, Yubna, Haifa, Safad, and Askalan.

Jews were allowed to return to Jerusalem after a 500-year ban stipulated by the Romans and maintained by the Christian rulers.

Umayyad Rule: 661–750

The Umayyads were the first Muslim dynasty to rule Palestine. Renaming it Jund Filastin and establishing their political and military capitol in Ramleh, they maintained Jerusalem as a spiritual capital. The Caliph Abd al-Malik ibn Marwan (685–705) ordered the building of the Dome of the Rock in 691 on the site where the Prophet Muhammad began his nocturnal journey to heaven. This is the oldest existing Muslim shrine of prayer in Palestine. Just to the south of the Dome, Caliph Al-Walid I (705–715), had the Al-Aqsa mosque built.

Remains of Hisham's Palace, Jericho

Beyond Jerusalem, the Umayyads made architectural contributions in Ramleh, Jericho, and Tiberias. Christians (including Arabs, Greeks, and Armenians) and Jews were given the official title "Peoples of the Book," in reference to the monotheistic roots that they shared with Islam. With Umayyad rule came an increase of influence of the tribes of Yemen, one of the two main Arab tribal confederations.

Abbasid Rule: 750–969

Although the Baghdad-based Abbasid Caliphs al-Mansur and al-Mahdi visited and paid homage to Muslim shrines and sanctuaries in Jerusalem and built up Ramleh, Palestine was not as central to the Abbasid realm as it was to that of their predecessors. Still, historians of the period noted that Palestine was among the most prosperous and fertile regions of the Muslim empire at this juncture.

Under Abbasid rule, the coastal areas were fortified and developed. Port cities such as Acre, Haifa, Caesarea, Arsuf, Jaffa, and Askalan received financial support from the state treasury. On September 15th of every year, a trade fair took place in Jerusalem where merchants from Pisa, Genoa, Venice, and Marseilles converged on the city to buy and sell their goods. Spices, silks, soap, olive oil, glassware, and sugar were traded for European products. The Europeans prayed and made generous donations to the Christian shrines of Jerusalem and Bethlehem.

The Abbasids were allied to the Qays, a northern Arabian tribal confederation, who made up the vast majority of their ruling army. At this time enmity between those Palestinians allied to the Yemen (largely introduced by the Umayyads) and those allied to the Qais began. This division continued to be a significant factor in Palestine's political life until the beginning of the 20th century.

Fatimid Rule: 969–1099
The Fatimids, a dynasty claiming descent from the Prophet Muhammad through the line of his daughter Fatima, proclaimed themselves caliphs from their base in Tunisia and conquered Palestine after taking control of Egypt. Their rule in Palestine was marked by an architectural revival. Jerusalem, Nablus, and Askalan were rebuilt, expanded, and renovated.

In 1071, the Isfahan-based Seljuk Turks captured Jerusalem only to hand it back to the Fatimids in 1098.

Crusader Rule: 1099–1187
The Crusades effectively diverted the attention of a disgruntled European populace to Islam, an outside "enemy" that ruled the most holy sites in all of Christendom. Known as the "Latin Kingdom" of Jerusalem, the almost 200-year long European rule in Palestine (1099–1187) was as repressive as it was foreign.

The most notable architectural achievements were largely in the rural areas, although at least one spectacular urban remnant of this era remains in Acre. Many fortifications, castles, towers, and fortified villages were built, rebuilt, and renovated across Palestine at this time.

At the same time that Jews, Muslims, and Orthodox Christians were killed, expelled, or condemned to lives of menial labor, intermarriage with local women and conversions of smaller communities to Islam were not uncommon. Wars were periodically interrupted by truces.

In July 1187 the Cairo-based Kurdish General Saladin and his troops challenged European hegemony and won a decisive battle crushing Crusader forces at the Battle of Hittin, near Tiberias. Although Saladin liberated Jerusalem, an agreement granting special status to the Crusaders allowed them to stay in the country. In 1229, the German Frederick II negotiated a ten-year treaty that temporarily restored Jerusalem, Nazareth, and Bethlehem to Crusader rule.

But by 1270 the Mamluk leader, Sultan Baibars, expelled the Crusaders from most of the country with the exception of Acre, from which they fled in 1291. The surviving Europeans either went home or merged with the local population.

Mamluk Rule: 1260–1516

The Crusaders had challenged the right of non-Western Christians to live freely in Palestine and thus, almost as a reaction, Mamluk rule brought about a literary, cultural, and religious revival for Muslims and Arabs.

Palestine under early Mamluk rule saw a period of prosperity. In Jerusalem, the government sponsored an elaborate program for the construction of schools, lodgings for travelers and Muslim pilgrims, and the renovation of mosques that had been neglected or desecrated during the Crusader era.

During this period Arab and Muslim writers emphasized Palestine's role as the blessed land of the Prophets and Islam's revered leaders. Muslim sanctuaries were "rediscovered" and celebrated as places of pilgrimage. The Haram al-Sharif in Jerusalem, the Haram al-Khalil in Hebron, the shrines of al-Hussein in Askalan, Sukayna in Tiberias, the Shrine of Hashim in Gaza, the Nabi Salih, Nabi Musa, and Haram Sidna 'Ali (north of Jaffa) are but a few examples of Muslim pilgrimage sites that were reborn during this era.

Palestine formed a part of the district of Damascus, second in importance only to Egypt in the Mamluk domains. It was divided into three districts with three regional capitals– Jerusalem, Gaza, and Safad.

The Mamluk era can be divided into the Bahri Period (1270–1382) and the Burji Period (1382–1517). The former was a peaceful and prosperous reign, while the latter witnessed the last onslaught of the Mongols. Although Palestine itself was spared the pillaging, it could not escape the disastrous repercussions. In the ensuing century, the Mamluks were pitted against the increasingly powerful Ottoman Turks in a battle for the control of western Asia. Hostilities broke out in 1486 and reached their climax three decades later at the battle of Marj Dapiq (1516), when the Ottoman Sultan, Selim I, routed the Mamluk armies.

Ottoman Rule: 1516–1917

Prosperity and development were the landmarks of the first century of Ottoman rule in Palestine. The accomplishments of Suleiman the Magnificent in Jerusalem and elsewhere have yet to be matched. Ottoman Palestine initially consisted of five districts: Gaza, Jerusalem, Nablus, Lajjun (Jenin district), and Safad. During the 16th century, Palestine was the main producer of cotton in the Ottoman Empire. Cereals, olives, and grapes were also produced in large quantities and exported to Egypt and Istanbul.

Among the cities of Palestine, Jerusalem, Safad, Gaza, Nablus, and Hebron were the most prosperous. The local and regional trade routes were efficiently served with khans, wells, cisterns or pools, bridges, and in some cases castles for security control. Building activities flourished within and without the towns. Jerusalem's walls were rebuilt and an improved water system, which brought water from Suleiman's Pools in Bethlehem through the stone aqueduct Qanat as-Sabil, was constructed. Palestine was a culturally and administratively developed land, with dozens of towns and hundreds of villages, organized trade-routes, and cultivated fertile land.

The deterioration of the central government in Istanbul in the 17th century brought decline to Palestine, although in the beginning of the 18th century some of its prosperity was regained as cotton again became a significant export. A self-sufficient agricultural economy grew, relying largely on the cultivation of olives and the production of olive oil. Cotton-spinning, glass-making, tanning, and leather industries were expanding. The central and southern coastal plains were producing wheat, sorghum, and sesame, as well as cotton.

The healthy economic conditions in Palestine that coincided with the overall weakness of the central

Throne Villages

With the weakening of centralized Ottoman authority, strong local leaders emerged throughout Palestine. These leaders, often tax collectors for the Ottomans, assumed the status of rural nobility and achieved great political and socio-economic power in their local areas, and sometimes beyond. Their power bases were called *kursi* (throne) villages, where they ruled from semi-urbanized residential and administrative compounds.

The twenty-some throne villages in Palestine, with their grand rural mansions and castles, remained significant on some level well into the 20th century. Indeed, the castles still provide an architectural narrative of this historical period. But the true authority of the throne villages came to an end with Ibrahim Pasha's invasion of Palestine (1831–1840).

Jerusalem is a museum of Mamluk and Ottoman architecture

Ottoman administration of the 18th century led to the rise of local powers in many parts of the country. They included Dhaher al-Omar al-Zaidani in the Galilee, the Notables of Jerusalem and Nablus, and the Chiefs of the various central mountain regions.

Most important of these local powers was the Arab tribal leader al-Zaidani, who ruled the whole of northern Palestine for more than three decades (1840s to 1875), largely by monopolizing the cotton trade. He built many castles in Galilean towns, but his greatest achievement was the revival and development of Acre. After managing to bring the most important European cotton merchants to the town, he improved and reconstructed its walls, built bazaars, caravansaries, public baths, mosques, and even churches. Acre rose from a very modest port into a busy town of 25,000 inhabitants, the largest in Palestine, and the third largest in southern Syria. Al-Zaidani was one of the few ethnic Arabs to rule at least part of Palestine successfully in the post-Crusader era.

When Napoleon decided to invade Syria in 1799 with his army of 13,000 men, he stormed Gaza. Jaffa was sacked and plundered, and a massive attack on Acre followed. Acre resisted occupation, and after a two-month siege, Napoleon was forced retreated. For the Arabs of Acre, this defeat of Napoleon remains a point of pride to this day.

Still, it took decades for Palestine to recover from Napoleon's destruction. The reconstruction in Jaffa and Gaza did not start until the 1820s. In 1812 the villages around Nazareth, which had been depopulated by Napoleon's troops, were still empty. Nablus, Jerusalem, and Hebron witnessed a population explosion as the refugees from the Galilee and the Marj Ibn Amr area fled into these areas.

It was during this period that many local feudal families were able to obtain political, social, and economic powers that enabled them to amass relatively large fortunes. With them, they built large fortified residences, castles, and villages, which became known as Throne Villages.

Women chat in the Old City of Jerusalem

In 1831 the armies of the Albanian ruler of Egypt, Muhammad Ali, occupied Palestine, and for nine years he and his son, Ibrahim Pasha, gave it a centralizing and modernizing administration. Taxes were increased and urban rebellions broke out against the regime, which had also opened the door to foreign missionaries and religious zealots. When in 1840 the British, the Austrians, and the Russians came to the aid of the Ottomans, Ibrahim Pasha was forced to withdraw and Palestine was pulled back into the Ottoman Empire. Increased security in the countryside and a revision of laws (known as *Tanzimat*) in 1858 led to the development of private property, agricultural production for the world market, the decline of tribal social organization, growth of the population, and the enrichment of the feudal classes.

As the Ottomans extended Istanbul's new military, municipal, judicial, and educational systems to Palestine, a delegation of Palestinian representatives attended the first session of the Ottoman Parliament in Istanbul in 1877.

But the country also witnessed a marked increase in foreign settlements and colonies—French, Russian, German, and Austrian. By far the most important, though they seemed numerically insignificant at the time, were the Zionist agricultural outposts, which foreshadowed what was to come. Russian Jews established the earliest of these settlements in 1878, known as Petach Tiqwa.

Jews had lived in Jerusalem, Safad, Tiberias, and Hebron (except during the Crusade period) almost without interruption since the beginning of Muslim rule for a period of 1,300 years. They were almost entirely Sephardic Jews. The new immigrants were almost entirely Europeans, mostly not religious. By 1903, 25,000 had come to Palestine with the intention of creating a Jewish state and essentially evicting the Palestinians.

The population of Palestine increased from 275,000 in 1800 to 446,000 by 1878. It was an era of urbanization, in which the population of the twelve major Palestinian towns more than doubled between 1800 and 1880. And by 1909, the first Jewish city, Tel Aviv, was built north of Jaffa.

1900 to 1948

The Palestinian Arabs rediscovered their Arab identity when a split in the country, between those that supported Arab self-determination and those that supported pan-Ottoman/Islamic policies, came to the fore. But firm anti-Zionist stand was already well developed by all sides before the end of Ottoman rule in 1918, when the population of Palestine was about 700,000 (620,000 Arabs and 80,000 Jews).

PALESTINE IN 1878, SHOWING THE FIRST JEWISH SETTLER COLONY

- Jewish colony
- Palestinian village
- Palestinian town
- Mixed town
- - Frontier of Mandate Palestine
  (excluding the Negev) in 1922

Mediterranean Sea

Acre

Safed

Sea of Galilee

Haifa

Nazareth

Tiberias

Jenin

Beisan

Tulkarem

Nablus

Petach Tikva

Qalqilya

Jaffa

Lydda

Ramallah

Ramleh

Jericho

Jerusalem

Majdal

Bethlehem

Dead Sea

Hebron

Gaza

As World War I raged in Europe, Palestine's Arabs believed they would get independence in return for their support of Britain against the Axis powers. But by May 1916 the Sykes–Picot Agreement had already decided Palestine's fate as a British colony. To make matters worse, by 1917 the British government had issued the Balfour Declaration, which supported the Zionist aspirations for Palestine to be a national home for Jews.

By February 1919 the first Palestinian Arab Congress in Jerusalem voted to reject the Balfour Declaration and opted to unite with Syria under the leadership of Prince Faisal Hussein Ibn Ali. The French forced Faisal to give up his newly founded kingdom of Syria by June 1920 and some believe that this was the beginning of the Palestinian catastrophe.

After a reaffirmation of the Sykes–Picot plan at San Remo, the British government appointed Sir Herbert Samuel as de facto ruler of Palestine. Samuel, like Balfour, was a British Zionist of Jewish descent. The Palestinians became increasingly wary of the Zionist plan, and established an Arab Executive Committee to represent their interests. The Committee was never recognized by the British Mandate government and was dissolved in 1934. The Committee stood against the Balfour Declaration and decreed that Palestine's Arabs demanded an autonomous Arab entity and rejected the rights of Jews to a separate autonomy in Palestine. This remained the position of most Palestinians until 1988.

In 1922 the British government declared in its White Paper that Britain, did "not contemplate that Palestine as a whole should be converted into a Jewish National Home, but that such a Home should be founded in Palestine." Later that year the forerunner of the United Nations, the League of Nations, dominated by the European powers, supported British rule and policies in Palestine, giving the division of the country a semblance of international legitimacy.

Arab nationalist activities became fragmented and community leaders, largely led by feudal families, lost every opportunity to make gains for the population and country as a whole. Meanwhile, the Jewish national home project continued and consolidated itself with urban, agricultural, social, cultural, and industrial development. When clashes in which hundreds of Jews and Arabs were killed sounded alarm bells in London and led to a reconsideration of its policies, Zionists worldwide protested and the British government retracted.

As persecution of Jews in Europe grew in the 1930s, immigration to Palestine increased. By 1936, the Jewish population had reached 400,000 (30 percent of the total). The Arab population of

Administrative Boundaries under the British Mandate, 1940s

Administrative Boundaries in the West Bank under Jordan, 1948-1967

ADMINISTRATIVE BOUNDARIES OF PALESTINE THROUGHOUT THE 20TH CENTURY

West Bank and Gaza Strip According to the Israeli Administration after 1967

West Bank and Gaza Strip According to the Palestinian Authority Governorate Divisions, 1995

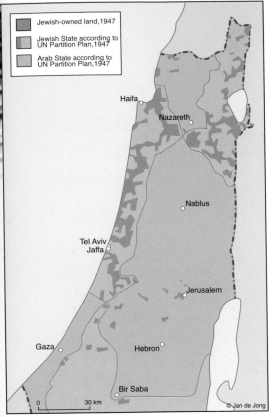

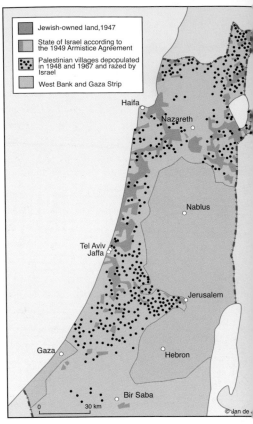

LAND OWNERSHIP IN PALESTINE AND THE UN PARTITION PLAN, 1947

PALESTINIAN VILLAGES DEPOPULATED IN 1948 & 1967 AND RAZED BY ISRAEL

Palestine also grew, partly because of natural increase, and to a lesser extent because the British and Jewish capital infusion to the country created jobs.

During this period, the disenfranchisement of the Arab peasantry increased and urbanization created a new working poor in the cities. The situation was extreme enough that although their livelihood depended on British jobs and Jewish industries, Arabs supported a boycott of British- and Jewish-owned goods. Thus the 1936 Arab revolt began. Thousands of Palestinians from all backgrounds and classes were mobilized and the British reinforced their occupation army with 20,000 more troops.

The revolt was led by followers of Izzedin al-Qassam, a Syrian-born opponent to colonialism in the Arab world, who had become popular with the new urban poor. Al-Qassam was able to channel their resentment at being dispossessed of their land and having to build Jewish housing for a living into a widespread rebellion; for this, the British killed him in 1935.

Leaders of the Palestinian general strike called for a nonpayment of taxes and the shutting down of municipal governments until national independence was granted. The rebellion was led by local rural leaders and fought by village partisans. The British decided that the only solution was to divide the country. The British government officially spoke of a Jewish state with a disproportionately large land allotment for the Jewish population and a mass transfer of the Arab population from the proposed Jewish state—in effect, they sanctioned ethnic cleansing.

The momentum of the Arab revolt increased and by 1937 the British declared martial law. Arab politicians were arrested and deported and Arab institutions shut down. Some 5,000 Palestinians were killed, 15,000 wounded, and 6,000 imprisoned.

Then, as World War II forced aside all concerns but the need for allies, the British seemed to retract their support for the Zionists. But it was already too late: the Zionist project in Palestine had progressed to the point where its own Jewish army of almost 20,000 was ready to go it alone. American Zionists, too, began playing an important role.

While 27,000 Jews enlisted in the British army, an almost equal number (23,000) of Palestine Arabs also served with the Allies. General Arab support of the Allies was stressed at the 1944 Alexandria meeting of Arab leaders, which urged European and Jewish leaders not to make the Palestinian Arabs pay for the crimes of the West against the Jews. In 1945, the Arab League appointed an Arab Higher Executive for Palestine (the Arab Higher Committee), which included a broad spectrum of Palestinian leaders, to speak for the Palestinian Arabs.

A UN Special Committee on Palestine recommended the partition of the country into an Arab and a Jewish state on August 31, 1947—with 55 percent of Palestine going to the Zionists. Jerusalem was to be international. The Arab and Islamic states attempted, unsuccessfully, to question the International Court of Justice on the competence of the General Assembly to partition a country against the wishes of the majority of its inhabitants (by 1946 there were 1,269,000 Arabs and 678,000 Jews in Palestine). Britain set its own date to withdraw from Palestine at May 15, 1948.

Soon after the UN resolution, fighting broke out. By the time a ceasefire was signed, Zionist forces occupied 78 percent of Palestine. The violent birth of Israel led to what amounted to the ethnic cleansing of more than 750,000 Palestinians. More than 400 Arab communities were systematically destroyed, and Arab life in many coastal cities ceased.

A schoolgirl in the alleyways of Hebron

2.

The Palestinians

Enough for me to die on her earth
Be buried in her
To melt and vanish into her soil
Then sprout forth as a flower
Played with by a child from my country
Enough for me to remain
In my country's embrace
To be in her close as a handful of dust
A sprig of grass
A flower

— "Enough for Me," *Fadwa Tuqan, translated by*
Naomi Shihab Nye, 20th century

Today there are an estimated 7 million Palestinians worldwide. About 4 million live in what was Palestine proper; just over 1 million of these are Israeli nationals, and the rest carry Palestinian National Authority (PNA) IDs, Jerusalem IDs, or refugee cards. Of the 3 million living in the diaspora, about 2 million live nearby in Jordan, Lebanon, and Syria. The rest are residents in the Arab Gulf countries, Egypt, Western Europe, and North and South America. Small communities exist in the rest of the world.

The Palestinians are ethnically and religiously diverse. Since the term "Philistine" became a point of reference more than 3,000 years ago, Palestinians have distinguished themselves by their ability to adapt to and absorb other cultures, ethnic groups, and even religious identities. Although today the vast majority of Palestinians define themselves as Arabs, many are an ethnic mélange.

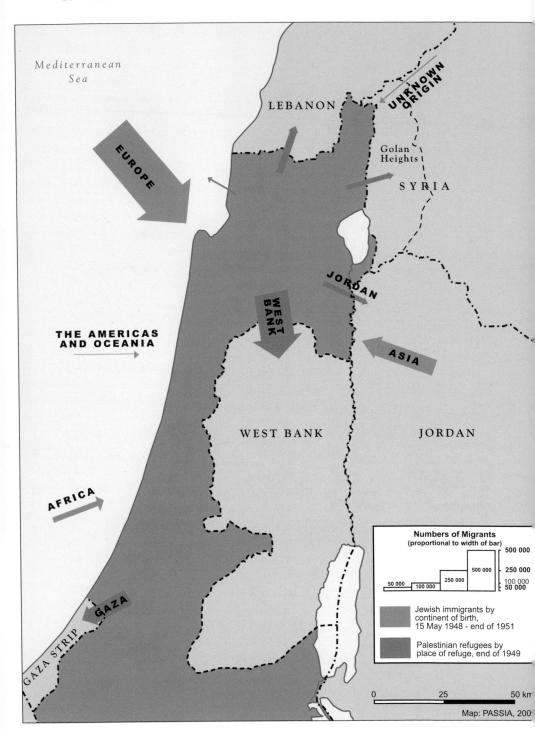

EXODUS OF PALESTINIANS AND INFLUX OF JEWISH SETTLERS

The Arabs of Palestine, even when tribal, tended to be socially inclusive. Mostly through intermarriage, outsiders—Europeans, Turks, Greeks, Armenians, Persians, Jews, East Asians, and Africans—became part of the Palestinian family. While many communities that made their home in Palestine maintained separate city quarters and neighborhoods, they were never excluded if they wished to join the majority. This was, and to some extent still is, a quality that distinguishes Palestinian society; it has comparatively little prejudice toward peoples of "other" races, ethnic groups, or religions. Thus Palestinians can be black, white, Asian, Muslim, Christian, Jewish, agnostic or atheist.

Official figures don't always reflect this diversity. According to the registrars, some 85 percent of Palestinians are officially Muslim, a category that can be broadly divided into practicing Muslims and secular Muslims. Though most of the 15 percent of Palestinian Christians live in the diaspora, they play a visible role in the political, economic, social, and cultural life of the entire Palestinian community.

The multiculturalism that exists like a second skin in Palestinian society has been partially suppressed since Israel took over Palestine. The essentially non-inclusive nature of the occupation has created a sometimes reactionary and certainly more defined sense of self and "otherness" among the Palestinians.

In Israel

Approximately 150,000 Palestinians were "allowed" to stay in what became Israel in 1948. Those that remained were mostly from rural areas, but with their agricultural land confiscated by the newly established state, they migrated to the cities and many became unskilled wage laborers, working in Jewish industries and construction companies.

As citizens of the state of Israel, they are guaranteed equal rights with Jewish citizens, in theory. In reality, however, they lived under military jurisdiction until 1966. Their political rights and personal freedoms were restricted and it was not until the 1990s that they became politically active in a significant way.

Israel sought to block the development of a cohesive national consciousness among the Palestinians by administratively dividing them into "minority" groups, such as Druze, Circassians, Bedouin, and Arab. By focusing on media and education as a means of creating a new Israeli–Arab society, which lived alongside but was not equal to the Jewish society, Israel tried to placate the Palestinians.

For almost twenty years after the establishment of Israel, Israeli Arabs were isolated from other Palestinians. But the years following the 1967 war brought resumed contact with the Palestinians of the West Bank and the Gaza Strip. By the late 1960s, with the total decline of Palestinian agricultural communities and a change in social consciousness, many Palestinian Israelis began identifying with left-wing politics. Some married Israeli Jews and began working toward creating a society that would not differentiate among its citizens.

By the 1980s the Palestinian–Israeli economy had gained some autonomy, as the community made the transition from farming and unskilled work to business ownership. During this time, as the Islamist movement grew throughout the Middle East, the traditional left-wing and secular tendencies of Palestinian Arabs shifted. Today the more than 1 million Arab Israelis are politically divided, about 40/60, between Islamist religious parties and secular parties. The emergence of charismatic leaders and the proliferation of Arab satellite television stations have brought Palestinians inside Israel closer today to the rest of Arab society than they have been since 1948. The inability of the Israeli establishment to relinquish rule of the West Bank and Gaza and its unwillingness to be a state of all its citizens rather than simply a Jewish state, has reinforced the believe among Palestinian Israelis that Israel does not seek a fair and just solution to the conflict.

In Jordan

Prior to 1948 social, clan, and economic relations between Jordanians and Palestinians had been strong and marked by multiple unifying factors. Borders were open and intermarriage was both common and encouraged by an Arab tradition that fostered tribal alliances to boost prestige, wealth, and strength. The Jordanian monarchy did not find it difficult to integrate Palestinians into its population. From 1948 until its recognition of the PLO as the "sole legitimate representative of the Palestinian people" in 1976, Jordan often acted as a surrogate speaker for the Palestinian people. It provided education and, in 1949, extended citizenship to Palestinians within its administrative borders. Initially educated, middle-class Palestinians lived in Jordanian cities and were free to compete for positions within the government and establish commercial establishments, while less fortunate Palestinians filled the UN-established refugee camps.

During the late 1960s and early '70s, a majority of Palestinians, from both rural and middle-class backgrounds opted to support "nationalist" Palestinian aspirations against the surrogate state, Jordan, in what was essentially a class struggle. Most Palestinians and many Jordanians supported pan-Arab and socialist policies toward the State of Israel, rather than the more cautious positions of Jordan's King Hussein. But with the Israeli occupation of the West Bank in 1967 and the birth of an independent Palestinian fighting force, the PLO, a line was drawn in the sand.

After the 1967 war, an understanding was reached whereby the Jordanian government allowed PLO guerrillas independent control of their own bases in the Jordan Valley, but relations between the government and the guerrillas remained uneasy. Tensions between the Jordanian army and the Palestinian guerrillas erupted in a brief but bloody war in September 1970, known as Black September, in which up to 5,000 people are believed to have died. Backed by the US and regional powers, the Jordanian army defeated the Palestinian guerrillas, who sought new bases in Lebanon.

Today most Palestinians in Jordan have become Jordanians, much as American Jews are American. Their advocates consider them social, economic, and cultural assets; their critics claim they are a fifth column.

In the Gaza Strip with Egypt

The relationship between the Gaza Strip and Egyptian administrators (1948–1967) can only be fully understood in the context of the historical relationship between Egypt and Palestine, which dates back nearly 4,000 years. Despite a lack of democratic and economic participation, Palestinians did not see the Egyptians as occupiers.

During the 20-year Egyptian rule of the Gaza Strip, this formerly glorious Philistine stronghold turned into a giant reservation for refugees, who made up some 80 percent of the population. Unlike West Bankers and refugees in Jordan, Palestinians living in the Gaza Strip were not given citizenship. Thus they were legally stateless. Yet though Gazans had relatively little control over local administration, they were allowed to attend Egyptian universities, which were considered among the best in the Arab world.

The Gaza Strip, 25 miles long and 4 or 5 miles wide, has become one of the most densely populated areas of the world. While the Israelis confiscated much of Gaza's agricultural lands and Egypt allowed for only a little industry, commerce flourished. Gaza became a kind of duty-free port for Egyptians. Although some Gaza Strip Palestinians were able to find employment elsewhere, most had no alternative but to stay in Gaza, despite its lack of natural resources and jobs. The Egyptian rule of the Gaza Strip ended when Israel occupied the Gaza Strip in June 1967.

In Lebanon

Palestinians from the northern parts of Palestine considered Lebanon as much a part of their natural geographic and cultural domain as West Bankers saw Jordan. Prior to 1948, Palestine was home to many Lebanese landowners and peasants. They shared a culture, language, culinary tradition, and a host of regional particularities that resulted from their sharing an extended part of the Mediterranean coast. At various periods in history Palestine and Lebanon were administered by the same rulers. Borders were non-existent, intermarriage was the norm, and trade relations enriched both communities.

Many of the wealthiest and most educated Palestinians made Lebanon their home-in-exile after 1948. West Beirut, once dominated by Sunni Muslims and Greek Orthodox Christians, became reinvigorated as a capital of culture, learning, and commerce. Beirut flourished as the Palestinians brought their airlines, their banks, their businesses, and their know-how to the Lebanese capital.

But that was only one element of the Lebanese–Palestinian relationship in the post-1948 period. Along with thousands of upper-income merchants and intellectuals came nearly 200,000 destitute refugees. Living on the economic, political and social periphery, they espoused the radical politics of the dispossessed. When the Palestine Liberation Organization (PLO) was expelled from Jordan in 1970 and regrouped in Lebanon, they found a population thirsty for liberation— from poverty and political and social disenfranchisement.

Initially the PLO found support among poor Lebanese, notably Shiite Muslims. But the PLO's creation of an armed mini-state within Lebanon and the subsequent Israeli attacks on both Palestinian and Lebanese population centers were more than enough to pitch the already delicately balanced sectarian Lebanese society, and the Palestinians resident there, headlong into civil war.

In June 1982 Israel launched a full-scale invasion of Lebanon and over the course of two months, lay siege to the capital Beirut. Its aim was the establishment of a client regime in Lebanon and the liquidation of the PLO. The United States eventually brokered an agreement and the PLO left Lebanon. The Palestinian refugees who had found protection under the PLO umbrella were left defenseless and many were killed in the landmark massacres in Beirut's Sabra and Shatilla refugee camps.

Many Lebanese blamed the PLO and its policies for the destruction of their country and the combined deaths of some 150,000 Lebanese and Palestinians over the course of the war.

Political Parties and Movements

Before the official birth of the PLO (Palestine Liberation Organization) in 1964, the Palestine National Liberation Movement, known in Arabic by its acronym, Fatah, had begun the training of guerrilla fighters to liberate Palestine. The strategy of armed struggle had been decided upon in the 1950s. After its formal establishment at the 1964 Arab summit meeting in Cairo, the PLO, a political umbrella organization of several Palestinian political groups (including Fatah), consistently claimed to be the sole and legitimate representative of all Palestinians. Its first leader was Ahmad Shukairy, a member of the Palestinian bourgeoisie with little popular support. By 1969 a member of the Palestinian middle class and former student activist, Yasir Arafat, became chairman of the PLO's executive committee and thus the chief of the Palestinian national movement, a position he held until his death in November 2004.

The Palestine National Charter was the basis of the PLO's goals and principles. Palestinian spokesmen stated that they sought to establish a nonsectarian state in which Jews, Christians, and Muslims would live in equality in all of historic Palestine. This position was popular among Palestinians, but was rejected by the vast majority of Israelis, who saw it as a blue print for the destruction of Israel.

The Palestine National Council (PNC) was established to serve as a parliament of the PLO. An executive committee, which took on the functions of a cabinet, managed PLO activities. Initially, the PNC consisted of civilian representatives from various areas, including Jordan, the West Bank, the Gaza Strip, the Persian Gulf states, and other diaspora communities. In 1968, representatives of political organizations and parties were added to the executive committee.

After the Israeli occupation of the West Bank and Gaza Strip in 1967, Fatah launched a wave of attacks against the occupying forces. Throughout the 1970s and 1980s, the PLO, dominated by the secular, politically centrist Fatah party, acted as a state-in-the-making, while launching frequent military attacks on Israel. The proliferation of Palestinian guerrilla groups increased membership in the PLO, which emerged as a player in Arab regional politics. Fatah permeated and mobilized the Palestinian populations under occupation and in the diaspora, providing political leadership and in some cases social and cultural services and organizations.

On September 22, 1974, the UN General Assembly, overriding strong Israeli objections, included the "Palestine question" for the first time as a separate agenda item, rather than as part of the general question of the Middle East. On November 13 of the same year the

General Assembly heard Yasir Arafat plead for the Palestinian people's national rights. By the end of the decade, the PLO had diplomatic representatives in more than 80 countries.

International recognition of the PLO had important repercussions within the Arab world. At an Arab summit conference held in Rabat, Morocco, on October 26–28, 1974, the conference held that any "liberated" Palestinian territory "should revert to its legitimate Palestinian owners under the leadership of the PLO."

Under the PLO umbrella a number of very vocal, mostly leftist, parties vied for leadership of the armed struggle. They included the PFLP (Popular Front for the Liberation of Palestine), Popular Front for the Liberation of Palestine–General Command (splinter group from the PFLP), As-Sa'iqah, DFLP (Democratic Front for the Liberation of Palestine), PSF (Popular Struggle Front), and the PPP (Palestine People's Party, formerly the Communist Party). Despite their differences in tactics and ideology, the guerrilla organizations were united in rejecting any political settlement that was not based on the premise of a one-state solution to the conflict. These political positions changed over time. By the late 1960s, the DFLP and the PPP became front-runners in openly advocating a two-state solution and accepting a Palestinian state in Arab-Palestinian territories occupied in the 1967 war. In 1988, Fatah took that same position, which ultimately led to what is known as the Oslo Peace Process.

Still, the United States continued to refuse to recognize the PLO so long as it did not recognize the legitimacy of Israel to exist in Palestine. In 1991, the PLO officially recognized the right of Israel to exist in the territories captured prior to 1967, in return for Israeli recognition of the PLO as the political representative of the Palestinian people. These developments, however lopsided, ingratiated the PLO to Washington temporarily. Although Europe and the rest of the world have generally supported the Palestinians, the political establishment in America still has not.

Top: A vigil in Ramallah; Middle: In Beirut in 1982;
Bottom: Funeral in Ramallah, November 2004

Yasir Arafat
"Abu Ammar" 1929–2004

Born Muhammad Abdel Rahman Abdel Raouf Arafat al-Qudwa al-Husseini, Yasir Arafat was senior architect of the Palestinian resistance and founding member of the Palestine Liberation Organization. For half a century he was instrumental in keeping Palestinian identity and the struggle for independence and statehood alive. Arafat, whose *nom de guerre* was "Abu Ammar," went from guerrilla leader to Nobel Prize winning statesman. For the last ten years of his life he was the most recognized world figure, in his black-and-white checkered headdress, the embodiment of the Palestinian resistance and nationhood.

For Palestinians, Arafat's spartan lifestyle, fatherly manner, and unwillingness to compromise on core Palestinian issues, even under enormous political pressure, made him a leader who was both loved and respected, even by those who differed with him. That Arafat did not live to see the establishment of a Palestinian state, or bring about a just peace, was not, as many of his critics claim, for lack of trying, but rather a result of the unequal balance of power between the two sides in the Israeli-Palestinian conflict.

Arafat's defining moment, his 1974 speech on the floor of the United Nations General Assembly, will always be remembered for the Palestinian motto he coined there: "In one hand I carry the olive branch, in the other a freedom fighter's gun. Do not let the olive branch fall from my hand… Do not let the olive branch fall from my hand."

3.

Geography, Flora, and Fauna

P alestine is located north of the equator between the latitudes N30º 30 N15º 32, and longitudes E15º 34 and E40º 35. On the southeastern coast of the Mediterranean Sea, it touches the eastern boundaries of Africa and the western boundaries of Asia. This geographical location places Palestine at the juncture of the European, Asian, and African continents, and at the center of the Arab world, which extends from the Atlantic Ocean to the Arabian Gulf.

All of historic Palestine covers an area of some 34,000 sq km (21,250 sq mi). The West Bank is 5,800 sq km (3,625 sq mi), and Gaza at the north of the Negev desert and the southeastern corner of Mediterranean Sea, is only 365 sq km (228 sq mi). The topography of Palestine creates diverse climate systems. Daylight lasts 14 hours in the summer and 10 in the winter, which explains the summer's heat and the winter's cold.

Mountains of median height help to decrease the high temperature in the summer and to increase the amount of rain in the winter. The Jordan Valley is much warmer than the mountains, so between the two—as mountainous areas are planted in the summer, and the valley regions in the winter—vast numbers of vegetables and fruits grow year round. This diversity in habitat also makes for unusually high biodiversity.

While Palestine may be most famous for its history as the nexus of monotheism, its rich and varied topography have, as much as anything, enhanced the images associated with Biblical life and the many lores and legends associated with the country and its people. Romanticized, often Orientalist, images of the countryside, such as those of 19th-century artist David Roberts have often failed to capture the intense character, colors, and varieties of nature in Palestine.

Flower of Palestine

The country is abundant with fertile fields of fruits and vegetables and lush Mediterranean valleys dotted with olive, carob, and almond trees, as well as sand dunes and arid deserts abound with Biblical shrubs and bushes. The climate changes from semi-arid to temperate to subtropical with the rapid alternations of mountain and plain plateaus and the rift of the Jordan Valley, and the contrasts between green mountains, the sea, and the desert.

In the Bible, Hebron is described as the "Land of Milk and Honey." Indeed, Palestine is inhabited by thousands of living species: an estimated 115 species of mammals, almost 500 kinds of birds, over 90 types of reptiles, and 7 types of amphibians are all native to the country. In addition, over 2,700 types of plants have been identified as currently growing across the country.

Hillsides of Palestine

Flora

On the coast and in Gaza, purple, red, orange and white bougainvilleas brighten even the shabbiest refugee camp. According to local lore every garden in Gaza was once surrounded by them. In the Jordan Valley and Jericho too, bougainvilleas spread across homes and public spaces with their lanky branches to beautify every corner that they touch. In the West Bank, aromatic Arabian Jasmine, white lilies, and honeysuckle greet visitors with their sweet, romantic smell. In the Galilee, scarlet tulips and purple gladioli mix in the springtime to welcome pilgrims at Easter.

Throughout the country oak and sycamore trees are integral to local mythology and are often labeled "holy," more often than not because a Biblical or Quranic figure is believed to have rested under the tree. Calliprinos oaks in particular blanket the mountains near

Haifa, the upper Galilee, and large parts of Marj Ibn Amr. As spring approaches thorny broom and rockrose spring to life in almost every garden, blossoming in yellow, pink, and white. During the fall, narcissus, crocus, hyacinth, as well as cyclamen, iris, anemones and daisies dot the hills and mountains of much of northern Palestine. The most striking and perhaps most common of all the flowers in Palestine are the lilies of the field, which grow in great abundance along the roadsides and all across the country.

As the demographic make-up of Palestine slowly began to change with an influx of European Jews at the beginning of the 20th century, so did the flora and fauna. Trees and plants native to northern Europe, mainly Germany, Poland, and Russia were planted in the country en masse. Some survived and flourished, some died, and some have been hybridized by growers attempting to make the new vegetation viable. Today there are over 200 million trees in the country, including forests of eucalyptus, pine, carob, and tamarisk.

Poppy and flax plants still grow across the hills of the Galilee, with blue and red pimpernel, pink cyclamen, and dark blue and white lupine pervading for a good part of the spring season.

In the mountains and the deserts, wildflowers and medicinal plants, such as arnica, grow in abundance. On the sites of destroyed Palestinian villages, cactus spring from the rubble of destroyed homes. Strangely, the Israelis born in Palestine call themselves "Sabra," meaning cactus, perhaps aware that on the site of Palestinian communities destroyed by Israel stand endless growths of cactus.

As the winter or rainy season sets in, a green carpet of fields dotted with red poppy flowers, pink and white cyclamen, and red, white, and purple anemones bloom. Some plants, such as the crocus and squill, are geophytes, which store nourishment in their bulbs and tubers and bloom at the end of the summer.

Fruit trees bloom from January to April. Apricots ripen in June, grapes in July, and olives in October. Grapes, olives, and apricots grow in almost every backyard across the West Bank. Strawberries, bananas, oranges, and other citrus fruits dominate the coastal plain from Gaza northward. Dates, bananas, avocado, guava, and mango have been introduced in the Jordan valley. In the Negev highlands, massive Atlantic pistachios strike a dramatic note among the dry riverbeds, and date palms grow wherever there is sufficient underground water.

Popular lore has it that in the "old days" the country was filled with forests and that the Ottoman rulers of the late 19th century cut down and used the wood as fuel during wartime and to built railroads. While this cannot be entirely verified, it is true that during the Israeli occupation of the West Bank and Gaza, tens of thousands of olive and orange trees have been uprooted because they obstruct the "visibility" of the Israeli army. This uprooting has been widely photographed and well documented. This destruction has taken place alongside the Israeli state's spending millions of dollars annually to plant trees.

Fauna

The history of animal life in Palestine stretches back some 60 million years. About one million years ago the hippopotamus, rhinoceros, warthog, striped hyena, and various species of gazelle arrived in the area, with some remnants found in Wadi Khareitun. Wild horses, asses, wolves and badgers, migrating from western and central Asia arrived later.

Climatic changes and human actions caused the extermination of many of these species. Over-hunting caused the rapid disappearance of roe deer, fallow deer, Arabian Oryx, Syrian bears, cheetahs, ostriches, and Nile crocodiles.

Birds

Because of its location between the northern and southern hemispheres, Palestine is somewhat of a central station for migratory birds, which travel three basic routes over the country. Cranes, sparrows, starlings, pigeons, larks, warblers, and eagles are but a few of the seasonal visitors. There are also about 65 families of wild birds in Palestine. The most well known are warblers, buntings, gulls, wheatears, terns, and falcons.

There are also some 120 species of vagrant birds, which visit the country in irregular periods. The most important of these are the pelicans, who stay on the Gazan shore. Water birds pass over land east of the Mediterranean Sea, flying by the shore. The numbers of these birds increase toward the south. Quails migrate in large numbers along the Gaza shore in the winter time.

While with the exception of the Qalqilia Zoo, there are no reserves in the PNA-controlled areas, both Jericho and Gaza are teeming with birds, especially in the early hours of the day.

Mammals

According to recent estimates, historic Palestine is still home to about 115 different species of mammals. While their numbers and variants decline, still existing mammals include mountain gazelles, wild boar, foxes, jungle cats, Nubian ibex, leopards, hyenas, jackals, and wolves. Since the 1960s, the Israeli Nature Reserves Authority has been reintroducing ostriches, roe deer, Asiatic wild asses, Persian fallow deer, and white Oryx to the wild.

There are several fox types in Palestine, including the reddish-gray Egyptian fox in the Hebron region, the Mediterranean fox in the Jerusalem–Ramleh corridor in the south and to the borders of Lebanon in the north, the tawny fox in the Galilee, the Fennec fox in the extreme southern parts of the country and on the border with Egypt, and Rueppel's sand fox in the Negev.

Gazelles, signifiers of beauty and elegance, have often been the subjects of poetry. The most common species is the red gazelle, seen both in the mountains and plains, where it lives in the southern and eastern deserts. The black-nosed gray gazelle (gazella Arabica) is more common in the coastal plain and in the deserts.

The Libyan cat, a probable ancestor of the domestic cat, is rare, but

still present, in the Negev. The Palestine jungle cat looks like an ordinary cat, except for its short tail, and lives along the reed-beds of the Jordan River. The sand-colored Caracal lynx, recognized by its long ear tufts, lives mostly in the Negev and the Dead Sea area. The spotted lynx lives mostly in the Galilee. A small number of cheetahs still live in southern Palestine, mostly in the Negev and its surrounding mountain ranges. Although generally thought to be at home in northern Palestine, the leopard also lives in deserts, from south of Hebron to the Ein Gedi region, to the Dead Sea and the Egyptian border.

The brown furred marbled polecat is most abundant in the hills and mountains, although it is also found in the coastal plain.

The common badger lives in the West Bank and woody areas of Jerusalem, while the tropical honey badger and the hedgehog inhabit the Negev and the Jordan Valley. The Palestine hedgehog lives as far north as Tulkarem.

The Mediterranean hare lives along the coast, while the smaller Egyptian hare is most common in the Negev, Gaza, and the Jordan Valley. The jackal lives in the lower Jordan Valley, the Jerusalem region, and the desert of the Negev. The Nubian ibex lives in mountainous areas of the Negev and Jerusalem.

The natural habitat of the Otter was once the Al-Auja River, north of Jaffa, but today they are known to survive in the upper part of the Jordan River.

Marine and Freshwater Life

Almost 250 bottom dwelling species have been identified off the coastal waters of Gaza while another 285 fish species are found in its waters. A lack of sufficient nutrition, high salinity and high temperatures have long limited the amount of marine life on the shores of Palestine, but the building of the Suez Canal in 1869 created an influx of marine fauna species, including jellyfish, prawn species and swimming crab.

Before 1978, Gaza fishermen were allowed to work off the coast of Gaza and the Sinai. After the 1978 Camp David Peace Accord between Israel and Egypt, the Sinai waters became off limits to the Palestinians and Gaza fishers were restricted to an area extending outwards 20 nautical miles. The outward limit was reduced to 12 nautical miles and subsequently to 6 nautical miles.

Honey bee in Gaza

Barghouti

Darwish

I Saw Ramallah

Selected Poems

The Secret Life of Saeed
THE PESSOPTIMIST

A Woman of Five Seasons

SHAMMAS

ARABESQUES

A BALCONY *over the* FAKIHANI

A LAKE BEYOND THE WIND

Israel
NEW INTERNATIONAL LITERARY VOICES

Palestine
NEW INTERNATIONAL FOREIGN VOICES

Palestine

EMILE HABIBY

LEILA AL-ATRASH

LIYANA BADR

YAHYA YAKHLIF

4.

Literature and Music

L anguage, rather than race, creed, or geography, defines who is an Arab. And poetry is what the early speakers of Arabic, the pre-Islamic dwellers of sixth-century Arabia, have left us as their artistic legacy. A North African traveler, some thousand years ago, was impressed that

> When there appeared a poet in a family of the Arabs, the other tribes round about would gather together to that family to wish them joy for their good luck... they used not to wish one another joy but for three things: the birth of a boy, the coming to light of a poet, and the foaling of a noble mare.

Poetry, to this day, has remained the Arabic literary form with the widest popular appeal. In Palestine, when a poet recites from his or her work, the audience can number in the thousands, more resembling rock concerts than the poetry readings of the West. Fans range from urban sophisticates to ploughmen and refugee camp dwellers, even though the poets use the classical Arabic of literature. Until a generation ago, almost every Palestinian village could boast a folk bard or two. Often illiterate, they commanded respect as the voice of their community, giving luster with their verses to its events, its sorrows, and its celebrations.

Poetry and Politics

The pre-Islamic poems are to Arabic what Shakespeare is to English; every Arab child is made to memorize at least some of their words. These poems are elaborately composed odes, *qasidas* that are related in their content. They have in common the qasida meter, which comes in a number of variants though each poem adheres throughout to the form of its opening lines. Each poem also maintains a single rhyme for its duration—forty, sixty or a hundred verses threaded onto one recurring sound, which is echoed down the entire composition. In English this would be tedious even if it were feasible. But the vast vocabulary, the complex grammar, and the multiple forms of each Arabic word permit the poet this extensive flexibility. For the listener there is a pleasurable tension in the unfolding of the poet's skill as, line-by-line, he achieves the pre-set rhyme.

The qasida form has endured to our time, even though by the end of the nineteenth century, French and British colonialism, education abroad, emigration, and translation had brought contact with other literatures and ideas. In the early 1900s, the *Mahjar*, the "Emigrant Poets" of South America and the members of the New York "Pen League," of whom Khalil Gibran is best remembered, wrote in Arabic though living overseas and injected a freshness into the canon of the countries they had left behind. In the 1940s, a revolutionary "New Poetry" or "Free Verse" movement, which first became identified with some Iraqi poets, liberated writers from the rigidities of the past. Blank verse, prose poetry, interrupted line and meter—all became acceptable.

The pre-Islamic poet was essentially a communicator for his tribe. His qasidas were dedicated to the glorification of his own people and the derision of their enemies: his art served a political purpose in the power struggles of ancient Arabia. Even within memory, a celebrated Saudi Arabian folk poet could make the boast that he was as powerful as a general, that without stirring from his corner by his coffee pot, he could move armies. Indeed, with a qasida, he had once summoned allies for a factional fight all the way from Damascus.

And verses survive in the Palestinian folk archive that persuaded a Turkish governor of the Hebron district to repeal a burdensome tax, and a satire which shamed a village into paying what it owed its neighbors. The power of poets' words has always been a cause for concern for the foreign occupiers of Palestine. The Ottomans, British, and Israelis have all thrown poets into prison and suppressed their works.

Resistance Poets

For hundreds of years the land in Palestine was life itself for the *fellaheen*. They cleared it of the overabundant limestone rocks, tilled its rusty red soil, coaxed bread and olives, onions and herbs from its uncertain rainfalls for their everyday fare, and grazed sheep and goats on its scrubby hills for the meat of feast days and celebrations. Their relationship with the land was their identity, the colors of its wild irises, tulips and anemones embroidered on their women's dresses, the rhythm of its seasons dictating the pattern of their occupations. For this largely agricultural society the sudden loss of the land, brought about by the flourish of a distant politician's pen, has been a wound that, more than 50 years later, has yet to heal.

The Palestinians who remained within the borders of what became Israel in 1948 found that they were second-class citizens in a state whose language, schooling, laws, and religion denied their identity and their relevance. They had become aliens in what had been their own land, and they were cut off from the rest of the Arab world. These Palestinians have produced the best known and the most frequently translated contemporary Palestinian poets: the Poets of Resistance. Their unusual circumstances have set them apart and give their work its distinctive tone.

The poems of Mahmoud Darwish, Samih al-Qasim, and Tawfiq Zayyad will be found in every English anthology of modern Arabic poetry. Like most Resistance Poets, they embraced the freedoms of the "New Poetry." Early in his career Mahmoud Darwish declared that

> If poetry does not carry a lantern from door to door
> If the poor don't know what it "means"
> We had better discard it!
> It is better that we seek immortal silence.

If not from door to door, Samih al-Qasim took his poems from village to village in the Galilee region where he was born and Tawfiq Zayyad incorporated folk sayings into some of his poems. Combining an accessible classical vocabulary with the looser, more immediate new poetical forms, the Resistance Poets adopted an ideal medium for conveying their urgent message to a wide public.

"When the Arab world heard of Darwish, al-Qasim and Zayyad, there was a deep and quiet joy, for this was a sign that Palestine was still Arab and that the Arab heart there had not stopped beating," writes one of their translators. Arab hostility to the alien state in their midst had isolated Palestinians who remained inside the "Green Line," the partition boundary. It was not until novelist and short story writer Ghassan Kanafani published an anthology of their work in 1966 that the Resistance Poets became generally known to Arabs beyond Israel's border. Kanafani himself was killed by an Israeli bomb in Beirut in 1972, at age 36.

Resistance Poems

With his poem "Identity Card" from the 1960s Mahmoud Darwish illicited an instant heartfelt response. Its defiant tone struck a cord in a Palestinian population long resentful of Israeli regulations which, among other things, required Palestinians to carry identification at all times. Darwish has known firsthand the full range of the Palestinian experience under Israeli rule. He was six years old when in 1948 his family fled on foot to Lebanon and their village of Berweh, near Acre, was burned and leveled to the ground. He has been a displaced person, a refugee, and an exile. His work has been censored and he has lived under house arrest and been jailed. A precocious talent, still in his teens when a first collection of his verse was published, Mahmoud Darwish through his very personal poetry has made comprehensible the extent of the trauma resulting from the tearing apart of Palestine to accommodate a Jewish state: no small achievement to have pierced with his art the world's silence on this subject.

Samih al-Qasim, a few years older than Mahmoud Darwish, published six collections of poetry by the time he was 30. He too challenged Israel's denial of Palestinian rights and in "Enemy of the Sun," clearly declared his position:

> You may take the last strip of my land,
> Feed my youth to prison cells.
> You may plunder my heritage.
> You may burn my books and my poems
> Or feed my flesh to the dogs.
> You may spread a web of terror
> On the roofs of my village,
> O enemy of the sun,
> But
> I shall not compromise
> And to the last pulse in my veins
> I shall resist.

The following excerpt, from Tawfiq Zayyad's often quoted poem "The Impossible," likewise embodies the Palestinian commitment to resistance. Born in the Galilee in 1932, Zayyad studied literature in Russia. Upon his return to Palestine, he was not only a poet but a political leader: a Communist Party representative and many times mayor of his hometown, Nazareth.

> Here upon your chests
> We shall remain
> Like the glass and the cactus
> In your throats
> A fiery whirlwind

In your eyes…
Here we shall remain
A wall upon your chests.
We starve,
Go naked,
Sing songs

And fill the street
With demonstrations
And the jails with pride.
We breed rebellions
One after another.
Like twenty impossibles we remain
In Lydd, Ramleh, and Galilee…

Israel's victory in the 1967 war and its seizure of control over the whole of Palestine rocked the Arab world. Palestine was now on every Arab mind and the sentiments of the Resistance Poets found echoes everywhere. The great Syrian poet of love, Nizar Qabbani, wrote after the 1967 defeat,

O my sorrowing fatherland,
In a single moment you changed me
From a poet writing of love and longing
To a poet writing with a knife.

Style and Content

Not surprisingly, a sense of loss pervades the work of Palestinian writers wherever they live. Born in Bethlehem a generation before the Resistance Poets, Jabra Ibrahim Jabra grew up during the British Mandate and went to Cambridge University in England for his studies. He was an adult well into his thirties when he left his home in 1948 never to return. A displaced Palestinian living in Iraq, he achieved a distinguished career as poet, novelist, and literary critic. His translations of James Frazer's *The Golden Bough* and of T.S. Eliot proved significant for Arab writers in a period of modernizing change. In his poem "The Deserts of Exile" Jabra's recollection of the land of his childhood is steeped in nostalgia. It is a verdant Palestine whose

…month of March is an inlay of anemone and narcissus across the hillsides
April—a burst of bridal blossom on the plains
May—a love song sung at noon under the lowland olive's blue shade….

The poet finally despairs, "Where can we go with our passion, as one springtime follows another and our eyes have nowhere to rest but on the frosts and dust of exile?"

By contrast, Rashid Hussein, from a village near Haifa, defiantly claims the memory of Palestine as a right, in a poem set in a refugee camp. In Israel, where he grew up, the history of Palestine was erased in the school books and its traces ploughed under in the countryside.

> Tent number fifty on the left—that is my present
> But it is too crammed to contain a future
> And, "Forget," they say
> But how can I!
> Teach the night to forget to bring
> Dreams showing me my village
> Teach the winds to forget to carry me
> The aroma of apricots in my fields
> And teach the sky too to forget to rain.
> Only then may I forget my country.

Rashid Hussein translated Hayim Byalek's poetry into Arabic and Palestinian folksongs into Hebrew. But his own writings and his activism on behalf of Palestinians in Israel landed him in prison more than once and he was barred from his professions of choice, teaching and journalism. After the 1967 war he chose to exile himself in New York where he died ten years later in a fire in his apartment at the age of 40.

Mahmoud Darwish also left Israel soon after the 1967 war, in 1971. Since then he has lived in Egypt, Lebanon, the West Bank, and France, where his books are bestsellers. His interests have widened and his poetry is constantly alive to new ventures. Musing about home, Darwish, for whom "the smell of coffee is geography" and who "travel[s] like other people but return[s] to nowhere," must reflect the melancholy of stateless exiles everywhere regardless of country of origin. The poem called "Homeland" can speak for any person who has been forcibly displaced:

> My homeland is no bundle of legends...
> This land is the skin on my bones,
> And my heart
> Flies above its grasses like a bee...

Two poets from different generations have treated an identical subject so differently as to illustrate the change in style over time. Fadwa Tuqan (1917–2004), from an old and prominent family in Nablus, was encouraged to write by her brother Ibrahim Tuqan

(1904–1941), who was the leading poet of his generation. Like his contemporaries, he wrote in the traditional meters. He could be playful in a love poem, but, having witnessed the defeat of the Ottomans, the coming of the British to rule in their place, and the Palestinian uprising against the British Mandate of the 1930s, he inevitably devoted much of his poetry to politics. Appearing in the newspapers of the day, his poems assailed the British for their treachery, Balfour for his promise to the Zionists, and Arab landowners for selling their estates to Jewish immigrants. He eulogized in stately, heroic style the men, "firm of heart and tread who... joyfully welcomed death for God and country," or who met "with head held high" their British executioners.

The same heroic nationalist mood colors a 1954 poem by Fadwa Tuqan. Her "Call of the Land" tells of a youth standing at the border that divided Palestine in 1948. He looks longingly at the fields that had nurtured him. Then, defying the artificial barrier, he crosses and, like a child upon its mother's breast, he throws himself on the precious ground, a loyal son reunited with his land at last, and dies content, with the echo of the border guards' bullets. Even when using the older forms, Fadwa Tuqan wrote with unprecedented openness, for a woman of that time, about her own intimate feelings. She went on to explore the new and experimental forms. After the occupation of her city, Nablus, in 1967, Tuqan's emphasis became more political. She aimed her pen at the enemy tanks patrolling her streets, the young students filling the jails, the rubble of rooms that had housed dreams deemed punishable by demolition. "With angry lips" she called for "My liberty—my liberty—my liberty!"

Prison has long been a hazard of the Palestinian poet's calling. A folk qasida by Hleiweh Barghouthi, whose clan has contributed richly to the oral tradition, dates back to Ottoman days. It describes in some detail how he was marched by Turkish soldiers from his village of Kafr 'Ein to prison in Jerusalem, fainting with thirst by the time he passed the water trough of al-Bireh, and finally being flung into a cell with no bedding but the ground. Mousa al-Rahhal, village poet born in 1895 in Artuf near Jerusalem, dwells humorously and at length on the discomforts of prison, the size of the fleas and the price of a cigarette, and he mocks the pink-cheeked British officer who counts and recounts his prisoners then causes a riot when he knocks off an old shaykh's turban. More recently, Samih al-Qasim's "End of a Discussion with a Jailer," set in an Israeli prison, concludes,

From the window of my small cell
I can see trees smiling at me
Roofs filled with my people
Windows weeping and praying for me
From the window of my small cell
I can see your large cell.

Folktales

If much of Palestinian poetry is pervaded by a profound sense of loss
and its subsequent longing—"My country is desire in chains," as
Darwish put it—Palestinian folktales invariably offer instead the
satisfaction of a just and happy ending. The villain is disposed of in any
number of unpleasant ways and Clever Hassan marries the king's
youngest daughter. Better still, the king's crier shouts through the
streets, "All who are present tell all who are absent that: For the next
forty days, everyone come, take your food from the palace kitchen!"

The storyteller may end her tale with "Tutu, tutu, finished is my
haddutu (story)" or with "The bird has taken flight, God bless you
tonight." She might also say, "If my house were not so far, I'd bring the
raisins in my jar. Some for myself, some for the teller of this tale, and
some for Imm Suhail (if that is her name)" or, with some other rhyme,
hint that a snack would be welcome about now. Storytelling in rural
Palestine almost always begins with an invitation to the listeners to say
God's prayers and blessings upon the Prophet Muhammad (in a
Christian village, upon the Virgin Mary) or to testify to the uniqueness
of God. Then follows the traditional opening "There was or there was
not, in the oldness of time…" Unlike the certainty of "Once upon a
time," the Arab storyteller leaves open the question of fact or fiction.

Palestinian storytellers share such formulaic elements with those
from other Arab countries. Though the rhymes may differ the intent
is the same. Their tales also share the same cast of supernatural
characters: Giants whose every tread makes the earth tremble, djinns
who can cross the Seven Seas in a blink, ghouls with eyes red as
embers and teeth of brass—all of whom, fearsome as they are, can be
appeased, by the way, with a polite greeting, a small grooming service,
or the correct answer to a riddle. And as in most folklore, it is the
youngest son who, at the meeting of three paths, knows which one to
take, who rubs salt into a cut in his arm to keep himself awake so as to
catch the bird with the golden feather; it is the least fortunate girl,
always beautiful as the moon when it is full, who, by being patient,
kind, or devout—or sometimes by being smarter than all the men—

eventually wins the respect of the king and the heart of the prince.

Two features that distinguish the Palestinian versions of the Arabic repertoire of stories are the farming culture of the Palestinian *fellaheen*, and the fact that Palestine was the scene of significant events in the history of the three monotheistic religions. The older folktales can be recognized by their wealth of accurate agricultural detail—they are, after all, the fantasies of tillers of the earth. The Palestinian Cinderella, for instance, is shoved into a *taboon*, the domed clay oven found in the yard of most village houses and on which, at the end of the story, the rooster perches and resolves the plot by crowing "The beauty has been hidden away! The ugly ones are on display!" The girl hounded by the ghoul hides among farmers driving donkeys laden with grapes from their vineyards in the hills to sell along the coast. The poor woodcutter, given the chance for ease and plenty in the Garden of Eden on condition that he stay silent, cannot stop himself from exclaiming out loud when he sees an old man pruning fig trees incorrectly and finds himself back where he started. Princes are as familiar with the practicalities of sheepherding or olive pressing as any *fellah*. A beautiful girl may be described as being "shapely just as if she had been turned on a carpenter's lathe," with arms "smooth as peeled cucumbers," and teeth "like shelled almonds." Familiar place names abound—the Good Apprentice and the Bad are baker's boys in Nablus who want to earn extra cash working the early wheat harvest in Gaza and so set off on their fateful journey. The wonders of the stories are brought almost within reach of those listening in the dim light of an oil lamp after a weary day.

A group of artless tales embroidered onto incidents in the Bible attest to this being the Holy Land. The Virgin Mary, on the flight to Egypt, passes through villages of the Palestinian countryside attended by miracles. In one story she evades Herod's soldiers by spending the night in a dry well but leaves it brimming with water—it has not run dry since. In another narrative, Moses, digging a trench like any farmer, greets the Angel Gabriel with a distinctly Palestinian accent. Adam, Abraham, and any number of local Muslim saints find a place in the tellers' imagination.

These stories told in the spoken *'ammieh*, the common dialect of everyday talk, were the evening entertainment of the extended family before the advent of radio and TV. The men might go to the coffee house or the village guest house to pass the evening but women and children amused themselves at home. Their tales were considered harmless fun, not matter fit for print in the classical Arabic of literature. It was therefore Europeans who, with help from Palestinian friends, first thought to write down the stories; Biblical scholars doing research in Palestine or Orientalists interested in capturing samples of the dialect. Not until the 1920s, in alarm at the erosion of the Palestinian culture under British rule, did Palestinians begin to record their own folklore. With the occupation of the West Bank and Gaza by Israel and Golda Meir's notorious question "Who are the Palestinians?" there grew a sense of urgency about preserving the Palestinian heritage. In 1975, the In'ash al Usra society of al-Bireh, originally founded to provide social services, began to include folklore and stories in its research division and its quarterly publication. Birzeit University developed an active oral history and folklore department under the guidance of the late Abdullatif Barghouthi. Palestinian artists have incorporated traditional embroidery patterns into their paintings, poets have quoted folk sayings in their work, and motifs from folktales have appeared in the fiction of authors like Emile Habiby, who is best known for his satire on the plight of Palestinian citizens of Israel, *The Secret Life of Saeed.*

For the English reader interested in Palestinian folktales, the largest collection currently available is Sharif Kanaaneh and Ibrahim Muhawi's *Speak Bird, Speak Again*, (University of California, 1989) In addition to the texts, which are faithful to the narrators' exact words, there is a fund of information about Palestinian life. The stories are grouped according to the stages of the life cycle and the authors examine how they illustrate relationships within the family and the community. Another highly-praised collection edited by Salma Khadra Jayyusi is *Abu Jmeel's Daughter and Other Stories* by Jamal Sleem (Interlink Publishing, 2002).

In the recorded life stories of Palestinian folk poets, time and again they cite weddings as the scene of their first interest in poetry and their apprenticeships. The close-knit, patriarchal clan system has been the one dependable social unit in Palestine, regardless of who governed the country. Marriage, because it reinforces blood ties and secures family assets, therefore becomes an event of significance beyond the couple concerned. A wedding is also an opportunity to show the legendary Arab virtue of hospitality. Traditionally celebrated over the course of several evenings and attended by the whole community, weddings were showcases for every folk art, but the presence of one or more folk poets marked the really grand events. Qasidas in praise of the hosts and bridal couple were mandatory, but the well wishers would also be entertained with recitations of well known folk epics and with *zajal*, a form of virtuoso poetic jousting in which two poets display their verbal skills and ability in on the spot improvisation.

As the conditions of Palestinians worsen under Israeli occupation and funerals become the major community gatherings of the intifada, wedding celebrations have been severely curtailed. Young poets and folk poets in the West Bank and Gaza dedicate their compositions to martyrs of the struggle and to individual towns that have endured or resisted Israeli attacks. Cassette recordings of their works pass from hand to hand, inspiration to counter the dismal newscasts that punctuate the day.

The highly regarded Lebanese singer and composer, Marcel Khalife, has set to music a number of the poems of Mahmoud Darwish and other Resistance Poets, including one by Samih al-Qasim excerpted below. It compels audiences to join in the chorus wherever it is performed in the Arab world: an anthem to the Palestinian capacity for endurance, whether as *fellaheen* facing the challenges of nature or as nationalists struggling for independence.

> I walk.
> Straight as a ramrod
> Head high
> I walk.
> An olive branch
> And a dove
> In my palm
> And on my shoulders a coffin
> And I walk.
> My head is a red moon,
> My heart is a garden
> My lips a rainy sky,
> At times
> Love
> And I walk—walk!
> Straight as a ramrod
> Head high…

As a young student attending university in Egypt, the poet Mourid Barghouthi was trapped by the 1967 war and excluded from re-entry to his home and family. After an exile lasting 30 years he was at last permitted to return to Palestine. It was a shock for him to see an Israeli soldier manning the bridge across the River Jordan and he wrote, "His gun took from us the land of the poem and left us with the poem of the land."

Palestinian Fiction in Translation

Fiction always tells what history books hide. Not surprisingly, the conditions of terror or exile in which most Palestinians live figure prominently in Palestinian novels and short stories. But although many Palestinian writers have utilized their talents to create an awareness of their plight and give voice to the aspirations of their people, they remain first and foremost writers, acknowledged and respected as masters of their craft.

The Palestinian novel as a distinct literary form came into existence after al-Nakba, the catastrophe of 1948. (Although there were several attempts at novel writing when Palestine was under British rule, such exercises by Palestinian academics, educated mainly at British universities, had been largely unsuccessful.) Three literary figures who lived under different circumstances in three different countries and whose novels are arguably the finest in Palestinian fiction spearheaded the new literary movement: **Jabra Ibrahim Jabra** (1920–1994), **Ghassan Kanafani** (1936–1972), and **Emile Habiby** (1920–1995).

Jabra, an award-winning writer, literary critic, poet, painter, and avid reader and translator of western literature, moved to Iraq in 1948 where he became a university professor. His novel ***The Ship*** (*Al-Safeena*, 1970), translated by Roger Allen and Adnan Haydar—with its themes of spiritual and physical displacement, yearnings for the homeland, and struggle for survival as depicted through the interactions of his characters on a ship sailing from Beirut to Europe—established his place as a towering figure in 20th-century Arabic literature.

In contrast to Jabra's western-influenced literary style and his use of characters drawn primarily from the wealthy and educated classes, Kanafani, whose family fled to Lebanon as part of the 1948 exodus, honed his craft as a journalist on the beat in Beirut, as an editor of the Palestinian weekly *al-Hadaf*, and as political activist in the refugee camps. His artistic motives were formed by his journalistic awareness, especially his deep understanding of the Palestinian street: the loss, misery, anger, suffering, despair, day-to-day struggles, and the desire to return home. Kanafani adopted a fresh novelistic style steeped in symbolism and where elements such as time, place, the desert, the earth become characters crucial to the plot and flow of the story. This is seen in several of his wonderful short stories and his powerful novellas ***Men in the Sun*** (*Rijal fi al-Shams*, 1956), translated by Hilary Kilpatrick, ***All That's Left to You*** (*Ma Tabaqqa Lakoum*, 1966), translated by May Jayyusi and Jeremy Reed, and ***Returning to Haifa*** (*'A-id ila Haifa*, 1970) published in English as part of the collection ***Palestine's Children***, translated by Barbara Harlow and Karen Riley. Indeed, the Arab world lost a major literary talent when Kanafani was killed in July of 1972 in the explosion of his booby-trapped car in Beirut.

No less important is the work of Emile Habiby, a brilliant thinker, writer, and politician (he was a three-time member of the Israeli Knesset) who remained in Palestine after 1948, became an Israeli citizen and in 1974 wrote ***The Secret Life of Saeed*** (*Waqa'i al-Ghareeba fi Ikhtifa' Sa'id Abi al-Nahs al-Mutasha'il*), translated into English by Salma Khadra Jayyusi and Trevor LeGassick. Influenced by his love for classical Arabic prose and drawing on his close acquaintance with the absurdities of Israeli politics and the sociopolitical dilemmas of the time, this novel—hailed as one of the masterpieces of contemporary Arab literature—is a lament for the fate Palestinians in modern times. It combines fact and fantasy, tragedy and comedy in a story of a simple man intent on survival, and perhaps, happiness.

The 1970s and Beyond

The continued dispossession of the Palestinians, their shattered hopes for peace, and the worsening conditions on the ground contributed in many ways to a literary intifada of sorts and the emergence of a new generation of writers eager to have their voices heard. While many lacked the experience and aesthetic sensibility of Jabra, Kanafani, or Habiby, a few have produced works of distinction and received much praise for their literary and intellectual creativity. One such writer is Nablus-born **Sahar Khalifeh**, Palestine's foremost feminist and author of the compelling novel *Wild Thorns* (*Al-Subbar*, 1976), translated by Trevor LeGassick and Elizabeth Fernea, in which she gives us a true picture of social and personal relations in the Israeli-occupied West Bank. Together with her later novel *The Inheritance* (*Al-Mirath*, 1997), translated by Aida Bamia, these two are considered the most important Palestinian novels of this generation of creative artists.

Two other writers who succeeded in their portrayals of Palestinian history and society from a woman's perspective are **Liyana Badr** and **Leila al-Atrash**. Badr's *A Balcony over the Fakihani* (*Shurfah ala al-Fakihani*, 1983), a remarkable collection of three novellas translated by Peter Clark and Christopher Tingley, delves into the lives of Palestinians living in refugee camps in Lebanon and allows us a glimpse of the joy and despair of these lives rooted in exile and resistance. Similarly, in *A Woman of Five Seasons* (*Imra'at al-Foousool al-Khamsah*, 1990), translated by Nora Halwani and Christopher Tingley, Al-Atrash through her characters tackles the complexities of interpersonal relationships, official corruption, and the Arab woman's cherished ideals of independence and intellectual life in predominantly patriarchal Arab society.

Yahya Yakhlif, whose unique style is marked by exceptional simplicity, is another accomplished Palestinian novelist of note. He has written seven novels and several collections of short stories and is best known for *A Lake Beyond the Wind* (*Buhayra Wara' al-Reeh*, 1991), a novel translated by May Jayyusi and Christopher Tingley that revolves around events taking place in Samakh, a small town on Lake Tiberias, north of Jerusalem, in 1948, that most catastrophic year in Palestinian history.

Palestinian poet and novelist **Ibrahim Nasrallah**'s poetic novel *Prairies of Fever* (*Baraari al-Humma*, 1985), translated by May Jayyusi and Jeremy Reed, deserves a mention for its contribution to postmodern Arabic literature. At times disturbing, evocative, and deeply moving, it gives a harrowing account of the psychological and physical anguish of a young Palestinian teacher hired to teach in a remote part of Saudi Arabia.

An impressive talent who took the literary scene by storm and received wide international acclaim for his first novel **Arabesques** (*Arabeskot*, 1986) is **Anton Shammas**, the first Palestinian to write a novel in Hebrew. Shammas is a poet, playwright, and essayist writing in Hebrew, Arabic and English. He was born in 1950 in Galilee, lived in Haifa and Jerusalem, attended Hebrew University, and is now professor of Near Eastern Studies and Comparative Literature at the University of Michigan. His novel—chosen by the editors of the *New York Times* as one of the best books of 1988 and in its front-page review called it "an ornate twining and twisting of memory, myth, history and self-consciousness"—touches on the theme of identity exploitation and challenegs Israel's exclusive ownership of the language.

Lastly, any discussion of Palestinian literature in translation would be incomplete without acknowledging the vast contribution of **Salma Khadra Jayyusi**—distinguished scholar, author, poet, and literary critic—who for nearly three decades as founder and director of the Cambridge-based PROTA, the Project of Translation from Arabic, has championed the translation of works by leading Arab creative writers and made it possible for English-speaking readers to sample the once-unheard voices of writers who have achieved wide acclaim at home, but were not recognized beyond the borders of the Arab world. Her **Anthology of Modern Palestinian Literature**, called a "living monument to the culture of a nation" by the late Edward W. Said, offers translations of poetry, short stories, and excerpts from novels—a must-read for anyone interested in Palestinian literature.

Copies of the above mentioned titles may be purchased from the bookstore at the **American Colony Hotel, Educational Bookshop, al-Deira Hotel Bookshop (Gaza)** *or online by visiting* **www.interlinkbooks.com** *and* **www.rienner.com**. *For a complete listing of literary events visit the website of* **Khalil al-Sakakini Cultural Center, www.sakakini.org**, *pick up a copy of* **This Week in Palestine** *or visit* **www.thisweekinpalestine.com**.

Palestinian Music and Dance

A visitor to Palestine will instantly feel the flow of musical energy emanating from the place and its people. In Palestine, music is simply all around you: from the unforgettable melodic chanting of the muezzin's call to prayer—often juxtaposed against the ringing of church bells—to fruit and vegetable vendors in the market singing praises about pickling cucumbers (as small as babies' fingers) or prickly pears (so delicious they melt in your mouth); from the cheerful foot-thumping sounds of *dabke* dancers at weddings or village festivities to the powerful emotional songs performed at political rallies and martyr funeral marches.

Like poetry, the art most cherished by Palestinians, music occupies a significant place in society. It is enjoyed and played everywhere and at all times. To a people living under occupation, the pleasant, soothing emotions produced by Arabic musical expressions are as indispensable as water or air is to human survival. Now, more than ever, music has become the therapy that can temporarily lift one's spirits, the prescription an embattled people administer in daily doses to ease their pain, suffering, and despair.

Local Palestinian music is multi-faceted and can take on many forms and styles. It involves different sounds and instruments and ranges from classical to folk to commercial popular music, both homegrown and from neighboring Arab countries. Even hip hop—with its themes of statehood, freedom, loss of homeland, and resistance to Israeli occupation—has gained popularity in recent years and is attracting huge crowds at sold-out concerts in major cities throughout Palestine.

A little knowledge and understanding of how the music works will greatly enhance a person's appreciation of the art form and make one want to hear more.

Classical Arabic Music

Throughout history, Arab culture has honored musicians and poets to a great degree. In the courts of the Omayyad and Abbasid caliphs, and later in the Andalusian courts of Seville, Granada, and Cordoba at the height of the Islamic Empire, musicians enjoyed unmatched prestige and were very handsomely rewarded. The same is true in the contemporary Arab world where the likes of **Mohammad Abdel Wahab**, **Farid el-Atrash**, **Abdel Halim Hafez**, **Riyad al-Sunbati**, **Zakariya Ahmad**, **Sayyid Darweesh**, **Asmahan**, **Leila Murad** and others were considered musical giants in the twentieth century and were adored by the masses. The Egyptian singer **Oum Koulthum** was, and continues to be, by far the most loved female artist in Palestine and the rest of the Arab world. Her voice was the voice of the Arab nation and it was often said that when she sang, "life in the Arab world came to a stop." She mesmerized millions with songs of emotional yearnings such as *al-Atlal* (Give me freedom, set my hands free... We haven't chosen to be born sad) and touched the hearts of almost all Palestinians, who interpreted some of her abstract lyrics that deal with love and loss as expressions of political support and sympathy with their plight.

Classical Arabic music has a distinctive sound—an enveloping sound with unique and haunting rhythms called *iqa'at*; it has a defining structure based on ancient modes developed in the 9th century called *maqamat* (melodic modes), singular *maqam*, but allows plenty of improvisation (*taqasim*, singular *taqsim*). It is known to include more than 100 musical scales, each associated with a particular mood, as compared to western scales that only have two: major and minor. Unlike the western tempered musical scale that consists of seven basic notes and is divided into 12 equal halftones, the Arabic *maqam* or musical scale is divided into 24 quartertones. And it is those quartertones that give it its special feel and character. To a western ear, the music may at first sound out-of-tune but will invariably win people over once it becomes even slightly familiar.

The traditional Arabic music instrumental ensemble (known as *takht*) consists of six musicians playing *oud* (a fretless, pear-shaped string instrument with a short neck and five double courses of gut or nylon strings, plucked with an eagle's feather), *qanoun* (a flat, trapezoid, zither-like plucked instrument, played on the lap, and has 78 strings arranged in triplets and held by a bridge over a fish skin patch), *nay* (a reed flute, open at both ends, with finger holes, played by placing the lips at an angle and blowing), *kamanjah* (a spike fiddle, now replaced by the western violin with Arabic tuning), *riqq* (a wooden, fish-skinned, small tambourine with five sets of cymbals), and *tabla* or *derbakkeh* (a goblet-shaped, clay drum with fish skin, today replaced by a more durable aluminum and plastic version).

The heart and soul of Arabic music is improvisation (*taqsim*), both vocal (known as *layaali*, plural of *ya layl*) and instrumental; it sets it apart, defines it, makes it unique, and gives it its unpredictability and excitement. In a *wasla* (a traditional suite of vocal and instrumental pieces) the singer (*mutrib*) may insert a *mawwal* (vocal improvisation in dialect) after a *muwashshah* (a measured poetic composition of Andalusian origin) and before embarking on a *qasida* (vocal improvisation on a classical poem); he or she may during the course of a performance use ornamentation or embellishment to showcase his or her musical ability, lend more charm to a tune, and ultimately induce *tarab*, and bring the audience to a state of ecstasy and enchantment. Instrumental improvisations function in more or less the same way; they are both spontaneous and organized. The soloist, be it on the *qanoun, nay, oud*, or violin, has unfettered freedom to express his or her own perspective on the music so long as he or she stays within the chosen *maqam* and *iqa'* (rhythmic cycle that can range from two beats to 176).

The works of **Simon Shaheen**, a Palestinian composer, performer, and music educator born in the village of Tarshiha in the northern Galilee, are good starting points for sampling classical Middle Eastern music. His highly praised anthology *Turath* features solo improvisations and ensemble works by 19th and 20th century master composers. His virtuosity on the oud and violin is brought to the fore in his later recording *The Music of Mohammad Abdel Wahab* featuring selections from the vast body of masterworks of the Egyptian composer.

Palestinian Folk Music

Although such times as when a male villager would be inspired to sing after casting an admiring look at his girl when she came to fill her jar at the village spring are long gone, it is still possible to get a taste of the folk traditions of the people of Palestine. Palestinians never miss playing the *tabla* and dancing the *dabke* (a line dance with energetic leaps and spins) during festivals and family celebrations. But to witness traditional Palestinian folk songs and dances at their most rudimentary and ancient, a visitor would need to get away from the big cities and take a trip to the villages and refugee camps, where men and women of the entire village or camp would gather on festive occasions to sing and dance together.

The most popular folk songs in Palestine are the *Meejana* and *'Ataba*, where a singer starts with "Ooaaf, ooaaf, ooaaf..." followed by four verses of sung poetry, often spontaneously composed depicting a singer's skills at word-play. The *Dal'oona* and *Ya Zareef et-Tul* are the songs most favored for *dabke* dancing and usually accompanied by traditional instruments such as the *shabbabeh* (a small nay), the *yarghoul* (a single-piped, wooden clarinet that gives a sound similar to that of bagpipes), the *mijwez* (a double *yargoul*), the *rababa* (a long necked, single-stringed, instrument with a rectangular bottom covered in hide and played with a bow made of hair from a horse's tail), and the *tabl* (a shoulder-held, wooden drum covered with hide on both sides and played with two sticks).

Several recent recordings give a good introduction to Palestinian folk music. Of note is *Traditional Music and Song from Palestine* put out by The Popular Art Centre in el-Bireh, a Palestinian NGO founded in 1987 during the first intifada by El-Funoun, the Palestinian Popular Dance Troupe, to teach and promote traditional dance and provide a forum for local dance groups, musicians and artists. It features the powerful voice of Mousa Hafez, a leading poet-singer living in the Jenin refugee camp. Other worthy recordings include *Zaghareed: Music from the Palestinian Holy Land,* featuring contemporary interpretations of old folk songs and *Lost Songs of Palestine* (www.interlinkbooks.com), which includes both instrumental and vocal favorites such as *Weyn A Ramallah, Arrozana, Marmar Zamaani*, and *Ala Dal'oona.*

Popular and Fusion Music

As the day-to-day experiences of Palestinians became more involved in the politics of resistance, so changed the musical output of the people. Instead of lyrics, for example, that tell of a "suffering heart burning with love, which is satisfied only by the sweet lips of a lover," artists began to sing about the day-to-day hardships of life under occupation and the dream of statehood. In the aftermath of the 1967 tragedy, a young Palestinian *oud* player and composer by the name of **Mustapha al-Kurd** inflamed peoples' emotions and received wide popularity with his 1970 recording of *Kullee Amal* (in Arabic, Full of Hope). **Marcel Khalife**, a Lebanese singer-songwriter, touched the souls of Palestinians with his defiant music, especially his use of poetry composed by the Palestinian poet Mahmoud Darwish on his recording *Tousbihouna Ala Watan.* Palestinians also have great respect and admiration for the Lebanese diva **Fairouz** who sang eloquently about beloved Jerusalem in *Zahrat al-Mada'en* (The Flower of All Cities) and *al-Quds Albaal* (Jerusalem on Our Mind) and about return in *Raji'oon* (We're Going Back).

The group **Sabreen** achieved international acclaim with their lively concerts and lyrics that convey messages of hope for freedom and a better life. The voice of their charismatic lead singer, Akka-born **Kamilya Jubran**, who is also an accomplished qanoun player, and the group's eclectic style that fused Arabic music with western influences, contributed to their 20-year success.

The new voices of resistance within the Palestinian struggle for peace and justice are those of Palestinian rappers living in Gaza, the West Bank, and inside the Green Line. A new documentary called *Sling Shot Hip Hop: The Palestinian Lyrical Front* by Jaqueline Salloum spotlights the alternative voices of young rappers such as Arapeyat (Akka), DAM (Lydda), RFM (GAZA), Zilzal (Akka), WE7 (Nazareth), Abir (Lydda), Boi Kutt and Stormtrap (Ramallah), Rami (Jenin), No Fear (Tamra) and others. It gives insight into Palestinian youth culture and emerging musical talents and explores the role their music plays within their social, political and personal lives.

Culinary Traditions

A ttention to detail is an aspect of Palestinian cuisine that could deter the initiate cook. We roll vine leaves and chard into cigarette size morsels, we stuff bite-size pastries with infinite patience and care, and we chop meat and vegetables into diminutive chips, undaunted by the lure of modern appliances. Yet for all this refinement and delicacy, Palestinian cuisine has not gone public; it is within the confines of private homes that the Palestinian repertoire unfurls an extensive variety of culinary delights.

Recent visits to the old marketplace and to the many vegetable and fruit shops about the towns have been disheartening lately: displays are a caricature of what we used to have in summer. Supply to the towns has been irregular and poor as a result of the isolation of agricultural villages, irreverent attacks on planted expanses, and a persistent ban on the passage of goods in the Palestinian areas. One has to be content with basics; yet unfortunate as the situation might be, it is during times as hard as those we are living in that one comes to appreciate the ingenuity of Palestinian cuisine and its adaptability to dire circumstances. A lack of products can be an incitement for cooks to pull out old recipes from the bottom of their drawers and infuse what they learned from their mothers and grandmothers with the ingenuity of acquired experience.

Traditional Palestinian cuisine offers a rich variety of dishes characteristic of the eastern regions of the Mediterranean. Geographic differences change methods of food preparation, as do the lifestyles—nomadic migrant to urban sophisticate—that have left their imprint on Palestinian life. Successive occupations left their mark, too. The many foreign communities who settled in the Holy Land in the aftermath of the Crimean war in 1855 have greatly contributed to the character of Palestinian cuisine, especially in urban centers such as

Jerusalem, Jaffa, Ramallah, and Bethlehem. And of course, the changes of the last 50 years have influenced culinary trends, too, and cannot be underestimated.

Special Features of Palestinian Cuisine

Palestinian cuisine has shouldered the tides of history by accommodation rather than rigid resistance, yet certain features have remained constant. Lamb, for example, holds a place of honor at every Palestinian table, and the slaughtering of lamb especially for an important occasion is still a vital element of Palestinian life, even if one has to borrow money to do it. Easter and *Adha*, two major feasts based on the concept of sacrifice for Christians and Muslims alike, are the focal points of this long-standing tradition.

Rice is a staple—and a symbol. The fact that it is not sown in Palestine is an indication of the worldliness that has long been a feature of Palestinian culinary tradition, with the country's position both as a station on ancient trade routes and as a destination for foreigners who wanted to make the Holy Land theirs. Rice is the basic ingredient in ceremonial dishes. It invariably accompanies stews and is an essential component of *mahashi*, all dishes that involve stuffing, from whole lambs to chicken to daintily cored vegetables.

Samneh baladieh, or clarified butter, is another important element of the cuisine. Extracted from sheep's milk, *samneh* is strained butter that has been boiled with cracked wheat, nutmeg, and *curcuma*, a bittersweet spice that gives the samneh its musk flavor and distinctive bright yellow. It is one of those ingredients that cannot be bought off the shelf in a grocery store, but must be obtained through a network of contacts among the nomadic bedouins who breed the sheep and make the butter. In recent years, as consumers have become more wary of saturated fats, samneh is being used sparingly as an added flavor. Many younger people living in urban centers have given it up totally, instead using more and more olive oil.

Left: Breads and sandwiches, Jaffa
Below: Aubergine Mahashi

When the milk is churned to extract the butter, the by-product, *laban mkheed*, another essential ingredient in many Palestinian dishes, is also processed for year-round storage. This buttermilk is left to drip through cheesecloth for a few days. The resulting pasty cheese is then kneaded with salt, cumin, and *curcuma*, shaped into balls and dried over a wooden board in a dark room for a few days and then stored in cloth bags. Individual balls of *laban jmeed*, as it is called in its new state, are diluted as needed for sauces for *mahashi*, *mansaf*, *fatteh*, and a variety of stews.

Typical Palestinian Dishes

Mansaf and *kidreh*, without which any celebration does not deserve mention, are de rigueur at every traditional wedding, funeral, baptism, and circumcision. *Mansaf*, a dish with lamb, rice, and *laban jmeed*, comes originally from Trans-Jordan but was adopted wholeheartedly by the Palestinians as a dish for special occasions, most particularly in the Hebron area and the Negev. It is traditionally served in a large common plate, without the use of western tableware. *Kidreh*, another dish typical of the Bethlehem, Ramallah, and Jerusalem areas as well as the Gaza Strip, is also based on rice and meat, with minor regional variations, particularly in the use of spices.

Mahashi dishes are popular all over Palestine and have the advantage of being prepared the day before. The preparation of stuffed vegetables—eggplants, zucchini, baby pumpkins, potatoes, carrots and cucumbers—is a delicate operation requiring great dexterity and infinite patience. Coring vegetables requires a special tool that one can buy for a pittance from the local souks. It can also be bought in Middle Eastern food shops or in the Arab quarters of big cities. *Mahashi* also includes the stuffing of vines leaves, cabbage leaves, and chard into small cigarette size portions, an elaborate and time consuming job, unless the family's large enough to have many women who can chip in.

Fatteh, another popular dish often based on rice, derives its name from the cut up bread which, soaked in sauce, is a basic component of the dish. *Fatteh* can be cooked with meat, chicken, or fish and the added rice and sauce are prepared with their broth. Originally a peasant dish, it is convenient for recycling left-over bread.

Stews are basic fare for every day family cooking and are always served with vermicelli or plain rice. They are popular because they provide a wide range of nutrients from the meat, the vegetables, and the rice, and supply the extra liquid so essential in a climate where dry weather is the norm for most of the year. They also have the advantage of being economical, as a relatively small amount of meat can go a long way.

Mussakhan, an all-time favorite among Palestinians, originates in Tulkarem and Jenin. A succulent dish consisting of grilled chicken served on bread smothered with a mixture of onions and sumac and cooked in plenty of olive oil, it competes with *mansaf* and *kiddreh* as the representative dish of the Palestinians. The ideal bread for this dish is the local *tabun* bread. The tabun is the famous clay oven that was a centerpiece in every garden or backyard. When this bread is not available, *kmaj* bread is thick enough to carry the stuffing.

Further north, in Acre, Haifa, Nazareth, and the Triangle, the differences that we encounter in the cooking styles between the rural and the urban areas are as sharp as those in the rest of Palestine. One marked regional difference is that rice, though a staple in these parts too, is a less important ingredient in ceremonial dishes. While oriental rice—a mixture of rice with chopped meat and nuts, flavored with an

Modern Musakin

Lubia

assortment of spices—accompanied by meat or chicken, is quite a
favorite, it is a variety of meatball and potato dishes that are ubiquitous
at special occasions. *Kubbeh*, a mixture of meat and burghul ground to
a paste and shaped into oblong balls and stuffed with spicy meat and
onions is often served raw, a practice directly imported from Lebanon.
It is often served at social gatherings to officially put an end to a period
of mourning.

Food Preparation and Lifestyles

One eats with one's eyes first, an Arab saying goes, so it is no surprise
that Palestinian cuisine is colorful, and none more so than a table
spread with *mezze*. A whole assortment of salads and dips and fresh
bright vegetables cut and prepared in a variety of ways; generous
dribbles of olive oil smoothing the sharpness of pickles and hot
peppers; fried or baked pastries stuffed with all manner of savory
fillings; and the ubiquitous bowl of olives, home grown and home
pickled according to grandmother's recipe.

   Mezze, typical of most countries of the Mediterranean basin,
suggests leisurely meals consumed over hours of nibbling and sampling
and dipping, with languid after-meal siestas or long summer evenings
on the terrace stretched by endless puffs on the nargila. But the ease

implied in the consumption disguises the time and effort invested in the preparation of an assortment worthy of the name.

Traditionally, food preparation has been the domain of the many women of an extended family living under one roof. Changing life styles in urban centers, a shift toward the nuclear family, and a growing number of women joining the work force, have inevitably brought about new food habits. Starting from the shopping for food to the actual sharing of a meal, middle-class urban Palestinians increasingly show signs of Western standardization: pizza nights, frozen food, pasta salads, Chinese takeout. The social dimension of the collective preparation of food and sharing of favorite dishes has almost disappeared. Yet during these last few hard months, one sees a reversal in cooking and eating habits, and a return to some of the creative old country cooking of the past.

Olives in Nazareth

6.

Traditional Dress

To tell the story of the *thob*, the traditional Palestinian dress for women, is also to tell the story of the women of rural Palestine. For more than a thousand years, the color, style, fabric, and stitching on the thobs have served as letters and words for women who did not have the privilege of literacy. The record the women of rural Palestine have left for anthropologists is these long, flowing dresses. They tell of Palestinian history, identity, and endurance through the ages.

The color scheme of traditional Palestinian dresses—unlike the bleak black, gray, and beige Islamic dress code of the modern Muslim world—embraces bright colors, reflecting both Palestine's pre-monotheistic traditions and its natural, rural way of life. Reds and purples, indigo blue, saffron yellow, and vibrant green run across Palestinian fabrics as flowers dot the country's fields.

The quality of fabric, the brightness of its colors, and the simplicity or elaborateness of the embroidery all reflect the social status of its wearer. A thob displays a woman's hand skills, her social standing, and even her regional identity. Anthropologists have described the thob as a map, since it indicates what village a woman is from, whether she is single, married, divorced, widowed or remarried, rich or poor, Christian or Muslim, from the plains, mountains or coast, settled or nomad.

As in many cultures, fineness of embroidery was regarded as the hallmark of a desirable bride. Women from wealthy villages, especially in the Jerusalem (including Bethlehem and Ramallah) and Hebron areas, considered themselves of a different class than other village women, who, with less free time, were less likely to have fine embroidery.

Ramallah area dress

Ancient Fabrics

Traditonally, a thob was made either of local or imported cotton, linen, or silk. Both linen and wool industries flourished in ancient Palestine. Linen was cultivated as a major crop on the plains of Jericho, and the "wool of Canaan" is often mentioned in ancient texts. These commodities were sought after throughout the Mediterranean world, as was cotton, which the Assyrians brought to Palestine in 750 BCE.

Dyes

The art of dyeing has been practiced in Palestine since the days of the Canaanites. A dyer typically had his workshop next to that of a weaver. Indigo plants were cultivated in the plains of Bisan, around Tiberias, and along the Jordan Valley. In the environs of Nablus, madder, kermes, and cochineal were cultivated for red dyes. Sumac berries were crushed to obtain purple; yellow was extracted from saffron flowers. These natural dyes display a subtlety of hue not found in contemporary synthetic dyes.

Embroidery Traditions

Women's embroidery gatherings contributed to solidifying and intensifying community ties, whether they took place under the shade of carob trees or grape arbors, or at home around a fire. Women gathered to exchange patterns and discuss new stitches and color schemes. Girls would start embroidering their own dresses at the age of nine or ten, and many spent their spare time as young teenagers embroidering their wedding dress and trousseau under the supervision of their mothers, older sisters, and sister-in-laws.

Although women were free to choose their own designs for their embroidery—and they did, varying stitch, color, density, and pattern—they were also bound by tradition and the context in which they lived. A woman who feared the evil spirits would embroider a protective eye into her dress; pious women wove in religious motifs, such as crescents or crosses. The use of vibrant colors on a densely stitched bodice was believed to protect the vulnerable chest area from illness and to enhance the woman's ability to breastfeed her children. A camel meant the woman came from a desert region, while grapes, flowers, and orange blossoms meant she came from an agriculturally rich community. Geometric patterns tended to indicate a coastal region. The eight-pointed star and S-shape designs that recur across the regions are believed to be inherited from ancient, pre-monotheistic times.

Colors

While the colors red, purple, indigo blue, and saffron are part of the ancient color schemes of Canaan and the Philistine coast, Islamic green and Byzantine black have more recently been added to palette of "traditional" embroidery colors.

Red, the most prominent color for embroidery, served several purposes. The tribe of Yemen, one of the two Arabian tribes in Palestine, used red as an identification symbol. Hence, brides of the tribe of Yemen wore red dresses on their wedding day. The other major Arab tribe of Palestine, the Qais from northern Arabia, was identified with white. According to lore, red is also the color of sensuality and sexual maturity, so unmarried girls and women never embroidered their dresses with red thread.

Beit Dajan/Jaffa regional dress

Stitches

Cross-stitch is the most commonly used stitch in embroidery, whether for thobs, cushions, doilies, or headdresses. Couching stitch, a more complex, sophisticated stitch, involves ample silver and gold *qasab* threads to achieve the Bethlehem-style embroidery. Other stitches such as *manajel* (sickles), *tinbeeteh* (plant sprouts or shoots), daisy-chain, and satin stitch were used as decorative stitches, as well as for appliqué, edging, and hemming.

Density of stitches on a thob could imply its origin. Thobs of the Hebron area are famous for their remarkably dense embroidery; thobs from the Ramallah area are much more lightly embroidered. Thobs of the Jaffa area are marked for the finesse of their stitches, while Gazan thobs are characterized by striped cotton fabrics with minimum embroidery.

The Traditional Wardrobe

The Palestinian traditional wardrobe does not begin and end with the thob. (Indeed, a man's attire is no less an indicator of social standing and income than a woman's.) In addition to the thob, a typical woman's costume includes: a highly decorated headdress, often coin-loaded, whose importance is revealed in its many names (*shatweh, smadeh, saffeh, wuqqaieh*); a loose veil, which covers the headdress and drapes over the shoulders, meeting the thob at about two-thirds its length; *sirwal*, ankle-length pants worn under the thob; and *jillayeh*, an

Jerusalem area village dress

exceptionally beautiful short-sleeved, richly and flamboyantly embroidered or appliquéd coat-dress.

The Bethlehem dress, whose beauty influenced some Jerusalem village dresses, is considered the queen of the dresses, so heavily laden with golden and silver embroidery. It is accompanied by a refined velvet jacket that is also embroidered with ornate silver and gold thread.

A woman's traditional *jhaz* (trousseau) includes all dress requirements for her future life: everyday and ceremonial dresses, jewelry, veils, headdresses, kerchiefs, girdles, belts, undergarments, and footwear.

Times of Crisis

The first Palestinian intifada (1987–1993) produced a new kind of thob. In response to the Israeli banning of the Palestinian flag (the penalty for flying the red, white, black, and green flag was arrest and imprisonment), many village and refugee women showed their support for the liberation struggle by embroidering their dresses with the colors of the flag, daring Israeli soldiers to arrest or shoot them. Instead of being first an individual belonging to a clan, a tribe, or a village, Palestinian women showed their desire to become part of a larger entity by simply wearing the flags embroidered on their dresses.

Of course modernity, urbanization, and globalization have changed fashion in Palestine. No doubt Palestinian dress will change in the 21st century according to the the needs and aesthetic of the times. But with the Palestinian national identity under constant assault, it is unlikely that the thob will die out. Rather it is likely to be reinvented again and again, by the increasingly literate female population.

7.

Jewelry

Canaan was a society that valued the arts, and in particular the art of jewelry-making. The vast amounts of exquisitely crafted jewelry found at excavated sites across the country indicate advanced knowledge of metal and silversmith techniques. Indeed, ancient records found in Egypt document that the Canaanites traded olive oil for Sinai copper, Egyptian faience beads, and alabaster.

Among the first finds in Palestine date to the Chalcolithic age and include pendants and beads of ostrich egg shells, ivory, turquoise, and mother-of-pearl. The latter were believed to protect their wearer from evil.

An exquisite gold jewelry collection was unearthed at Tell el-Ajjoul in the Gaza Strip. The Gaza jewelry, dating to the late Bronze age (1300–1200 BCE), attests to the wealth of Canaan shortly before its demise. Archeologists now cite Tell el-Ajjoul alongside Troy (Asia Minor), Enkomi (Cyprus), and Ras-Shamra (Syria) as among the most important jewelry arts centers of the ancient world.

The Tell el-Ajjoul collection includes a gold amulet portraying the female head of the mother goddess, a gold eight-pointed star pendant, and gold crescent-shaped earrings. The crescent was the symbol of Ashtarout, the Canaanite love and fertility goddess. Both the eight-pointed star and the crescent were early Canaanite symbols long before they were integrated into Byzantine, Islamic, and modern art traditions.

Jewelry found at other excavation sites revealed a substantial Egyptian influence, in such pieces as gold-set faience beads, a signet ring with a pharoahs's name inscribed on it, and many eyes of Horus. Carnelian beads became popular after the Assyrian conquest of Palestine in 730 BCE.

Much of the jewelry discovered at sites across the country were Byzantine or Hellenistic prototypes, with heads of gods and sacred creatures such as snakes predominating. Twenty-one-karat gold snake-head bracelets are still part of the wedding dowry (*shabkeh*) of the Palestinian bride.

One of the most important archeological finds related to jewelry-making is a porcelain mold of an earring found near Jerusalem, probably dating back to the first century BCE. The existence of a mold suggests that such pieces were mass-produced. Another major find in the Nablus region, a gold diadem (crown) dating back to the times of Julius Caesar, was apparently crafted by a local artist.

Islamic designs were introduced during the rise of the Abbasid Caliphate (circa 750) and diverged completely from the long dominating Byzantine/Hellenistic style. Calligraphy, especially phrases from the Holy Quran, was integrated into jewelry designs, as well as floral patterns, seemingly endless scrolls (sometimes called arabesques) and extensive use of filigree and granulation. Animal and human figures were discouraged by teachings of Islam. Some Fatimid gold hollow beads discovered in a grove in Caesarea, and many other gold pieces found in Askalan and elsewhere, revealed the use of the intricate granulation and filigree work that are characteristic of Islamic jewelry.

Modern Traditional Jewelry

Most of what is left to us from the Ottoman and British era in Palestine is silver jewelry. Collections can be found in small local museums, usually run by private collectors, or at the antique bazaars in

Jerusalem, Hebron, Gaza, or Nablus. Vanity and the desire for adornment were not the over-riding reasons for wearing jewelry in traditional Palestinian society. Much as their ancestors did, modern Palestinian women wore their jewelry for protection against schizophrenia, the evil eye, the envious eye (*ein el hasood*), and in general against the penetration of evil into their souls.

Wearing blue beads to keep away the evil eye was ultimately a remnant of pre-monotheistic traditions. The talismanic and amuletic powers of jewelry were thought to relieve the difficulties of labor and childbirth, to heal, to protect newborns, to bring fertility and love. Such powers were induced by the presence of a certain component in a jewelry piece: a symbol, a shape, a stone, a color, a number, an inscription.

Traditionally, amber was thought to have healing powers, agate to induce fertility, turquoise or imitation blue beads to ward off the evil eye, and coral to safeguard the soul. A baby's first jewelry would always have an inscription (either Christian or Islamic) and a blue bead. The famous good-luck charm called the "Hand of Fatima," or "*kaf*" (palm), is a symbol of patience and abundance.

Odd numbers, especially three, five, and seven, bring good luck. Tradition has it that dangles suspended from any kind of jewelry should be in odd numbers. A triangle, with its three sides, is a

Bir es-Saba area headdress

popular shape for earrings and necklaces, and is thought to ward off evil spirits.

Beauty and the Bead

Hardly any women are fonder of jewelry than Bedouins, who as a matter of daily existence wear large and colorful jewelry, beads in particular. Perhaps the extensive use of colorful beads, genuine or imitation—red and yellow amber, coral and turquoise—livens the sometimes monotone desert landscape, or more contemporarily the slums provided for them by the state of Israel. Perhaps it is the heritage of the nomad: to wear riches openly, rather than hoard or install them in buildings.

Silver Bedouin jewelry is historically influenced by the Yemeni tradition and vaguely to Anatolian tribal jewelry. Jingling jewelry—earrings, anklets, many bracelets—proclaim a Bedouin woman's presence without her having to utter a word. She wears most of her jewelry most of the time—equally for ceremonies and funerals, making dough and filling water jugs, shepherding, and even sleeping. This often gives the jewelry an antiqued *niello* color, a look modern jewelers use chemicals to achieve.

Several standard pieces are most noteworthy. One is the remarkable *burkou* (face cover), which the Bedouin woman wears when around men who are not part of her clan. Revealing only her kohl-lined eyes, the *burkou* is densely embroidered, stitched with colored beads and amulets, and loaded with all the silver coins that the woman owns. Village women generally also wore a *shatweh*, which covers the hair and is draped over by a long veil. The *shatweh* also holds almost all of a woman's precious coins (often received as part of her wedding dowry). The delicate *shnaf* (nose-ring) is a strictly Bedouin accessory. Pierced through one nostril, the piece is highly ornamental with filigree work and granulation. Depending on the husband's fiscal standing, the *shnaf* may be reduced to a plain metal ring or simply a loop of thread. Although considered a traditional Bedouin piece of jewelry, the nose ring resembles a common Byzantine earring.

Urban and Rural Traditional Jewelry

Urban and town jewelry, including bangles, earrings, hair ornaments, chokers, and other items, were typically silver. Gold started to make a regular appearance only in the 1920s. Though each locality had its own particularities of style, it is not surprising that much of the Palestinian

Kafat Fatima

jewelry resembled that of the larger Arab world. Necklaces and chains often have a theme that involves the number 8 and many are composed of silver or gold coins.

The following jewelry pieces, though, are noteworthy for their uniqueness and particular place in the lexicon of Palestinian jewelry.

The *kirdan* (neck in Persian) is one of the most sophisticated traditional neck chokers found in the Palestinian collection. Exclusively manufactured in the Nablus area, and more recently in Hebron, the kirdan has a sister design manufactured in Egypt and in the northern Lebanese city of Tripoli where it is known as *sha'ariyah* (noodles).

The *khyarah* (cucumber) necklace has a hollow cucumber amulet from which dangle silver coins; a scroll with religious writings thought to have protective talismanic powers fits inside the hollow. This popular piece of jewelry is attached from both sides to thick durable long chain.

The *saba' arwah* (seven spirits) necklace is a type of chain-and-coin jewelry given to a bride as part of her wedding *shabkeh* (dowry). Worn attached to the sides of her wedding hat, the necklace comprises seven chains and one Austrian Maria Teresa coin (a leftover from the Ottoman era). Palestinian tradition is superstitious about the number seven. A cat has seven lives. God created the world in seven days. These are but two of the local folk traditions that have spread around the world.

Hibbiyah (with seeds, grains, or granules) refers to a necklace or bracelet done in the granule technique. The most famous and beautiful hibbiyah is a three-stranded gold choker. The hibbiyah was originally manufactured in the village of Hamama, between Gaza and Askalan. After the destruction of the village in 1948, the design was made famous in Gaza by the town's refugees. The centerpiece is a gold coin from which a gold filigree crescent is suspended.

Saba' arwah necklace with Maria Teresa coin

By the beach in Gaza City

8.

Refugees and Refugee Camps

Visitors may find it curious that this guide book contains a special section dedicated to the Palestinian refugees and the camps within which many of them reside. Indeed, the construction of historical Palestine as the Holy Land serves to draw a visitor's attention away from the living people of Palestine. But modern day Palestinians are the living part of a historic, religious, and cultural continuum.

The last century has forced great changes and challenges upon the Palestinian people that threaten their attachment to their history and environs. The success of the Zionist movement in establishing the state of Israel on the ruins of Palestine came at a huge price to the indigenous Christian and Muslim community. By the end of 1948, more than 750,000 Palestinians (two-thirds of the entire indigenous population) were forced into exile by the newly established state and more prevented from returning to their homes. In a massive ethnic cleansing, 530 Palestinian villages, towns, and cities were depopulated of their inhabitants, with most destroyed, and in some cases, resettled with new Jewish immigrants. Palestinians refer to these events as the *Nakba* (catastrophe).

The experience of 1948 is, however, not the end of the story of Palestinian dispossession. Events since the establishment of the Israel state have resulted in significant waves of new refugees. These include the June War of 1967 (350,000 refugees from the West Bank) and the 1990–91 Gulf War (400,000 Palestinians displaced from Kuwait). Additionally, regular Israeli governmental policies and practices within the Green Line and in the Occupied Territories such as massive house demolitions, deportations, and land confiscation have also created a significant number of refugees. Overall, it is estimated that three-quarters

UNRWA Refugee Camps

Mediterranean Sea

Neirab
Quarantine
Khan Abu Bakr

Hama

Homs

Nahr Al-Bared
Beddawi

LEBANON

Gouraud
Wavell

Dbayyeh
Beirut
Dekwaneh
Shatila
Jisr Al-Basha
Mar Elias
Burj Al-Barajneh

Damascus

Ein Al-Hilweh
Mieh Mieh
Alliance
Khan Dannoun
Khan
Ashieh
Nabatiyyeh

Al-Bass
Burj Ash-Shemali
Rashidiyyeh

SYRIA

Golan
Heights

Haifa

Dera'a

Irbid

Jenin

Tulkarem
Nur Shams
Camp No. 1
Far'a
Balata
Askar

JORDAN

Zarqa

Tel Aviv

Deir Ammar
Jalazoun
Al-'Amari
Nuweimeh
Qalandia
Ein
Sultan
Jericho
Al-Karameh
Amman
Amman New Camp
(Wihdat)
Jabal
Al-Hussein

Jerusalem
Akabat Jabr
Aida
Beit Jibrin
Dheisheh
Arroub

ISRAEL

Shati (Beach)
Jabalia
Nuseirat
Deir
Al-Balah
Bureij
Al-Maghazi
Khan Younis
Rafah

Fawar

0   25   50   75 km

Map: PASSIA, 2002

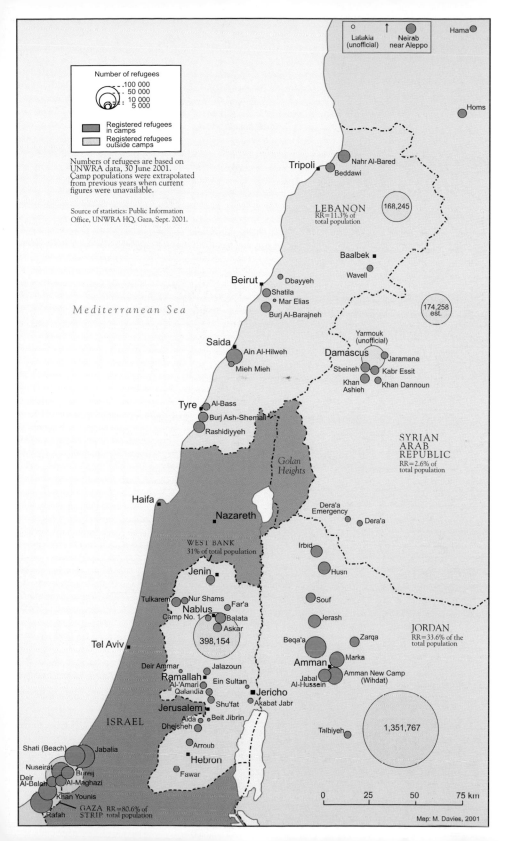

Lalakia (unofficial)   Neirab near Aleppo   Hama

Number of refugees
- 100 000
- 50 000
- 10 000
- 5 000

Registered refugees in camps
Registered refugees outside camps

Numbers of refugees are based on UNWRA data, 30 June 2001. Camp populations were extrapolated from previous years when current figures were unavailable.

Source of statistics: Public Information Office, UNWRA HQ, Gaza, Sept. 2001.

Mediterranean Sea

Homs

Tripoli
Nahr Al-Bared
Beddawi

LEBANON
RR=11.3% of total population
168,245

Baalbek
Wavell

Beirut
Dbayyeh
Shatila
Mar Elias
Burj Al-Barajneh

174,258 est.

Yarmouk (unofficial)

Saida
Ain Al-Hilweh
Mieh Mieh

Damascus
Jaramana
Sbeineh   Kabr Essit
Khan Ashieh   Khan Dannoun

Tyre
Al-Bass
Burj Ash-Shemali
Rashidiyyeh

SYRIAN ARAB REPUBLIC
RR=2.6% of total population

Haifa

Golan Heights

Nazareth

Dera'a Emergency   Dera'a

WEST BANK
31% of total population

Irbid
Husn

Jenin

Tulkarem   Nur Shams
Nablus   Far'a
Camp No. 1   Balata
Askar

Souf

Jerash

398,154

Tel Aviv

Beqa'a

Zarqa

JORDAN
RR=33.6% of the total population

Amman   Marka
Jabal   Amman New Camp
Al-Hussein   (Wihdat)

Deir Ammar   Jalazoun
Ramallah
Al-'Amari   Ein Sultan
Qalandia
Jerusalem   Jericho
Shu'fat   Akabat Jabr
Aida
ISRAEL   Beit Jibrin
Dheisheh

Talbiyeh   1,351,767

Arroub

Hebron

Fawar

Shati (Beach)   Jabalia
Nuseirat
Bureij
Deir   Al-Maghazi
Al-Balah
Khan Younis
Rafah
GAZA   RR=80.6% of
STRIP   total population

0   25   50   75 km

Map: M. Davies, 2001

of the Palestinian people are refugees or the descendents of refugees. That this has extended for more than half a century makes the Palestinian refugee issue one of the greatest unresolved refugee tragedies in the world. Understanding the experience of these refugees, therefore, is essential to understanding the Palestinian people.

There are approximately 5.5 million Palestinian refugees today, dispersed throughout the West Bank (700,000), the Gaza Strip (820,000), Israel (259,000), Jordan (1,866,000), Syria (477,000), and Lebanon (437,000). Almost 80 percent reside within 100 kilometers of their original homes. But they are barred from returning by Israel, which also refuses to acknowlege relevant UN resolutions and international law.

Israel has expropriated Palestinian refugee property by enacting a series of laws, the most explicit of which is the Law of Absentee Property (1950). This law decrees that Palestinians not present on their lands during the 1948 War be defined as "absentee," thus allowing the property's seizure and transference to the Israeli government, administered by the Custodian of Absentee Property. In many cases, the Custodian has transferred the properties to a "Development Authority" which authorizes the development, rental, and selling of these properties to Jewish foundations only. All Palestinian refugees are considered to be "absentee," including those who remained in the territory that became Israel, and who may have gone merely to a neighboring village to flee the fighting.

West Bank and Gaza Strip Camps
Throughout the 1967 Occupied Territories, UNRWA administers 26 camps (19 in the West Bank, 8 in the Gaza Strip), with a total refugee population of 1.5 million people. UNRWA established the main Palestinian refugee camps in 1949. Much has changed since then, when relief meant providing tents and blankets, emergency medical attention and vaccinations, and food. When it became obvious that the Palestinian refugee issue would take time to resolve, UNRWA widened its activities.

The land upon which the camps were located (usually on the periphery of what then were small cities or towns) was rented by UNRWA from their original owners at going rates, usually with a 99-year lease. Around the mid-1950s, UNRWA began building more permanent shelters for the refugees, who by that time had been living in tents for several years, directly exposed to harsh winter and summer conditions. The new shelters or "units" constructed for the refugees were 3-by-3 meters square made of cheap building blocks with asbestos or zinc sheeting for a roof. Families composed of five members or less were given one unit, while those of six or more were given two units. (The average Palestinian refugee family size at the time was 6.7 persons). Every 25 units were allotted two public bathrooms (one for women, another for men) and water was piped to a community spicket. Needless to say, refugee camp elders recall the early years of the camp as times marked by great difficulty and suffering—compounded by their collective shock and the pain of prolonged exile from their native lands.

Today, the original unit structure of the camp is difficult to discern. With the propitious rise in the camp population, as well as the rapid urbanization of the West Bank and Gaza Strip, refugee camp residents have been forced to build vertically, often several stories high, upon original structures that were intended for no more than two floors. Due to city growth, many refugee camps no longer exist upon the periphery of a given city or town but rather are fairly centrally located, causing the price of local real estate to rise. This has made it more difficult for refugees to leave the camp, because they are unable to purchase plots of land outside. Over 50 years, this has resulted in a fairly clear visual distinction between refugee camp and city, with the camps being characterized by a dense concentration of unfinished (without facades) concrete structures.

The distinction is not merely visual but penetrates to the social relations between camp and town or village. Urban refugee camps dwellers, particularly in the West Bank, experience social marginalzation from their host communities. Refugees are considered outsiders—and burdensome and undesirable outsiders at that. This phenomenon is less prominent in rural refugee camps and in the Gaza Strip where refugees outnumber locals by at least three to one.

Visitors to Palestinian refugee camps will notice certain similarities: high rates of unemployment, the density of the construction, the numbers of children who seem to be incessantly running around the labyrinth of alleyways, and so forth. Yet beyond this superficial impression, Palestinian refugee camps have distinctions between them, as well as diversity within each camp. Camps are a potpourri of village peasants, city folk, and Bedouins, and each group brings their unique traditions, customs, culinary techniques, dress, and regional accents.

From the beginning, Palestinian refugee camps have often been hotbeds of nationalist political activity. Refugee camps have developed networks of political organizations, as well as distinct

Refugees celebrating a wedding

histories, even if these are often unknown to those outside the camp.

It is not uncommon for refugee camps to routinely suffer curfews, house searches, and house sealings (a house is filled with concrete) or demolitions as punitive measures against those involved in resistance activity against the Israeli occupation. The difficulty of governing the

refugee camps was one of the main reasons Israel sought to withdraw from the Palestinian cities when they signed the Oslo Accords with the PLO in 1993. As result of these Accords, most of the major nineteen refugee camps in the West Bank and all those in the Gaza Strip were transferred to the self-governing Palestinian National Authority.

The refugee camps listings in this guide consist of the official UN-registered camps of the West Bank and Gaza Strip and include the basic histories of each camp community. Also provided is contact information which will enable visitors to visit each camp. First-hand visits, more than any synopsis or statistical data, are the best means to understanding what it means to be Palestinian. Additionally, UNRWA will always be able to provide the accurate statistics and information on each camp and generally are able to arrange tours.

Refugee camp residents, while often struggling on many levels, tend to be exceedingly warm and welcoming to concerned foreign visitors, and visitors will invariably discover a Palestinian life much richer than media and tourist stereotypes.

9.

The Conflict and the Wall

My country's brokers are a band
Who shamefully survive
Even Satan went bankrupt
When he realized their temptation
They lead an easy, splendid life
But the bliss is the prize of the country's misery
They pretend to be its saviors,
Whatever you say, they claim to be its leaders
And protectors! But they are its ruin
It is bought and sold through their hands
Even the newspapers
Shield them, though we know the truth

—from "Brokers," Ibrahim Tuqan, translated by
Salwa Jabsheh & Naomi Shihab Nye, 20th century

Most guidebooks offer advice and information on touring countries that have internationally recognized borders and carry the political status of "state." This, however, is a guidebook to the homeland of the Palestinian people, a primer to the largely ignored indigenous narrative of Palestine, its people, their culture, and their history. Since the state of Israel rules most of this homeland—the rest is known as "Palestinian Autonomous Areas," zones A, B, and C—any guide to Palestine cannot ignore this reality. What follows, then, is a brief summary of the political situation.

Most beatings take place out of the sight of cameras.
al-Am'ari Camp, 1989.

The Politics

Realpolitik dictated that a 1947 United Nations decision dividing Palestine into two states, one Arab (Palestinian) and one Jewish (Israeli) never went into effect. The UN Partition Plan had envisioned the country being split 55–45, but after the cease-fire ending the fighting of 1948 went into effect, the newly created Israel held 78 percent of Palestine. Despite international outcry, Israeli forces refused to pull back from Palestinian territories acquired through force of arms. Half a century later a Palestinian state still has not come into existence.

At the end of hostilities, the remaining 22 percent of what was Palestine became known as the West Bank and the Gaza Strip. Jordan and Egypt ruled them as "administered" entities. Jerusalem was divided into Eastern and Western sectors, with the former under Arab rule.

In retrospect, Palestinians were slow to register that Palestine as they had known it ceased to exist almost overnight. Hundreds of thousands became refugees, living in tents and later in tin and cement dwellings, waiting to return home. Their homes were expropriated and given to Jewish colonists and hundreds of their towns and villages razed to the ground and erased from maps. Calls by the international community to allow the Palestinian refugees to return home were

The Wall surrounding Ramallah, as seen from the Qalandia checkpoint

ignored by Israel. Israel was built on Palestine. With the support of Western Europe and United States and by forging military alliances with the apartheid regime in South Africa, Israel has been able to ignore international law and world opinion for the past five decades.

For the first two decades after al-Nakba nearly a million refugees turned into two million—all with dreams of returning home. The 1967 war resulted in Israelis occupying the remaining 22 percent of Palestine.

So much has been written about this "conflict" that it is hard to identify one central way of describing what happened. But Akiva Orr, an Israeli historian, summed it up best when he wrote: "Palestine was Arab; foreigners came and took the land; the rest is detail."

In late 1987, after enduring twenty years of military occupation, a grassroots revolt erupted in the West Bank and Gaza Strip. A new generation of Palestinians born under Israel's military government fueled the new struggle for freedom. Unlike the refugees who lived in exile in Lebanon, Jordan, Syria, and across the globe, the young rebels who led the *intifada* (uprising) lived on their ancestral homeland and wanted the Israeli army gone.

The Map after Oslo

It must first be stated that the Oslo peace process has basically fallen apart; Israeli settlements and the Wall have ensured that, and now all of the Palestinian Autonomous Areas are again under Israeli military jurisdiction. But the redrawings of the map that were part of Oslo are important to know, because people still refer to Areas A, B, and C.

Oslo I, or the Gaza–Jericho Agreement (1994), amounted to the "redeployment" of the Israeli military from Jericho and Gaza and the beginning of self rule in those two areas.

Oslo II, the Interim Agreement on the West Bank and Gaza Strip (1995), extended the partial autonomy of the Palestinians to a series of cities and rural areas, including Jenin, Tulkarem, Qalqilia, Nablus, Ramallah, Bethlehem, and Hebron. The West Bank and Gaza Strip were divided into areas A, B, and C until further agreements could be made.

Area A: "Full" Palestinian civil jurisdiction and internal security.

Area B: Administrative and municipal jurisdiction by Palestinians, with "joint" Palestinian/Israeli jurisdiction over Palestinian internal security.

Area C: Full Israeli jurisdiction over all civil and security matters.

In August 2005, Israel disbanded 17 illegal settlements and military outposts in the Gaza Strip, though it continues to control all borders, airspace, and the sea.

0   20 km

Jenin

Tulkarem

Nablus

Qalqilya

Ramallah

Jericho

Jerusalem

ISRAEL

Bethlehem

Green Line

Hebron

Area A - Palestinian limited autonomy

Area B - Palestinian civil responsibility

Area C - Israeli exclusive rule

Map: PASSI

Demanding freedom and equality, their rallying cry was independence from foreign rule. For almost seven years they battled the Israeli army with slingshots. Over 1,200 Palestinians died and more than 10,000 were injured. But the long-term result of the intifada was the only true diplomatic gain the Palestinians ever made.

Pressured by international outrage at Israel's behavior, the United States intervened. In October 1991 in Madrid, Spain, a Palestinian delegation, working under the umbrella of the Hashemite Kingdom of Jordan, were allowed to represent themselves for the first time in peace talks with Israel. It was considered an historic breakthrough.

Three years later, the process known as the "Oslo Accords" began. The PLO came to an agreement with the Israelis—not an agreement between equals, but many Palestinians and Israelis were willing to call it a start.

The Palestinian Yasir Arafat and the Israeli Yitzhak Rabin led the two camps. "Interim" steps were taken to "ease" the occupation. Israeli tanks withdrew from "parts" of the West Bank and Gaza and tens of thousands of Palestinian political prisoners were released from Israeli jails, were many had languished for decades.

The Palestinians had two things to offer: recognition of the right of Israel to exist in Palestine and a helping hand in ending an embargo of Israel by an international community that had backed the Palestinians. While Israel had grown with the help of the United States and Western Europe, most of the rest of the world supported the Palestinians and economically and diplomatically boycotted Israel. The Palestinians paved the way for Israel to be accepted by the nations of the Third World, in exchange for forfeiting their claim over 78 percent of the Palestinian homeland.

In return Palestinians were allowed to police themselves in well-defined ghettos, called "Autonomous Areas," and to run municipal services such as garbage collection. Control of the border, airspace and territorial waters, the right to a national defense force, the ability to issue passports, currency, and regulate trade with the outside world—all were controlled by the Israelis.

A decade passed. Conditions for Palestinians continued to grow worse. Palestinians remained imprisoned in their ghettos, while not one illegal Israeli settlement on the West Bank or Gaza was dismantled according to the terms of Oslo. Indeed, seizure of Palestinian land dramatically increased in the West Bank and Gaza, dispossessing more and more Palestinians. The fuel of a massive rebellion was in place when General Ariel Sharon backed by 2,000 armed men, "visited" Palestine's

most holy shrine, the gold-domed, Haram al Sharif violating a 500-year-old Ottoman law on the status of religious sites in Jerusalem.

Another intifada, the al-Aqsa intifada, started almost immediately. Israeli soldiers firing live ammunition met stone-throwing crowds. Palestinian police responded by firing back, prompting a full-scale Israeli invasion of the Palestinian Autonomous Areas, using air strikes, backed by ground troops and helicopter gun ships. Palestinians responded with suicide bombings, and Israel countered with mass arrests, home demolition, land confiscation, and death squads. Finally, "the Wall" became the 21st-century emblem of Palestinian–Israeli relations.

A Wall in Palestine

In June 2002, Israel began implementing the building of a wall inside the West Bank that would run at least the West Bank's entire length. The Wall follows the logic of land confiscation and colonial control, annexation of land, the implanting of settlements and the caging off

Qalandia checkpoint

of urban, Palestinian areas. The Wall (also referred to as the "fence," "separation barrier," and particularly deceptively the "security fence") does not even mark the 1967 border known as the Green Line, but is a major land grab, attempting to seal the fate of the Occupied Territories and of Palestine.

The Wall has turned Palestinian towns and villages into essentially large open-air prisons. In its first phase alone (one-third of the Wall, in its shortest form), 65 communities and over 200,000 people in the Qalqiliya, Tulkarem, Jenin, Jerusalem and Bethlehem districts have been affected. Massive destruction preceded the Wall: the razing of agricultural land, the demolition of homes and community infrastructure, and loss of water. The Wall has cut farmers off from their land and markets, thrown thousands of workers into unemployment because they are barred from traveling to work, and has isolated thousands of families from one another.

When completed, the Wall will snake up to 6 kilometers (3.7 mi) deep inside the West Bank, effectively confiscating a substantial amount of Palestinian land. Israel is nearing the approval of an expanded plan, which will move the Wall even further east, up to 16 kilometers (9.9 mi) inside the West Bank, annexing its illegal settlements of Ariel, Immanuel, and Kedumim, among others. With the construction of the second Wall along the Jordan Valley, east of the Green Line and running parallel to the first Wall, Israel will isolate—amidst plans of direct control— full one-half of the West Bank, as the Wall will run the length of over 650 kilometers (400 mi).

In Jerusalem, the Wall is causing the city's complete isolation from the rest of Palestine. Jerusalem has become inaccessible to most Palestinians under the Israeli closure system that began ten years ago and which the Wall is making permanent. In Bethlehem, the Wall has severed the city's connection with Jerusalem and the rest of the West Bank. The Wall is both the stark embodiment and agent of Israel's closure and siege policy, as it shrinks already shrunken Palestinian ghettos further.

The Wall's Structure

The Wall takes on several physical forms, each massive and horrific. In Qalqiliya, the Wall is 8 meters (26 ft) high, made of concrete and lined with watchtowers and gun emplacements. In other areas, the Wall is a series of fences (some electric), trenches, military roads, barbed wire, surveillance cameras, trace paths for footprints, and buffer zones, all spanning a width of 70 to 100 meters (230 to 328 ft). In Bethlehem, the Wall consists of both structures: electric fences, remote sensors, trenches, and barbed wire. An Israeli-only bypass road, forbidden to Palestinian vehicles, and a concrete Wall encircling the city has completely isolated Bethlehem from the outside world.

The Wall is an old idea. Talk within Israeli establishment of erecting barriers to further cut off Palestinian communities from the wider world precedes the start of the intifada. The totality of the Wall's future continues to be kept secret by the Israeli military and government.

Sealing the Fate

The expanded Wall and the Jordan Valley Wall together form a map of the West Bank sliced on two sides, with two large, disconnected areas in the middle, and within them numerous ghettos comprised of villages and towns cut off from the outside world, with no freedom of movement, surrounded by settlements, military bases, Israeli-only bypass roads, and checkpoints.

When the walls are completed, the West Bank will be divided into three disconnected cantons with movement between them nearly impossible. As a façade of negotiations is being brokered over the creation of a Palestinian state, in actuality the Wall—known to Palestinians as the Apartheid Wall—is shaping the future of Palestine as it solidifies imprisonment of Palestinian people.

On July 9th, 2004 the International Court of Justice (ICJ) in the Hague declared the Wall Illegal.

The main premise of the court ruling was that the construction of the wall and "its associated régime" are contrary to international law and that Israel is under "obligation" to cease works on the construction of the wall and to "dismantle forthwith the structure therein situated," and to repeal or render ineffective forthwith all legislative and regulatory acts relating thereto.

Leaving Ramallah at the Qalandia checkpoint

PART TWO

Northern Palestine

Al-Jazzar Mosque

10.

Acre (Akka)

When he raised his head, something appeared in front of him.
Through the pale blue mist were the domes and rooftops of Akka.

—from *Dr. Qassim Talks to Eva About Mansour Who Arrived*
in Safad, Ghassan Kanafani, 20th century

Acre, a fabulous port city with a natural bay was first mentioned in in the *al-Amarna* tablets of the 14th-century BCE. To the Greeks, Acre was Aka; to the Egyptians, Ptolemais; and to the Romans, Colonia Claudia Felix. The Arabs, like the Canaanites and Greeks, called it Akkah, while the Crusaders named it Saint Jean d'Acre. Although Acre was to be a city in the Arab state of Palestine under the 1947 UN partition plan, the Israelis seized it and named it Akko.

Since earliest times it has been a pivotal seaport, situated on the sea at the mouth of the river Na'aman, on two important trade routes: the coastal highway and the road leading from the Mediterranean Sea to Syria and modern Jordan. A Canaanite city specializing in glass manufacturing and royal purple dye, it was much coveted by the Egyptians, who repeatedly launched expeditions to conquer the city (Thutmose III, 1504–1450 BCE; Seti I, 1291–1271 BCE; and Ramses II, 1275 BCE, all succeeded). On its shores, the Murex shells from which the Canaanites first extracted the color purple can still be found.

Ugarit and Akkadian documents attest to the city's importance during the Canaanite era, though it is mentioned just once in the Old Testament. (Judges 1:31 reads, "Asher did not drive out the inhabitants of Acco….")

Despite the Egyptians, Acre remained a Canaanite city until the reign of Sennnacherib (8–7th century BCE), when it was captured by the Assyrians and presented as a gift to the Phoenician king of Tyre. Later, under Artaxerxes II (405–359 BCE), it became a military and administrative center of the Persians who used it to attack Egypt.

Alexander the Macedonian's troops overran Acre on their march to Egypt and the city became predominantly Greek as colonists from the Aegean poured into the conquered port. After the death of Alexander it was captured by Ptolemy II of Egypt who renamed it Ptolemais in the third century BCE.

Herod captured it for the Romans and subsequently Acre enjoyed a rebirth under the Emperor Claudias (41–54 CE). It was a full-fledged Roman colony at the time of Nero (54–68 CE) and was subsequently enlarged and improved. Local industries continued to produce silk and purple dye. It took part in the First Jewish Revolt during the reign of the Roman Vespasian (69–79 CE).

Acre is only mentioned once in the New Testament. Luke relates that Paul of Tarsus, traveling aboard a Roman ship, "stopped over at Ptolemais during the spring of 59 CE... and stayed for one day." Despite being overlooked in the Bible, Christianity took an early foothold in the city.

After the Muslim conquest of Palestine, the Umayyad Caliph Mu'awiyah Ibn Sufian (639–681) built fortifications and renovated the harbor. Acre became a central launching pad for Arab-Muslim conquest of Cyprus, and ultimately North Africa. According to the historian al-Maqdisi (985 CE) Acre was an unfortified city until Ahmad Ibn Tulun (883–868) ordered that it be made as "impregnable" as Tyre. The builders worked for three years and used sycamore trees and stones to build the immense fortification. These walls still stand today.

At the time Acre had several significant pilgrimage sites. One was the Tomb of the Prophet Saleh (Nabi Saleh), said to have foretold the coming of the prophet Muhammad and performed miracles. He is most famed for turning a stone into a female camel, from whose milk a hungry population was fed. There are Nabi Saleh tombs in Ramleh and the Ramallah area. Another site is the garden inside the main al-Jazzar Mosque compound, which, according to Palestinian lore, was planted by the biblical Adam. And outside the eastern city gate, Ein al-Bakr (the Oxen Spring), is where Adam is believed to have brought his oxen to drink.

The Crusader Era

Acre has been a point of reference in the West since 1104 when King Baldwin I, with the support of the fleet of Genoa, overran the city in a 20-day siege. It was renamed St. Jean d'Acre and new city districts were founded to accommodate the Italian sailors, merchants, and soldiers who occupied the city. A refortification of the now popular city took place almost immediately and a new harbor was built.

In 1185 Ibn Jubair, the Andalusian traveler, wrote:

> Akkah is the chief of the Frank cities of Syria, the great port of the sea, and the great anchorage of their ships, being second only to Constantinople. It is a meeting place of Muslim and Christian merchants of all lands. No *maidan* (racing track) for horses can be finer. The lords of the town go there every evening and morning, and the soldiers also, for exercise.

The city remained in the grip of the Crusaders until 1187, when their armies were crushed by Saladin at the Battle of Hittin. Two years later, a new wave of Crusaders returned. The battle for Acre lasted two years and cost the Europeans 60,000 lives. Richard the Lionheart and Philippe August eventually joined the troops at the battle front and by reducing the Muslim troops inside the city to starvation, obtained their capitulation. It was during this siege of Acre that the famous military order of the Teutonic Knights was founded by the Germans of Jerusalem.

The victorious Europeans declared Acre the capital of the Crusader Kingdom in Palestine in July 1191. Richard the Lionheart concluded the Jaffa Pact with Saladin in 1192, by which they agreed to divide Palestine into two. The agreement declared that the Crusaders would rule the coast and the Muslims the inlands and mountain ranges.

For the next hundred years the Europeans of Acre fought off would-be conquerors, including the Mongols in 1259 and the Egyptian Mamluks in 1272. Additional quarters were established to accommodate European reinforcements such as the Teutonic Knights, the Order of the Knights of Saint John (Hospitallers), the Knights Templar, and the Order of St. Lazarus.

In 1219 St. Francis of Assisi stopped in Acre on his way to Egypt. During his brief stay he established a convent for women, the Order of St. Francis, the remains of which are now part of the Khan al-Franj.

Intrigue between the European merchant communities and the different military orders weakened Crusader rule and stirred up at least one civil war. The city became the last Crusader stronghold in Palestine to fall to Egyptian forces in 1291. The Cairo-based Sultan El-

Malik El-Ashraf Saladin al Khalil, who arrived at the city gates with 200,000 men, carried off thousands of Europeans as slaves, while some 30,000 others fled to Cyprus and the rest were killed.

The Ottoman Era

Two centuries later the Ottoman ruler Suleiman the Magnificent reintroduced European merchants to the city by inviting them to work and reside in Acre. Most of the existing churches and mosques in Acre date back to the Ottoman Era. But it remained a secondary city until the beginning of the seventeenth century when the Arab Emir of Mount Lebanon, Fakhr Eddin II (1572–1635), became ruler of the city and encouraged European traders to expand their presence in the city. It was another Arab ruler, Dhaher al-Omar al-Zaidani (1730–1775), who truly restored Acre to its previous glory, when he made the city his residence and capital, and Acre became the central export station for Syrian grain.

Ahmad Pasha al-Jazzar (1775–1804), an Ottoman Bosnian, continued the work of his two predecessors and had an elaborate aqueduct built to supply the city with water. He also had a mosque, a bathhouse and a citadel constructed over the convent of the Hospitaliers. Ahmad Pasha was an ally of the English, whose navy helped him defend Acre from conquest by Napoleon in 1799.

In 1831–1832, the Cairo-based Albanian renegade general, Ibrahim Pasha, wrested Acre from Ottoman control after a six-month siege. To maintain the existing balance of power, the British and Austrian empires helped the Ottomans defeat Ibrahim Pasha and bring Acre back under the yolk of Istanbul in 1840. In order to regain the city, the three "conquerors" bombarded it from the sea, destroying many historical sites. By 1904 Acre began to decline after a railroad link between Damascus and Haifa sidelined its port in favor of Haifa's harbor.

The British and the Israeli Era

According to twentieth-century local lore, if the waters of the Na'aman reached the eastern gate of the city, Acre would fall into the hands of the English. In 1910, the river came close. Practicing an ancient pagan rite of sacrifice, the people of Acre killed hundreds of sheep to appease the gods and avert the rising of the river and the rule of the English. That winter the direction of the river changed, but after World War I, Acre, along with the rest of Palestine, was British war booty. The new rulers turned the Citadel (once the Castle of the Knights of Saint John) into a prison. Despite the economic decline of

Acre, the population doubled during the British Mandate; by 1944, 12,300 people lived within the city's walls. Most were Muslim, though a substantial majority—15 percent—were Christian.

The British imprisoned in the Citadel as many as 10,000 Palestinians from all over the country in response to the uprising of 1936–1939, the first major show of resistance to their rule. Three of its prisoners were killed while allegedly trying to escape. Their names—Fou'ad Hijazi, Muhammad Jamjoum, and Ali al-Zir—became battle cries for the resistance and they remain icons of the Palestinian struggle against occupiers.

Terra Sancta Church

On May 17, 1948, the militant Jewish underground group Haganah wrested the city from its Arab inhabitants and expelled all but one quarter of the population, despite the fact that the UN division of Palestine had placed Acre in the Palestinian state. Today, about a quarter of the Israeli Acre's population is Arab. A plaque on the Citadel mentions only the Jewish victims of the British rule of Acre.

Visiting Acre

On the way to Acre from Haifa is Tel al-Fukhar (mount of potsherds), also known by the Israeli name of Tel Akko. It is believed to be the site of ancient Acre. Excavations indicate that Tel al-Fukhar was inhabited since the 2nd century BCE and that a lagoon existed on the southern part of the Tel. In more modern times Napoleon allegedly placed his artillery at Tel al-Fukhar and used it to bombard the modern city.

As you approach the old city from what is called Weizman Street (known before 1948 as Tariq el Qala', the road of the fortress) you can see small portions of what was once the Crusader wall. The most prominent parts of the still existing city wall were built by Ahmad Pasha al-Jazzar.

During the Ottoman Era five mosques and five churches were built in Acre and they are the only ones to have survived.

Mosques

Sinan Pasha Mosque or al-Bahr Mosque
Named in honor of one of the greatest architects of the Ottoman world, this white domed mosque next to Venice Square must have been built around 1600. Sinan lived and worked during the reign of Suleiman the Magnificent. Few remains of this mosque exist, but in 1816 al-Bahr mosque was built adjacent to its ruins, at the orders of Suleiman Pasha.

Al-Ramal Mosque
Built on a sandy site beginning in 1704 on what were the remains of a church from the Crusader era (Latin inscriptions can be seen on some of the walls), this mosque is used today as a youth club for Acre's Arab community. It is located south of the al-Jazzar Mosque.

Al-Mu'allaq Mosque
According to local tradition, Dhaher al-Omar al-Zaidani prayed at the al-Mu'allaq Mosque more frequently than all others. Built in 1748, it was financed by a Shaykh Suhail, a religious man of letters. Israelis say a synagogue once stood here.

Al-Zaytouna Mosque
This mosque was built in 1754 through the endowment of a wealthy and pious pilgrim Haj Muhammad Sadiqi. The proliferation in mosque building at the time reflected Acre's growing population. Al-Zaytouna is sometimes called the Olive Mosque, because it was build next to an olive grove.

Al-Jazzar Mosque
Built in 1778 during the reign of Ahmad Pasha, al-Jazzar was known as the Mosque of Light. Unlike the other mosques built in the 18th century, which were built to accommodate the growing Muslim

population, al-Jazzar was built specifically to legitimize a ruler through a religious endowment. It is believed to have been modeled on the Hagia Sophia in Istanbul. It is richly endowed with ancient marble columns that were brought from Askalan, Caesarea, and Tyre.

The mosque stands in a part of the city that was part of the quarter of the Knights of St. John, before its destruction in the last Crusader war. The compound includes a courtyard and cloisters, which housed civilians during times of siege and war. On the second floor, an enclosed area contains a box said to contain a hair of the Prophet Muhammad. Once a year, on the 27th day of Ramadan, the box is opened and shown to the faithful. And in the western courtyard, a twin-domed building holds the sarcophagi of Ahmad

Al-Jazzar Mosque

Pasha and his adopted son and successor Suleiman Pasha (1804–1818). Beneath all of this lies a vast underground water cistern built by the Order of the Knights of St. John.

Churches

During the reign of Dhaher al-Omar al-Zaidani, Arab Christians appear to have had a most favored status in Acre and it is believed that the majority of the city's merchants were Christian, with Greek Catholics the majority. Thus as many churches as mosques were built during this era.

St. John's Church

In 1737, Franciscans built Acre's first eighteenth-century church on the spot where it is believed that the Crusader Church of Saint Andrew once stood. The area around the church, including the remnants of the "lighthouse" known as the Tower of Flies, was once the Templar quarter of the city. Behind the church a plaque names British soldiers and officers that died in battle at Acre.

St. Andrew's Church

Built in 1764 at the orders of the Greek Catholic Church, St. Andrew's is the largest church in Acre. It may have been built on the ruins of an older Crusader church, which in turn was built on the remains of a Byzantine structure. The beautifully ornamented church serves Acre's Greek Catholic community of Palestinians.

St. George's Church

One of the most beautiful churches in the country, St. George's is central to the spiritual life of Acre's still surviving Palestinian Greek Orthodox community. This oldest continually used church in the city was built around 1730. It was renamed to honor a young Cypriot martyr who was executed in the nineteenth century.

St. Mary's Church

A Maronite Church built to accommodate the influx of Maronites from Lebanon and Syria who came to trade and at times flee persecution at home, St. Mary's was established in 1750. It is located between St. Andrew's and St. George's Church.

Terra Sancta Church

This Franciscan church is the largest in Acre. The original church seems to have been built in 1620, but the existing church (including a school and inn) was almost certainly built in the 20th century. The Franciscans themselves have been in Palestine at least since the visit of St. Francis of Assisi in 1219.

Khans

Khan al-Shawardeh (Merchant's Inn)

South of Souq al-Abyad this khan, part of a group of inns built after the Crusader rule, now serves as a location of shops, cafes, and parking lot. South of the khan is the **al-Ramal Mosque** (1705), which was built over the remains of a Crusader Church (its Latin inscriptions are still intact). It is used as a youth center today. The adjacent **Burj al-Sultan** (Sultan's Tower) is the city's only remaining thirteenth-century tower.

> ## Khans
>
> Khans, also called caravansaries, were rural inns with large courtyards situated on trade and travel routes. The khans that remain in Palestine date almost exclusively from the Mamluk and Ottoman periods—not surprising, since the establishment of the khans required stability and a commitment on the part of the central government to provide safety for merchants and pilgrims (and their horses, donkeys, and camels) even in the far reaches of the realm.

Khan al-Franj (Frankish Inn)

The oldest continually existing khan of Acre, it was built in 1600 by the Emir Fakhr Eddin II in what had been known as the Venetian quarter. At the beginning of his reign, Suleiman the Magnificent, who had strong ties to Paris, encouraged the return of French merchants to return to Acre.

The khan has incorporated what was left of a convent established during the visit of St. Francis of Assisi. Legend has it that its occupants committed suicide rather than be ruled by the Muslims.

Exit onto **Venzia Square** for ice cream vendors and another important khan.

Khan al-Umdan (Pillar's Inn)

Built in 1784–5 during the reign of Ahmad Pasha, this is the best kept of Acre khans and takes its name from its impressive granite and porphyry columns. Built where the Genoese quarter and a Monastery of the Dominican Order once stood, the Khan al-Umdan was used during the Ottoman era by rural traders and farmers who came to the city to sell their goods. It was also known as the Grain Inn.

The Ottoman clock tower at one of the exits was built in 1906 to commemorate the 30-year rule of the Ottoman Sultan Abdel Hameed II.

Khan al-Shuna (Pisan Inn)
Pisan Harbor, which is now occupied by several restaurants, was originally a Phoenician port. The Pisans built upon the ancient port to allow vessels to come to their part of the city and stay at Khan al-Shuna. Built by al-Zaidani in 1764–5, though the city's smallest khan, it still plays an integral part in life of the Arab community.

Other Sites

Underground Crusader City or Quarter of the Knights
Situated opposite al-Jazzar Mosque is what remains of the quarter of the Knights of St. John (or the Hospitaliers knights). Originally much of the complex, which can't be excavated for fear of endangering the Citadel, was above ground as well, but was razed in the last war between the Mamluks and the Crusaders. Seven big halls were excavated (only three of them are open to the public). It is believed that each hall was used by different orders and nationalities of the Knights. The **Chamber of the Grand Maneir** is where the Grand Master of the Orders and his entourage resided. The chamber leads to the crypt, which is the most elaborate of all the halls in the compound. The name of Louis VII, the date 1184, and the *fleur-de-lys* cut into stone, marks one of Acre's best kept architectural remnants of the Crusader era. Legend has it that Marco Polo once dined here. A long tunnel connects this hall with another building known as al-Bosta. The Crusaders used this building as a hospital; the Mamluks converted it to a post office.

Hamam al-Pasha (Pasha's Bath), and the Municipal Museum
Built like the Cairo bathhouses of the same era, the Hamam al-Pasha opened its doors to the city's elegant society in about 1780. Situated just behind the Ahmad Pasha Mosque, it remained in use until May 1947, when it was confiscated by the Israeli state as "abandoned property."

In 1954 it was turned into a museum and despite its lack of interesting contents, its architecture makes it worth a visit. The marble floors and walls, domed ceiling, and tiled glass evoke the

Stone tablet in the Quarter of the Knights

grandeur of another age. A theatrical recreation of the story of the last bath attendant is performed for visitors today.

Zawiyat al-Shazilia (Prayer Niche of al-Shazilia)

West of the Hamam is this Sufi zawiya, established in 1862 in honor of the Tunisian-born Ali Nurridin al-Yashruti. The Sufi Shaykh established orders as far north as Beirut. Today the movement has some 1,500 followers in several cities, including Acre, Jerusalem, and Jaffa.

Citadel/Prison (or Burj al-Qurayim)

Built by al-Zaidani and added on to by Ahmad Pasha in the eighteenth century, the Citadel has served as a residential palace, army barracks, and prison. Its 40-meter-high **Burj al-Khazneh** (Treasurer's Tower) offers a stunning panoramic view of old Acre and the Mediterranean.

The Citadel's most famous prisoner during the Ottoman era was Mirza Husayn 'Ali Nuri (also known as Baha'u'allah), the founder of the Bahai faith. Incarcerated here in 1868, he spent the next 24 years in prison writing the Bahai holy scripture, *Kitab al-Akdas*.

During the British Mandate, the vast majority of the Cidadel's 10,000 prisoners were Palestinians who struggled against British rule. Some 500 Jewish opponents to the British were also incarcerated here. Today it is used by the Israelis as a museum to commemorate the Jews killed during British rule.

Souq al-Abyad (White Market)

So named for its well-lit passages, Souq al-Abyad remains the principle market in Acre. Once compared to the Souq al-Hamidieh in Damascus, it was built by al-Zaidani at the start of the eighteenth century. After much of the original market was laid waste by fire in 1817, Suleiman Pasha oversaw its reconstruction. At the junction between the al-Jazzar Mosque and Saladin Road, it serves as a Middle Eastern version of a mall, with souvenirs, toys, clothes, and household items for sale, along with fruits and vegetables.

Near Acre

Shrine of Baha'u'allah or Bahai House

About 2.5 km north of Acre, near Shomrat, is the home of the founder of the Bahai faith. Originally a rural mansion that had been "abandoned" by its owners, the Ottoman government placed Baha'u'allah under house arrest on its premises. He lived here from the time of his release from prison in 1870 until his death in 1892.

His burial tomb and the lush surrounding gardens provide a peaceful environment. The **50-acre gardens** are maintained by volunteers from around the world, who typically come for a year of service to their faith.

Kabri Springs

Several kilometers north of the Bahai shrine are the Kabri Springs, next to what was the Palestinian village of al-Kabri and is now the Kibbutz Lohamei HaGeta'ot. According to Arab legend, Adam stopped here with his oxen so they could rest and drink. It was from here the first Ahmad Pasha and later his adopted son Suleiman Pasha built aqueducts to supply Acre with water. Although partially destroyed by Napoleon and not easily accessible by road, the Ottoman archways are well preserved and worth seeing.

Purple Beach

Known to Israelis as Argaman beach, here Canaanites came to gather murex shells for the distinctive purple dye of their imperial robes. Today, it is simply the best beach in the Acre area.

Feline residents of the Old City

Nasir Mosque and Israeli skyscraper

11.

Haifa

The village of Haifa lies on the seashore, and there are here palm-gardens and trees in numbers. There are in this town ship-builders, who build very large craft.

—Nasir-i-Khusrau, Persian pilgrim and traveler, 1047

For the first 40 years of the twentieth century, Haifa was the most sophisticated city in Palestine. As the de facto capital of the north, it was home to the country's main port, the most important rail system and a 1,200-mile oil pipeline that connected Palestine to Iraq.

Its population was cosmopolitan and its urban landscape well designed. Along with the Arabs of Haifa were smaller communities of Armenians, Greeks, Persians, Indians, Germans, and other Arabs, mainly from Lebanon. Nestled at the meeting point of the Carmel mountains, the Bay of Haifa, and the plain, the city is geographically blessed. The father of modern Zionism, Theodore Herzl, thought so too, and after his visit, he encouraged Jews to settle in Haifa.

Early History

The area in and around Haifa has been inhabited since Paleolithic times (500,000–40,000 BCE). The remains of a fourteenth-century BCE port northeast of the city at Tel Abu Hawwam indicates that it was once a medium-sized Canaanite city. There were two towns where Haifa stands today: Porphyrion (Purple) to the north of today's cape and Sycaminos to the south. It is not clear whether Porphyrion was a secondary city to Acre, or a regional Canaanite power in itself. Sycaminos has only been partially excavated, but significant remnants from the Hellenistic and

Byzantine era were found. Remnants of eight mosaic floors can be seen at the Haifa Museum of Art.

The Talmud refers once to Haifa and a Jewish burial ground lies nearby. Archeological evidence suggests that while the city had a Jewish population, it was probably a minority in the largely Greek city of Sycaminos.

After the Byzantine era, the city flourished under the reign of the Muslim Fatimids, who established a substantial ship-building industry by the bay. The Crusaders, however, put an end to Haifa's prosperity in 1099, when they killed and enslaved the population and reduced the city to a village. It became an endless battleground between the Crusaders and Saladin, and later the Mamluk Baibars. After the last Crusades, the city lay fallow for some 200 years, only to be revived with the coming of the Ottomans.

When Sultan Suleiman the Magnificent reinstated trade with Europe at the beginning of the sixteenth century, the port of Haifa was rebuilt and it again became a city of consequence. Its harbor was fortified to protect it from pirates and much of the city was re-populated with Ottoman, Arab, and European merchants.

Napoleon briefly occupied the city during his siege of Acre and the Egyptian Ibrahim Pasha passed through. The German Emperor visited in 1898 on his famous state visit and was thought to have been instrumental in pushing for the establishment of the Haifa railway in 1904. After the Haifa–Damascus–Mecca railway was built, the economic future of the city was sealed. By 1919 there was also rail service to Egypt and Haifa became the second most important port city in the Mediterranean, superceded only by Marseille. By 1929 the Kirkuk–Haifa pipeline was inaugurated and Iraqi oil found its outlet to the Mediterranean and the rest of the world here.

With the influx of workers and business people, immigrants and intellectuals, labor unions and newspapers thrived in the city. It was to the urban slums of 1920s Haifa that Izzedin al-Qassam came to teach migrant workers about labor rights and independence. The Syrian-born civil rights activist eventually turned militant when he led 800 men into battle against the British forces in the area around Jenin. He lost his life, but his ideas continue to inspire anti-colonialists in Palestine. The Izzedin al-Qassam Brigades of the Islamic Resistance Movement, Hamas, are named in his memory. Today the decrepit Independence Mosque (built in 1923) marks the location where he gave his first speeches, calling for resistance to the British occupation and Jewish colonizers and warning of their inherent dangers.

Post-1948 Haifa

Of the city's six quarters in 1948, four were Arab and included Muslims, Christian Arabs, Armenians, and Bahai Persians; one was Jewish; and one was German. According to the 1947 UN partition plan Haifa was to be part of the Jewish state, naturally against the wishes of its many Arab citizens.

Before the date of the partition, some 5,000 Jewish militia men surrounded Haifa, whose Arab neighborhoods were defended by about 500 Palestinians. In 1948, most of Haifa's Arab residents fled the city and took refuge in Lebanon. Of the city's 61,000 Arabs, only 3,500 remained. The rest were never allowed to return. As happened all over Palestine, their homes were expropriated by the state of Israel and given to Jewish families. Today, most of Haifa's Arab residents come from destroyed villages in the Haifa area or in the Galilee. In 2003, Haifa's population of 300,000 is ten percent Arab (with half Muslim and half Christian). Arab life still predominates in many parts of the city, particularly in Wadi Nisnas and the areas around the German colony and the Bahai temple.

Some consider Arab–Jewish relations in Haifa to be more civil than elsewhere in the country and some Israelis believe it to be a model of coexistence.

Port of Haifa

Mosques

Ahmadi Mosque

Built in 1984, this mosque serves as a hub for the small Ahmadi community. As followers of an Indian Muslim named Mirza Gulam Ahmad al-Kadiani, who declared himself the 12th Imam of Islam, the Ahmadi community has long been at odds with mainstream Islam. It is located in the suburb of Kababir.

Hajj Abdullah Mosque

Built in 1932 in Halissa, the only predominantly Muslim quarter built during the British Mandate, by a local businessman Hajj Abdullah Abu Youness. The mosque was closed after 1948 by the Israeli government and proclaimed absentee landlord property. The Muslim community of Haifa struggled for 30 years to have the mosque reinstated as a religious shrine, and were finally successful in 1981.

Independence Mosque

Built in 1923 near Kikar Faisal, the mosque was considered the main location of incitement against British rule. It was bombarded by the Italian navy in 1940 as part of the showdown between the Axis and the Allies.

Nasir Mosque

The oldest mosque in Haifa was built during the rule of al-Zaidani in 1761. Today it stands in ruins, closed by the Israelis in 1955. In 1977, parts of it were torn down during renovation work in the old part of the city, where it is located.

Churches

Carmelite Monastery

Every July 20th on St. Elias day, a huge popular festival staged by Haifa's Catholic community takes place here, to commemorate the deeds of this local hero. Built in the twelfth century, the monastery was seriously damaged during the Crusader wars (1291) but rebuilt in 1769 under the rule of al-Zaidani. During the siege of Acre, Napoleon's troops used it as a hospital to treat their wounded. The Carmelites paid bitterly for this alliance with the French; after the Ottomans returned to power, part of their monastery was destroyed. Today's building on Stella Maris Road dates from 1836.

Bahai Temple and Gardens

The Carmelites

The Carmelite order was established in the 12th century after the third Crusade, when a group of hermits began practicing their Christianity in caves on Mt. Carmel. There are really two branches of Carmelites: the Ancient Observance Calced Carmelites, and the Discalced Carmelites or Teresians (established in 1592 in Spain). The latter followed the ways of St. Teresa of Avila. St. Teresa believed that the Order should be dedicated to poverty, so her reformed order of Carmelites became known as Discalced (shoeless). Their spiritual home is in Haifa.

Maronite Church

Built in the 19th century, it served Haifa's once-large Maronite community, most of whom had come from Syria and Lebanon. Community leaders, who were successful merchants, financed the building of the church and an adjacent community center.

St. Gabriel's Church

Built for the Melkite community (Greek Catholic Church) in 1930 by a local patron, Gabriel Saad. It ceased to function in 1948 when the community fled to Lebanon and to neighboring Wadi al-Salib. The church, though still standing, is no longer a place of worship, but is under the "protection" of the Israeli government. It is situated in the part of Bat Galim, formerly known as Karmel, once a Christian Arab community and now a Jewish neighborhood.

St. Joseph's Church

This Catholic Church, built in 1961, is the last in the country to be designed by the Italian architect A. Barluzzi.

Museums

Archeological Museum

Concentrates on grain handling in ancient Israel and the Near East. It has artifacts dating back to the Iron Age period (12,000–600 BCE) but completely omits the city's Arab history.

Maritime Museum

While it has some interesting items from the Egyptian, Phoenician, Greek, as well as British and French eras, the museum fails to mention anything significant of the Arab world's 1,400-year history in Haifa.

Nevertheless, the Ram of Atlit is well worth seeing. Considered to be one of the largest bronze finds from antiquity, it is the only known ram of its kind in the world. Discovered in 1980 in the waters of Atlit (south of Haifa), this three-pronged ram has contributed much to the knowledge of naval warfare. Since the 8th century BCE, ships bearing a single ram were well known. The three-pronged ram developed at the end of the 6th century had the advantage of shattering an enemy ship's hull. It was used in naval battles by the Phoenicians, Greeks, Romans, and Etruscans. The ram, which features mythological symbols including eagles and a thunderbolt, was probably made in Cyprus. The museum is located on Allenby Street.

Railway Museum

An early 20th-century monument commemorates the establishment of the Hijazi railway line, next to a small museum with some interesting railway paraphernalia.

Other Sites

Abdullah Pasha's Palace & Stella Maris Lighthouse

Built in 1821 as the governor's residence for the Egyptian envoy to Haifa, Abdullah Pasha, the palace was given by Abdullah (perhaps to spite the Ottomans) to the Carmelite Order before the rule of Palestine reverted to Istanbul. A lighthouse was built on top of the house in 1928, known today as Stella Maris Lighthouse. It is still in use.

Bahai Temple and Gardens

The beautiful golden-domed shrine is located on Mount Carmel, and serves as the spiritual center for the world's 5 million adherents of the Bahai faith. Said Ali Muhammad, one of the two founders of the Bahai religion, is buried inside the modest interior of the shrine.

The Bahais

The Bahai religion is an independent, mono-theistic religion based on the teachings of the Persian, Baha'u'llah (1817–1892). He is regarded by his follo-wers as the most recent in the line of Messen-gers of God. He fled Persia and settled in Palestine toward the end of the 19th century.

Their mecca, the Shrine of the Ba'b, is run with the help of about 600 Bahai volunteers from more than 55 countries. The Haifa-based admini-strative center comprises several buildings in neo-classical style, including the Seat of the Universal House of Justice, the International Bahai Archives, a library, and other administrative institutions.

The Bahai Gardens, planted in 1909, are the best kept in the entire country.

German Colony

East of Wadi Nisnas, at the foot of the Bahai gardens, stands the German colony, one of four such communities in the country. In 1868, devout Protestants from Wuertemberg purchased land that was far from the city and began to build the first planned agricultural community in Palestine. The two founders, Hardegg and Hoffman, eventually split when the latter set up the German community in Jaffa. Introducing advanced agricultural knowledge, the Germans also introduced a new style of urban planning and landscaping. European styles of architecture can be seen in the homes they built.

Khader's Grotto (Elijah's Cave)

During Canaanite and Philistine times, Carmel was dedicated to Baal; the Greeks replaced him with Zeus to whom they built an immense statue, of which a marble foot was found. The Jews and the Christians dedicated it to the prophet Elijah and later to the Virgin Mary. Muslims dedicated it to Khader, patron of the heavens and fertility.

The Israelis confiscated the grotto in 1948 and renamed it Elijah's Cave. According to Jewish and Christian tradition, this is one of the caves that protected Elijah in his flight from the Baal-worshipping Jezebel.

The only scientific evidence of the grotto's history is Greek graffiti dating back to the 4th century CE. The cave is accessible via a steep path from the Carmelite monastery on Stella Maris Road.

Kikar Faisal (Faisal's Column)

One of the main streets to old Haifa is Derekh Ha'Atzma'ut, previously known by its Arabic name of al-Mulouk Street. This street leads to what used to be downtown in the old days, and also to Kikar Faisal, named in honor of the former Iraqi King Faisal I. The column is inscribed with one of his favorite sayings: "Freedom is not given; it must be taken."

Organizations

Al-Balad Cultural Association

The backbone of a new generation of young Arabs in Haifa, the organization gives literacy classes and does community work. It teaches young people about the Arab history of Haifa and its environment, something they are not allowed to learn at Israeli-controlled schools.

Ittijah
This umbrella organization, the Union of Arab Non-Governmental Organizations in Israel, includes everything from child's rights organizations, to women's groups, to land reclamation organizations. It is the biggest, most active organization founded by Palestinians inside Israel.

Social Development Committee of Haifa
This civil service organization creates awareness about civil rights and liberties and protects Haifa's Arabs from discrimination in employment, health care, education, and housing. In recent years the committee has also championed the protection of Haifa's Arab and Islamic cultural heritage.

Israeli Haifa
Most of the Jews who settled in Haifa and later took over Arab homes were from Europe. Known to Israelis as the laborer's city, jokes were told about how the sidewalks were "rolled-up" early in the evening, leaving nothing to do. Today Haifa is home to many of Israel's high-tech firms, and it is still the only city with (limited) underground transportation. The famous Israeli university Technicon is located in Haifa. Unlike in many other Israeli cities, street signs in Haifa are in Arabic, English, and Hebrew, which is often advertised as a sign of good Arab–Israeli cohabitation.

Emile Habiby (1922–1996)

Emile Habiby was one of the Palestinians who remained in Haifa after the Israeli assault "cleansed" the city of its Arab population. A radio presenter in the 1940s and editor of the daily *al-Itihad* (union) newspaper, he continued to write opinion pieces all his life. He was famous in the Arabic-speaking world for his novels, most notably *The Secret Life of Sa'eed*, an account, over 20 years and two wars, of the life of the Palestinians remaining in Israel.

Habiby's contribution to the literary world was acknowledged by Israelis and Palestinians alike, although many Arabs opposed his acquiescence to Israel's rule over Palestine. Nevertheless, he represented the Arab community's most prominent organ, the Communist Party, in the Israeli Knesset for 19 years.

In a famous line from *The Secret Life...*, he revealed the constant discomfort of being an Arab in a Jewish state: "I'm afraid that the stones and trees will speak to me and ask me, 'Where have you been all this time?'"

Beit-Hagefen (Arab–Jewish Center)
Beit-Hagefen (House of the Vine), the Arab–Jewish Center, was established in 1963. It offers a number of guided tours (primarily for groups) all centered on the theme of coexistence. The center has an art gallery and an Arab language theater. Its two festivals include the Holiday of Holidays in December and the Arab Theater month in May and June. It holds meetings between Jewish and Arab students, workshops for community dialogue, and works toward democracy and coexistence.

Near Haifa

Atlit
This village, including Wadi Mughara, is home to some of the most amazing prehistoric caves in the country. Human settlement seems to have existed here for thousands of years. Early Arab travelers mentioned the site in their writings and later, the Crusaders built pilgrims rest-houses and a small community settled nearby. Both German missionaries and Armenian refugees settled amongst the Arabs in Atlit in the 19th and 20th centuries. Jewish settlers established a colony nearby as early as 1903 and used it as a base for military activities. Today no Arabs live in Atlit; they have all become refugees.

Balad al-Shaykh
Named after a Sufi cleric, Shaykh Abdullah al-Salhi, who had preferential status with the first Ottoman Sultan, Saleem I (1512–20) and whose tomb is still visible in the north end, this village is thought to have been inhabited since Byzantine times. The village was adjacent to the Haifa–Jenin highway and was one of the few villages to get a school while still under Ottoman rule (1887). Izzedin Qassam was laid to rest here, and his tomb is still visible, though all the marble slabs have been removed.

The village was "emptied" in 1948 and officially no longer exists. It has been renamed Te Chanan by the Israelis. Remains of Arab houses and the Muslim graveyard can still be visited.

Druze Villages
The villages of Usfiya and Daliat al-Carmel are located on the Carmel summit. Both villages were established during the reign of Emir Fakhr Eddin II (1572–1635). The former is the less commercial of the two, but both have good restaurants and tend to cater to people

Arab shop in Wadi Nisnas

who want to have an "Arab experience." Despite this leaning toward all things Eastern, all signs are in Hebrew only, although Arabic is spoken by all villagers. Israelis tend to frequent the villages on Saturday. In the center of Daliat al-Carmel, a colorful market sells carpets, brass coffee-pots, pipes, and Indian furniture.

Ein Houd

One of the most famous villages not destroyed in 1948, it was established by one of the generals in Saladin's army, Abu al-Hayja, who died after the battle of Hittin. Although it remained small throughout the Ottoman era, it had its own mosque and a school that was built in 1888. The village was rich in carob trees, wheat, and sesame seeds. The village merchants sold carob molasses and sesame seeds in the markets of Acre and Haifa. After the fall of other villages and the city of Haifa, the residents of Ein Houd were driven out and not allowed to return. Eventually, the less than a hundred of the original 700 inhabitants who remained inside what became Israel established a new village, which they also called Ein Houd. The village is not recognized by the Israeli government as legitimate, and is thus denied all municipal services, including water, sewage, electricity, and roads.

In 1954 Israelis established an artist's colony in the old village of Ein Houd, renovating the old Arab homes and turning the mosque into a bar.

Ijzim

This village was home of the powerful Madi clan that ruled parts of Palestine in the 19th century. Several influential judges during the Ottoman era came from Ijzim. The village was depopulated of its Palestinian residents in 1948, but several of the villages' original buildings can still be visited. Although both mosques have deteriorated, the 18th-century two-story residence of Shaykh Masoud al-Madi has been turned into a museum. The village school now serves as a synagogue, and the town café, a post office.

Tantoura

Tantoura was built at the site of the Canaanite Dor. Archeological evidence indicates that it was inhabited since 1600 BCE. The seaside town was mentioned in several Egyptian texts from 1300 and 1100 BCE. It was inhabited by the Tjeker, one of the Sea People who accompanied the Philistines. It became a center for the Phoenicians and was administered through Sidon in the 4th century BCE. By the 2nd century, it was a Greek colony and much later the Crusaders built the Merle castle, which Napoleon had burned by his retreating army. In Ottoman times, Tantoura was a renowned fishing village with a considerable inland area devoted to the growing of bananas, citrus, and cereals.

Underwater excavations have revealed anchors from most of the town's historical periods, and the remains of both Byzantine basilicas and Crusader castles have been recovered. A shrine, fortress, and several houses still stand. The fortress, which is run by the Israelis living at the Kibbutz Nasholim, has been turned into a museum.

In line with official Zionist policy, the entire area from Haifa to Tel Aviv was to be cleared of Arab habitation, and thus after a brief battle, the inhabitants of Tantoura were expelled or killed. American, Polish, and Greek Jews settled in Tantoura, establishing a new community, which they gave the name of the ancient Canaanite community, Dor.

Tirat Haifa

This village south of Haifa was, with 5,000 inhabitants, the second largest rural community in the district, before the attacks and destruction of 1948. Called St. Yohan by the Crusaders, it was the olive oil center of the extended Haifa community. It has the ruins of St. Brocardus Monastery. Today the village lands have been incorporated into the Israeli Elyaqim.

Prehistoric Caves

About 20 kilometers south of Haifa, near the Valley of the Caves, excavations began in the 1920s and 1930s. Among the most significant finds were:

Tabun Cave (Cave of the Oven)

Inhabited 500,000 to 40,000 years ago, excavations indicate that this cave is one of the longest continuously inhabited sites in the history of the Levant. Among the impressive finds was a Neanderthal-type burial of a female, dated to about 120,000 years ago. It is one of the ancient human skeletal remains found in the country.

Skhul Cave (Children's Cave)

Fourteen skeletons were uncovered here, including three complete ones defined as an archaic type of Homo sapiens, closely related to modern humans in physical appearance. It is believed that these humans, with delicate facial features, a protruding chin, and a straight forehead, were fully developed about 100,000 years ago. The finds from these graves also show evidence of cult and death-related rituals.

Al-Wad Cave (Valley of the Caves)

Although there were finds here dating back to 45,000 BCE, the most important ones date back to the Natufian culture (10,500 to 8,500 BCE). The large number of skeletons found provided anthropologists with the opportunity to study the physical characteristics of the Natufian population. The average height was 1.58 to 1.65 meters (5.2–5.5 ft), with relatively large heads and wide, rather low foreheads. These characteristics were typical of populations of this period in the eastern Mediterranean Basin. The Al-Wad cave is now open to the public.

12.

Caesarea

It was of old a fine grand city, the very mother of cities, with broad lands and wide domains.

—Yakut, Muslim geographer, 1220

Initially built by the Phoenicians in the 4th century BCE, the city was rebuilt by Herod in 22 BCE, on the remains of the Phoenician and Greek port town known as Straton's Tower. It was named Caesarea in honor of Augustus Caesar. This seaport of ancient Palestine is probably the best-kept archeological site in the country. Its Roman builders provided the city with an amphitheater, temples and public buildings, excellent water supply and drainage systems, and a magnificent harbor protected by a breakwater.

When the First Jewish Revolt erupted in 66 CE, the Romans made Caesarea their headquarters and most of the Jewish inhabitants were slaughtered after the Romans reestablished their authority in the city. During the next couple of years, General Vespasian was proclaimed emperor of the Roman Empire in Caesarea and the city was proclaimed the capital of Roman Palestine. According to Josephus, the destruction of the temple in Jerusalem in that same year (70 CE) was celebrated by special events in the ampitheater of Caeseria where over 2,500 Jews perished in "games."

Although it remained a pagan city, Caesarea played an important role in early Christian history. Here Peter converted and baptized the Roman officer Cornelius, who is often described as the first Gentile to accept Christianity. It is from Caesarea that Paul set sail for his journeys in the eastern Mediterranean.

Arches of Crusader structure in Caesarea

During the Byzantine era, Caesarea became an important Christian center. Church father Origen founded a Christian academy in the city, which included a library of 30,000 manuscripts. The theologian Eusebius, who served as Bishop of Caesarea in the 4th century, composed here his monumental *Historia Ecclesiastica* on the beginnings of Christianity and the *Onomasticon*, a comprehensive geographical-historical study of the Holy Land.

Side by side with the Christian population and its numerous churches, Jewish and Samaritan communities built elaborate synagogues. During this period, the Roman inner harbor was blocked and buildings were constructed on what had become dry land. A row of vaults serving as shops was built against the podium wall facing the port. The main church, the Martyrion of the Holy Procopius, was built

The last vestige of Muslim Caesarea

in the 6th century upon the remains of the Roman temple on the podium. The floor was paved with marble slabs in a variety of patterns. Of the rows of columns in the building, several Corinthian capitals decorated with crosses were found.

In 639, the Arabs conquered Caesarea and expanded the harbor and developed the countryside around the city. The population during the Umayyad and Abbasid era declined, and some of the urban areas were replaced with well-groomed agricultural terraces. Remains of the 10th-century 3-meter-thick (9.8 ft) wall which surrounded Arab Caesarea were found during the excavations.

Tourists from Italy in Caesarea

In 1101, the Crusaders conquered Caesarea and it became the seat of an archbishop. The Genoese found a green-colored glass cup in the city and declared it to be the Holy Grail. It was taken to Genoa and placed in the Church of San Lorenzo.

Saladin captured Caesarea in 1187 after a short siege, but four years later the Crusaders retook the city, and the Muslim inhabitants were exiled. During each historical period, it seems that Caesarea's wall was further fortified. By this time, the wall was four meters (13 ft), and access to the city was via gates, which were closed on the inside with wooden bars and protected on the outside by an iron grill, which was lowered through a slot from the ceiling.

The Crusaders built their cathedral on the city acropolis. The end of Crusader Caesarea came in 1265, when the Mamluk Sultan Baibars took the city, after a short siege. Fearing a return of the Crusaders, the Mamluks razed the city's fortifications to the ground.

Centuries later, Bosnian Muslims, who were citizens of the Ottoman Empire, established a farming and fishing community by Caesarea. In 1948, just over a half-century later, they comprised half of the approximately 1,000 residents of the town.

Caesarea was the first Palestinian town to be ethnically cleansed in a systematic manner. On February 20, 1948 all but six of the town's homes were destroyed. Although almost half of the lands around Caesarea had been bought by Edmond de Rothschild, Palestinian Muslims living on the other half were evicted. Their homes were either destroyed or taken from them.

Only two Arab communities in the entire vicinity of Caesarea were allowed to stay, Jisr al-Zarqa and Furaydis. Settled nomads and villagers, they provided the labor pool in Jewish towns and thus were not expendable. Many of Caesarea's refugees settled in these villages. All that remains of Palestinian Caesarea, as it existed in 1948, are the remnants of a mosque next to the port. It has been turned into a café-bar.

Sites

Caesarea is a most impressive archeological site. One can visit the Roman-period theater, King Herod's palace and the amphitheater. One can also cross the moat, enter the restored Crusader city and look toward the harbor from the top of the podium.

Amphitheater
First built in the Herodian period, the amphitheater on the city's southern shore seated 8,000 spectators, and after it was expanded in the first century CE, 15,000. This venue for racing horses and chariots had two well-preserved sides, although the sea largely destroyed the western side.

Aqueduct
The Roman aqueduct provided an abundant supply of water for several eras. The upper aqueduct begins at the foot off Mt. Carmel. Entering the city from the north, the water flowed through a network of pipes to collecting pools and fountains throughout the city. Many inscriptions in the aqueduct ascribe responsibility for its maintenance to the 2nd and 10th Roman Legion.

Mediterranean seafront of Caesarea

Herod's Palace

In use throughout Roman rule, the palace was a large architectural complex with a decorative pool surrounded by porticoes.

Roman Theater

Herod commissioned this earliest of the Roman entertainment facilities. The theater faces the sea and has thousands of seats resting on a semi-circular structure of vaults. The semi-circular floor of the orchestra, first paved in painted plaster, was later paved with marble.

This staircase marked the boundary of Safad's Jewish and Arab quarters

13.

Safad

A fortress on the summit of Mount Canaan .... It was originally but a village and they built there a fortress, calling it Safat, and afterwards Safad.

—al-Dimaski, 1300

S afad lies in the hills of eastern Galilee and was long an important town in northern Palestine and southern Lebanon. Its strategic and economic value stemmed from the fact that it lay along historic trade and communications lines between Syria and Egypt.

Safad is believed to be the Canaanite Triphot mentioned in Egyptian texts from the 14th century BCE. At the time of the Romans it was known by the name of Sepph (strong castle), but it is not certain if Romans or Greeks lived there before it was written into "western" history.

Most of its recorded history begins around 70 CE when it became a haven for Jews revolting against Roman rule who set up a spiritual center away from Jerusalem in nearby Tiberias.

The first mention of consequence in Arab Muslim writings came in the 10th century when it became known as the town in which the ruler of Damascus, Ahmad Ben Ata'Abu Abdullah, was buried. Indeed, its geographic proximity to Damascus was reflected in the dialect spoken by its city residents, its cultural references, and its population's mercantile character.

Until the Crusades, Safad appears to have had a large Jewish population. The Crusaders banished all the city's residents and the Knights Templar built a grand fortress, of which only remains can still be seen. Baibars subsequently sent the Crusaders marching in 1266 and destroyed their main fortress, but left most of the rest of the city intact. The Mamluks later rebuilt parts of the fortress and the city walls.

During the Mamluk period, Muslims who had come mainly from the Damascus region, along with some Jews, dominated the city. In the late 16th century a large number of Muslims and Jews fleeing Spain settled in Safad. During this era, which marked the beginning of Ottoman rule, Safad was part of the district of Damascus. The Spanish Muslims and Jews brought arts and literary talents with them and Safad became a center of learning and of Jewish mystics.

Emir Fakhr Eddin II (1572–1635), the Galilee native Dhaher al-Omar al-Zaidani (1730–1775) and the Bosnian Ahmad Pasha al-Jazzar (1775–1804), successively worked to undermine the importance of Safad and increase the commercial importance of neighboring Acre.

In 1769 a powerful earthquake and a decline in Safad's economy appears to have created an exodus in the Jewish community. By 1849, the majority of the local population was Muslim, with a very substantial 40-percent minority of Jews. Although the numbers fluctuated, Arabs, mainly Muslims along with a small community of Catholics, dominated the cultural and religious character of the city for the next 100 years. At the time Safad was known for its many

shops, mills, and bakeries. Safad merchants were middle men who bought and sold cereals and agricultural goods from the peasants of the northern Galilee and resold them in Acre and Tyre.

Safad vied with Acre as a regional capital, and became an administrative center of the sub-district carrying its name in 1886. In 1888, Safad (with Tiberias, Nazareth, Acre, and Haifa) became part of the Province of Beirut and remained so until 1918. Governmental presence led to the establishment of schools, beginning in 1880. Safad was a relatively large Palestinian town during the first half of the twentieth

Son of Safad: Palestinian President Mahmoud Abbas

century. Economic life centered on trade of agricultural products, artisan production (especially wool and cotton textiles), and, given its location in the hills, summer tourism.

Remains of a Palestinian mosque in Safad

By 1948, the population was 13,300, and 20 percent Jewish. The 1947 UN division plan allocated Safad to the Jewish state, arguing that it was one of the four holy cities of Judaism in Palestine.

Safad's strategic location made it a site of conflict during the Arab–Israeli fighting of 1948. Zionist forces made the capture of Safad their main objective in the days prior to Britain's evacuation of the country. Of Safad's 13,300 inhabitants, only the 2,300 Jews remained. Of the rural Arab communities in the Safad district, 77 were destroyed and their inhabitants sent into exile. Most of the Arabs from the Safad district became refugees in South Lebanon and Syria, while a few went to Nazareth. One of those to flee was a young boy called Mahmoud Abbas. In 2005 he was elected president of the Palestinian National Authority. Another famous Arab child of Safad whose family was expelled is Inam al-Mufti, the first woman to hold ministerial rank in Jordan in the early 1980s.

Today Safad, known to Israelis as Tsfad, has a population of about 30,000. Many Russian and Ethiopian emigrants along with Orthodox Jews live there. Ceramics, diamonds, and handicrafts are produced in the town. The only Arabs still in Safad are those who work as day laborers and live elsewhere.

Visiting Safad

Arab Safad was divided into four historic quarters, three Arab and one Jewish.

Haret al-Akrad

The eastern part of the city, between the bus station and the market area. Once a working-class neighborhood, now only a few architectural remains attest to its Arab past.

Haret al-Sawawin

This was the middle and upper-middle-class neighborhood of Arab merchants and traders, close to the Citadel, near the contemporary location of the Israel Bible Museum.

Haret al-Wata

Located in western Safad, small shop-keepers and small traders lived here, close to the Jewish quarter. The area is currently enveloped into the Artist's quarter. The mosque, built during the rule of Emperor Abdul Hamid II, is no longer in use.

The synagogue quarter (Qiryat Batai HaKnesset) now encompasses what was Haret al-Wata. A staircase that once divided the Jewish and Arab part of this middle-class merchant quarter is still in use.

Sites

Citadel

"Safad has a strong built Castle which dominates the Lake of Tiberias," wrote Abu al-Fida in 1321. By the time the Damascene writer recorded his impressions, the castle had already been destroyed and rebuilt once. Originally constructed during the rule of King Fulk in 1140, it was reconstructed by the Mamluks, only to be leveled in the 1837 earthquake. Today the remains of the castle are housed in a small park on the summit of Safad's main hill.

Remains of an Arab home in Safad

General Exhibition Hall
This pedestrian mall and exhibition area contains a mosque renovated in the 19th century, which is used as part of the exhibit arena. An ongoing court case against the Israeli "owners" by the Islamic Waqf, which maintains it must be preserved as a place of worship.

Mamluk Mausoleum
Built as the final resting place for the Mamluk ruler of Safad, Haj Musa Eroktai (1372). Arabic inscriptions are engraved in the stone of the southern wall. The building can only be viewed from the outside. Today, the area around it is an artist's makeshift gallery.

Museum of Art and Printing
Dedicated to the history of printing in the Arab world, with special emphasis on the Jewish involvement. The first Hebrew books ever were printed in Safad in the 16th century during the Ottoman era.

Ottoman public building converted into an Israeli Center

Ottoman Mansion/Israeli Bible Museum

In the home of a former 19th-century Ottoman ruler of Safad, Israelis have set up the Israel Bible Museum. It is a fine example of late Ottoman architecture. Next to the Wolfson Community Center stands the fourth clock tower that the Ottoman Emperor Abdel Hamid II built in Palestine.

Red Mosque

Constructed soon after the Baibars wrested Safad from the Crusaders in 1266, paid for by Damascene migrant merchants and built by Mamluk architects, it is in abominable condition and often used by young artists. Along with the mausoleum is the oldest building in Safad besides the Citadel.

Near Safad

Safad's most famous contemporary village, Birim or Kufr Bir'im, is listed among the more than 400 Arab communities that were destroyed in 1948. The village surrendered in early November 1948, when Galilee fell to the Zionists. Its residents were "temporarily" expelled for "security reasons." Some of these expelled across the border were later allowed to return to Israel, but not to Birim. The army leveled the village in 1953. The Israeli settlement of Dovev, established in 1963, is northwest of the village site. The only standing structure is a church and its bell tower. The village has been closed off and the surrounding area declared an archaeological and tourist site. The nearby village of Rihaniya (5 km away) is home to what remains of Palestine's Circassian community. Unlike most of this ethnically Caucasian Muslim group, the villagers of Rihaniya did not leave the country after Israel took over this part of Palestine in 1948.

Mosque and its courtyard turned into Israeli artists' quarter

14.

Tiberias (Tabariyya)

...backyard for the first paradise.

—*"The Death of the Phoenix" Mahmoud Darwish, 20th century*

If Palestine was the first paradise, then Tiberias, the easternmost city in the Palestinian Galilee, is well described as its backyard. From the time of its founding by Herod Antipas in 18–22 CE, its location on Lake Tiberias (also known as the Sea of Galilee), its fertile soil, and its public baths and hot springs made it a popular place for relaxation and rest in the winter. (In the summer, insects and flies drove local residents away.)

Herod attracted people to Tiberias, which he had built near the Canaanite settlement of Raqqa, by allotting gifts of land. Until 61 CE, the city was considered the capital of Galilee, largely because the royal Roman treasure houses and archives were here. Tiberias had its own currency, the Tiberian dirham, which featured reed plants indigenous to the shores of the sea of Galilee and later a palm tree.

The city was settled by pre-Islamic Arab tribes, some of whom were Jewish, though at first Orthodox Jews refused to live in Tiberias because it was built over a burial site. The Arab tribes that resided in the Tiberias included the al-Ash'ariyyin (named for their long, luxurious hair), the Lekhm, and the Khutham.

In the 2nd century CE, Shimon Bar-Yohai "purified" the town and settlement by Orthodox Jews began. After their banishment from Jerusalem, Jews made Tiberias another Jewish holy site (along with Jerusalem itself, Hebron, and Safad). During the Jewish revolt against the Roman empire, Tiberias was divided into two camps: the revolt's supporters and Roman collaborators. The latter prevailed, and Roman armies conquered the city without any resistance, in return allowing

Mount Bernice

The mountain that dominates Tiberias is known as Bernice, name of Herod's great-grand-daughter. The remains of a large building used between 3rd and 8th centuries can be seen on the mount's summit. On the slope of the mountain is an ancient theater from the 2nd and 3rd century, and an aqueduct, which led spring water to the center of the city. On the mount itself are remains of a 15-meter (99-foot) wall with towers that was once part of Roman Tiberias.

the Jews to practice their religion freely. The city was said to have thirteen synagogues.

When Christianity became widespread in the rest of Palestine, Tiberias followed; by the 4th century, many locals had converted to Christianity. At the Council of Ephesus in 449 CE, Bishop John of Tiberias represented the city's faithful.

In 634, Shurahbeel Bin Hassaneh conquered Tiberias and its environs. Soon after, the Caliph Othman Bin 'Affan sent the city elders a copy of the Quran known as the Othman Quran, so that they could spread the Propher's message. This famous copy of the Quran remained in Tiberias for almost 500 years. When the Crusaders approached Tiberias, it was sent for safekeeping to Damascus, where it remains to this day.

Tiberias was host or home to many a luminary, among them Suleiman Abu al-Qasem al-Tabrani (981–873), the great adventurer said to have traveled the world for 33 years in a row, and the famous poet Abu al-Tayyib al-Mutanabbi, who lived for a few years as the guest of the local ruler, Wali Abi Hasan al-Asadi al-Tabristani (939), writing odes to the waters, warm valley, and birds of Tiberias—and the lions kept by his host.

In 1998, three large storage jars containing 1,000 rare objects (candelabras, lampstands, scissors, bowls with Arabic writing, and 58 Byzantine coins), were unearthed in Tiberias. The stash was the largest collection ever found of these coins, which featured the image of Jesus with Greek inscriptions of praise. They were probably brought to Tiberias by pilgrims from Constantinople. Archaeologists believe that the jars belonged to a Fatimid artisan who hid his treasures from the approaching Crusaders.

Although Crusader rule lasted less than a century, it was devastating for the local population. The Crusaders exiled or killed the city's Muslim inhabitants, but left a tiny Syriac community in place, and eventually made the city capital of a new principality of the Galilee. As elsewhere, the Crusaders took control of towers and built fortresses and a cathedral.

The Sea of Galilee

The sea of Galilee is mentioned in the Bible under several names: the sea of Chinnereth, the sea of Genesar, the lake of Gennesaret, the sea of Galilee, and, most commonly, the sea of Tiberias. It is the backdrop to several well known stories, such as the ones about Jesus walking upon the waters (Matthew 14:24–32) and calming the stormy sea (Matthew 8:23–26).

The historian Josephus found its waters "both sweet and excellent to drink" and Pliny described it as "encompassed with pleasant towns: on the east, Julias and Hippo; on the south, Tarichea, by which name some call the lake also; and to the west, Tiberias, healthful for its warm waters." Though pollution has rendered the once-sweet waters undrinkable, 22 kinds of fish both large and small inhabit the lake.

Six main valleys (wadis) replenish the lake with their winter waters. These are the valleys of Musallekheh (or 'Usheh), Abadan, al-Jammouseh, al-Amoud, al-Rabadiyyeh (also known as Tuffah or Sallameh), and al-Hamam. Near to Wadi al-Amoud are two archeologically significant caves that contained prehistoric artifacts. The first, known as the Princess Cave, is located 2 kilometers from where the wadi's water pours into the sea. Nearby is Zuttiyeh cave, where a 200,000-year-old skull known as the "Skull of the Galilee" was discovered in 1925.

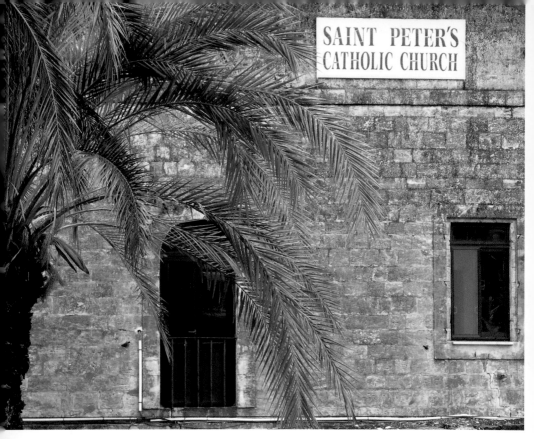

Church of St. Peter

Archaeologists have unearthed pillars of the cathedral, which was destroyed in an earthquake, in the courtyard of the Jordan River Hotel.

In 1187 Saladin gathered his troops on the eastern bank of the sea of Tiberias and set off for the southern shore, crossing into Palestine over the Sunbarah Bridge and setting up camp in the village of Kufr Sabt. His army defeated the Crusaders at the Horns of Hittin, and afterward Saladin destroyed the city walls, making it difficult for the Crusaders to retake Tiberias.

More than 100 years later, Tiberias was still described as a "city of rubble" by the writer Abu al-Fida. The famous Arab traveler Ibn Battuta (d. 1388) confirmed this, writing that "You can tell it once was a grand city, but all that remains are drawings that indicate its former greatness." Ibn Battuta's work gives many interesting details about Tiberian life at that time: He writes of the "strange baths" with separate entrances for men and women, its Mosque of the Prophets, and lists many well known mystics or religious leaders buried here.

Grand Mosque

Tiberias played a relatively marginal role for much of the Ottoman era (1517–1918). The Jewish population of Tiberias grew, however, as Sephardic Jews received permission from the Ottoman caliphs to reside in the city after they were expelled from Spain in 1492.

The leader of Portuguese Jewish refugees, Joseph Nasi, settled in Tiberias and began a silk industry.

The city became a center for trade with the migrating tribes of the Arabian Peninsula. Most prominent of these was the Zaidani tribe of the Hijaz, who settled throughout northern Palestine. In 1730, al-Zaidani built a great fortress at the entrance of the city and extended and rebuilt parts of the city wall. From this fortress, the Zaidani fought and defeated the Ottoman vassal from Damascus, Suleiman Pasha al-Athem.

Napoleon briefly controlled Tiberias during his sojourn in Palestine. After his defeat, Tiberias came under the control of Mohammed Ali in 1832, who instructed his engineer Todoraki, to reconstruct the city's famous hot water baths in 1833. Five years later, an earthquake destroyed them, killing some 600 people.

Soon after, in 1848, a traveler noted that Tiberias was nothing more than "a small village with a broken down surrounding wall, beyond which you will not find one standing house or tree," strangely echoing Ibn Battuta five centuries earlier.

During the Ottoman empire's last century, many European travelers came to Palestine, and they kept diaries of their observations. According to the Swiss-German traveler Johann Ludwig Burkhart, a community of Afghans from Kashmir had settled in Tiberias. He also wrote about the city's Jewish community, estimating that it was comprised of "160–200 families, of which 40–50 are of Polish origin. The remainder are of Spanish and northern African origin as well as from various parts of Syria. The Jews of Tiberias enjoy complete religious freedom."

The British Mandate and the 1948 War

Despite the fact that the Jewish community of Tiberias had co-existed with Arab Muslim and Christian populations throughout its history, the British mandate and Zionist colonialist practices and settlement soured relations between the two communities. The relationship deteriorated to the extent that clashes broke out in 1929, 1933 and 1935, and during the Great Revolt of 1936–39.

According to the UN Partition Plan, Tiberias was to be part of the Jewish state. By March 1948, clashes intensified and fighting was widespread within the city, with the Palestinians gaining the upper hand. Hostilities were halted by a British cease-fire order. The British orders held until mid-April, when Jewish forces launched a surprise attack and took the city. This time the British commander did not impose a cease-fire, but instead ordered 60 trucks to "load" the Palestinians and send them to Nazareth. By late April (before the official war began), Tiberias was already under Jewish rule, the first Palestinian city to be surrendered to Zionist forces by the British. The entire Christian and Muslim population of Tiberias, along with virtually all nearby villagers, became refugees. Most Tiberian Palestinians became exiles in refugee camps in Syria, Lebanon, and Jordan.

Afterword, the 6,000 Jewish residents of Tiberias quickly became 7,700 by 1951 and 23,000 by 1965. Many of these new immigrants were from Arab countries. They settled in the homes the Palestinians had fled. The al-Zaidani Mosque, located on the shore of the Sea of Galilee, was turned into a local museum.

The Sea of Galilee has been witness to several Arab–Israeli skirmishes, though nothing comparable to what has taken place over the Israel–Lebanese or Israeli–Jordanian border. In 1955, Israel attacked the Syrian army in an operation that began from the Israeli settlement of Ein Jib, where Jordan meets the sea of Tiberias. Again in August of 1966, Israel led a sea assault into the demilitarized zone on the Syrian shores accompanied by aerial cover in events known as the Battle of the Lake.

Today, Israel advertises Tiberias as a resort town, though without much success.

Religious Sites

Church of St. Peter (Miracle of the Fish)
The Church of St. Peter is one of the few remaining Crusader churches. Franciscans took control of the church around 1641. A neo-classical facade was built during the 19th century at the entrance of the church and statues from the studios of the Delin Brothers of Paris were brought to decorate its interior. The apse of the church features a large scene painted by Edward S. Patzolt (1902) of St. Peter at the bow of a boat. Hidden within the painting are the coat-of-arms of the Holy See, with the Tiara and Keys, as well as the coat-of-arms of the Franciscan Order and the Custody of the Holy Land. The Church features a replica of a famous statue of St. Peter found in the Basilica of St. Peter in the Vatican and was given to the sanctuary by the second French "Pilgrimage of Penance" in 1883.

Near to the statue of St. Peter and in the outer courtyard stands a monument to the Virgin of Czestochowa erected by Polish soldiers of the Third Army in dedication of their stay in the Casa Nova of Tiberias in 1945.

Bordering the church on the north side, the Casa Nova (b. 1903)

has been recently renovated. It is a 25-room bed & breakfast inn, featuring a balcony overlooking the sea.

Franciscan Friary
Bordering the Church of St. Peter to the south, the friary also claims to be located on the site of the "miracle of the fish." The church is open for prayer and celebrations of the Eucharist.

Grand Mosque
Built in the 18th century during the reign of al-Zaidani, the mosque has fallen into disuse, but is one of the few Muslim shrines in Tiberias that has not been destroyed. Even in bad condition, its former splendor still shines through.

Greek Orthodox Monastery
A Christian shrine has stood in this place since the 4th century. Today's monastery, built upon the ruins of a Crusader fortress, was completed in 1868. The adjacent garden is used for community events.

Rabbi Moses Ben Maimon's Grave
Located near the small park off what is today Elhadeff Street lies the grave of the Jewish Scholar of the 12th century, Moses ben Maimon, also known as Maimonides.

Other Sites

Roman and Byzantine Tiberias
The archaeological remains of Roman and Byzantine Tiberias are found less than 3 km (1.864 mi) south of the present-day city center, near what is known as Sironit beach. Here stand the remains of a square building with colonnades dating to the second century. Orginally built by the Romans for administrative purposes, the building was transformed into a church four centuries later.

Tiberian Baths
On the site of the destroyed Canaanite village Hammat ("hot springs") stand the remains of a Roman bath house dated to the 4th century. The Romans named the hot springs Ammathus; they were

Top: Church of Beatitudes
Below: Druze Sanctuary of Nabi Shueib

said to heal rheumatism and nerve and skin disorders. The bath was used for 800 years. Today a roof protects the coloring of the floor mosaics, which depict birds, fish, and other animals. Three domes, which were built during the Islamic reign, and the baths are on property once owned by the Islamic waqf, until they were forcibly transferred to "state ownership" during the British mandate.

Near Tiberias

The area around Tiberias is as important as the city itself, for it is the location of several important historical sites.

Capernaum and the Mount of the Beatitudes

Capernaum, on the sea of Galilee, was Jesus' headquarters during his brief ministry in the area. In 1894 the site was bought by Franciscans. Just a short ride up the hill is the Mount of the Beatitudes, with the beautiful **Church of the Beatitudes**. Built in 1938 and designed by Antonio Barluzzi, its octagonal shape (representing the eight blessings of the Beatitudes) provides an unbroken panorama of the sea of Galilee.

Horns of Hittin

Imbedded in a now extinct volcano are the Horns of Hittin, which overlook the site of one of the most important battles in world history. The fields still seem burned where the army of Saladin put fire to them and defeated the Crusaders on July 3, 1187. Some 12,000 of Saladin's troops defeated 17,000 Crusaders. With sun in their eyes, searing summer heat, and heavy armor, the Crusaders were exhausted even before the battle began, and Saladin's agile archers won the day.

Al-Majdal

Al-Majdal, four kilometers from Tiberias, was destroyed in 1948 by the Israeli state and its 360 residents sent into exile. Frequently referred to in historical records, al-Majdal was called Tarichea by the Romans. A shrine honoring local sage Muhammad al-'Ajami still stands here.

Tabgha

Some Christian historians believe that Jesus came here in search of solitude and meditation. It is near Capernaum (Kufr Nahum), the place understood to be the site of two of Jesus' miracles: the loaves and fishes and St. Peter's primacy.

Nabi Shueib (Druze Sanctuary)
Seven kilometers northwest of Tiberias is the Druze sanctuary of Nabi Shueib, site of a festival every spring on the occasion of the prophet Jethro's birthday. Mentioned in the Quran as a messenger to the Prophet Muhammad, Jethro was also the father-in-law of Moses. For the occasion, many lambs are slaughtered and shared with Druze families, neighbors, and the poor.

The Nabi Shueib compound consists of the **Tomb of Jethro** (Shueib in Arabic), an encased stone in the wall with a footprint believed to be Jethro's, and a prayer hall. A large meeting area for Druze elders, a youth center, a picnic plaza, and fresh springs make it a mountain refuge.

The Druze

The Druze sect, with 65,000 members in Palestine and another million in Syria, Lebanon, and Jordan, is shrouded in secrecy. The founding fathers of the Druze were supporters of an 11th-century Egyptian caliph who belonged to the Fatimids, a Shiite sect. Though he was called al-Hakim, "the just one," he was known for his extreme intolerance. He declared himself a manifestation of God, and the new sect took its name from one of his followers, Muhammad al-Darazi. After al-Hakim's mysterious disappearance in 1021, the sect was persecuted and driven into the mountains of Syria and Lebanon, where it still has its main base of support. A disciple encrypted what were to become the six secret books, which are accessible only to chosen Druze elders.

Technically, the Druze stopped proselytizing in the 11th century—one cannot convert, but can only be born a Druze. The Druze believe in reincarnation. They do not circumcise their men, and avoid the popular Middle Eastern vegetable dish *mlokhia*, the consumption of which the Caliph al-Hakim personally banned 1,000 years ago. (The Druze, though, have made their own contributions to the culinary scene in Northern Palestine, with restaurants, especially in Daliat al-Carmel, that attract many Jews from neighboring villages.)

The exact origins of the Druze community in Palestine are not clear. They probably began coming from Syria during Ottoman rule, forming enclaves close to Palestine's northern borders. Living in separate, tucked-away communities and practicing secret ceremonies, they did not represent part of mainstream Palestinian life. Muslim and Christian communities, whose traditions were more transparent, often looked at them with suspicion. Unlike the Druze of Lebanon and Syria, Palestine's Druze as a community never held real political, economic, or social power.

The British and later the Israelis focused on their desire for separateness in order to attain their loyalty and cooperation. Unlike the Druze of Syria and Lebanon, who have taken a staunchly pan-Arab stance, Palestine's Druze have added to their historic political and social isolation by appearing to have sided with Israel in the struggle for Palestinian freedom. In return for basic municipal and public services such as electricity and running water, building permits and health care, the Druze elders agreed that their youth would serve in the Israeli army. The subsequent stigma that the Druze of Palestine acquired still exists. They remain a marginal part of the Palestinian community, both inside modern Israel and inside Palestinian autonomous areas. A few, like the Druze poet Samih al-Qassem, have broken the mold, and younger, more politically conscious, members of the community have joined Arab political movements inside Israel.

Inscribed stone in ancient Bisan, with the fortress mound in background

15.

Bisan

Bisan is now a purely Arab village situated on the plain at the extreme edge of the southern descent to the Jordan. Very fine views of the river can be had from the housetops, and on a clear day the Mountains of Moab across the valley are very sharply defined.... Many nomad and Bedouin encampments, distinguished by their black tents, were scattered about the riverine plain, their flocks and herds grazing round them.

— Lawrence of Arabia in *The Railway Magazine*, 1934

L ocated in the northeastern portion of Palestine's historic fertile plain, about 6 kilometers (3.7 mi) from the Jordan River and 32 kilometers (20 mi) south of the sea of Galilee, Bisan (or Beisan) is one of the world's longest continuously settled cities (at least 6,000 years). It owes its longevity largely to its location along ancient trade routes connecting Syria with Egypt and northern Palestine with Jordan and its water supply, which flows from Wadi al-Bireh, Wadi 'Aisheh and the Jordan Valley, ensuring the flourishing and survival of its agricultural communities.

Bisan's setting is picturesque, located where the valley plain drops down a precipitous 300 feet to the level of the Jordan Valley (Ghor), which sweeps gracefully southward. The surrounding region was originally volcanic, like the region around Tiberias, making most of the stones and ancient structures black and basaltic in nature.

Modern Bisan is south of the original town, which was situated on a small hill north of the modern city, known as Tel al-Husn (Fortress Mound). Visible from a considerable distance from both east and west, Tel al-Husn is a treasure trove of archeological ruins containing some twenty layers of settlement and at least 9 different ancient cities.

The mound rises 80 meters (262 ft) above the surrounding landscape and has a 30-degree slope on all its sides, forming a large plateau on top. The mound's black color makes it look like a crater.

Bisan has had several names, including Beit Shan, Beth Shan, Scythopolis, and Scythopolis-Nysa. The Arabic (Bisan), English and Hebrew (Beth Shean) all derive from the original Canaanite name Beit Shan, meaning "house of the God Shan," or the "house of tranquility."

Early History

Shards of pottery of Yarmukian and Jericho culture found at Bisan indicate that it was settled during the Bronze Age, 3500 BCE, but sparsely, until at least 2,200 BCE when evidence of a larger and more settled population living in multi-roomed structures and traveling on intersecting streets appeared.

In the 19th century BCE the Egyptians conquered Bisan and turned into an important administrative center, according to the texts at the Great Temple of Amon in Karnak (1468 BCE). It is also mentioned in several other texts including the Tel Amarna letters (1350 BCE), the inscriptions of Seti I (1300 BCE), his son Ramses II (1280 BCE) and the Anastasi Papyrus (13th century BCE).

The Egyptians left significant archeological ruins in Bisan, among them a mid-14th century BCE Canaanite-style temple complex dating back to Thumose III. According to an Egyptian stele found on site, the temple was dedicated to "Mekal the great lord of Beth Shan" and had a basalt relief of a lion and a dog fighting in combat.

A temple used around 1300–1150 BCE dedicated to the goddess Astarte was built on top of this site and a large number of Syrian–Hittite seals and an axe were found at the site.

An elaborate combination of cult objects related to the Egyptian rule in Bisan have been found, including cylinders with serpents and doves, pottery duck heads and other objects with snake motifs. The prevalence of this motif has led experts to believe that Bisan was the center for a serpent cult.

Roman colonnade of Bisan

Philistine rule began in Bisan after they defeated the Egyptians in 1127 BCE and resided in the city for more than 100 years. According to an Old Testament tradition the Philistines fought a battle at nearby Mt. Giboa in 1005 BCE, which ended when they impaled the headless bodies of Saul and his three sons "to the wall of Beth Shan."

After the Philistines left, Bisan reverted to the Canaanites, who resisted the attacks of the Israelites using weapons left for them by the sea people. According to the Old Testament the Israelites failed to drive out the Canaanite inhabitants of Beth Shan, "for the Canaanites were determined to live in that land" and they had "iron chariots" (Joshua 17:16).

During Pharaoh Sheshonk I's incursion into Palestine in 918 BCE, a huge fire is said to have engulfed the city, destroying most of it. Subsequently the Israelites controlled the city until the Assyrian King Tiglath-Pilesar III destroyed it in 732 BCE.

Hellenistic, Roman, and Byzantine Era

Bisan seems to have been more or less abandoned between 587–332 BCE. It appears that Scythians (warriors from the Black Sea area) may have taken up residence in the vacant city during their years of alliance with Assyria. According to Herodotus, the Scythians made an incursion through Palestine into Egypt in the 8th century. Alexander the Macedonian conquered the city in 332 BCE and built a new and adjacent Bisan, at the foot of the mound. The new and enlarged city was called Scythopolis (city of the Scythians) and existed as such for 900 years.

Though little is known of the town during Hellenistic times, remains of a temple to Dionysus and a temple dedicated to Zeus "of the high mountain," as well as fountains, markets, a theater, and an odeum, imply a substantial urban population.

During Roman rule, beginning in 63 BCE, Scythopolis was incorporated into an alliance of ten city-states known as the Decapolis. The others cities of the Decapolis were Damascus, Opoton, Philadelphia, Raphana, Gadara, Hippondion, Pella, Galasa, and Canatha. As the largest city, Scythopolis was declared the capital of the Decapolis.

It became known as a production center for wine, cotton fabrics, and textiles. Impressive new amphitheaters, baths, and a theater were built; they remain the best Roman archeological sites in Palestine.

According to Mark (7:31) Jesus passed through the Decapolis region after leaving Tyre and Sidon, healing "a man who was deaf and could hardly talk."

By 324 CE, Scythopolis had become a Christian city, and the gladiator scenes in the local amphitheater stopped. The theater, bathhouses, and fountains continued to function, however, until 363 CE, when a huge earthquake destroyed the city. It was reconstructed, but not at its original site, which was thus able to retain its pagan character.

Thereafter it was described as "a flourishing Christian city of saints and scholars, churches and monasteries" by Eusebius and Jerome in the 4th century. It had its own bishop, Patrophilus, who participated at the Council of Nicene in 325.

In 409, Emperor Theodosius named Scythopolis the civil and ecclesiastical metropolis of the region, which incorporated the Galilee, Um Qais, Scythopolis, and Tiberias and had a population of 30,000–40,000 inhabitants.

By the sixth century, the city had four churches, dedicated to St. Thomas, St. John, St. Procopius, and St. Basil, a local martyr. Many monks lived in the town and its environs, making baskets and fans from the palms trees, which were sold in Damascus.

Arab Muslim Era

In 634 the Muslim armies reached the gates of nearby Tiberias, which was conquered in the Battle of Yarmouk and moved south to Bisan against the Byzantine forces that resisted with water-filled moats, though to no avail. The day of the victory became known in Arabic as "Youm Bisan" (the day of Bisan).

In 749 the city was devastated by another earthquake, which turned much of Bisan to rubble. A small group of refugees returned to rebuild the city, but few remains of this period exist.

Among the noteworthy descriptions of Bisan made by Muslim and Arab chroniclers during this era are that of al-Maqdisi (d. 990) who wrote of Bisan as "being on the river, with plentiful palm trees, and water, though somewhat heavy (brackish)" and Abi Obeid al-Andalusi (d. 1094), who found the wine delicious.

Crusades

The Crusaders built a fortress on top of Tel al-Husn and ran it as an independent fiefdom that in 1117 CE declared a French man, "Count Adam de Bethune," the "first Baron of Bessan."

After fending off the Muslim armies in 1182, the Crusaders deserted the town in the next year after the defeat at Battle of Hittin. Saladin had the fortress destroyed, to avoid any possible return of the Crusaders.

Nevertheless, the Crusader armies waged an attack against the city in 1217. The Muslims defending Bisan were few and greatly outnumbered and abandoned the city to the Crusaders, who sacked and looted what remained. Because they had no fortress to protect them, they also abandoned the city and took their booty to Acre, which they still controlled.

Mamluks and Ottomans

During Mamluk rule Bisan became the principal town of the district of Damascus and a relay station for the postal service between Damascus and Cairo. It was the capital of sugar cane processing, which was the most important industry in Palestine in this period.

The Mamluks' most enduring architectural feat in Bisan is Jisr al-Maqtua' (the cut-off bridge). It consisted of a single arch that spanned 25 feet and hung 50 feet above the stream.

During the 400 years of Ottoman reign Bisan appears to have disappeared from the map of important places. Only during the reign of Sultan Abdel Hamid II and the building of the Haifa–Damascus railway did a short and limited revival take place. A feudal system that leased tracts of land to tenants, collected taxes, and largely impoverished the local peasant population was the hallmark of the Ottoman era. The Swiss-German traveler Johann Ludwig Burkhart, who visited Bisan in 1812, described it as "a village with 70 to 80 houses, whose residents are in a miserable state." By the early 1900s, it had become a small, obscure village, though still known for its plentiful water supply, fertile soil, and sun, and its production of olives, grapes, figs, almonds, apricots, and apples.

British Mandate

After the British occupied Bisan in September 1918, they encouraged the growth of agricultural production, but with prejudicial land policies that worsened the economic state of the Palestinian peasants—often forcing them to sell their land to the Zionist settlers. The Zionists then prospered in the production of bananas and citrus fruits, and their movement expanded in Bisan throughout the Mandate period.

A 1922 census estimated that the population of Bisan was 10,500 inhabitants of which 9,500 were Muslim, 300 were Christian, and 700 were Jewish. By 1945, Zionist efforts to colonize the Bisan district had been very successful; entire communities, including Shatta, Tel al-Firr, Jisr al-Mujami', and al-Zarra'a, had disappeared under British rule. Out of an overall population of 23,500, 16,500 were Palestinian (Muslims and Christians) and 7,000 were Jewish. Entire communities had disappeared under British rule

As elsewhere in the country, the British facilitated the excavation of many ruins. From 1921 to 1933, a team from the University of Pennsylvania excavated many sites in the Bisan area.

War of 1948

The UN Partition plan allocated Bisan to the Jewish state. Joseph Weitz, a leading figure of the Zionist movement, wrote in his diary on May 4, 1948 that "The Beit Shean [Bisan] Valley is the gate for our state in the Galilee.... [I]ts clearing [of the Palestinian Arabs] is the need of the hour."

Attacks against Bisan began in February 1948. First to be attacked and expelled were the Bedouin populations of the Bisan district (February and March 1948). The expulsion was facilitated by fears of the local population of massacre. Bisan fell to the Zionists three days before the end of the British Mandate.

A few days after Bisan became part of the state of Israel, 6,000 Arabs were expelled from the city. Many were loaded into trucks and expelled across the Jordanian and Syrian borders. Today no Palestinian residents of Bisan remain. All their possessions, homes, businesses, gardens, orchards, land, schools, churches and mosques were confiscated and held as property of the state of Israel. Demolition of Bisan's homes began in June 1948, but was halted to allow Jewish immigrants, mostly from North Africa, to settle in what remained of Palestinian homes.

Of the 44 villages in this region only 8 remained. Three of these were later occupied and their residents expelled. By the end of May 1948 the name of the town was changed from Bisan to Beth Shean. Much of Bisan's Jewish-Ashkenazi population moved elsewhere and thus by 1949, the population was 1,200. But by 1966 it had reached 12,800, mostly through an influx of Morrocan and Yemeni Jews. Textile and plastic factories were established. The kibbutzes in Bisan's periphery (which were largely settled by Ashkenazi Jews) prospered, in large part as a result of the fact that they took over the Palestinians' large tracts of fertile land and crops.

Today, Bisan's population is about 18,000. The town's main tourist attraction is the Beit She'an National Park, and some water parks including Gan Hashlosha National Park (Sahne), and the Hogah Springs near the present city. A total of 33 Jewish settlements now reside upon the land of Bisan and its villages.

20th-century Arab architecture in Bisan

Visiting Bisan

These main archeological sites are located in Beit She'an National Park (including remains of the Byzantine city), and in Nahal Harod Park, a park that runs the length of the Jaloud River. The park has picnic grounds, remains of an ancient aqueduct, a waterfall, and walking trails.

Bath Houses

Built during the Byzantine era (324–640), the western bath house stayed in use until the Umayyad period (7th century). An absolution pool with a red cross painted above, suggests that was used for baptisms. The eastern bath house was built during the Roman period and renovated during the Byzantine period (324–640 CE).

Jisr al-Maqtu'a

This Mamluk bridge spanning the Jaloud River made possible the postal service from Gaza to Damascus during the Mamluk and early Ottoman era. A bit downstream is a large waterfall.

Mosaic Inscription

In the summer of 1998, a twenty-foot wide street leading to the southern city gate was discovered. Alongside the basalt paving stones was a walkway paved with mosaics. It was, in essence, an ancient pedestrian mall lined with shops. In front of one shop, an inscription read: "May the victory of the Blues come." The Blues and the Greens are thought to be two chariot-racing teams. Fanatical support turned the teams into formidable political forces, with supporters who organized the crowds and could whip up riots or empty the streets at will. Their protection was sometimes essential for finding employment or safely operating a shop. Similar inscriptions wishing the Blues luck have been found in other Middle Eastern cities, while slogans encouraging the Greens have been discovered in Eastern Europe and Turkey.

Nymphaeum

A public fountain (built 2nd century and remodeled in the 4th century) at the end of Palladius street dedicated to the water nymphs of Roman and Greek mythology.

Palladius Street

This nearly 500-foot long colonnaded street was built by the Romans and renovated at the beginning of the Byzantine period. On the northwest side, a roofed double colonnade sheltered a row of shops faced with marble. After the discovery of a 4th-century mosaic documenting the construction of the road during Palladius's rule as provincial governor, the street was named for him.

Public Lavatory

Located east of Palladius Street near the eastern bath house, this public lavatory contained 40 seats. Water from a large tank flowed into a deep channel beneath the seats to wash away waste.

Roman Temple

A semi-circular temple, built in the 1st to 2nd centuries CE, dominated the center of the city. It was probably dedicated to Dionysus, god of wine and the city's patron deity, whose image is seen on a Corinthian capital.

Colonnades of Bisan

Roman Theater

Just south of Tel al-Husn, this large Roman theater (capacity 8,000) is considered to be the best preserved specimen of Roman architecture in western Palestine. A now dismembered statue, probably of Hermes Psychopompus (1st CE), was found in the western hall. It was later upgraded and renovated by the Byzantines under Justinian (518–27 CE), when apparently water was introduced for water ballet performances.

Tel al-Husn (Fortress Mound)

North of the current city, this mound with its layers of nine cities is the site of the most important Egyptian archeological findings in the entire Levant. The oldest city dates back to the 5th millennium BCE

and the most recent, to medieval times.

Among the diverse ruins discovered atop Tel al-Husn are five different Egyptian temples and Corinthian capitals of a Roman temple of Zeus.

Other Sites

Amphitheater/Hippodrome
Just south of the theater outside the city limits, the amphitheater was originally much larger and was used as a hippodrome for chariot-racing. In the 3rd century CE, it may have been converted into a venue for gladiatorial contests, a concession to the many Roman legionnaires stationed in the area. To protect spectators from the wild animals in the amphitheater, a limestone wall was built, covered with plaster, and decorated with frescoes. The word arena, the floor of the amphitheater, is Latin for sand, which was spread there to absorb the blood shed during the contests. The amphi-theater ceased functioning in the second half of the 4th century.

Tombs and Cemeteries

Philistine burial customs, probably already intermingled with that of the Canaanites and the Egyptians, included burying their dead in lightly fired clay coffins, ceramic sarcophagi, accompanied by portraits of the dead. Objects found in graves included lamps, pilgrim flasks, stirrup jars, cups, necklaces, earrings, and anklets typical of the early Iron Age.

In their tombs, their hair is arranged simply up to the cheek, leaving the ears exposed in some cases. Their faces are clean shaven and smooth, and the arms are placed on the chest, at times with the hands grasping a lotus or other objects similar to Egyptian religious symbols.

Burial chambers from the Hellenistic period included glass, terracotta figurines, statuettes, and bronze bells. An interesting feature of the Roman burials is the inclusion of crude portrait busts of the dead, a custom apparently confined to the Bisan area.

Saraya
During the Ottoman era, the saraya was the equivalent of town hall. Many of them were seized by the Israeli government. In Bisan it remained closed for nearly five decades before being renovated as a tourist center with shops and restaurants. Now the actual building is an artist's house.

Panoramic view of Nazareth with the Basilica of the Annunciation

16.

Nazareth (al-Nasira)

A thousand forgotten conquerors have passed over my country and melted like the snow.

—from *"Six Words,"* Taufiq Zayyad, 20th century

Nazareth lies in a hollow plateau about 1,200 feet above sea level, between the most southerly hills (about 1,600 feet) of the Lebanon mountain range.

Historically Nazareth is often portrayed as less important than other cities in the country. Archaeological evidence, however, shows that Nazareth was inhabited by the Canaanites since the Middle Bronze Age (2000–1500 BCE). The Romans and Byzantines had burial grounds on the hill across from the Church of the Annunciation. The recent discovery of an extensive Roman bathhouse implies that there was a Roman colony in Nazareth, about which not much is yet known.

The origins of the name are most probably Canaanite adapted to Hebrew, possibly meaning either "monk" or "branch." Others believe that "Nazarenes" was the derogatory name Jews gave to early Christians. In any case, Nazareth, or Nazereth, is most famous as the town where Jesus lived and preached, and where the Archangel Gabriel appeared to Mary to announce the impending birth of her child, though it was then but a small agricultural town settled by a few dozen families.

Historical accounts indicate that although Christ's own clan and family was from Nazareth, most of its residents did not accept or convert to Christianity until the 6th century. In 326, the Emperor Constantine allowed the building of a small church over the Grotto of the Annunciation, which was Mary's home. By 570, there were two churches.

The first detailed description of Nazareth came under Muslim rule, when Christian pilgrims started coming to Palestine in large numbers and larger churches were built. During the Crusader period Nazareth became a "Christian city," and all Muslims and Jews were expelled and monastic orders set up. The city became the seat of an archbishop.

Significant parts of Nazareth were destroyed after Sultan Baibar's final expulsion of the Crusaders. Not until the reign of the Ottomans were Christians welcomed back to the city, when in 1620 Emir Fakhri Din encouraged them to settle in the city. Still, the community seemed in peril until the reign in 1730 of Dhaher al-Omar al-Zaidani (1730). Al-Zaidani encouraged the Franciscans to build a new church over the Grotto of the Annunciation.

Throughout this time (from the 17th to 19th centuries), Nazareth was settled by various Muslim clans from Albania and elsewhere in southern Europe. Though in World War I it was made into a regional command center under German control, throughout the Ottoman era it had been an area of little importance.

Nazareth gained preferential status during British Mandate rule, for the British made a habit of preferring Christian to Muslim Arabs. The Mandate government employed many Nazarene Christians and facilitated scholarships and business opportunities. According to the UN partition plan, Nazareth was to be part of the Arab state of Palestine, but the Israelis wanted it to be part of their state and tried to have all the Arabs evacuated during the war. The act of a single volunteer commander from Canada, who refused to accept verbal orders to evacuate the Arab population, insisting he get a written order instead, allowed for the continued presence of the Arabs here.

In order to force a Jewish presence in Nazareth, the Israeli government established Nazareth Illit (Upper Nazareth), on a mountain opposite Nazareth. It is an almost entirely Jewish city, which receives preferential treatment from the Israeli government but has no tourist sites.

Nazareth has about 50,000 inhabitants, many of whom are refugees from the 1948 war. Like all Arab populations in Israel, the Nazareth community lived under martial law until the 1960s. Local politics has tended to be a competition between members of the communist party and the Islamists; thus far the communists have always won the municipal and parliamentary elections. Israel has frequently tried to interfere in local politics, inadvertently supporting Islamists, to the chagrin of the largely secular population.

In 2000 Nazareth was the site of major unrest after the Israeli army had killed a large number of Palestinian protesters in the West Bank and Gaza.

Altar in the house where Mary was born

Visiting Nazareth

Nazareth's Old City is a wonderful Mediterranean mountain town. To make sure it stays that way, a municipal team has identified architectural and historical sites that should be preserved. One of them, at the foot of the ridge, is a large concentration of traditional two-story houses of Galilee stone, with tile roofs, patios, and inner courtyards. Most of these were built in the 1800s or the early 1900s.

Religious Sites

Basilica of the Annunciation

This large basilica stands over the Grotto of Annunciation and Home of Mary, where the Latin Church believes she received the news of her son's impending birth. The first church on this site was a small one, built in 326 by one of Nazareth's first converts, Joseph of Tiberias, after he applied for and received a building permit from the Emperor Constantine.

The church was re-built during the mid-fifth century and yet again during the Crusader period. It was destroyed during or after the battle between the Mamluk forces and the Crusaders in 1263. During the next 500 years, it was built and demolished at least half a dozen times. The current church dates from 1969, and was constructed on the site of a church built by the Franciscans in 1730. The Italian design of today's church is one of the most unusual in the country.

Church of St. Joseph

This church, sometimes called the Church of the Carpentry Shop, stands north of the Basilica of the Annunciation. Built in 1914 over an earlier church from the Crusader period, it preserves the home and workshop of Joseph, husband of Mary. It is a one-room church that monks use for meditation.

Maqam of Shihab ad-Din

Shihab ad-Din was a nephew of the Prophet Mohammad who settled in Nazareth. This early Ottoman shrine (16th century), was built over what is believed to be his grave, just south of the Basilica.

Mary's Well and the Church of St. Gabriel (Orthodox Church)

The Church of St. Gabriel houses a first century spring of water believed to be the source of Mary's Well. The spring is connected to the site of the well by an underground aqueduct.

White Mosque
Built in 1812, this popular mosque stands at the center of the Muslim community's quarter in Nazareth, next to the covered marketplace. The tomb of Abdullah el-Fahoum, governor of Nazareth in the 1800s, is in the courtyard.

Other Sites

Roman Bathhouse
Near Mary's Well, inside a local tourist shop called Cactus, is what appears to be a bathhouse that was possibly used by Jesus. Archeologists agree that the bathhouse dates from the Roman empire.

Saraya Museum
The Saraya, in which the Nazareth Museum is located, is one of the most important historical buildings in the city. It was built in the 18th century by Dhaher al-Omar al-Zaidani, the governor of Galilee, under whose reign Nazareth developed from a village into an urban center. Al-Zaidani encouraged the Christian population to settle within its borders. He built his summer residence in Nazareth, the state of security improved greatly, and trade flourished. It was during this period that the Saraya was built.

Al-Zaidani turned one of the rooms of the 2-story building into a prayer chamber for Muslims (it was not until 1812 that the White Mosque was erected next door). Until the 1990s, the Saraya fulfilled its original purpose, serving as Nazareth's town hall.

The Saraya is now being restored, with its original facade conserved. Museum exhibits will be displayed in the rooms of the original building, from whose windows visitors will have a scenic view of the city, preserving an architectural link with the nearby market and the urban surroundings of the city.

Plans for the museum are quite elaborate. Olive trees, vines, pomegranates, and herbs remniscent of the Galilean countryside will greet visitors as they leave the commotion of the market behind and enter the courtyard of the Saraya. An old carpentry workshop suggestive of the Christian tradition associated with Nazareth will stand in one of the corners of the reconstructed yard, part of the exhibition that will recreate Nazareth as it was 2,000 years ago. The exhibition will feature state-of-the-art presentation with models and special technical effects, original exhibits, ancient manuscripts, and textual and graphic material.

The White Mosque, Nazareth

Near Nazareth

Arraba

Arraba (south of Nazareth) is a surprising tourist site. It looks simply like a beautiful, well-kept village from the highway, but it is also full of historical interest, including Canaanite tombs and many mosques (one dates from the 12th century). Arraba is also home to many of the north's displaced Bedouins. Several bed-&-breakfasts, as well as hiking spots, make this a worthwhile stop. Up the street is another nice Arab village, Deir Hanna, which contains a mosque, church, and an 18th-century fort built by Daher al-Omar.

Kufr Kana

Also known as Cana of the Galilee, this vibrant Palestinian village of 10,000 (6 km/3.7 mi northeast of Nazareth) marks the place where Jesus is believed to have turned water into wine at the wedding feast. In 1879, Franciscans built the **Church of the Wedding Feast** to commemorate the miracle. The Greek Orthodox Church also built a house of worship here. Several mosques serve the town's Muslim population, which includes a small Circassian community, originally from the Caucasus.

Mt. Tabor

As the highest mountain in the region Mount Tabor has been a coveted site for all invaders. It was the site of a major battle between the Canaanites and Hebrews but later (4th century CE) became famous as the site of the **Transfiguration of Christ**. Consequently a church was built to mark the spot; first by the Byzantines, then the Crusaders, and in the 1920s, the Franciscans. Next to contemporary basilica is an earlier Greek Orthodox Church dedicated to St. Elias. A smorgasbord of remains—a Canaanite temple to Baal, Hebrew caves, remnants of a 13th-century Mamluk wall—make the trek a journey through time.

Saffuriya

Three kilometers northeast of Nazareth, Saffuriya (Zippori) is one of the Galilee's well known villages ethnically cleansed in 1948. In Roman times, it was capital of the Galilee. According to Christian tradition, Anne and Joachim, the Virgin Mary's parents, were natives of this village, then called Sepphoris. It was a Hellenized town, with theaters and public spaces, and a popular center for Jews. The Crusaders built a castle and started their fatal march to the Horns of Hittin from here. Later al-Zaidani renovated the Crusader Castle and

Northern Palestinian Culinary Traditions

The northern regions of historic Palestine have been part of Israel since 1948, but traditional cuisine has continued to thrive among the Palestinians who became citizens of Israel. In fact, resistance to change is a means of cultural survival in the midst of an ever-encroaching Israeli culture. From the Mediterranean coast to the Jordan valley, and from the stretches of Bisan all the way north to the Syrian and Lebanese borders, the Arab population forms cultural enclaves where food traditions have remained generally impervious to Jewish influence.

In the large urban centers such as Haifa and Acre, where sizable Arab communities are established, or in Nazareth, which has remained a purely Arab city in both population and culture, there lurks a disarming provincialism in culinary tradition. One explanation is demographic: after 1948, many urban Palestinians left the country and many villagers from the surrounding countryside moved to the city looking for job opportunities. Another reason is the deep importance to Palestinians of everything to do with the land, most of which was lost to Israel's expansion. (Let it be noted, however, that up until 1992, the Arab population of Israel in Galilee still outnumbered the Jewish one.)

This is not to say that Palestinian cuisine is without its influences—but they are older than the last fifty years. In Northern Palestine, first and foremost is the influence of Lebanese cuisine. In Ottoman days, open borders between Lebanon and Palestine allowed for extensive trade and interaction between communities. From Acre to Nazareth, throughout the north, Palestinians seem to have adopted the Lebanese preference for goat meat, as opposed to the sheep favored by Palestinians in general. Their favorite dish is *ouzi*, a whole goat stuffed with rice and meat and cooked for hours until it melts into the mouth. *Ouzi* is for special occasions: engagements, weddings, housewarmings, or the welcome of a long absent loved one. For such occasions, the goat is rubbed from the inside with nutmeg, cinnamon, cardamom, and laurel leaves, stuffed with a mixture of rice and chipped meat seasoned with salt, pepper, cinnamon, and nutmeg, and finally left to cook all day, until the guests are ready for the main dish (after having indulged in a spread of salads and appetizers, or *meze*).

A Persian influence is also felt in certain circles in the larger cities such as Haifa and Acre. This influence is due to the presence of the small but privileged Bahai community, who have assiduously maintained their traditions, which they share on special occasions such as Nairuz, the Persian new year, when it is customary to eat fish, to ward off evil.

Broom and lamp in a Nazareth home

turned it into a school, which became a stronghold of Arab resistance against the Zionists in the 1930s. Today the former school functions as a visitor center. Zippora National Park displays some of the historic finds uncovered in the village.

Sakhnin

Sakhnin was probably founded by the Canaanites around 1500 BCE. Only a 15-minute drive from Nazareth, this town of 30,000, like almost all Arab communities under Israeli rule, suffers from a lack of public funding and is largely underdeveloped. Nevertheless, it is home

Elias and Martina Shama discovered Nazareth's Roman Bathhouse

to one of the few Palestinian heritage museums in Israeli-occupied
Palestine. Next to the town's main Omari Mosque housed in a
traditional Arab home with an outdoor courtyard is the **Museum of
Palestinian Folk Heritage**.

Every fall Sakhnin hosts an olive oil festival, which is attended by
many villagers from throughout the Galilee. On March 30, the town
marks Land Day, a Palestinian memorial for those who died protesting
Israeli confiscation of Arab lands.

Um al-Fahem

Um al-Fahem (mother of burning coal) is one of the most famous
Arab-Israeli towns, known mostly for its defense of Palestinian rights
within Israel. In more recent years it has also become a center for
conservative social philosophies. With a population of 30,000 it is the
capital of the "triangle" that also encompasses the still Arab villages of
Taibe and Musmus. The town is full of good cafes and restaurants and
an unusually large congregation of mosques. The highest point of the
town, Jabal Iskandar (**Mt. Alexander**), gives visitors a panoramic view
of the whole region.

Fatimah Khatoun Mosque

17.

Jenin

We may never know how many Palestinians died in Jenin. In the end, however, it is not the number that died that will tell the story. It is the savage cruelty experienced by those who survived Israel's assault that will ultimately define the legacy of that devasted square mile of earth.

—James Zogby, Arab American Institute, 20th century

The story of the Palestinian town of Jenin was essentially a simple one before the spring of 2002. Jesus passed through, the Mongols were defeated nearby, and the land was always green, producing some of Palestine's best produce. Since the Israeli invasion in the April of 2002 (see page 185), the name Jenin has not been the same. It is a code-word for massacre and resistance in the battle between the occupier and the occupied.

Located about 43 km/27 mi north of Nablus and only 5 km/3 mi from the village of Jalama on the border of the Green Line, it is the northernmost city in the West Bank and the southern tip of the fertile Marj Ibn Amr triangle. It is known for its produce: wheat, olives, dates, carobs, and figs. Since 1995, it has been home to an American University.

Built at the site of the Canaanite city "Ein Ganeem" (garden spring) or Tel Jenin, the city's existence was first documented in the Egyptian Amarna Letters. It was incorporated into the district of Sabastia during Roman rule, when it was called "Jinae" and considered the agricultural marketplace for the Roman colonies. The Bible describes it as a beautiful place with plenty of water and gardens. It is a holy site for Christians because Jesus passed through on his way from Nazareth to Jerusalem on several occasions.

The Crusaders called Jenin "Le Grand Gerin" and fortified it with a wall and fortress. They renovated the Byzantine church and built a new one. After their eviction, Jenin, like many inland cities, was built up by the new rulers, the Mamluks. Pathways, khans, and public service buildings were commissioned by the Prince Tajar al-Dawadar. The daughter of the Mamluk Sultan al-Ghuri, Princess Khatoun, commissioned the building of the still-existing city mosque over the ruins of the Crusader church. Next to it she also had built a girl's school, now—at 800 years—one of the oldest in the country.

The Jenin area was the site of the Battle of Ein Jalout (1260 CE), in which the Mamluk King Baibars defeated the Mongols, forever ending their rule of the Arab east.

The area of Jenin was famous for its pigeon towers and pigeons, which carried letters back and forth between the leaders of Egypt and the Levant. It represented a main way-station between Gaza and Damascus for the Mamluk mail service.

Ottoman Era

During the rule of the Ottomans, olive oil exports from this region were so great that an ever-increasing number of wealthy families sprung up, even in the countryside. As a result, the peasants and village folk, unlike elsewhere in Palestine, were treated as serfs. This is one of the very few areas in the country where rural women did not—and still do not—wear richly embroidered dresses. Social and economic historians note this as a sign of the absolute subjugation of even the women to the local landowners. Although many peasants had owned land, excessive and often cruel taxation by the Ottoman rulers made many dependent on the feudal classes for their survival.

Modern Era

During World War I, the Germans built an airport here to serve their own and the Turkish air force. Today there is a war memorial for German and Turkish pilots who perished in that war.

Another war memorial commemorates Iraqi soldiers who came to help the Palestinians fight the Zionists in 1947–48; it stands at the southern edge of the city. According to local lore, many Palestinian women, hiding from the fighting in their homes, heard Iraqi-accented Arabic voices outside their homes and believed them to be Iraqi soldiers who had come to protect them. As they emerged from their homes singing songs of welcome, they found that the voices where those of Iraqi Jews fighting with the Zionists.

Hashemite rule (1949–1967) came as relief, as locals considered themselves lucky not to have fallen under the jurisdiction of the Israelis. Many of the local population migrated to the Gulf countries for work during the Jordanian reign. A daughter of Jenin notables, Ferial Irsheid, married Prince Muhammad, King Hussein's brother, giving Jenin an intimate connection to the royals across the river. And long after Jordanian rule was over, Jenin notables, including members of the powerful Jarrar clan, served in the Jordanian parliament and held cabinet positions.

Israeli Occupation and Self-Rule

The years of Israeli occupation (1967–1995) were dominated by a vibrant economy and political turmoil. Palestinian Israelis and Israeli Jews alike were prime customers in the markets of Jenin. Saturdays and

Entrance to Jenin

Women make up a substantial part of the rural labor force

Sundays were shopping days in Jenin, and competitive prices and Jenin's location fostered interaction between Palestinians, Israeli Arabs, and Israeli Jews, which was exceptional.

The district of Jenin was the single largest tract of land to be ruled by Palestine's National Authority (PNA) under the terms of the Oslo agreements. With the fewest number of Jewish settlements in its vicinity, Jenin was free to grow and expand under Palestinian self-rule, which began in October 1995. That year, the Arab American University, a private institution affiliated with the California State University at Stanislaus and Utah State University in the United States, was founded.

Over 50 percent of the male working force in the Jenin district work as construction workers, cooks, gardeners, and day laborers inside the Green Line. As a result of the closures during the al-Aqsa intifada, unemployment reached unprecedented levels, in some cases as high as 60 percent. The name Jenin has come to be associated with Islamist politics, as the number of militant young men and women involved both in the resistance and in acts of violence against Israelis was disproportionately high.

Near Jenin

A'rrabeh

"The whole courtyard was lit by torches and populated with handsome horses tethered there…One would have believed oneself to be in an enchanted palace." Thus Count Leon de Laborde described the Throne Village of A'rrabeh after a visit in 1827. The original homestead of the Abdul Hadi clan, which ruled most of the northern West Bank for almost 200 years during the Ottoman reign, it was then a regional rural capitol. Today A'rrabeh is a town of some 15,000, with considerable town planning. Many town residents made money working in the Gulf countries and have invested their savings in large homes. The most impressive building in town remains the early-19th-century Abdul Hadi mansion, a fine example of the Ottoman architecture of the rural feudal classes.

As allies to and governors of the Muhammad Ali dynasty, the Abdul Hadi clan acquired vast amounts of real estate in the Jenin and Nablus districts and became governors of faraway Haifa. They established themselves in the heart of Nablus in the 19th century.

Under the rule of the PNA and with the support of the UNDP, two of the thirteen Abdul Hadi Palaces are being restored for public use. The Abdel Qader Abdel Hadi Palace is being turned into a cultural center, which will include a library and computer center, museum, and art studio. The Hussein Abdul Hadi Palace is being turned into a children's center.

Today A'rrabeh is an agriculturally rich area, with lots of expatriate investment that has kept it afloat, even during the al-Aqsa intifada, when the town had long closures by the Israeli army (although the town itself lies in Area A).

At the entrance of the town is a shantytown, where Israel resettled Palestinian collaborators and their families from Gaza. Local townspeople do not socialize with this group, whom they consider outcasts.

The town's most famous contemporary figure was Abu Ali Mustapha, a political activist and head of the PFLP. He was assassinated by the Israelis, who fired into his office window with helicopter gun ships in Ramallah in 2001. His death almost single-handedly spurred on an unprecedented round of bloodshed, at a time when his party had been considered comatose.

Burqin and the Church of St. George

Although less than ten years old, the PNA Department of Antiquities has already overseen some major work in Burqin (3 km west of Jenin), home of the third oldest church in the world. According to Christian tradition, Jesus performed the miracle of curing lepers near a cave here.

During the 4th to 5th centuries, the cave was a pilgrimage destination, and a church was built over the cave to commemorate the site and miracle. It was expanded several times during the 6th to 9th centuries. The Byzantines built an altar and erected a stone wall with a door at the cave entrance. The church was damaged several times, though during the Crusader period it was enlarged, and a courtyard and wall added. A new hall and nave were built in the 18th century. It is now run by the village's Greek Orthodox Church.

Khirbet Belameh (Jeblaam or Ibleam)

This Bronze Age site is situated near the northwestern entrance to the city of Jenin. Most of what we know of this ancient settlement comes from Egyptian sources. The city of Ibleam, as the Egyptians dubbed it, was among the sites named as significant Canaanite cities in the list of Thutmose III's conquests in the 14th century BCE.

The pottery collected during an archeological survey (1967–68) indicated human habitation and settlements from the Bronze and Iron ages, as well as from the Roman, Byzantine, and late Islamic periods. On the summit of the hill, ancient ruins of buildings are still seen. The tunnel excavation, in the eastern slope of the hill, unearthed pottery from the Roman, Byzantine, and Islamic Eras.

In 1996 the Palestinian Department of Antiquities began excavations on a tunnel shaft, the most elaborate feature in Belameh. The excavation of the tunnel, which is not yet finished, indicates that the southern tunnel was cut during the Late Bronze period and the entrance of a fortress and gate built onto it. It allowed people of the city to access their water source safely, even during times of siege. The tunnel fell out of use in the 8th century. Through the support of UNDP, some 150 meters (492 ft) of tunnel is being transformed into an archeological park, which will feature an educational sound and light show.

In the Bible, Jeblaam, as it was then called, was cited for its fierce defense against the Hebrew tribe of Manasseh. It was also the site of several Samaritan attacks against Christians from the Galilee traveling toward Jerusalem.

On the same eastern slope are many cisterns and tombs from the Roman period. The high-vaulted Mamluk shrine on the summit of the hill is known as the **Mosque of Shaykh Mansour**, and remains in use today.

Sanur

This scenic village is home to the Jarrar clan who, along with the Abdul Hadi clan, represented the rural revolution against the urban-dominated feudal lords of this part of Palestine. Although both clans ended up being just as feudal and oppressive for the peasant class as the urban Ottoman tax collectors, they nevertheless stemmed the tide of history. This village once stood at the center of the regional universe when, some 150 years ago, the Jarrar clan challenged the powers of the central Ottoman govern-ment and governed most of today's West Bank and large parts of the Galilee and Jaffa. Several rural mansions built at this time dot the village.

Tel al-Hafireh (Tel Dothan)

Tel al-Hafireh is an archeological site that lies 6 kilometers south of Jenin, close to the village of Bir al-Basha. Here, Old Testament Joseph was sold by his brothers to traders and taken to Egypt. Earliest human habitation here dates back to the Chalcolithic era. During the Early Bronze Age, it was the site of a major Canaanite city. Evidence suggests that the city was fortified by a large wall, which probably was about 4.5 meters (13 ft) high. It appears to have been inhabited until its destruction by the Arameans in the 9th century BCE.

Massive storerooms and elaborate burial sites attest to great wealth. By the end of the 9th century, the site was rebuilt, and additional storerooms added. Tel al-Hafireh flourished under the Assyrian period from 722 BCE.

Later, the Mamluks had a relatively large settlement, at whose center was a complex consisting of no less than six courtyards and 150 rooms. One courtyard and 25 rooms around it were cleared.

A traditional Palestinian village sits on the western edge of the archaeological site.

Tel Ti'innik

The archaeological site of Canaanite Taanak lies on the northwestern edge of the village of the same name (8 km northwest of Jenin). The earliest reference to Taanak is in a Karnak inscription from the 15th century BCE describing Thutmose III's first campaign into Asia. He mentions this site in his 1468 BCE account of his conquests, and he is believed to have destroyed the settlement.

Potsherds found at the beginning of the 19th century indicate that the site was inhabited during the Early Bronze Age. Palestinian archeologists and their students at Bir Zeit University working extensively on the site found 64 burial chambers. Most of them contained large jars with corpses of what appear to be children. The jars are a testimonial to a high mortality rate among children and an interesting clue to Canaanite burial traditions. Some 40 tablets of clay written in the Canaanite cuneiform script and dating to the 14th century BCE were also found, giving archeolgists and historians great insight into the administrative and socio-economic workings of the Canaanites.

Remains of an Abbasid palace, built sometime between the 10th and 11th century CE, can still be seen, as can the ruins of a Mamluk complex on the eastern side of Taanak. Byzantine potsherds were found within the same complex.

During the Ottoman era many grandiose buildings were built for the town's residents, several of whom became wealthy as tax collectors for the Ottomans.

Refugee Camps

Jenin Camp

Jenin camp was established in 1953, on 373 dunums (93 acres) by refugees from nearby villages and also from quite far afield. Many refugees in Jenin camp descend from distant villages in the Carmel region of Haifa. Their experiences in 1948 trekking day and night, southeast through the mountains before reaching the plain of Marj Ibn Amr (Esdraelon Valley) after 24 hours walking, are seared in their collective memory. Other camp residents took refuge in Jenin after fleeing from villages that can be seen from the camp, but which lie inside the Israeli state.

The camp is situated on the side of a mountain, looking out over beautiful fertile plains and scattered villages. Approximately 14,000 people live in Jenin camp, making it the third largest camp in the West Bank, behind Balata (Nablus) and Tulkarem.

The camp came under PNA control in 1995. It still suffers, however, from poor sewers, water shortages, blackouts, and over-crowding.

The Jenin Camp received international attention because of the fighting and destruction that happened there during the al-Aqsa intifada (see next page). No doubt, Jenin camp and the events of April

2002 have entered Palestinian national consciousness as a symbol of steadfastness and resistance against immeasurable odds. Residents of the camp speak proudly about how they were able to withstand and resist the Israeli invasion.

Far'a Camp

Far'a, like many West Bank refugee camps, was named after a nearby spring that Palestinian refugees gathered around as their source of water. Established in 1949 on 255 dunums (64 acres) in the foothills of the Jordan Valley, 17 kilometers northeast of Nablus, Far'a camp lies

April 2002

In April 2002, the Jenin refugee camp was the scene of one of the most well-known and defining moments of the al-Aqsa intifada. In an effort to crush the Palestinian revolt the Israeli army launched "Operation Defensive Shield," its largest military deployment since its invasion of Lebanon in 1982.

At the beginning of the assault, resistance forces inside the camp announced the formation of the "General Command for the Defense of Jenin Camp," which unified all political forces who attempted to defend the camp. Indeed, for three days, lightly armed resistance forces successfully repelled continuous attempts to penetrate the camp, despite Israeli aerial bombardments and use of artillery, heavy armor, and battle tanks backed by hundreds of troops.

The turning point in the battle took place on April 9, when Israeli forces requested a cease-fire to recover the bodies of 13 dead and 8 injured soldiers from within a building that resistance forces had ambushed. Thereafter, Israeli bulldozers razed the entire Damj and Hawwashin neighborhoods, near the center of the camp where resistance fighters were holed up.

An Amnesty International research team sighted evidence of serious Israeli human rights violations, including allegations of extra-judicial executions, failure to allow humanitarian assistance for 13 days to people trapped under the rubble of demolished houses, denial of medical assistance to the wounded, deliberate targeting of ambulances, excessive use of lethal force, using civilians as "human shields," beatings of Palestinian detainees, and extensive damage to property with no apparent military necessity. In total, 441 dwelling units and 25 uninhabited structures were completely destroyed, 419 homes suffered what UNRWA classified as "major damage," and 3,340 homes suffered "minor damage." Literally nearly every family in the camp had members who were injured, dead, or imprisoned, and property that was damaged, if not destroyed.

Today the Hawasheen neighborhood, which suffered the brunt of Israeli bulldozer destruction, is informally referred to as "Ground Zero" by the UNRWA project office for the Reconstruction of Jenin Refugee Camp. Victims are laid to rest in the camp's cemetery at the base of the camp.

Urban homes and shops bombed in the Israeli strike of April 2002

within the municipal boundaries of the nearby Palestinian village of Toubas, 5 kilometers to the north.

Unlike most West Bank camps, whose residents originate from the Lydd, Ramleh, and Jaffa regions, the 6,500 residents of this camp come from villages in the northeastern Haifa region, including al-Rehaniyeh, al-Kafrin, Sabbareen, Qannir, Sindiyani, Khubbaizi, Umm al-Tout, Um al-Shouf, al-Mansiyyeh, and Um al-Zeinat.

According to local legend, the Far'a spring earns its name from the daughter of Haj Bin Yousef al-Thaqafi, a local Arab leader during the

Umayyad period renowned for her slender beauty. (*Far'a* in classical Arabic means "tall" or "towering.") Now the spring is less plentiful than it once was, largely because of the many wells that have been dug for agricultural use throughout the surrounding region. Indeed, it is precisely this northern part of the West Bank that represents the beginning of Palestine's fertile agricultural plain, Marj Ibn Amr, which supplies a large percentage of the West Bank's agricultural produce year round.

Far'a camp's agricultural setting, as that of other rural camps (such as Fawwar, Arroub, and Jalazone), allows it to maintain a high level of self-sufficiency. Much of its produce is grown locally, local power generators supply the camp's electricity, and Far'a is one of the few camps in the West Bank that UNRWA is able to supply water to by pumping from the nearby spring. Despite its otherwise sleepy village setting, the camp was a hotbed of political activity during the first and second intifadas.

Most Palestinians know Far'a as the location of an infamous jail used by the Israeli occupation authorities. Also, during the first intifada, Israel took advantage of the wide expanses of the camp's geographic plain and established several prison camps there.

The jail, located just opposite the camp on the main road, dates to the British mandate period and has been used by every successive authority, until the PNA converted it to a youth headquarters and sports facility. Just behind the former jail, on a small precipice looking south, stand the ruins of a Crusader lookout post. The ruins, known locally as the Salahed-Din al-Ayyoubi Castle, must have once been a place from which to warn of invaders from the Nablus region.

Today, high unemployment rates exist throughout the camp, due to the loss of jobs from camp residents who used to work as laborers inside the Green Line. Those few who still have jobs, work in Palestinian National Authority ministries or on local farms.

A favorite thoroughfare in Tulkarem

18.

Tulkarem

A mare was leaping in the vision of the world
when the sycamore tree becomes
a tree of myth and wonder
of cloudy sorrow

—from *"Death at Night's End,"* Waleed Sayf, Tulkarem poet,
20th century

The traditional and best way to get to Tulkarem is via Nablus (perhaps a 30-minute drive), but if the road is closed by the military, then driving to one of the Arab villages along the Green Line, such as Baqa al-Sharqia, is next best.

The city and district of Tulkarem lay at the westernmost reach of the northern West Bank. It boasts great agricultural lands, a population of 140,000 people, and at least a dozen historic sites. Tulkarem is relatively small, and historically had limited autonomy from centralized powers in Nablus or Acre. Its physical seclusion within rich farmlands and its nearness to the Mediterranean combine to make a relaxed environment.

It is not certain when humans first settled in the Tulkarem area, but some Arab sources indicate it was a Canaanite settlement. Archeological findings have not been able to confirm any settlement prior to the Roman Era, but then Tulkarem has not been an archeological priority. It seems that Tulkarem was built on the ruins of the Roman village "Birat Soreqa." Some historians speculate that the name Tulkarem comes from the Aramaic *"tur karma"* (vineyard hill); others suggest an Arabic source, *"tur karm"* (generous mountain). All names clearly refer to the area's wealthy agricultural lands.

As with other inland towns and cities, Tulkarem was built up by the Mamluks and in the 13th century, the Mamluk Dhaher Baibars reportedly gave Tulkarem to two of his generals, as thanks for their good work. One of these generals was the progenitor of the Jayyusi clan, who had their rural base at Kur, in what became a Throne Village. Their rule, later on behalf of the Ottomans, extended to 24 villages in the Tulkarem area. The area was one of the few that was ever ruled by a woman, Saliha al-Jayyusi.

The area was categorized as a district by the Ottomans in 1892. The Bani Sa'ab district, as it was called, consisted of 44 villages and two cities (Tulkarem and Qalqilia) by the end of the Ottoman era. At the end of the British mandate, the district consisted of one city (Tulkarem) and 70 villages, in which Qalqilia was included.

Tulkarem's strategic location between Nablus and the coast gave the town commercial and military importance. Two railway lines passed through, creating a commercial center and the easy export of the town's agricultural produce. In the 1930s, however, the establishment of highways leading to Jewish settlements and kibbutzes made Tulkarem peripheral.

The Arab–Israeli war in 1948 created an influx of refugees that brought the town to an economic standstill. Two refugee camps, Tulkarem and Nur Shams, were established. Contingents of the Iraqi army were based in Tulkarem during the 1948 war.

Like the rest of the West Bank, Tulkarem came under Jordanian rule in 1948 and most of its citizens were given Jordanian passports and had access to Jordanian institutions. In 1967 it came under Israeli rule and, along with Jenin and Qalqilia, was a site of economic prosperity due to its proximity to the Green Line. Israelis would come to the market town on the weekend to buy cheaper goods, and many Palestinians from the town and camps worked in Israeli cities and towns.

During Palestinian self-rule (1995) Tulkarem began to prosper, both as a result of international development projects in the city and because of increased work with Israeli businesses inside the Green Line. In Tulkarem as elsewhere, "peace" brought projects and financial support from the international community.

Today

With the rest of the West Bank, Tulkarem is being walled in by the immense concrete Wall that the Palestinians call "apartheid wall" and the Israelis sell to the world as a necessary "barrier." Walled in and out of work with nowhere to go, the youth of Tulkarem will undoubtedly emigrate or become more adamant in their struggle for freedom.

Tulkarem is still officially under the jurisdiction of the PNA, although Israeli military invasions are common.

The city of Tulkarem has a population of about 50,000, while the district has a population of 194,000, including the refugee camps. Most of the population is Muslim, but there is a small Christian minority, most of whom are refugees from the 1948 war. It is thus that a small Greek Orthodox Church is found in the center of town.

Tulkarem prides itself for its two semi-professional soccer teams, *Markez Shabab Tulkarem* and *Thaqafi Tulkarem*, both in the Palestinian League Division One. Tulkarem has a two-year college, the Khodori Institute, and four high schools, two for girls and two for boys.

Most of the people in Tulkarem continue to work in agriculture, producing citrus fruits, melons, olives, olive oil, tomatoes, potatoes, wheat, sesame seeds, peanuts, eggplants, chili peppers, green beans, and guavas.

The town of Tulkarem

Near Tulkarem

Within the city and its environs are tombs from the Early Bronze Age and various Roman ruins, such as foundations, cisterns, wine presses, rock-cut tombs, a mausoleum, and a stone altar with Greek inscriptions. Although the city itself does not contain important historical sites, there are several sites of interest in the vicinity.

Khirbet Irtah

The archeological site of Khirbet Irtah is threatened by extensive construction in the modern village of Irtah, whose expatriates (mostly from the Arabian Gulf countries) are building palace-like structures as retirement homes.

The site was mentioned in the Amarna Letters and is known to have been inhabited during the Roman, Byzantine, and Islamic eras, although perhaps not continuously. Tombs, caves, and a Roman pool are still visible, if not always recognizable. A Byzantine olive press and a vine press have been cut in the bedrock of the hill.

A Muslim shrine, **Binat Yacoub** (Jacob's daughters), dating to the late Mamluk and early Ottoman eras is still in good condition. It has two rooms and a courtyard in front of the shrine, and its two high vaulted domes can be seen from a distance.

The Palestinian ministry of tourism and antiquities, with the support of UNDP, is turning the area around the archeological site into a park for the local community. Maintenance on the shrine of Binat Yacoub and the refurbishing of neighboring pottery workshops promise to make the site a local tourist and recreational attraction.

Kur (Fort Kur)

Off the beaten path, this Throne Village falls in the middle of the Nablus, Tulkarem, and Qalqilia triangle. Known to have existed in the 12th century under Mamluk rule, some say the local clans are of Crusader origins; others claim they are decendents of Mamluk generals. The only inhabitants of the village are descendents of the Jayyusi clan, landowning tax collectors who acted as rural lords for centuries.

Several of the most prominent village mansions, including **Qasr al-Shaykh, Abu Naman al-Jayyusi's home,** and **Abdullah's Fortress** (Qa'la) are being renovated and restored (through USAID and UNDP) in order to revitalize village life for its some 300 residents. The architecture of the three palatial structures is still quite something, despite their dilapidated condition.

In the fields of Tulkarem

The village consists of a complex of simple peasant houses with one or several rooms arranged in a row and a courtyard in front of the house, and a more elaborate structure called "Ilye," which wealthier families employed. The Ilye structure also features a courtyard in front, but the houses themselves have two or more floors. Concrete buildings are scattered among the old traditional houses.

Shweikeh and Tel al-Ras

Three kilometers north of Tulkarem, Tel al-Ras dominates Shweikeh, a Mamluk-era village. The archeological site here has yet to be excavated, but a survey of potsherds and the ruined appearance of the earth's surface provide hints of human habitation from as far back as the Bronze Age. An Ottoman structure on the top of the main mound is in good condition.

Zababdeh

Modern Zababdeh is built over the site of a Byzantine village, with the Latin Church of Visitation at its center. According to tradition, Mary and Elizabeth came through Zababdeh on their way from Nazareth to Bethlehem for the census. The town lies on the old

Remnants of the Ottoman era

Roman road that was the main thoroughfare of the day. Zababdeh has been a predominantly Christian town since the 3rd century CE. Today it has 3,000 inhabitants.

Refugee Camps

Tulkarem Camp

Tulkarem camp was established in 1950 on the northwestern edge of the West Bank, near the demarcation line with Israel. It is the second largest camp in the West Bank. The camp's 16,000 residents come from Lydd, Ramleh, and Jaffa as well as Umm al-Fahem and nearby villages.

Before the outbreak of the al-Aqsa intifada, Tulkarem camp residents were almost entirely dependent upon work inside Israel. After Israel imposed a lock-down on towns throughout the West Bank,

the residents of Tulkarem camp were not able to get to work and unemployment soared to 40 percent, and some 80 percent of the camp's residents have received emergency aid since then.

In the first days of the revolt, Israeli tanks and infantry stormed Tulkarem, making it the first refugee camp to be totally occupied during the intifada. An unprecedented 600 residents were arrested in one day. During this time the Israeli military's practice of numbering handcuffed and blindfolded Palestinians by writing on their arms was caught on film, provoking international outrage.

Needless to say, Tulkarem, like other large refugee camps, has regularly been the subject of military assaults and invasions. Visitors should be sure to call in advance to see what the situation is like on the ground.

Nur Shams

Nur Shams, a smaller version of Tulkarem camp, was established in 1952 on 226 dunams (55 acres), 3 kilometers east of Tulkarem. Its approximately 8,000 residents all come from the same area of central and northern Palestine. Because of the rich agricultural lands that surround the camp, many Nur Shams residents have studied at the nearby Keddouri Agricultural College. The college was established before 1948 by a wealthy Iraqi Jew who established a similar agricultural college on the other side of the Green Line, giving institutional life to his hopes for peaceful coexistence between Israelis and Palestinians. Before the intifada, Nur Shams's residents worked as day laborers in construction and agriculture inside Israel. Today, Nur Shams residents have had virtually all of these options cut off, sending rates of unemployment skyrocketing, and forcing the camp to develop its own internal economy. The Tulkarem area particularly suffers from the Israeli closure because the Wall literally cages in the entire region, cutting off the city from its lands, which have been expropriated by Israeli settlements. Israeli closure policies concentrated on the Tulkarem district because of its proximity to the Green Line and its close connection to the neighboring Palestinian villages just inside Israel.

Mssakhan: A Favorite Northern Dish

Less exposed to foreign presence than the rest of Palestine, the northern region, with its main cities Jenin, Tulkarem, and Nablus, has maintained a more traditional lifestyle, which is reflected in their food habits. Their restaurants offer traditional menus; it is rare to find a pizzeria or a hamburger place, though in Nablus, these Western establishments have sprung up around the university.

Probably the most important northern ceremonial dish is *mssakhan*, which comes from Tulkarem and Jenin. Its importance is such that it competes with *mansaf* and *kiddreh* as the national dish. Even in other parts of Palestine, you are bound to find *mssakhan* on the menu of the better restaurants. The secret to successful *mssakhan* is the bread, which should be neither too thick nor too thin, and spongy enough to absorb the olive oil sauce. *Tabun* bread is perfect. But if you don't have a *tabun*, the clay oven at the center of every *hosh* (compound in which an extended family shares the common space, with private rooms allocated to individual families), *kmaj* bread will do. *Kmaj* (more commonly known by the Greek name pita in the West), is thick enough to carry the stuffing and widely available.

The dish is easy to prepare if you follow the steps carefully. The key ingredient is sumac, a red spice with a warm, slightly acidic flavor, best bought from a reliable *'attar* (spice vendor), since adulterated sumac can be camouflaged with coloring. And prepare your own chicken broth—any commercial broth might contain preservatives or spices incompatible with the dish.

1 whole chicken (serves 4)
salt
pepper
1 cup chicken broth
3 medium-sized onions
½ teaspoon black pepper
¼ teaspoon allspice
2 heaping tablespoons of sumac
½ cup extra-virgin olive oil

1. Cut the chicken in four pieces and season them with salt and pepper to taste. Broil them in an oven or grill until they are done through and the skin gold.

2. For the sauce, chop the onions and cook with a pinch of salt in a pan on low heat for a few minutes, until transparent. Add black pepper, allspice, and sumac. Add 1 cup of hot broth and the olive oil. Heat to just boiling, and the sauce is ready for serving.

3. Spread pieces of hot bread in a circle on the four plates, smother with the sauce, but leaving some to add over the chicken. Add a piece of chicken to each, and extra sumac if desired.

Bon appétit! And no forks and knives if you please!

The fields of Tulkarem

Nur Shams camp has two schools, which, because of their particularly poor condition, have made UNRWA's priority list for replacement, pending funding. No one in the camp is hopeful that this will happen, since UNRWA usually operates with a chronic budget deficit.

Old man from Qalqilia

19.

Qalqilia

*When Israel conquered the West Bank in 1967, Moshe Dayan
remembered his old threat to raze Qalqilia, and his victory enabled him
to carry it out. His troops drove out all the inhabitants and brought in
bulldozers to plough the town under and erase it from the map, just as
they had done with the villages of Bayt Nuba, Yalu, and Imwas.*

—Mamdouh Nofal, Palestinian peace negotiator & former
military commander, "Memories of Al-Nakba,"
Middle East Studies, October 1998

In the past, Qalqilia was not a town or a city but an important
village that lay on the caravan and trading route. Invading armies,
many of which came from the Mediterranean coast just 12 km/7.5
mi away, also came through Qalqilia. Its Canaanite origins are murky,
but its current name comes from the Roman "Qala'alia," meaning high
fortress. Medieval European sources refer to it as "Kalkelie," a name
used today by its contemporary residents.

Today Qalqilia has 45,000 inhabitants and is a regional
agricultural center. Residents established an independent local council
in 1909, and by 1945, a municipal council. Local politics are run by
several clans with successful negotiators among them. For example,
their intervention prevented Israel from annexing Qalqilia in 1948.

Thousands of landless refugees swarmed the city after the Arab defeat
in 1948 and made one city quarter their home. Known as the people of
Kufre Saba and Arab Abu Kishek, the refugees got UNRWA help, but a
refugee camp was never created because local politicians negotiated UN
help for the whole city in return for integrating the refugees.

Between 1967–1995 almost 80 percent of Qalqilia's labor force worked for Israeli companies or industries in the construction and agriculture sectors. The other 20% engaged in trade and commerce, and many if not most of their traditional markets are across the green line, i.e. Israel. As elsewhere, Israeli military closures and the building of the separation wall has destroyed the local economy and made Qalqilia dependent on outside support.

Even during the closures, Israel's "guest" workers from Thailand and Romania used to come to Qalqilia's Saturday markets to buy their week's worth of household items and food at nearly half the price, but since the construction of the Wall the city has been cut off from the world. It is not only one of the first cities to be effected by the apartheid Wall, but it has been doubly hit because of its absolute economic dependence on work in and trade with Israel. To make matters worse, most of Qalqilia's agricultural land falls outside the wall premises, making it impossible for the city's farmers and landowners to work or harvest their fields and crops.

Sites

Al-Omari Mosque
Most cities and towns in Palestine have an "Omari" Mosque, mainly to mark the advent of Islam as it was introduced by Omar Ibn Khattab, the commander of the Muslim armies that conquered the Levant. This particular Omari Mosque was built in the 20th century. It stands over and encases a 19th century Ottoman version of the same sanctuary.

Qalqilia Zoo
The city's main attraction is the zoo, which was established in 1986. Well kept and run by the municipality, it includes an amusement park for children, a swimming pool, a wildlife museum, and a cafeteria. Crocodiles, giraffes, ostriches, deer, gazelles, camels, zebras, lions, tigers, snakes, birds, peacocks, hippos and monkeys are among the many inhabitants of the zoo.

Near Qalqilia

A'zoun
To the west of Qalqilia, the village of A'zoun is the site of ruins from an ancient settlement. Potsherds from the Iron Age were found;

Animals at the Qalqilia Zoo

Reconstructed Canaanite village in Qalqilia

it may have been a Philistine site. It has been inhabited continuously since the Ottoman Era.

Deir Istya

Deir Istya was once a majestic village, but today it is home to only 30 families. Built during the reign of the Mamluks, Deir Istya became a Throne Village during the Ottoman era. The village was the home of the Qasim al-Ahmad family, rural feudal lords who also dominated nearby Bayt Wazan.

Deir Istya is a good example of a typical Mamluk village with Ottoman additions. It is still in very good condition, with the original architectural design, so Deir Istya is a good case study for how town planning was conducted by the Mamluks and Ottomans. The traditional heart of the village is wrapped by a wall with four main gated entrances and *madafa* (guest houses) and watchtowers on both sides. The main streets are paved with flagstones. The houses in the village are huge Ilye constructions (see page 199). Small alleys leading from one quarter of the village to another pass underneath the houses.

This type of construction exists only in cities with Mamluk traditions, such as Nablus, Hebron, and Acre; it is not usually seen in villages. Today, there are many houses built with concrete and cut stone.

Many of the village's old mansions are being turned into women's organizations, cultural heritage centers, and a children's recreational institution, with the help of the UNDP, among others. Renovation and revitalization of old homes, the municipality believes, will encourage village expatriates to return.

Faro'un

Located five kilometers south of Qalqilia, the village of Faro'un was built on the Canaanite Jiljal. Known by the Romans as Galgulis, the village contains remains of a mosque and a pool from the Mamluk era, a large Ottoman khan and a mosaic floor. The tomb built for Shams al-Din, one of Saladin's commanders, is here.

Khirbet al-Basatin

The remains of a large farm from the Byzantine period is located 8 kilometers east of Qalqilia. The remains of hewn stone walls enclose a large structure and a courtyard. In the center of the courtyard stand a large structure and a complete olive oil press.

Khirbet Ras al-Tira

A Palestinian village located 6 kilometers southeast of Qalqilia contains the ruins of a settlement from the Roman, Byzantine and Crusader periods. There are remains of many buildings and a complete olive oil press here, too.

Walking home from school in Qalqilia

A main street in Nablus on a weekday

20.

Nablus

Its beauty can hardly be exaggerated ...Clusters of white roofed houses nestling in the bosom of a mass of trees, olive, palm, orange, apricot and many another varying the carpet with every shade of green ... Everything fresh, green, soft, and picturesque with verdure, shade, and water everywhere. There is softness in the coloring, a rich blue haze from the many springs and streamlets, which mellows every hard outline."

— Pathways of Palestine, 1881, Tristam

The city of Nablus is often referred to as the "uncrowned queen of Palestine." Unlike the surrounding sites and villages, it is relatively new—that is, it was founded in 72 CE by the Roman Titus. Flavia Neapolis (the new city of Flavia), as he called it in honor of his father the emperor Flavius Vespasian, was built on top of the ancient village of Maborta, between and on the slopes of two mountains, Ebal (Jabal Aybal/Jabal Sit Sulaymiyya, 940 m/3084 ft) and Gerizim (Jabal al-Tur, 881 m/289 ft).

After Titus settled his army of legionnaires here, the Romans built a theater, hippodromes, aqueducts and springs, and paved streets lined with columns and stores. Most of the Roman temples, including one honoring Zeus, were built up Mt. Gerizim, where the Samaritans were living. Although the initial inhabitants of the city were Roman, Semitic tribes soon began to settle here as well, and Philip the Arab reinforced Arab settlement as well as Roman rule in 244. Byzantium eventually increased in strength, however, and in 484 the Church of Mary replaced the temple to Zeus. Nablus is shown as a major place in the Holy Land on the 6th-century Mosaic map in Madaba, Jordan.

With the coming of Islam, a new era began in Nablus. Many of the churches were transformed into mosques and Arabic replaced Greek as the language of the people. In 636, the Arab General Amr Ibn Al'as, who had played an important role in the Islamization of Egypt, made Nablus one of Palestine's most famous and richest cities. An Arab cartographer in the 10th century dubbed it "Little Damascus," recognizing another favored city surrounded by fertile land with plenty of water.

During their brief stay (1099–1187), the Crusaders christened the city Naples. Queen Melisande, mother to the Crusader King Baldwin III, made Nablus her home (1152–1161) after her son exiled her from Jerusalem. In 1259, when Jerusalem was sacked and destroyed by the Mongols, many Jerusalemites fled to Nablus and settled there.

The Mamluks, after overturning Saladin's Kurdish dynasty, brought in architects and builders from the Balkans to construct mosques, schools, and entire cities. The Ottomans continued this tradition in a more Anatolian style, adding caravansaries in the countryside and soup kitchens and public baths in the cities.

The rural areas around Nablus were dominated by a tribal group known as the Beni Haritha, which was affiliated with tribes north of Ramallah. Until the mid-1750s, when other tribal conglomerations from Transjordan, Anatolia, and Syria became the "lords of the land," the Beni Haritha ruled the countryside. By the 1800s new, more urban clans had become the strongmen. Tuqan, Nimr, Abdul Hadi, Jarrar, Jayyusi, and Rayyan clans are still considered the most prominent landowning families of the northern districts, Nablus in particular.

The 19th century was the golden age for the Nablus area. It became one of the most prosperous cities in Bilad al-Sham (Greater Syria), with the production of soap, olive oil, and processing of cotton its economic backbone. It was a main supplier of these products to all the countries of the Levant, and of soap to Egypt and Anatolia. In fact, in one decade in the late 1800s, the number of soap factories doubled from 15 to 30 in order to meet the demand for Nablus's high quality products.

Trade expanded toward Transjordan, Egypt, and Syria well into the 20th century. But after the British and French divided the Arab world in the aftermath of World War I, the region's economic trade patterns were disrupted by new and often illogical borders. With the resulting economic deprivation came politicization. Although the Nablus elite tried to moderate the rhetoric of activists—mainly journalists and writers—in order to maintain good relations with the colonial power, Britain's apparent collusion with Zionist expansionism made anti-British sentiment run deep among Palestinians. Despite this, certain groups continued to profit and export, and large new houses in Europeanized styles sprung up.

In the struggle against Zionist settlement, many Palestinian partisans were drawn from rural areas of the northern West Bank. Nablus was the host to conferences and rallies in support of Arab sovereignty and against the White Paper and the Balfour Declaration. Despite this atmosphere of resistance and nationalism, a 1946 Franciscan tour guide to the Holy Land, recommended Nablus to travelers, mildly stating: "The town contains a post and telegraph office, comfortable hotels and a hospital. Trade is brisk."

In 1949, the Nablus elite played an important role in legitimizing the rule of King Abdullah of Jordan in what became known as the "West Bank." The rule was patriarchal, and a quid pro quo among Arabs. The clans of Nablus, for the most part, gave their consent to Jordanian rule, in return for posts and positions in the Jordanian government.

But Nablus, like all of the north, was never easy to rule. The undercurrent of leftist and nationalist feeling came out in shining colors after Israel occupied the whole of the West Bank after the June 1967 war. The youth of Nablus took to the streets and hurled fury at the Israeli occupation soldiers, while their elders were exiled, assassinated, imprisoned, or maimed. Bassam al-Shakaa, the city mayor, had his legs blown off when the Israelis placed a bomb in his car. During the first intifada (1987–1993) Nablus was one of several centers of rebellion.

Palestinian Rule

On December 12, 1995, Nablus came under the administrative and security jurisdiction of the PNA. The city of Nablus and some of its surrounding towns were categorized as "Area A," and most villages and sites are in "Area B." Still other villages and much agricultural land were designated "Area C."

Since the re-occupation began in 2000 Nablus has been under one form or another of permanent Israeli assault, leaving an estimated 70 percent of the city partly or totally destroyed. Hundreds of Palestinians have been killed and thousands wounded, while historic sites in the city center have been bombed from the air or bombarded by tanks. Public buildings and private homes, many dating to Ottoman and Mamluk times were bulldozed or bombed from the air. An international drive, spearheaded by the Palestinian Department of Antiquities and Cultural Heritage and largely supported by the Japanese government and the UNDP are doing much to rebuild and renovate wherever possible.

Nevertheless, for the first time since 1967, the city has witnessed an exodus of its mercantile and industrial class, as Israel continues its occupation parallel to nominal Palestinian self-rule.

Still, as throughout history, Nablus industries have continued. Even its renowned traditional soap industry survives, though it has been surpassed in economic importance by other industries, including the production of olive oil and vegetable oil, leather, textiles, plastic, aluminum, paints, wool, metal furniture, cartons, marble, and building stones.

The city is largely administered by modern-day clans that have all but replaced the old. The Shaka'a, the Masri, and the Allul clans take turns holding the seats of governor, mayor, and other posts. More than any other city under Palestinian rule, Nablus has seen a good deal of private sector investment by its own expatriate community. The city is well run, with many new homes and factories. Old family homes have been renovated and cultural centers founded. While the city, like all throughout Palestine, still needs substantial development, it can boast of 50 public schools, a university (al-Najah National), a library, 49 mosques, 36 kindergartens, 7 local television stations, 4 hospitals, and many public and private clinics. The Palestinian Stock Market (Boursa), the Palestinian Communication Company (PALTEL), and the Standards and Measurements Control Center are all located here.

Sites

Al-Manara Clock
Built in 1895 on the orders of Sultan Abdul Hamid, this clock is an icon of his reign. It has sister clocks in all major Palestinian cities.

Old City
At the center of modern Nablus and the base of Mt. Gerizim, lies the Old City. It boasts large residential and market areas, colorful alleys, religious and administrative buildings from the Ottoman period, a cultural center, and old family mansions. The Abdel-Hadi, al-Nimr, and Tuqan mansions are architectural and social remnants of the prosperous side of the feudal Ottoman past. **Tuqan Palace** has largely been renovated (it was damaged by various Israeli invasions), and although private property, visitors are welcome to look at the architecture and garden. The Abdel-Hadi and al-Nimr mansions await a face-lift.

Soap stacked in Tukan soap factory in Nablus

Al-Qasbah Museum

The Qasbah Museum is a tribute to traditional life in Nablus as it existed in Ottoman times. Founded in 1997, when the museum director called on city residents to donate or loan family antiques and heirlooms so that they could be preserved as part of the city's collection, the museum now boasts some 700 objects. The collection has traditional clothes, kitchen utensils, and tools from working in the fields, in pastry-making, and in the soap industries. It features a city house, a village house, and the library. The museum also contains an open showcase to which anyone can contribute objects considered important for the community.

Rafidia

Originally one of two predominantly Christian villages in the Nablus region, today Rafidia is an upper-middle-class neighborhood in the city. Crusaders once built a settlement here, and there are remains of walls, foundations, a church, a press, and a cave. A prominent Palestinian spokesman and writer, Naim Khadre, came from Rafidia.

Roman Cemetery

Encased behind steel bars, this Roman cemetery lies close to the now decrepit Joseph's tomb. The PNA has closed off the area to prevent looting until a time when they can renovate the surrounding area and make it accessible to the public.

Soap Factories

Nablus was the center of the Arab soap-making industry, with over 30 factories in 1882. Abundant local production of olive oil gave rise to the industry, for *Nabulsi* soap is made of olive oil and caustic soda. Visit the **al-Bader Soap Factory** (20 al-Nasir Street) and see how the soap is made. Al-Bader, established over 250 years ago, has exported soap to Arab countries and to Europe.

Sweet Shops

Nablus is also famous for its sweets, especially the Nabulsi *kunafa*, which comes *na'ma* (smooth) or *khishna* (crunchy). People line up at night to order them from vendors with huge, round, hot trays.

Top: Panoramic view of Nablus
Bottom: A Samaritan elder in downtown Nablus

Lightning-fast, the vendor makes square-shaped cuts with a large spatula. A quick flick of the wrist flips the *kunafa* into the paper take-out tray; another drizzles extra sugar syrup on top. A *kunafa* is thin and golden brown on the top, with stretchy mozzarella-like *Arisheh* goat cheese in the middle, between fine filo dough oozing with ghee. There are at least a dozen sweet shops in Nablus, and every one of them is worth visiting.

Tile Factory

Traditional floor-tile designs found in homes of the late Ottoman and early Mandate periods were made with tiles produced almost exclusively in the Nablus and Ramallah region since the 19th century. These tiles, which are intricately ornamented with variously colored geometric shapes such as rosettes and stars, are produced today by only a few craftsmen. One, in northern Nablus, is well worth a visit.

Turkish Baths

For centuries, Nablus was famous for its Turkish baths, which used the water from natural springs. A continuous fire burned under the main room and was maintained with olive stones. **Al-Shifa**, in the Old City, is the oldest working Turkish bath in the country. Built in about 1624 at the start of the Ottoman period, it was beautifully restored in the 1990s. In addition to the steam rooms, a central hall with cushion-strewn platforms to recline on provides a delightful place to sip black coffee or mint tea and puff on a *nargila*.

Hamam al-Hana was built in the 1800s, and though it is neither as renovated nor old as al-Shifa, it is equally enjoyable.

Religious Sites

There are about 30 historic minarets punctuating the Nablus skyline. Al-Kabir Mosque is the largest, with its beautiful arch at the corner of al-Nasir and Jamaa al-Kebir streets.

Jacob's Well (Bir en-Nabi Ya'qub)

Jacob's Well is where, according to tradition, the Samaritan woman offered a drink of water to Jesus, who was resting by the well. Jacob, like many biblical figures, is transformed into a prophet through local lore and became part of the Palestinian popular tradition.

Additions to the church compound were made in the 6th and 12th centuries by the Crusaders, and the most recent renovations in 1908, by the Greek and Russian Orthodox churches. PNA-authorized

A tilemaker and his tile in Nablus

The Samaritans

The Samaritans live on the sacred mountain of Gerizim. Unlike other Jews, the Samaritans never left the Holy Land and lived side by side with the Palestinians throughout most of history. Their brand of Judaism subsequently evolved differently from Jews elsewhere. The Samaritans believe that Abraham sacrificed Isaac at Mt. Gerizim and not Mt. Moriah in Jerusalem, as other Jewish groups would have it. During Passover, Samaritans spend 40 days on the mountain just below the summit. The highlight of their celebration is the sacrificing of a lamb, still carried out in strict conformity with the ritual prescribed by Moses, pouring water over the lamb and shearing its fleece.

Some Samaritan legends have it that it was on Gerizim that Moses received the Ten Commandments. To get a better insight into the Samaritan world, visit the Samaritan Study Center on 26 Omar al-Khatab Street, in the Samaritan quarter. The Palestinian parliament has one seat allocated to a representative of the Samaritan sect.

renovation and restoration is now ongoing. A small museum displays remnants found during the restoration work.

Al-Kabir Mosque

This silver-domed mosque was once a Byzantine church, and parts of the current shrine were built by the Mamluks. Local lore has it that Joseph's brothers showed his "coat of many colors" to their father Jacob here, to make him believe his son was dead.

Al-Nasr Mosque

Situated off Midan al-Manara, this mosque was built in 1935 after an earthquake demolished the Ottoman mosque that stood here. The green-domed house of worship is one of the most popular in Nablus.

Near Nablus

Beit Furik

Ten kilometers (6.2 mi) southeast of Nablus, Beit Furik was built on the site of an ancient Roman city, Perekh (Plant Home). Three kilometers east of the village structures, stone fragments and graves at Khirbet Tana al-Fouka are what remain of the Canaanite village Tanna Shelwa. The villagers of Beit Furik, with their neighbors in Awarta and Salim, produced lime and sold their goods to their tax collectors, the Nimr family of Nablus, throughout the 18th and 19th centuries. Nearby Awarta was also built on a Canaanite village, Giba' Phinehas, and graves, tombs, and ancient dwelling places have been found there.

Mt. Ebal

Unlike Gerizim, its sister mountain, Mt. Ebal is rocky and hardly green at all. From its summit, you can see Jaffa to the west and Safad and Mt. Hermon to the east. But the importance of the mountain is related to its domination of the Tel Balata site of Shekem (see page 218). Excavations at the summit suggest the performance of animal sacrifices. What appear to be Canaanite-era finds include 4-room houses, adjoining the cult center and paved with medium-sized stones. One of the rooms contained pottery—an oil lamp, storage jars, bowls, and a colored-rim pithos. Two scarabs were ascribed to the reign of Ramses II (13th century BCE).

The structure of a Muslim shrine dedicated to Imad al-Din and built in the Mamluk period is still visible on the southern side of the mountain. Some of urban Nablus creeps up the lower slopes of that side of the mountain. 'Askar village lies on the eastern slope.

Mt. Gerizim

Gerizim offers a **magnificent panoramic view of Nablus** and the surrounding area. Local tradition has it that Adam was made from the soil found on this mountain, that its peak was the only earth not covered during the biblical floods. It is *the* Holy Mountain. The Samaritan community believes that the Jewish Temple stood here and not in Jerusalem. A small museum run by the Samaritans celebrates and explains the origins and beliefs of their community.

Ancient ruins at the summit include an octagonal church built by Zeno in the fifth century, and the remains of a mosque and fortress. Roman coins dating back to 159 CE appear to show a great monument on the summit (known in Arabic as Tel al-Ras); archeologists believe it was a temple to either Zeus or Jupiter. Steps leading to where the temple once stood have been unearthed.

Sabastiya

One of the most interesting sites in the all the Palestinian countryside is Sabastiya, which lies 14 kilometers (8.5 mi) northwest of Nablus. The ruins of ancient Sabastiya extend over a hill overlooking the existing village with the same name. It was first inhabited as far back as 4000 BCE, and during the time of the Canaanites it was important enough to have had a royal quarter, the ruins of which are still visible on the top of the hill. Canaanite Sabastiya had strong links with the Phoenicians, with whom they traded and shared deities. Remnants of an altar to Baal and ivory produced in Tyre have been discovered here.

The existing town of Sabastiya was built over a Canaanite settlement between 885–874 BCE, during the reign of Omri VI, an Israelite. At the time, the site was called "Shamer" (Guardian) in the Canaanite language. Omri renamed it Samaria, the first known instance of that famous name. His son Ahab built temples for the Canaanite deities Baal and Astarte to honor Jezebel, his pagan wife.

In 721 BCE the Assyrians defeated the Israelites and a good number were carried off into what is known as the "Babylonian captivity." Historical record indicates, though, that the majority of Israelites stayed, and probably merged with the large influx of Chaldeans and Assyrians. Alexander the Macedonian (333 BCE) quelled Samaritan revolts against his rule by sending them to Nablus and repopulating Sabastiya with Macedonians. Subsequently John Hyrcanus destroyed the city in order to cleanse it of its non-Jewish elements.

Later Herod rebuilt the city and named it Sabastia (Greek for Augustus), honoring his patron Caesar Augustus. The visible remains at ancient Sebastia include Roman tombs, a Hellenistic tower, a Severan basilica, a Herodian temple dedicated to Augustus and Herodian gate towers at the entrance to a colonnaded street with 600 columns on both sides.

Christian tradition very quickly identified Sabastia as the site of the infamous party during which Herod Antipas executed John the Baptist. Two churches were built in honor of St. John, one near Herod's temple and the other in the old village.

The Mamluk and Ottoman eras have remained visible partly due to the durability of their architectural remains, especially in the old town. One of the churches was later reused as a mosque, also in honor of St. John, whom Muslims call Nabi Yahya. The tradition of honoring holy men and women has been maintained, and continues, across the religious divide.

Salfit

Originally an Ottoman-era village, Salfit is located 26 kilometers (16 mi) southeast of Nablus. Under Palestinian rule, it became a separate governorate, with a population of 7,000 in the town and 50,000 in the district, which includes some 22 villages.

Tel Balata

First mentioned in Egyptian texts, the Canaanite Shekem (High Place) was located on Tel Balata at Nablus's eastern outskirts.

Mtabbaq: A Nablusi Sweet

Nablus is especially renowned for its sweets—stop and sample them in any of the city's many sweet shops. *Mtabbaq* is a classic cheese pastry.

White cheese from sheep's milk is typical of Palestine, and its processing has remained unchanged for generations. It is usually made in the spring, when pastures are green and milk bountiful, and preserved with salt for year-round consumption. Although dairy plants have been supplying the market with a selection of white cheeses, many households still boil and preserve their own cheese for the year.

The essential components in the preparation of this cheese are *izha* (black cumin), *mahlab*, and gum arabic, which are added to the water for the boiling process. The cheese is then cooled and preserved in large glass jars or large tin containers and desalinated in small batches for consumption by soaking it in water for a few hours. For the preparation of desserts, it needs to soak overnight.

10 sheets filo dough
1½ lbs white desalinated cheese
1⅜ sticks butter
2 cups sugar
1½ cups water
1 cinnamon stick
1 teaspoon lemon juice

1. Mash the cheese with a fork and set it aside while you prepare the dough. Preheat the oven to 200°. Grease a large cookie sheet. Spread out a filo sheet and brush it all over with butter. Repeat, until 5 sheets are evenly stacked. Then spread the cheese over the entire surface, brush with butter, and top with the remaining 5 filo sheets, brushing each with butter, especially the top layer. With a sharp knife, cut the surface into diamond shapes, barely allowing the knife to touch the bottom layer. This allows for easier cutting upon serving and prevents the cheese from seeping to the bottom of the tray during baking.
2. Bake for approximately 45 minutes; the top should be golden & crisp.
3. While the *mtabbaq* is baking, prepare the syrup. Place sugar, water, and cinnamon stick in a pan over medium heat. Once the sugar syrup comes to a boil, add lemon juice and cook for 8-10 minutes.
4. Pour the syrup over the *mtabbaq* the minute you take it out of the oven. Let it cool slightly, no more than a few minutes, and serve in warmed dessert plates. For special occasions, sprinkle some crushed pistachios on every portion.

Archeological digs have uncovered remains from the Chalcolithic to Roman periods, including city walls, towers and temples, a cuneiform Akkadian inscription, and an Iron Age seal. The first human habitation appears to have been in the Neolithic and Chalcolithic period. But Shekem did not become a town until the 19th century BCE. Destroyed and abandoned until the end of the 17th–16th century BCE, Tel Balata became prominent again during the 15th century, when the Canaanite King Labayu fortified the city with impressive gates and built temples for rulers and the public alike.

A fortress temple on the summit of the hill is the largest and most impressive surviving Canaanite temple in Palestine. Other visible ruins include two monumental gates, massive city walls, and a governor's palace with a small private temple, guardrooms, an assembly, living quarters, and a kitchen.

Tel Balata was destroyed several times and archeological finds, including bronze weapons are currently housed in the Berliner Museum in Berlin.

Canaanite Shekem was the first place the biblical Abraham stopped and rested when he came from Mesopotamia. Subsequently many Jewish notables settled in Shekem.

Refugee Camps

Askar Camp

Askar, home to approximately 14,000 people, lies 3.5 kilometers (2.2 mi) east of downtown Nablus. Once on the fringes of the city, the camp has been absorbed into Nablus's urban sprawl. Askar camp is actually composed of two different camps established at different times: "Old Askar" was established in 1950 on 209 dunums (50 acres) of prime agricultural land known as Sahal Askar (Askar Plain). In 1964, as a result of severe overcrowding problems, "New Askar" was established on a 90-dunum plot (22 acres) of land adjacent and east of Old Askar.

The residents of Askar camp were exiled from 36 villages, primarily in the Lydd, Jaffa, and Haifa regions. Integrated into Askar's population are about 100 families of non-roaming Bedouins, a great many of whom are Afro-Palestinians.

The land around Askar is known for its carrots and fertile soil. A cemetery for Iraqi soldiers who perished in the War of 1948, rests nearby, not far from a trade college the Ministry of Education has run since 1995.

Like many of the refugees in the Nablus region, residents of Askar recall a tense relationship with the original inhabitants of the area, primarily the feudal classes in Nablus. These families continue to control many of the key positions in local municipalities and governing bodies. Though this tension has decreased over the years, still a line is drawn that divides the refugees from the native population.

An arch in the old city

Balata Camp

Balata lies about two kilometers southeast of the center of Nablus. Established in 1950 on 252 dunums (63 acres) of land, Balata is the largest West Bank refugee camp with a population that tips the 20,000 mark. The camp is named after the nearby Canaanite town of Tel Balata to the east. The site is strategically located at the junction of two important ancient commercial routes: one connecting the coast to the Jordan Valley, and the other a mountain route running north to south.

Balata's residents originate from 69 different villages and cities in the central Palestinian regions of Jaffa, Lydd and Ramleh. It also includes a large number of Palestinians of Bedouin origin (as many as 6,000) from the Hashashin, Abu Kishik, and Sawalmeh tribes.

Balata, perhaps more than any other West Bank camp, is renowned for its vanguard position in Palestinian national movement. From the onset of the 1967 occupation, Balata was consistently a thorn in the side of the Israeli army, which tried vainly to control the camp. As early as 1968, Israeli occupation forces were breaking up the political cells that marked the beginning of organized Palestinian political resistance to the occupation in the West Bank. Balata residents boast that the first intifada did not start in Jabaliya camp in

Gaza in 1987, but rather in Balata in 1985, where much of the intifada infrastructure of popular committees, collaborator arrest units and daily confrontations with the occupation army occurred. The camp proudly produced three Palestinian Legislative Council members (including one woman) who earned respected positions as independent and critical voices in the Oslo era.

Visitors to Balata will immediately notice its poverty, population density, and lack of decent infrastructure. An intricate network of alleyways dissects the camp. Two doctors provide health services to the entire camp. Official statistics show that visits to the clinic have averaged 6,092 per month, which amount to about 100 patients per doctor per day. Both the boys' and the girls' school run double shifts; still class size averages 40 students per class. Unemployment is rife, averaging about 50 percent. In the first three years of the al-Aqsa intifada (September 2000–2003), Balata had no less than 80 of its residents killed, thousands wounded, and six full-fledged invasions of the camp—to say nothing of the almost routine arrest campaigns the camp has witnessed.

Balata has a proud tradition of community organizing. The Refugee Committee to Defend Refugee Rights was established in Balata in early 1994, and is run by the prominent Palestine Legislative Council member Husam Khader. (Khader was subsequently arrested and as of publication is still incarcerated). Additionally, youth and women's initiatives are very active.

Ein Beit al-Ma' (Camp #1)

Ein Beit al-Ma' was established in 1950 on a meager 45 dunums of land (10 acres) on the main Nablus–Jenin road. Though the smallest of the three Nablus camps, Camp #1, as it is officially known, is also the most densely populated. Situated on the steep northern slope of Mt. Ebal, the residential conditions are extremely cramped. During funerals, the deceased are passed through windows from one shelter to another in order to reach the camp's main street.

Camp #1's approximately 6,000 residents are exiles from an assortment of Palestinian villages and cities in the Haifa/Western Galilee, Lydd, and Jaffa regions. The camp also has a minority Bedouin population, as well as a handful of families from destroyed villages in the Gaza region.

The camp's double name can be traced to two sources: "Camp #1," the official UNRWA-registered name for the camp, because it was the first of the three Nablus camps, and "Ein Beit al-Ma'," from the name of the local spring that was the camp's primary water source in the early days of its establishment. Most residents prefer this version, usually shortened to Ein Camp (Mokhayyam al-Ein).

In its early history, the camp was situated much more on the outskirts of Nablus, but the camp now seems very much integrated with the urban sprawl of the West Bank's largest city. Many residents of the camp were initially self-employed in small local workshops that made traditional Palestinian reed mats (husr), though this handicraft is, sadly, no longer practiced.

Sports were an important part of early camp life, too. In 1964, the camp's soccer team won the "both banks of the Jordan" competition, proudly beating their Palestinian refugee brethren in Amman's Wihdat camp. Sadly, the lack of open space and increasingly difficult economic conditions have relegated such activity to the sidelines.

UNRWA constructed two new schools on land donated by former Nablus Mayor Thafer al-Masri outside the camp's boundaries, after the original grossly inadequate facility had to be abandoned. A clinic that serves the rural communities northwest of Nablus was also built on the camp grounds.

Daughter of political prisoner from Balata refugee camp

PART THREE

Central
Palestine

21.

Jaffa (Yaafa)

It is the ocean …
It stretches out
And out
And out
Embraces the sand on Jaffa's coast,
Frolics with the houses in Assailant …
And here I am
Standing still.
I do not give my heart up to the sea.
I did not brave the water and its proud eddies.
Here I am
Chained by the city …

—from *"On the Shore,"* Naji Allush, 20th century
translated by Lena Jayyusi and Thomas G. Ezzy

Jaffa has been inhabited for at least 4,000 years, making it one of the oldest seaports in the world. Its builders, the ancient Canaanites, named it Yafi (beautiful). The city is referred to as Yaafa in Arabic, Yafo in Hebrew, Yoppa in Greek, and Yapu or Iapu in Egyptian inscriptions.

Jaffa has been conquered no less than 22 times, notably by the Egyptians, Phoenicians, Babylonians, Philistines, Assyrians, Maccabeans, Seleucids, Persians, Greeks, Romans, Crusaders, Mongols, Mamluks, Ottomans, French, British, and Israelis, and destroyed perhaps as many times, if not by invasions, then by earthquakes.

Balcony over Jaffa

The Legend of Andromeda's Rock

Queen Cassiopeia, wife of Ethiopian King Copeus, made the tragic error of boasting that her daughter, Andromeda, was more beautiful than any mermaid. Cassiopeia's arrogance infuriated Nireus, father of the mermaids, and he beseeched Poseidon to settle the score. Poseidon sent a horrible sea monster to terrify Queen Cassiopeia and the residents of Jaffa. Attempting to assuage the beast, Copeus chained his beautiful daughter to the rocks off Jaffa's port as a sacrifice. But just as the monster was about to take away the fair maiden, gallant Perseus flew down from the heavens on his trusted winged horse, slew the beast, and rescued the beautiful Andromeda.

According to the Roman geographer Estrapo, the chains used to lash Andromeda to the rock were said to be visible at the time of the Roman conquest in 63 BCE. The chains and bones of the sea monster were supposedly taken back to Rome and shown off as a wonder of the world on orders from Scaurus, the Roman governor of Palestine. Pliny recalls their length to be 40 feet long. (Historians believe these must have been the remains of a whale). An image depicting the scene of Andromeda and the sea monster has been discovered on coins minted and found in Jaffa. To this day, the natural rock barrier 300 meters off of Jaffa's shore is called Andromeda's Rock and can still be seen from the port of Old Jaffa. The rescue of Andromeda became a favorite scene in Roman art.

First mentioned in Egyptian sources, Jaffa appears in the list of conquered cities in the 15th century BCE in the Temple of Karnak. The Egyptian soldiers used the equivalent of a Trojan Horse and took the city with ease, enslaving the local population. At the time Jaffa was as a fortified port on the central Canaanite coast, belonging to "the Empire"—an assembly of small states governed by local rulers under the control of Egypt.

During the 12th century BCE, one of the Sea Peoples, the Dannuna, took Jaffa from the Phoenicians, who had wrested control of the city from the Egyptians in 1450 BCE. Most scholars have linked the Dannuna with the Danaoi, of Homer's *Iliad*. Historians and archeologists have suggested that the Dannuna eventually converted to Judaism after the death of their leader Samson, becoming known as the Tribe of Dan by the 11th century BCE.

The oldest archaeological layers in Jaffa show that the city had a wall and gates, and a rampart leading up to the gates. These were destroyed at the beginning of the 13th century BCE, around the time the Dannuna conquered the city. The name Ramses II (the Egyptian pharaoh) is inscribed on one of the doorjambs of the Bronze Age gates. Archeological evidence of the Sea Peoples reveals a temple with two columns supporting the roof, of which only the bases are left. On the floor of the temple a lion skull was found with fierce teeth and a scarab seal near its teeth. Since lion skulls were found in other nearby sites as well, there may have been a lion cult in Jaffa at this time.

Jaffa's only period under definite Hebrew control seems to have begun 200 years after the landing of the Dannuna when David conquered the city, and Jaffa became a port city for Jerusalem. The Phoenician King Hiram of Tyre sent the famous cedar logs of Lebanon to Jaffa for the construction of Solomon's temple. "And we will cut wood out of Lebanon, as much as thou shalt need: and we will bring it to thee in floats on the Sea of Jaffa; and thou shalt carry it up to Jerusalem" (II Chronicles 2:16).

In 701 BCE the Assyrians conquered the city, which fell in rapid succession to the Babylonians, and then the Persians. The latter victory is made known by the inscription on the famous sarcophagus of the Phoenician King Eshmunezer of Sidon (6th century BCE), which relates that Jaffa and Dor were put under the tutelage of the King of Sidon. Although under Persian rule, Phoenicians inhabited Jaffa from the end of the 6th century BCE to the end of the 4th century BCE, as a temple in honor of the Phoenician god Eshmun attests.

Alexander conquered Jaffa and the Persians in 332 BCE, and the Greeks settled in, expanded, and modernized the city, using it as a place to mint coins, some of which depicted the scene of Andromeda and the sea monster (see sidebar).

The Roman Mark Antony reportedly gave Jaffa to Cleopatra as a token of his undying love. After her death in 30 BCE, Jaffa became Herod's. The city lost much of its importance during this period, though, when a new port city, Caesarea was founded just 63 kilometers (40 mi) to the north.

Jaffa had a sizeable Jewish minority that participated in Jewish rebellions against the Roman Empire. The emperor put down the rebellion and renamed Jaffa "Joppa Flavia," and declared it a free city, and permitted it to mint its own coins. One of the coins found in Jaffa shows a portrait of Athena, goddess of wisdom.

Jaffa is mentioned in the Old Testament as the port of embarkation for Jonah, who set sail on his fateful journey from the city (Jonah 1:1–3). Ignoring God's commandment to sail to the "evil city of Nineveh," he was swallowed by a whale—a story also mentioned in the Qur'an. Islamic tradition recalls that after the whale spat out Jonah (Yunis in Arabic), he landed on the shores of Palestine.

According to Biblical tradition, St. Peter came from Lydd, 12 miles away, and brought the virtuous Tabitha back to life in Jaffa. After his feat, he is said to have taken up lodging in the city with Simon the Tanner who lived by the sea. In Jaffa Peter experienced visions of "the clean and unclean animals" and also received the order that "the Gentiles too should be saved." The house of Simon the Tanner can be visited in Jaffa's old city, though it is now a private residence.

In the 5th–6th centuries, Jaffa came under Byzantine rule, though information on the city during that time is limited.

The Arab Era

The Arab Amrou bin Ala captured Jaffa in 638 and designated it the port for Ramleh, the new capital. During the early days of Arab rule, Jaffa was a center for prisoner exchange, mostly between the Byzantines and the Islamic Caliphate.

Near the end of the first millennium CE, al-Muqaddasi writes,

> Yafah, lying on the sea, is but a small town, although the emporium of Palestine and the port of Ar Ramleh. It is protected by a strong wall with iron gates, and the sea-gates also are of iron. The mosque is pleasant to the eye, and overlooks the sea, and the harbor is excellent.

Jaffa became known as home to early Islamic scholars such as Abu Abbas Ibn 'Amir al-Yaffawi (873–971), Abu Taher Abd al-Jabar al-Yaffawi, as well as the Islamic moralist Mohammed al-Kharaiti al-Samari (854–939).

Ja'far Bin Fallah al-Kutami invaded Palestine in 969 and Jaffa, along with the rest of Palestine, was in Fatimid hands. A massive earthquake devastated the country in 1033 and local lore has it that many of the fisherman who had embarked from Jaffa's port that day never returned.

Years of continuous warfare, as well as the natural disasters, earned Jaffa a reputation as a very modest and long-suffering town. It was described in 1050 as a "rainless town, where those who were born there were rare to live, and one cannot even find a teacher for young boys."

In 1074 the Seljuks took Jaffa briefly, in an ultimately failed attempt to establish a Turkmen republic. They were forced to relinquish it to the Fatimids in 1098. One year later, Jaffa fell to the Crusaders.

The Crusaders

Weakened by years of warfare, Jaffa was in no position to defend itself against the Crusaders, who landed their boats, stormed the walls, sacked the city, and exiled its Muslim residents.

Nearly one hundred years later, in 1187, Jaffa was taken back from the Knights of St. John by a Muslim army under the leadership of Malik al-Adel, the brother of Saladin.

Four years later, Richard the Lionheart re-occupied the city by launching a seaborne attack from the port city of Acre. Crusader

The coast of Jaffa

control of Jaffa finally ended when the Cairo-based army of Mamluk Sultan Baibars defeated the Crusader forces in 1267.

Mamluk Jaffa (1291–1516)

Jaffa was largely destroyed in the fighting with the Crusaders, a condition made worse when the Mamluk King Baibars called for the destruction of the Jaffa fortress to dissuade any attempts by the Crusader to retake the city. The wood and marble from the Jaffa fortress was taken to Cairo where it was used to construct the Baibars mosque.

Overall, the Mamluks largely ignored Jaffa, administering it from Damascus. The 15th-century traveler Barokiyya painted a bleak picture:

> As for now, Jaffa is destroyed, with nothing much in it but a few tents for pilgrims to hide from the evil of the sun's rays. Its port is shallow and dangerous owing to storms, and when the pilgrims come upon the shore, the Sultan's employees hurry to them to document their numbers, and take taxes from them.

Ottoman Jaffa (1517–1917)

The Ottomans, however, recognized Jaffa's strategic importance and made desperately needed improvements—rebuilding the city walls, reinforcing and improving its port. They also worked to halt attacks by marauding nomadic raiders from the south that plagued Jaffa during this period. The city was ravaged by particularly cruel sacking in 1689.

With its plentiful water supply, Ottoman Jaffa was known for crops that flourished even in the dry heat of summer, among them corn, sesame, watermelon, cotton, barley, and citrus fruits.

With the help of the Russians, Jaffa rebelled against Ottoman rule twice, in 1772 and 1775. The Russians aimed to destroy the Ottoman Empire from within by encouraging the Arab majority to revolt. In the first such siege, Jaffa's governor, Hassan Pasha Tuqan, led a revolt against Ottoman leader Ali Bek and took control of the city. Despite Russian support, the rebellion was eventually crushed in 1773. During the second uprising, Ali Bek sent the Ottoman wali Abu Dhahab to crush the rebellion. Abu Dhahab brutally killed more than 5,000 Jaffa residents and piled their heads in a pyramid.

Napoleon in Jaffa

A couple decades later, in 1799, Napoleon attacked Palestine, first invading Gaza in March and a month later attacking Jaffa. He began his campaign by sending a letter by messenger demanding that the residents of Jaffa surrender; if they did, their lives would be spared. But Jaffa's residents, who had gone through several sieges over the previous 50 years, were unwilling to give in so easily. They killed the messenger and flung him over the walls back at the besieging French troops. A long and bitter siege ensued, marked by great heroism on the part of the defenders. Eventually, the French breached the walls and took the city, killing at least 4,400 people. According to a witness, the "French went to kill their enemies like mad men all throughout the night and the following morning. Men, women and children, Christians, Muslims, and everyone with a human face fell in the frenzy of their madness."

The French victory would prove pyrrhic. Because of the high death toll and difficult conditions, half of Napoleon's troops became infected by the plague, which is thought to be a major reason Napoleon failed to conquer Palestine. Two months later his attack against Acre was repelled. The defeat forced Napoleon to retreat all the way back to Egypt. In total, the French occupation of Jaffa lasted less than three months.

By the 18th century, Jaffa witnessed a revival under the rule of Governor Mohammed Agha (Abu Nabut). Although Abu Nabut's rule was relatively short, (1807–1818), its impact on the city was long lasting. Many improvements made under his leadership are still visible today. Abu Nabut placed cannons directed toward the sea and the mainland, built a much needed moat surrounding the walled city, and a breakwater to protect the shorefront houses in bad weather. In 1810, Abu Nabut constructed Jaffa's main mosque, which today takes his name. On the southern side of the mosque, he had built a *sabil* (fountain) and a marketplace (site of today's flea market). A similar fountain was built on the Jerusalem–Jaffa road nearby.

Jaffa expanded and developed considerably in the second half of the 19th century, exporting sesame, beans, vegetables and fruit, while importing cotton, flour, sugar, tobacco, rice, coffee, and cloth. Together with Nablus, Ramleh and Lydd, though to a somewhat lesser degree, Jaffa was a center of soap and oil production. In 1872 Jaffa had five different soap factories.

Around this time, Jaffa's population grew with an influx of Austro-Hungarian, German, Russian, and French pilgrims. To make way for expansion, the city walls were dismantled and the moat filled. Jaffa's expanding middle-class and upper-class families, who had grown wealthy in trade, industry, and tourism, built luxurious villas in the gardens and rural suburbs. Some European pilgrims struck with "Holy Land syndrome" (and perhaps the hot sun) found walking in Jaffa's gardens like being transported to the Garden of Eden.

Jaffa's development was a European concern not merely because it was an important trading city, but because pilgrims landed here. A French association built a lighthouse in 1864 and in 1867, the road from Jerusalem to Jaffa was greatly improved, and regular wagon traffic to Jerusalem was established between the two cities. In 1892, a French engineering firm finished the construction of the 87-km (52-mi) Jaffa–Jerusalem rail line to facilitate trade and the travel of pilgrims. The train ran twice daily and took just under 4 hours. By that time, 80,000 pilgrims and traders arrived at the port every year.

In 1856, American missionaries intending to establish a pilgrim community purchased a plot of land in Jaffa that became known as al-Mallakan (from the Arabic word for American, al-Amarkan). Though the effort failed after 11 years, the land was purchased by German pilgrims who later founded the German colony in Jaffa. Nearby lies a second German settlement, Sarona.

The 20th Century

At the turn of the century, Jaffa blossomed as an urban port city and the most advanced Arab city on the Mediterranean, boasting trade unions, political parties, newspapers, boy scouts, and women's societies. In 1910, Jaffa had no less than 20 schools (public and private) and a population of 70,000. In 1913 alone, 665 ships from England, Austria, France, Russia, Germany, Italy, and America docked at its port. At the same time, Jaffa boasted seven newspapers, with an additional three emerging in the 1920s, two more in the 1930s, and another two just before the outbreak of the 1948 War. Jaffa also had a wide array of political parties and religious establishments (12 mosques, 10 churches, and 3 monasteries).

Its urban status made it an epicenter of emerging Palestinian nationalism, and anti-Ottoman, anti-Zionist, and later, anti-British sentiment. The original non-immigrant Jewish population of Jaffa before World War I was 3,000 to 4,000, but another 30,000 Jewish Zionists (mainly from Russia, Romania, Germany, Austria, and Hungary) resided nearby. Jewish numbers rose during the Constitutional phase of the Ottoman Empire, because progressive laws permitted the free practicing of religion, something from which European missionaries and pilgrims also benefited.

At the outbreak of World War I, Hassan Bek al-Jabi was appointed ruler of Jaffa. He made substantial improvements to Jaffa's buildings and infrastructure, beginning with the 1915 construction of Jamal Pasha Road (to the British, it became King George Street, and after the establishment of Israel, Jerusalem Road). Hassan Bek's most enduring accomplishment was the construction of Hassan Bek mosque in the Manshiyya neighborhood, now easily seen on the promenade walk south from Tel Aviv to Jaffa. In recent years the mosque has been subjected to attacks and desecration by fanatics who want to erase what remains of Palestine's Arab heritage.

British Mandate

Beginning in 1921, Jaffa was the scene of major demonstrations and labor strikes. After 320 Arabs and Jews were killed, Jaffa's Jewish population (both Zionist and indigenous) left for the newly emerging city of Tel Aviv. Similar events were repeated in 1929, when a Jewish police officer broke into the house of Shaykh Abdel Ghani Awn, the imam of Jaffa's Abu Kabir Mosque, murdering him and six members of his family and sparking a major uprising throughout Palestine. In 1933, a demonstration outside of Jaffa's main mosque was brutally put down by the British forces, who killed at least 30 demonstrators.

By 1936 Palestine's general strike had begun. The Palestinian

Hassan Bek Mosque stands in what is now Tel Aviv

demands were the establishment of independent parliamentary rule in Palestine. A six-month strike at the port of Jaffa wrought British anger and repression: lengthy curfews, arrest campaigns, the crushing of demonstrations, and the blowing up of over 1,000 Palestinian homes. In response to the Palestinian strike, a new port was built in Tel Aviv, rendering Jaffa's port obsolete.

The War of 1948

One of the first skirmishes in the war took place on the outskirts of Jaffa, one week after the UN passed its partition plan, which allocated

Jaffa to the Arab-Palestinian State. Jaffa was geographically disconnected from the rest of the Arab state-to-be and completely surrounded by the Jewish state-to-be. Zionist leaders understood that if their goal of an ethnically pure Jewish state was to be realized, it was necessary to expel as many Arabs as possible from the boundaries of the Jewish state. Jaffa became a particular target of Zionist militias because of its proximity to Tel Aviv.

Jaffa, and other Palestinian cities and villages within the proposed Jewish state, were the direct targets of Zionist militias before the end of the British mandate (May 15, 1948), and before the attempted intervention of the Arab armies thereafter. Zionist leaders understood that Jaffa had symbolic significance for Palestine, and that conquering Jaffa would strike a demoralizing blow to the Palestinian resistance forces.

On 4 January 1948, 30 Palestinians were killed when the Zionist militia Irgun destroyed Jaffa's Ottoman governmental building with a truck bomb. Palestinians moved to organize the city's defense, mobilizing 540 men armed with simple rifles. But they were out-gunned and out-numbered by the more experienced Irgun, which was said to have used 5,000 soldiers armed with artillery, mortars, and machine guns in the Jaffa campaign.

On May 5, 1948 the great majority of Jaffa's residents left fearing for their lives, terrified by the more than 30 massacres Zionist militias already had committed in Palestine. Of Jaffa's approximately 100,000 residents, only 4,000 non-Jews remained in the city.

Two days before the official end of the British mandate, four representatives of the remaining Arab community signed a pact of non-aggression and compliance with the Haganah in Tel Aviv, agreeing to comply with Zionist demands. A day later, Zionists hoisted the Israeli flag on the city's buildings. By the end of that month, 48 villages in the Jaffa region (with a combined population of over 69,000) had been occupied, forcibly depopulated, and in many cases destroyed. A widespread campaign of looting Arab properties took place. Almost immediately, homes and businesses were taken over by the Israeli state and settled with Jewish immigrants.

Jaffa's remaining Arab population was herded into the southern Ajami neighborhood on July 28, 1948 and surrounded by barbed wire. In total 1,300 Palestinians were killed in the battle to defend Jaffa.

The remains of Arab Jaffa

Post-Nakba

In 1954, Jaffa became part of the Tel Aviv municipality, known thereafter as the municipality of Tel Aviv–Jaffa. Palestinian refugee property was boarded up. In 1960, the Israeli government established the "Old Jaffa Development Corporation," which pushed for the Jewish gentrification of Jaffa. Today only small parts of the original town remain—it has been taken over by upscale Israeli galleries, antique shops, and restaurants. The sea front promenade now extends from Tel Aviv to Old Jaffa, but what is visible only represents a sanitized and hollowed-out shell. The main port of what was once Palestine's second largest city was closed in 1965. Palestinian fisherman were pushed southward to expand Tel Aviv's yachting aficionados.

Today, Jaffa has a population of 60,000, of which 25,000 are Palestinians with Israeli citizenship. Arabic is banned from street signs (they are English and Hebrew).

The Israeli Antiquities Administration has only two places it deems of historical value in Old Jaffa—the Biluim House (a home of early Zionist settlers in 1882) and the first Hebrew High School building (Gymnasia Hertzeliya). No structure of Jaffa's pre-20th-century history is a protected antiquity under Israeli law.

Visiting Jaffa

The Jaffa that Israel wants visitors to see is only a small corner of the northern neighborhoods of the original city, and can easily be reached on foot from Tel Aviv. Before arriving in the Old City, note the neighborhoods to the left. Though unimpressive at present, they constitute the remains of Jaffa's Manshiyya neighborhood, which was largely destroyed in the 1948 War. To see more of Jaffa the Palestinian city (depopulated from its original inhabitants though it is), travel directly south on Rehov Yefet.

The **Ottoman Clock Tower** (1906) commissioned by Sultan Abdul Hamid II is one of Jaffa's most recognizable landmarks. Twin clock towers were also built in Jerusalem and Acre at the same time to mark the ascension of the new sultan. On the historical square where the clock tower stands is a former British prison known as the Kishleh, which has been transformed into an Israeli police station. The square (now called Kikar Kedumim) marked the beginning of three historical trade routes.

The Jerusalem Road travels southeast through the burial ground of Abu Nabut, past a fountain bearing his name. Further along on the right stands a Russian settlement and the house of Tabitha, who was raised by the Apostle Peter.

The Gaza Road goes south, past an English cemetery, an English girls' school, and across from it the Hospital of St. Louis (founded 1876). Further are more missionary schools, including the Ecoles de Frere and the Sister of St. Joseph. Next door is the Orthodox Church, and immediately after, an English mission house and hospital.

The Nablus Road used to pass through orange groves on its way to the German colony, where the Germans ran two schools and a hospital.

Religious Sites

Al-Ajami Mosque
Located in the Ajami quarter, this mosque contains the grave of Shaykh Ibrahim al-Ajami. Little about this shaykh is known, beyond that he was a "righteous man." The mosque is the hub for the city's Muslim community.

Fisherman's Mosque
Located on the quay and built in 1820 to serve incoming fisherman, this mosque no longer functions. Just next door is the former Austrian post office, and nearby, the Hassan Pasha mosque.

Hassan Bek Mosque
Located in the Manshiyya neighborhood, along the Tel Aviv–Jaffa promenade, this mosque was named after Hassan Bek al-Jabi al-Dimashqi, general of Jaffa at the beginning of World War I. It is a classic example of late Ottoman architecture.

Hassan Pasha Mosque
Located on the road that leads to the port, this mosque takes its name from Hassan Ghazi al-Jazairli, an Ottoman sea captain who visited Jaffa after a 1775 massacre. It stands directly in front of Tel Aviv's Intercontinental Hotel.

Abu Nabut Mosque and Abu Nabut/Mahmoudiyya Sabil
Built in 1809 and extensively renovated three years later by Abu Nabut, this mosque sits in the southwest corner of the clock square. It is incorrectly called Mahmoudiyya Mosque in many tour books, after foreigners writing on Jaffa assumed that it carried the name of its sabil (fountain), which itself is called al-Mahmoudiyya, after Sultan Mahmoud II (1808–1839). It is said that some of the mosque's columns were taken from Askalan and Caesarea, but during

construction were placed upside down. The mosque features a tall slender minaret, two white domes, and a fountain dedicated to Suleiman the Magnificent on the mosque's southern wall. Diagonally opposite the mosque is the old road that used to lead to Jerusalem and the Abu Nabut Sabil along what is today Ben Tzvi Street, well worth seeing as it gives an indication of how Jaffa used to be.

St. Peter's Monastery

This Franciscan monastery dedicated to Peter the Apostle was built in 1654 on the ruins of a 13th-century Crusader castle. The Crusader architecture is still visible in the high vaulted chambers.

Al-Saksak Mosque

Located in the Eastern portion of the city, this mosque has a *sabil* of the same name. It was originally built as a school.

Shaykh Raslan Mosque

Also located in the Old City, near the Latin Monastery, this mosque takes its name from the notable Muslim Shaykh Arsalan of Ramleh who used to visit it in summer times.

South of Old Jaffa

Directly south of Old Jaffa is San Antonio's Roman Catholic (Franciscan) Church, which can be distinguished by its red-tile roof and tall steeple built in 1932. Dedicated to St. Antonius of Padua, the building was one of the only structures to have survived the 1948 war intact. Behind St. Anthony's is a Greek Coptic chapel and convent, recognized by its small red dome, arched cloisters, and square tower. Opposite San Antonius is the Church of St. Peter; just down the small side street is the Greek Catholic Church and convent built in 1924. Not far from that is the Maronite Church. To the east 2.5 kilometers (1.5 mi) lies the Russian monastery of St. Peter's (est. 1860), with its pink and white tower. The chamber beneath the monastery is the supposed site of the resurrection of Tabitha.

Al-Tabiyyeh Mosque

Located near the lighthouse, this is the oldest mosque in Jaffa. It was built on the foundations of a 10th-century mosque mentioned by Palestinian geographer al-Maqdisi.

Top: Staircase to St. Michael's Greek Orthodox Church
Bottom: The Abu Nabut Fountain on the Jaffa–Jerusalem road

Other Sites

Al-Ajami

Between Rehov Yefet and the sea lies the residential area of Jaffa's remaining Palestinian community, known as the Ajami neighborhood. This is where the Israeli government pushed Jaffa's remaining Arab population in 1948. Today, increasing numbers of Jews have bought property in this neighborhood, making for an awkward juxtaposition of luxurious villas and derelict Arab housing. It is however, the heart of modern Palestinian Jaffa, and is an essential visit for those willing to understand the modern Palestinian Jaffa experience.

Armenian Hospice

Founded in 1654, this hospice contains the "Hall of the Plague Stricken," where Napoleon's plague-stricken army attempted recovery.

Artist Quarter

A glimpse of the beauty and architectural heritage of lost Jaffa can be had in the Old City, now transformed into an upscale neighborhood of studios, galleries, and souvenir shops. Most of the original inhabitants of this quarter are living in Gaza or Nablus-based refugee camps.

Flea Market

Active since well before the establishment of the state of Israel, today this market has a wide variety of items including a few genuine antiques, and a whole lot of junk.

Jaffa Museum of Antiquities

This museum is housed in the 18th-century Ottoman government house (al-Saraya al-Qadima) located in the center of the Old City. Though the building itself, with a foundation that dates to Crusader years, is a testament to Jaffa's rich and varied history, the museum attempts to create an almost exclusively Jewish history for the city. It includes artifacts from the Neolithic period (7500–4500 BCE) through the 19th century, but the Arab and Islamic presence is remarkably absent. Just behind the museum is the former Turkish *hammam* (bath house), which has now been transformed into a theater and restaurant.

Top: The Ottoman Clocktower commissioned by Sultan Abdul Hamid II in 1906
Bottom: Jaffa was long known for its fishing fleet

Jerusalem Gate

Located at the entrance of today's Rehov Hatsorfim, this gate was until 1869 the sole entrance into the old city of Jaffa.

Manouli Khan

Now an antique store at 11 Yefet Street, this was once a caravansary run by an Armenian family.

St. Louis French Hospital

A community health center named after Louis ICX of the seventh crusade, who landed in Jaffa in 1251.

Simon the Tanner's House

The house of Simon the Tanner can be found at 8 Simat Shimon Haburski. Formerly the Mosque of Jami' al-Tabit, it is now a private house. According to tradition, here the Apostle Peter stayed after resurrecting Tabitha from the grave. Along the quayside of the port stand an assortment of religious institutions, including St. Michael's Greek Orthodox Church, the Armenian Church, St. Nicholas's monastery, and the Fisherman's Mosque (Jama'al Bahr).

Tabitha School for Girls

Named after Jaffa's favorite woman who rose from the dead, this school has been run by the Presbyterian Church of Scotland since 1863. Behind the school is a small graveyard within which is buried Thomas Hodgkin, the doctor who discovered Hodgkin's disease and died in Jaffa in 1866.

Tel Jaffa/Ramses Garden

The remains uncovered here include stone foundations of a Hellenistic citadel (332–140 BCE), a Persian wall (539–332 BCE), a late-Canaanite foundation (late 13th to early 12th BCE, the remains of brick walls dating to the middle Canaanite era (16th–14th century BCE), and structural remains from the Middle Ages, and a soap factory from the British Mandate.

Agriculture and the Jaffa Orange

At the turn of the 20th century, Jaffa farmers produced oranges, lemons, pomegranates, watermelons, and grapes, as well as other crops such as vegetables, cotton, and mulberries, which were used for raising silk worms. But Jaffa's most famous export by far was the "Jaffa Orange."

Although oranges were introduced to Gaza some 1,000 years ago, orange groves were not cultivated in the area until about 1750. By 1879, 5,000 people were employed in the harvesting and packaging of Jaffa oranges. By 1912, 2,100 hectares (5,189 acres) of agricultural lands were orange orchards, a third of which belonged to Jews. Just before World War II, two million boxes of Jaffa oranges were shipped to England alone. In 1947, the British government bought the entire citrus harvest of 12 million crates.

During the 1948 War, Arab and Jewish orange farmers had a shared interest in the preservation of the citrus industry, which resulted in the signing of a non-aggression pact between the mayor of Tel Aviv and Jaffa on December 9, 1947. The pact however, was violated; soon after winter's end, the Haganah attacked Arab-owned farms, along with the city and the surrounding villages.

After the mass expulsion of Palestinians from Jaffa and its villages, the Arab-owned citrus plantations were left to rot. Jewish citrus growers were barely capable of taking care of their own crops, because they had been dependant on the labor of Arab peasants, who were now refugees prevented from returning. A total of 150,000 dunums (37,000 acres) of citrus groves, the most valuable agricultural crop the Palestinians were forced to leave behind, remained untended. Kibbutz and moshavim preferred field crops to the oranges, which require high irrigation and high labor. Most of the orchards were cut down to make for housing and other construction.

Political reasons also motivated the abandonment of the groves. After the Nakba, "the stronger the international pressure for the return of the Palestinian refugees, the greater were Israeli efforts to destroy the agricultural infrastructure that might have made possible the absorption of returning refugees."

22.

Ramleh (ar-Ramleh)

Ar-Ramleh is the capital of Palestine. It is a fine city, and well built; its water is good and plentiful; its fruits are abundant. It combines manifold advantages, situated as it is in the midst of beautiful villages and lordly towns, near to holy places and pleasant hamlets. Commerce here is prosperous, and markets excellent. There is no finer mosque in Islam than the one in this city.

—al-Maqdisi, Arab historian from Palestine, b. 946

Founded in 716 during the rule of Umayyad Caliph Suleiman Ibn Abd al-Malik, Ramleh was indeed once a "fine city," very different from the sad, decaying metropolis it is today. For this region of the world, Ramleh was a new city—fresh and young and unimpeded by the burdens of history. Its name, a derivative of *"ramle"* (sand), is apt for a city built on sand dunes.

The Arab founders of Ramleh, wanting to be equally close to the two major cities of the country, Jerusalem and Gaza, measured the way and chose a spot in the middle. Located some 15 kilometers (9 mi) east off the Mediterranean coast, Ramleh lies at the crossroads of two major historical routes: the Via Maris, along the coast, and the Jaffa–Jerusalem road. The Arab armies were initially based in Jerusalem, but they felt that al-Quds was first and foremost a city of God, and not an appropriate seat for political power. The choice of the Muslim Arabs to build an altogether new, separate city was in line with their habit elsewhere, in which they established garrison cities and stayed out of the civil and religious life of the local population until a natural integration took place.

Tower of the 40 Martyrs at Nabi Saleh

Ramleh's marketplace is a rich mix of people

Ramleh became both the Umayyad and Abbasid capital of the Province of Palestine (Jund Filastin), and the seat of Arab provincial governors in the 8th and 9th centuries. While many of the soldiers which originally inhabited it moved to other cities once they married, enough brought their wives so that within one generation it was no longer a garrison.

During the 400 years before the Crusaders came, Ramleh was known for its religious tolerance, in particular toward peripheral and fringe groups. Sufi orders, which advocated spiritualism and meditation, flocked to the capital during the Abbasid era. It was also one of the few places in Palestine were followers of the Shia branch of Islam found a foothold. Along with a colony of Karaite Jews in nearby Matsliah, the Sufis, Shia, Orthodox Christians, and Sunnis combined to make Ramleh a diverse and cosmopolitan capital.

The al-Wazir Bathhouse

Economically, too, it thrived: its successful dyeing industry catered to cloth and carpet manufacturers as far away as Baghdad and Persia.

Much of the city was destroyed during an 11th century earthquake and while the Crusaders were trying to wrest the city from the Fatimids. The Crusaders controlled it for some 90 years, in which they used it as a stopover for pilgrims on their way to Jerusalem from the coast. It lost its political and economic importance for the entire interlude of the Crusades.

Although not much is known about the area before the founding of Ramleh, some Christian traditions believe it to be the site of Arimathea, home of Joseph, who carried Jesus off the cross and helped bury him. Thus the Crusaders built the Church of St. Joseph of Arimathea in Ramleh.

Both Saladin and Baibars are said to have made their base in Ramleh, in part because its location was convenient and in part to reiterate its importance as an Islamic city. Once the Mamluks came to power in the 14th century, Ramleh did once again regain some of its importance when it became a provincial capital and large parts of it were renovated and rebuilt.

Part of the former Ottoman city of Ramleh

Because it has been inhabited continuously since it was established, the early foundations of the city are buried underneath the existing structures, and archeologists wishing to dig have been seriously curtailed. Limited excavations carried out after the city was occupied by Israeli troops in 1949 indicate that the city is indeed still located at the same spot that it was in the 8th century.

Arab–Jewish relations seriously deteriorated during the 1930s and Ramleh, along with Lydd, saw some of the worst ethnic cleansing by

Zionist forces in 1948, during "Operation Dani." Initially Arab Jews from Yemen, Iraq, and North Africa were settled in Ramleh; today Russian and Ethiopian Jewish immigrants are encouraged to settle in the city. The Palestinian population, which consists of about 20 percent of some 60,000 inhabitants, is almost equally divided between Muslims and Christians.

Sites

Old Mamluk Ramleh

Only remnants of pre-1948 Ramleh can still be seen. Though in a state of almost total decay, the refined architecture of the Old City is still evident in what remains of archways, windows, and passageways. The Israeli government allegedly wants to turn the area into a parking lot.

Palestinian Homes

When driving around Ramleh the homes of what was the Ramleh bourgeoisie are still in evidence. Often closed off and abandoned, their owners are forbidden from reclaiming their property. Most cannot even visit—they cannot get visas from the Israeli government.

Radwan Baths

Unfortunately the Turkish bath in Ramleh shut down when much of Arab existence in the city went dead in 1948. A square structure built of carved stone and topped with a dome, this Ottoman vestige provides an interesting look at the past. According to Muslim lore, Radwan is the doorkeeper to the gates of paradise and decides who may enter and who may not. This bath was apparently bought from the Radwan family by the al-Wazir family of Ramleh some 150 years ago. Thus local Palestinians also refer to it as the Bathhouse of Khalil al-Wazir, also known as Abu Jihad, the Palestinian leader who was assassinated by an Israeli death squad in Tunis on April 16, 1988.

Vaulted Pools of St. Helena (Birket Anzia)

Built during the Abbasid rule, contemporary to the cisterns under the White Mosque compound, these arched vaults seem to be the forerunners of the Gothic architecture later used by the Crusaders. A tour of the underground vaults is possible with small rowing boats.

Ruins of the White Mosque

Religious Sites

Church and Hospice of St. Nicodemus and St. Joseph of Arimathea
The compound was built in the 16th century to honor Joseph of Arimathea and Nicodemus, the men who took Christ off the cross and buried him. Apparently Napoleon spent a night here on his way to Jaffa. Run by Franciscans, the current structure was completed in 1902.

Church of St. George
This blue-domed church is the main shrine of worship for the Greek Orthodox community, which has particular attachment to St. George, who is depicted slaying the dragon above the church entrance. The church complex includes monks' quarters, a pilgrim inn, stables, and underground water storage dating back to before the Crusades.

Omari Mosque (Kabir)

Built during the Mamluk period, this mosque is a startling mix of Crusader and Mamluk architecture. After driving the Crusaders out, the Mamluks turned the Church of St. John into a mosque and added a fine minaret and superb calligraphy to the basilica.

The White Mosque & the Tower of the 40 Martyrs

The most famous historical edifice in Ramleh is the **White Mosque** and the minaret next to it, known alternatively as the Tower of Nabi Saleh or the **Tower of the 40 Martyrs**. Built during Umayyad rule, this 7th-century mosque is believed to be the first Islamic house of prayer in Ramleh. Destroyed during the Crusader wars, it was rebuilt by the Ayoubites in the 12th century.

During the Mamluk reign the White Mosque and its adjacent tower covered an immense area of 10,000 sq meters (107,600 sq ft). A 1546 earthquake destroyed most of the compound. Broad pilasters which supported the barrel-domed ceilings of old water cisterns can still be seen. These were once filled with rainwater and water that flowed from an aqueduct from the hills east of Ramleh. The mosque was rebuilt by the Ottomans but destroyed again in 1927 during an earthquake. Under British rule the mosque was not rebuilt and today is hardly recognizable as a former mosque. The compound of the White Mosque today consists of the Tomb of Nabi Saleh, the Tower of the 40 Martyrs, the graves of 40 Muslim Martyrs and a large Muslim cemetery.

The Tower of the 40 Martyrs was a 14th century addition of the Mamluks. It was meant to commemorate 40 fallen Muslim soldiers, some of whom, according to lore, were companions of the Prophet Mohammad. At this time a popular local festival, the summer celebration of Nabi Saleh, a Muslim Saint that performed miracles took place around his tomb, which lies north of the mosque. The **Festival of Nabi Saleh** was celebrated until the 1940's with thousands of people coming from as far away as Jaffa and Jerusalem, converging on Ramleh. Palestinian tradition holds that the people of Ramleh and Lydd, carrying town flags and banners were the first to arrive and the last to leave in this summer celebration of a local saint known for his miracles.

Zeitouni Mosque

This is the most popular mosque in Ramleh, with a relatively uncomplicated history. It is closest to the lively marketplace and was built to honor a local cleric, Shaykh Zeitoun. His tomb is inside the mosque, which was most recently repaired in the 1980s.

Lydd at sunset

23.

Lydd

As of 11 July, the Israeli army began the systematic expulsion of the residents of Lydd and Ramleh... the largest single instance of deliberate mass expulsion during the 1948 war. Most were women, children, and elderly men, most of the able-bodied men having been taken prisoner. Memories of the trek of the Lydd and Ramleh refugees are branded in the collective consciousness of the Palestinians. The Palestinian historian Aref al-Aref, who interviewed survivors at the time, estimates that 350 died of thirst and exhaustion in the blazing sun of July....

—Spiro Munayyer in "The Fall of Lydda,"
Journal of Palestine Studies (Summer 1998)

First mentioned as a Canaanite metropolis in the city lists of Thutmose III, some experts estimate that Lydd was inhabited as far back as 7,500 years ago. Ideally located next to a stream and fertile fields, it appears to have been suitable for human habitation even in nomadic times. When the Canaanites ceased to play an important role in Palestine, Lydd was invariably conquered by Hebrews, Greeks, and Romans before becoming a Hellenistic Christian city and later an Arab capital.

Between the 1st century BCE and 66 CE, the Romanized population inhabited Lydd until the proconsul of Syria, Cestius Gallus, burned it en route to Jerusalem. Within a hundred years, it was rebuilt, and became famous for its large markets, textiles, dyes, and fine pottery. The recent find of the remains of a grandiose home with mosaic floors from this era implies that the city was indeed quickly rebuilt after destruction. By 200, the Arab emperor of the Roman Empire, Septimus Severus, had established a city in Lydd. During the rest of the Roman period and into the Byzantine era, a prosperous community of merchants thrived in Lydd.

The city was home to one of the first Christian communities and is cited as the place where the Apostle Peter healed Aeneas. In the 4th century the Byzantines renamed it "Georgiopolis" in honor of St. George, who had converted many city inhabitants to Christendom.

In 639, Lydd became under the Umayyads the Arab capital of Jund Filastin. By 716 the Muslim armies built a new capital in nearby Ramleh.

Some 400 years later, the Crusaders made Lydd a regional headquarters and built many churches, some of which can still be seen today. According to the travelogue of Benjamin of Toledo, only one Jewish family lived in Lydd in 1170. After the Muslims defeated the Crusaders, Muslims and Jews were allowed to live in the city. Although Muslims established a foothold and rebuilt the city, it was home mainly to Orthodox Christians.

In 1892 the Ottomans established the first railway station in the entire region in Lydd. During the British mandate, the railway services in Lydd were expanded and it became a hub for travel from Cairo to Constantinople. In the second half of the 19th century, Jewish merchants migrated to the city only to leave in 1921, when conflict between Zionists and Arabs became unbearable.

During World War II, the British set up many supply posts close to the Lydd railway station and also built an airport, which the Israelis later renamed Ben Gurion Airport. Palestinians still refer to it simply as Matar al-Lydd (Lydd airport).

Lydd was one of the most prosperous Palestinian cities in 1948 when its inhabitants were driven out. The city itself had a population of just over 20,000. During the war, as dozens of communities in the region were "emptied" of their Arab inhabitants by Zionist forces, the refugees came to Lydd. The city's population swelled to 50,000 within a matter of months. Although the UN partition plan allocated Lydd, like Ramleh, to the Arab State in Palestine, Jewish forces took it by force. In June 1948, Operation Dani "cleansed" Lydd of 40,000 citizens within a matter of days. Lydd was Arab no more.

Today, of the city's 60,000 inhabitants some 20 percent are Arab. Of these, only about half are indigenous to the city. The rest are dislocated Bedouins, who were driven out of the Negev by the Israelis. Arabs tend to make up the poorer elements of the community and thus many of the city's young Arabs move elsewhere in search of better job opportunities and a better quality of life.

Lydd's Jewish inhabitants are immigrants or children of immigrants from Arab countries, India, and the Republic of Georgia.

Sites

Baibars Bridge
Two kilometers north of the old city center stands a stone bridge built over a small river. Constructed in 1273, during the reign of the Mamluks, it is one of very few such architectural remnants of that era. An Arabic inscription dates the bridge and mentions Baibars, the ruler of the time. On either side of the inscription is a stone engraving of a leopard crushing a rat. The leopard symbolizes the Mamluks and the rat, the Crusaders. This same engraving is also found over the Lion's Gate in Jerusalem.

Hasuna Soap Factory
Built in the 19th century, the ruins of the Hasuna Soap Factory are an important landmark, because they attest to a time when the Arabs of Lydd ran flourishing industries. Despite its decrepit state, it is among the few remnants of better times of which the city's Arab inhabitants can be proud.

Remains of the Ottoman Khan al-Helou

St. George

Patron saint of Lydd (and England and Portugal), Saint George is claimed as a native son by both Lydd and Cappadocia in Anatolia. It is difficult to prove his place of birth either way, but it is known with some certainty that his mother, at least, was from Lydd. He enlisted in the Roman army and served under the reign of Emperor Diocletian (245–313 CE). According to lore, St. George refused to enforce an anti-Christian edict, was arrested as a result, and died a Christian martyr.

A more famous story involves St. George saving a damsel-in-distress. On the verge of being sacrificed to the dragon that terrorized Lydd, a local girl appealed to George to save her. He slew the dragon, rescued the girl, and became a hero. To give thanks, the local inhabitants all converted to Christianity and the church canonized George.

A third story, popular among Muslims, is that al-Khader (as Islam calls St. George), will defeat all the worlds' demons on the Day of Judgment.

The life of St. George is celebrated on two days in Palestine: April 23 and November 15. For the first, Christians and many Muslims from all over the country congregate in Lydd to celebrate. The November St. George's day, which coincides with the end of the olive-picking season, marks the day of his death and is thus more somber.

Khan al-Helou

This caravansary, despite its decrepit state, is also an effective reminder of the old Lydd: a thriving town with architectural treasures. The Israeli-run municipality has done nothing to renovate, restore, or protect this remnant of Mamluk rule in Palestine. It is one of two Mamluk and Ottoman khans in Lydd's Arab quarter.

Sabil Subakh and Bir Ali Zay Bek

Close to the Baibars Bridge are two relics from the past, Sabil Subakh (fountain of Subakh) and Bir Ali Zay Bek (well of Ali Zay Bek). Both were built to accommodate travelers and postmen who traveled from Gaza to Jerusalem. The Israeli government recently restored these two landmarks dating back to the Mamluk era.

Religious Sites

Church of St. George

The Church of St. George, which encases his tomb, is the most important landmark in Lydd and remains central to the Arab community's consciousness. With its Byzantine apses, Crusader arches, and Islamic columns, this church reflects the layers of Palestine's history better than most existing architectural remnants of the past.

Theodosius, a pilgrim, recounted visiting St. George's tomb in 530, so we know that the tomb, if not the church itself, has existed since then. The church was built to house the tomb. The church was destroyed and then rebuilt by the Crusaders, only to be destroyed again during the second half of the 12th century. The current church was built in 1870 by the Greek Orthodox Community and is richly decorated with Greek icons, candleholders, white marble, and frescos.

Dahmash Mosque

When in the early 20th century Dahmash, a local merchant, gave alms and had a mosque built in his name, little did he know that his shrine would one day be associated with tragedy. On July 10, 1948, some 100 unarmed Palestinians were killed inside the mosque by Israeli forces led by Moshe Dayan. Since then, the name Dahmash has been shorthand for Israeli brutality.

For decades the mosque remained closed, despite petitions from the local faithful to reopen it. On July 12, 1996, almost 48 years after the massacre to the day, the Israeli authorities finally permitted the reopening of the mosque.

Mosque of Omar or al-Khader

This mosque, which lies adjacent to the Church of St. George, is also dedicated to him. Built in 1268, its foundation stones were placed at the edges of a Byzantine church, whose remains the mosque has incorporated. The mosque, Lydd's most frequented, contains a courtyard, a small women's mosque, ablution fountains, and shares public gardens and spaces with the church.

The Mosque of Omar

Flying kites in al-Bireh

24.

Ramallah & al-Bireh

Ramallah of the cypresses and the pine trees. The swinging slopes of the hills, the green that speaks in twenty languages of beauty, our first schools where each one of us sees the other children bigger and stronger. The Teachers' College. The Hashemite. The Friends. Ramallah Secondary. Our guilty glances at the girls from the prep school swinging confidence in their right hands and confusion in their left and dazzling our minds when they look at us while pretending not to.

—This is Ramallah, *Murid Barghouti; translated by Ahdaf Soueif, 20th century*

Throughout history Ramallah was considered a passageway to cities in the north like Nablus, Nazareth, and Damascus. But today Ramallah and its twin city, al-Bireh, is the in place to be. They are home to the headquarters of the PNA, a cultural hub for intellectuals, and a base for civil rights activists. The city offers travelers a variety of outdoor cafes, garden restaurants, and even a few nightclubs. For the culturally minded, there are also many artistic hideaways and the Birzeit University. Many public institutions, foreign missions, radio stations, newspapers, and TV networks also have their headquarters in Ramallah.

Breezy summer evenings, women in sleeveless dresses, cultural centers, cinemas, and delicious mezze—all this is Ramallah. Though very few historic and archeological sites can be seen in the cities, many lie close by in the hilly villages and countryside. On scenic hikes you can inspect Iron Age burial sites, remains of Crusader castles, and Islamic sanctuaries.

St. Paul is believed to have traveled from Jerusalem to Damascus by way of Ramallah, but only parts of the road leading to the city are anywhere as rickety as the route the apostle took some 2,000 years ago. Omar al-Khattab in the 7th century and Saladin in the 12th took the same route. Yasir Arafat made Ramallah one of his headquarters after the 1993 Oslo Accords promised Palestinians self-rule. Most of the road was paved after the Accords, but is now full of so many potholes that biking is impossible.

The road from Ramallah to Jerusalem (which runs parallel to the old Roman route from Jerusalem to Nazareth that Jesus traveled) brings travelers to Qalandia checkpoint, the location of both a refugee camp and the Ramallah Wall. At the beginning of the al-Aqsa intifada, the Israeli army put up a roadblock, which turned into a military checkpoint, reinforced in 2004 by the Wall.

History of Ramallah

An Aramaic and Arabic word, Ramallah means God's Hill—and indeed both Ramallah and al-Bireh extend over several hills, about 872 meters (2,861 ft) above sea level. A number of prehistoric sites and Bronze Age tombs have been found in and around the city indicating that it was inhabited as early as 3000 BCE. Ras al-Tahuna (head of the mill), within Ramallah city boundaries, has been inhabited intermittently from the Chalcolithic era until the present day.

Despite remnants of Byzantine structures beneath Crusader remains, Ramallah as such does not appear to have been a location of note for many centuries; neither the pre-Christian nor Christian historians before 640 CE, nor the Muslim chroniclers after mention it in their histories.

In western Ramallah, however, in what is now the neighborhood of al-Tireh, Bronze Age burial sites indicate agrarian communities existed in the vicinity. Several Iron Age remains have been unearthed, including tombs chiseled into rock at Khallat al-Adas and remains of clay vessels and water pools dating back to 1200 BCE at Ein Abu al-Karzam. Some historians believe that al-Tireh was the site where the remains of St. Steven, the martyr, were found in 415 CE. The contemporary Greek Orthodox Church in Ramallah (built in 1852) is allegedly built in part from stones of a Byzantine church in the al-Tireh area.

Though French Crusaders built a stronghold at what they called "Ramelie" in the 12th century (remains of a tower in al-Tireh are all that mark the Crusader period), neither Saladin nor the Mamluks appear to have left any mark on Ramallah, and the city's modern

The Ramallah Municipal Gardens

history really begins with the Ottomans in 1520. With the coming of the Ottomans, Ramallah became, like many places in Palestine, a safe haven for persecuted and migrant communities.

According to local lore, a tribal confederation and several of its allies are said to have crossed the Jordan River to Palestine in search of a better life. Along with this Orthodox Christian clan of Rashid al-Haddad came the tribe of Hussein Tanash, their Muslim allies. Together they had migrated from the southern Trans-Jordanian governorate of Karak. The Tanash clan settled and intermarried with the Muslims of al-Bireh, known as the Ghazawneh, and then helped sell land to the al-Haddad clan, who made their home in adjacent Ramallah.

For the next 400 years Ramallah, was the exclusive domain of al-Haddad and his descendants. They built on a strong sense of community and fought alongside their al-Bireh allies whenever outsiders threatened their hegemony. Though many worked as traders, they appear to have been primarily farmers. In the municipality web site (www.ramallah-city.org) the "original" inhabitants of Ramallah are named as al-Haddad clan. In a country such as Palestine, where burial sites dating back to the Bronze Age can be found on almost every hill, deciding who was there first is usually tenuous at best.

During a brief pause from Ottoman rule in the early 19th century the Albanian ruler of Egypt and Palestine, Ibrahim Pasha, allowed Europeans (to a lesser degree Americans) and their missionaries to take an active role in trade, commerce, and cultural life. It was a trend the Ottomans could not stop, even after their return to rule, so by the mid-19th century, many church representatives and missionaries lived in the area, and Catholic and Protestant church institutions such as schools and hospitals proliferated. Until this time, education in Ramallah had been confined to parish boys whose parents were members of the Greek Orthodox Church. They were taught Arabic and Greek. The Sisters of St. Joseph opened Ramallah's first girls' school in 1873 and by 1889, the Quakers had followed, with the first boarding school for girls. This school became a landmark for Ramallah and provided schooling for much of the Palestinian intelligentsia for generations. In fact, as the ascendancy of the West became clear, styles, language, and education changed in Palestine to accommodate the new status quo.

As the Ottomans continued to fight wars in Europe, they drafted their Arab subjects to fight for the empire's survival. Many men left their homeland to avoid fighting for an empire they didn't consider theirs, and sought prosperity elsewhere. In Ramallah as across Palestine, most did not leave forever; they often came back to marry and make a home.

Although some large homes were built as the Ottoman era came to an end, it was not until the 1920s and the beginning of the British Mandate that people built two-story houses in Ramallah. Many homes had enclosed gardens with beautiful stone and masonry work, which were built, like the Jerusalem homes, by stonemasons from the Bethlehem district. Few maintained the inner courtyard that symbolized classical Arab architecture.

The 1920s were a time of great economic and social development. Money from relatives in America together with employment prospects under the British Mandate government created a new Ramallah elite. Many families moved from the village center to the lands around it, creating spacious residential compounds and villas. Ramallah grew, particularly along the main roads and in the direction of al-Bireh, bringing the two geographically closer.

During the next couple decades, the empty houses in Ramallah's old village center were rented out to migrant families from Hebron who were hired to work for the mandate government. To this day many of the people living in the older houses in this area are originally from around Hebron.

After the Nakba, thousands of refugees and displaced peoples flooded Ramallah. In the subsequent building boom, many remnants of the Byzantine, Crusader, and early Ottoman era became part of the city's infrastructure. Under Jordanian administration (1949–1967) Ramallah became both a refuge and a center for learning, integrating waves of urban and rural refugees from areas such as Jaffa, Lydd, and Ramleh. After the 1967 war, Ramallah became one of the hubs of resistance against the Israeli occupation. It went from being a town to a small city (pop. 80,000 today).

During the first intifada, the core group that became spokespeople for the Palestinians, (and later in Madrid and Washington) was made up of mostly Ramallah-based academics. Not surprisingly, the PLO chose Ramallah as its West Bank headquarters for the parliament and its bureaucrats and administrators. Very modest offices were set up for the president in the former compound of the Israeli occupation forces on Irsal Street.

During the al-Aqsa intifada, the Israel air force bombarded Ramallah with air-to-surface missiles on October 12, 2000 for the first time, after two Israeli soldiers were killed in the city. The presidential compound of Yasir Arafat became a local and international tourist site after it was bombed on several occasions and television pictures of Arafat under siege in his room by candle-light went around the world. Yet the rubble-filled compound remained the beleaguered Arafat's headquarters until he was flown to a hospital in France where he died in November 2004.

Visiting Ramallah

Abraham's Mausoleum (Maqam Abuna Ibrahim al-Khalil)
Located in the middle of town, this one room with its plastered walls and mosaic floor, became a mausoleum and official place of worship during Mamluk rule. (The structure was probably originally Byzantine, with some Crusader period remnants.) As late as the mid-16th century, the Ghazawneh clan of al-Bireh used to make offerings of candles and later oil lamps and ask for the blessing of the patriarch Abraham. The Haddadin adopted the tradition and continued it for generations. When visiting the mausoleum in 1904, the American historian Elihu Grant found 89 oil lamps inside the one-room structure.

Byzantine Watch Tower

Sometimes known as the Crusader Tower, this once served as a watchtower for agricultural communities. The remnants, most likely Byzantine in origin, are located in the Shakara neighborhood. As elsewhere, the Crusaders (and those who came in their wake) added on and renovated, building onto and over existing foundations.

Ein Misbah Tombs

In 1927, archeologists uncovered a tomb in the valley of Ein Misbah. The unearthed caskets, which were made of lead and engraved with both Christian and Pagan symbols, dated to the 3rd century. They now reside in the Jerusalem Museum.

Ramallah Cultural Palace

The largest and most modern in the region, the palace, built by the UNDP with funds from the people of Japan and operated by the Ramallah Municipality, opened its doors in the summer of 2004. It houses a state-of-the-art auditorium with seating for over 700 and is specifically designed to enhance the presentation and expand the possibilities of Palestinian artists, whether their concentration is dance, music, or visual art

Arafat's Tomb

Inside the presidential compound known as the Muqatia, previously British, Jordanian, and Israeli police and army headquarters, lies the temporary tomb of Yasir Arafat. Since his death in November 2004, the site has become something akin to a pilgrimage site and visitors, both local and international, come to visit his now glass-encased grave.

Al-Bireh

Ramallah's twin city, al-Bireh, is believed to have been inhabited as early as 3500 BCE, always with a variant of its current name: in the Canaanite language, Beroth (wells), and in Roman times, Bera.

Known as a resting place for trade caravans moving from Jerusalem to Nablus and the Galilee, al-Bireh was also mentioned as a stop-over for the biblical Joseph and Mary on their way back to Jerusalem from Nazareth. Al-Bireh was inhabited by Aramaic-speaking nomads before 640 CE.

The remains of the Church of the Holy Family, built by the Crusaders in 1146, are still evident in the town center. Some experts contend that the church was built on top of an older Byzantine site.

Ruqab Street, Ramallah

The Crusader church was destroyed during the wars. In 1225, the Muslim historian Yakut wrote, "It was laid in ruins by Saladin— as I myself have seen—when he took it from the Franks."

Adjacent to the church was the Omari Mosque, built in 1195 by Assad ibn Malik. Unfortunately it was destroyed in 1995 by those wishing to build a new mosque (also called the Omari Mosque). The remains of the church await restoration; the old mosque is lost forever.

Emigrants & Refugees

At the turn of the century, many Ramallah and subsequently al-Bireh men emigrated to the United States and became merchants. The missionary activities in Ramallah in particular of Protestant churches from the Americas can be linked directly to the onset of emigration from Ramallah and al-Bireh.

These men sent earnings back home to their families and most

returned to find brides. Although many of the brides, especially the Muslims, did not initially join their husbands, today almost 90 percent of the original Ramallah clans and some 70 percent of those of al-Bireh live in the United States.

If the towns lost population to the United States before 1948, by 1953 the population had doubled. Although emigration followed every political disaster that beset the Palestinians, Ramallah and al-Bireh continued to grow, as Palestinians from the diaspora, the villages, and even Arab Jerusalem continue to flock to the cosmopolitan and secular twin cities.

For the most part, al-Bireh is very proud of the fact that liquor sales are banned and that real estate is not sold to "outsiders." It has produced at least two feisty politicians. The former mayor, Abdul Saleh Jawad, was deported for his patriotic opinions in 1973 and only allowed to return twenty years later. Samira Khalil challenged Arafat in the 1996 presidential race, and although some may claim it was a bogus effort, many Birawis say she really had a lot more support than the 13 percent of the vote that showed up on the official tally.

Visiting al-Bireh

By far the most important archeological site to visit in al-Bireh is **Tel al-Nasbah**, on the southern edge of town. First excavated in 1897, it held remains from the Bronze Age, including burial chambers and living quarters. During the Iron Age, both the Hebrews and the Babylonians appear to have built small capitals in Tel al-Nasbah. Sections of a city wall with two towers were found. Exceptionally well preserved 9th-century BCE city gates once marked by an open square. Persian, Hellenistic, Roman, and Byzantine potsherds and coins were all found at Tel al-Nasbah. During the Roman period the Tel was probably an agrarian estate. The floor of a Byzantine church was discovered next to the western cemetery, and an Ottoman khan stands at the southern site of the tel. It is widely believed that inhabitants during the Roman era moved to nearby Khirbet Shuekeh, where archeological remains indicate more or less continuous human settlement until the 16th century CE.

Khirbet Radana is the Bronze and Iron Age site in the al-Bireh area, north of the city limits. Home to farming and hunting communities in the Bronze Age, there is also evidence of Iron Age settlements toward the end of the 13th century BCE.

Campaign rally in al-Bireh

Near Ramallah and al-Bireh

Aboud

Aboud, a renowned place of Christian pilgrimage, was once home to seven churches. Today only the Byzantine Church of the Virgin Mary, believed to have been built in the 4th century, still exists. It was restored and renovated by the Crusaders in the 11th century; thereafter it was neglected until Aboud came under PNA rule. The church was restored and renovated and its mosaic floors uncovered in 1997. The confines of the village contain remains of other Byzantine churches and monasteries.

Most contemporary Aboudis are Muslim. Most came from the cities where expatriate Aboudis had worked, namely in Jaffa and Lydd. Today the local population is 2,500, and some 4,000 natives of Aboud live in the diaspora.

Attara

Located north of Birzeit, this one-time Byzantine settlement is known in Palestinian lore as home of the shrine of Shaykh al-Qatrawani. Its name derives from the Canaanite "A'tarout" (crowns), but the only potsherds found indicate habitation during the Iron Age, Byzantine period, and in the Middle Ages.

Beitin

Beitin means "House of God" in Aramaic. Archeological finds dating back to the Chalcolithic Period include flint tools, pottery, and animal bones. Canaanite tombs from the Late Bronze Period and petrified olives attest to continuous inhabitation. During the Iron Age, an Israelite settlement replaced that of the Canaanites; apparently they traded incense with South Arabia.

Byzantines built a church and monastery here that the Crusaders turned into their stronghold, and Saladin into a mosque. Toward the end of the Ottoman era (1892) the mosque became an all-women's mosque.

Beitounia

This village, now largely part of Ramallah, is the site of the biblical Beth-aven. Remains of buildings, pools, and medieval mosaic fragments are found at Khirbet Bir al-Dawali. Here remains of structures are scattered over the place, including a tower, pool, and water cisterns. Nearby Khirbet al-Mayta has remains of a church,

Top: Students at Birzeit University
Bottom: Portrait artist Waleed Ayoub

columns, ruins of several buildings, and rock-carved tombs. West of Beitounia, Khirbet al-Ras contains ruins from an early Arab period.

Birzeit

The town of Birzeit (pop. 10,000) is a 10-minute car ride from Ramallah's Irsal Road. If the Israeli army is around, blocking normal traffic, it takes longer. Birzeit has been inhabited for thousands of years, the center of an agricultural community, but today its claim to fame is its university. **Birzeit University** sprung from humble origins in the old town of Birzeit, where in the 1920s a woman named Nabiha Nasir established a school in her family home. Today it is the most famous university in Palestine with both undergraduate and graduate programs. The university offers courses for international students in Arabic and related social sciences through a summer course and two three-month semesters. A number of interesting academic institutions are affiliated with the university: the archeological showroom in the former Institute of Archeology, a music conservatory, a law institute, a women's studies center, a media center, and institutions documenting health conditions.

Inhabited since Hellenistic times, Birzeit lies on the old Roman road connecting Jifna with Ras el-'Ain. It has been identified with the Roman settlement of Birzetho (2nd century BCE). Archeological findings indicate that in both the Iron Age and Byzantine times, wine was the region's main product. Later, olive oil took over.

Locals are mostly descendants of Christian Arab tribes who had settled and lived at Khirbet Birzeit until the beginning of the Ottoman era and then established the town. In the late 19th century a large number of the local population converted from Greek Orthodoxy to Catholicism due to an active Roman Catholic missionary presence, which opened schools and provided medical care. Anglican missionaries, too, helped one of the local families found a school based on missionary ideals.

Despite Birzeit's reputation as a center of learning, many townspeople have migrated to Jordan and the Unites States because of the unstable life created by the 20th century wars with the Israelis. Some of the émigrés set up a web site to keep in touch and inform the world about their town: www.birzeitsociety.org.

Deir Dibwan (al-Tell)

Northeast of al-Bireh stands the Canaanite site of al-Tell. Excavated in 1933–1935, al-Tell was a town of a considerable size in the Early Bronze Period. A massive defensive wall with a huge rounded tower encased a religious sanctuary. Egyptian influence on Canaanite religious and burial practices in the Early Bronze Age (2613–2494 BC) is evident. Archeologists discovered an alter with plaster and the remains of animal bones, benches on which the offerings were laid out, and an ivory-handled knife.

Destroyed by nomads toward the end of the Early Bronze Age, the site was resettled in the early Iron Age. Al-Tell is part of the Palestinian village of Deir Dibwan, a wealthy town kept afloat by its large expatriate community, most of whom live in the United States and come to visit only in the summer.

Deir Ghassaneh

As the capital of the Baraghitha clan, this Throne Village belonged to the larger tribal affiliate of Beni Zeid, who were tax collectors in some 50 villages until the 19th century. Today it is considered one of the most beautiful of Palestine's villages.

Ein Sinia

This village is home to the **Museum of Memory**, which is dedicated to the 1948 war and the time preceding it. It is housed in the village's most famous family home, which was built in about 1815. In the 1930s and 1940s the house was used by the Palestinian resistance, al-Jihad al-Muqaddas, one of whose leaders was Abdul Qader al-Husseini (1907–1948), to hide and rest. Those fighting the British and the Zionist colonizers could depend on finding food supplies here, as well as secret passages for hiding people and weapons.

Early in the century, a Jewish family from Odessa called the Shartouks became tenant farmers and rented space from Ein Sinia residents. Years later, one of the many Shartouk children became known as Moshe Sharett, the second prime minister of Israel.

Jifna

During Hellenistic and Roman times, Jifna was a regional capital. Today it is home to barely a thousand people. In history books it is known as the ancient Gophna of Josephus. The fourth Roman legion, which ruled Roman Palestine, was based here. Today it is known for its chicken restaurants, relaxing atmosphere, traditional village architecture, and apricot festival.

Kufr Aqab

Kufr Aqab was built on top of the Canaanite village of Ataroth.

Khirbet Attara, just west of Kufr Aqab, has remains of ancient walls, tombs, and a press with a mosaic floor.

Rafat

Rafat, an archaeological site with rock-cut tombs and remains of ancient building structures, is believed to be the location of the Canaanite village of Yerfe'el. Currently a large swath of the village is owned by the Latin Patriarchate, which has built a monastery here.

Ras Karkar

Built on a hill during Ottoman times, Ras Karkar is one of the Throne Villages. An 18th-century Ottoman official, Ibn Samhan, built a castle-shaped home here. Potsherds from Hellenistic, Mamluk and the Early Ottoman era have been found around the castle.

Al-Taybeh

First settled and built by Canaanites (2900–2200 BCE) who named it Ufra (deer), al-Taybeh is the spot where Jesus is believed to have rested on his way to Jericho when fleeing his persecutors, the Sanhedrin.

In the 4th century CE, the Byzantines built the Church of St. George in the village; eight centuries later, the Crusaders built a castle, Baubariya. Saladin gave the town its name in the 12th century after he found the local orthodox Christians to be generous and kind—"*taybeen*" means "kind" in Arabic. The village has five churches and its 1,300 residents are still largely Christian. The expatriate community of al-Taybeh, which numbers some 3,700, lives mostly in San Francisco.

In 1770 the Greek Orthodox Church built the first village school. Today the school library is named in honor of a village martyr, a young boy named Hanna Muqbal who was killed by the Israeli occupation forces.

A museum in the Greek Orthodox Church has some interesting artifacts of archeological and other historical finds from the village. An Ottoman-style house, restored in 1974 and called the Palestinian Old House, displays scenes from peasant life in Ottoman Palestine, which were similar to conditions at the times of Jesus.

Today al-Taybeh is known for its fine agricultural produce, including olives, grapes, and figs. A local hotel allows those wishing to experience rural life to stay overnight. Al-Taybeh is also home to the first Palestinian beer manufacturer, which started operating in 1994. To find out about their regular, light, or dark **Taybeh Beer**, go to www.taybehbeer.com.

Refugee Camps

Al-Am'ari Camp

Al-Am'ari camp was established in 1949 on 23 acres within the municipal boundaries of al-Bireh, on property belonging to the al-Am'ari family (they leased their property to the United Nations for 99 years). At the time of its establishment it was on the periphery of the town, but the cities have grown so that it is now close to the center of both al-Bireh and Ramallah.

The registered population of the camp is about 7,500, mostly from (or descendents of refugees from) 40 Palestinian villages in the Lydd (Beit Nabalah, Na'an'a, Sadoun Janzeh), Ramleh, and Jaffa (Beit Dajan, Deir Tarif, Abu Shousha) regions.

By 1957, all tents in the camp had been replaced with cement block shelters, with families with 1–5 members given a 3x3-meter housing unit, and those with 6 members or more given two adjacent units. The camp's geographical boundaries have remained the same, though the camp's population has increased five-fold since its establishment. Thus al-Am'ari suffers from severe overcrowding, and all the poor sewage and water networks and vertical construction that entails.

After the Israeli occupation of the West Bank in 1967, al-Am'ari became known as a hotbed for political activism and resistance activity (particularly of the Fateh party). During the first intifada, al-Am'ari was famous for its resistance to the Israeli occupation forces, which closed off the camp with a 5-meter fence and sealed off its entrances with concrete filled barrels. The large green-framed window apartment building at the entrance to the camp on the Jerusalem–Nablus Road used to have an Israeli army military post on the roof with snipers.

Following the redeployment of the Israeli army in 1995, the camp came under PNA control (Area A). Yet like other refugee camps used to operating more autonomously, the shift to PNA rule was not smooth. The camp gained a reputation as being somewhat "rogue" and "uncontrollable."

Al-Am'ari has active social committees operational within the camp boundaries. Both the youth activities center and the women's center are particularly well run. Furthermore, the camp's football team won the Palestine football championship several times and represents Palestine in regional and international competitions. An Am'ari youth, Lu'ai Husni, is the Palestinian national goal keeper who earned legendary status when the national team acquired semi-final berth in the 2000 Arab Cup.

Deir Ammar Camp

Deir Ammar camp is the smallest of Ramallah's three officially recognized refugee camps. It was established in 1949 on 40 acres of land. Most Deir Ammar residents are refugees from the destroyed villages of Beit Nabala, Deir Tarif, Jimzou (Lydd), Abu al-Fadhel (Ramleh), Sakiyeh, and Yazour (Jaffa).

Deir Ammar camp is home to approximately 2,000 people. Its bucolic and relaxed setting and relatively small population makes Deir Ammar camp feel less like a ghetto than most urban refugee camps. Because of its proximity to the Green Line, most of the men have traditionally worked as laborers in Israel, with a small minority working locally for UNRWA or the PNA. Though technically within Area B (Palestinian civil control, Israeli military and security control), neither the camp nor the adjacent villages receive many services from the PNA. Unlike more urban refugee camps, Deir Ammar camp has a fairly harmonious relationship with the neighboring villages, Deir Ammar and Jammal. Children from the camp attend some village schools, and vice versa.

Deir Ammar Camp and the surrounding villages have both the benefits and the misfortunes of being on the periphery: the slower pace and greater space on the one hand, not receiving basic services such as electricity (in the early 1980s) and water networks (1986) on the other. Camp residents take pride in the fact that many of their rank-and-file have become successful businessmen, some even dominating the local trading scene in Ramallah. The camp itself, however, has not benefited from these successes, since more prosperous camp residents tend to move out of the camp.

Jalazone Camp

Jalazone camp was established in 1949 on 63 acres of a rocky but lush hillside seven kilometers north of Ramallah on land leased by UNRWA for 99 years. Most camp residents originate from 36 villages primarily in the Lydd–Ramleh vicinity (Khayriyeh, Annabeh, Abbasiyeh) while a minority come from the North (Tiberias, Haifa, Sabarin, Um Zeinat) and from Hebron (al-Dawaymeh).

Established on land belonging to the nearby village of Jifna, and to a lesser extent to the lands belonging to the village of Durra al-Qarre', the name Jalazone has a variety of explanations attached to it. Perhaps it comes from "*halazone*" (snail), in honor of the plentitude of garden snails in the region. Or, the camp was founded in a "zone" replete with "*jalaz*" (bountiful springs). According to the original refugees, tens of springs were in the camp vicinity. Today, many have dried up or been polluted by the lack of a sufficient sewage system.

Summer dance under the pines, Ramallah

Many camp residents initially lived in the village of Birzeit after their expulsion from their villages. Those that did not move to Jalazone, but remained in Birzeit, became residents of the small, less recognized refugee camp in that village.

Despite the openness of the surrounding land, the camp itself cannot expand horizontally. Overcrowding and hygiene-related issues— wastewater from the camp flowing into neighboring fields, for example—have created a souring of relations with neighboring villages and communities. Though most of the issues of contention between the camp and the village are beyond the control of both, Jalazone problem's highlight the difficulties refugee communities experience as a result of living an extended period of time with an uncertain future, always subject to the hospitality of the communities where they are founded, all the time being politically, socially, and developmentally marginalized.

Like other camps on the vanguard of national political activity (Balata, Dheisheh, and Jabalia) the start of the first intifada was only the official beginning for what had been daily confrontations with the Israeli occupation and settlers for some time. The camp is infamous for the amount of days it spent under curfew (42 consecutive days in one session in 1989), as well as house demolitions by the occupation forces (12).

After the signing of the Oslo Accords in 1993, Jalazone was allocated to Area C, full Israeli military occupation. A high fence initially built to stop camp youth from throwing stones at settler cars still surrounds the camp, though a by-pass road built for settlers allows them to avoid the camp altogether. Military jeeps also travel the road, occasionally to raid the camp.

25.

Jericho (Areeha)

*The water of Jericho is held to be the lightest and best in all of Islam.
Bananas are plentiful, also dates and flowers of fragrant odor.*

—al-Maqdisi, *Arab historian from Palestine,* b. 946

The longest continually inhabited city in the world, Jericho has been home to human beings for 10,000 years, when the Natufians, at the very beginning of agriculture, moved from west of Ramallah and settled here. Its early name, Yareah (moon), perhaps came from the clarity of its skies or the Canaanites' extensive moon worship. Another theory has it that the name came from "*reeha*" (fragrance), for the abundant jasmine and nerolia. In any case, archeologists have unearthed the remains of some twenty successive human settlements dating back to at least 8000 BCE in and around this sleepy Palestinian town, one of the world's greatest archeological sites.

Here the very first nomadic hunter societies began to settle into a more sedentary life. Village settlements almost everywhere else, with the exception of outposts in what is contemporary Syria, are 2,000 years younger. The Pyramids were built 4,000 years after the first settlements in Jericho. Around 4500 BCE—after human habitation of already more than three thousand years—there was a major destruction of unknown origin (possibly an earthquake) that rendered the town temporarily uninhabitable. A revival took place by 3500 BCE, when it was inhabited by a community of potters, probably settled nomads.

By 3000 BCE, the city of Tel al-Sultan was expanded or rebuilt here. Discovered in the streets and courtyards of the Aqabat Jaber refugee camp, after the Israelis drove out the refugees in the 1967 war,

Mosaic school, Jericho

Bedouin shepherd with Nabi Musa in the background

the cemeteries contained a series of graves with 113 skulls arranged around a tomb's chamber. As was apparently customary in the region at the time, the bodies of the dead were placed in the open to decompose and were then cremated. The Jericho cemetery provided the first known physical evidence of this practice.

Written documents of this time do not exist; although it does not mention Jericho by name, the closest possibility is the Epic of Gilgamesh, written on tablets around 2000 BCE, some 700 years after King Gilgamesh himself passed the Dead Sea and saw a walled city. In this Akkadian epic, the hero travels across the "Sea of the Waters of Death" and prays to Sin, the Moon God. He is taken in by a veiled woman named Siduri, a wine-maker, who tells what is happening in the city. Some 1000 years later, in 1186 BCE, the Hebrews recounted a similar story, in which their spies contact the so-called "harlot" Rabab, who lives at the edge of the city and offers them lodgings. She informs them of events in Jericho, and when they destroy the city and its inhabitants, they spare only her. Subsequently Ajloun the King of Moab (southern Jordan), expelled the Israelites and declared Jericho his capital. Archeological finds, however, can find no evidence of the Israelite destruction of Jericho.

Later, during Roman rule (63 BCE–324 CE), Mark Antony gave the city as a present to his beloved Cleopatra. After her suicide it reverted to Augustus Caesar, who himself gave it to Herod. From this time, Jericho became a center of Christianity, and continued to be an important city throughout the Byzantine Period.

With the coming of Islam in the 7th century came the development of irrigated agriculture, which earned Jericho the name "City of Palms." At this time Qasr Hisham was built, one of the most important Umayyad monuments in all Palestine.

The Jerusalemite chronicler al-Maqdisi reports that 10th-century Jericho grew plentiful palms, indigo, bananas, and dates. In his brief description, he gives the impression of prosperity and calm. Strangely, neither he nor subsequent Muslim travelers note Hisham's Palace or Herod's building projects, as if they did not exist.

The remains of Hisham's Palace

Not a lot of information is available on the Jericho of the Mamluk era. And toward the end of the Ottoman Empire, in Jericho as elsewhere throughout Palestine, most of the landowners were feudal families who acted as tax collectors for Istanbul, enriching themselves and impoverishing the local population.

The 20th Century

Britain's archeological community had a field day once Palestine and Iraq came under British occupation. For the diggers working at Tel al-Sultan or Hisham's Palace, Jericho became a favorite hang-out during the pleasant winter months.

The socio-economic make-up of Jericho changed only a little during this time. The wealthy from Hebron who had settled in Jericho and a few investors from the Jordanian city of Salt joined wealthy Jerusalemites in acquiring land from the locals at low prices. Most of the Jericho people thus continued to be landless peasants who had sold their properties to tax collectors. They continued to be dependent on semi-feudal landlords for work.

Hashemite rule (1949–1967) saw an improvement in the status quo of the population. Garden restaurants opened during the winter months and thousands of Arabs and Jordanians as well as West Bankers flocked to Jericho to spend their weekends enjoying the warm weather and pleasant atmosphere. Those who could afford to bought property, and locals found employment as waiters, tour guides, and chauffeurs. Some locals managed to benefit from the newly established UN schools for refugees, whose directors often shut their eyes to the inclusion of poor (but non-refugee) students in their classrooms. The tourists, the investors, the refugees, and the UN created a bustling atmosphere in a previously quiet town.

According to the Israeli occupation forces, Jericho was a pleasant place to occupy during the formal occupation (1967–1994). Locals say that as long as the Israelis did not confiscate their land, which they did only in relatively small parcels here, the locals would wait out the duration of yet another foreign presence in their land until better days came. Locals catered to the needs of tourists and waited for the occupation to end.

According to Oslo, Gaza and Jericho were to be the first cities to come back to Arab rule under the leadership of the PLO. Hotels were packed and journalists were renting rooms in private homes when PLO chief Arafat arrived in Jericho. Pomp and fanfare accompanied the event, which carried hope for better days. Even the Orthodox Jewish group Naturei Karta showed up to ask Arafat for a ministry in his new government.

Under Palestinian rule Jericho continues to be an agricultural base, famous for its citrus trees, banana plantations, dates, flowers, and winter vegetables. With development aid, tourist attractions have been upgraded and expanded. The local population got a dance school and football fields, and concerts for up to 10,000 people take place in this winter resort. The high or low point, depending on who you ask, was the building of Palestine's first casino. Attracting an almost exclusively Israeli clientele, the casino and its adjacent five-star hotel gave the local economy an enormous boost.

For all this, Jericho, with its population of just over 30,000, is really no more than a large town. Saeb Erekat, one of the chief peace negotiators and a senior cabinet minister, is Jericho's only representative in the Palestinian Legislative Council.

Many of today's citizens of Jericho are descendents of migrants from the Hebron region or refugees from the Arab–Israeli wars. Others are descendents of African Muslim pilgrims or farm hands who came to grow sugar during the Umayyad period. Today many of these African-Palestinians work in the citrus and cotton industries. Palestinian society has always been a mix of races, and the African roots of the society are the most strongly felt in Jericho.

In 1983 the Hollywood film *Hanna K*, starring Palestinian actor Muhammad Bakri and the American actress Jill Clayburgh, was partly filmed in the Aqabat Jaber camp. The story is about the life of a Palestinian refugee trying to return to his family home.

The Road to Jericho

The road to Jericho begins in Jerusalem and winds past the Mount of Olives, the Garden of Gethsemane, and the ancient villages of Silwan, Abu Dis, and Bethany on its way to the Jordan Valley. Known in Arabic as Barriat al-Quds (Jerusalem wilderness), the road is the historical route traveled for centuries by the Bedouins of the region's Ka'abna tribes. Today their movement has been largely curtailed, partly due to the building of Israeli settlements. Along with the Jahhalin tribe, who were forcibly resettled from the Negev in the 1950s, the Ka'abna has been confined to settlements of tin shacks. Maale Adumim, the largest of all the illegal Israeli settlements in the Jerusalem area, perches on the mountains here, a giant city looking down over the villages and camps of Arabs. Built on land mostly belonging to the village of Abu Dis, the Israelis have pledged never to withdraw from this settlement.

About six kilometers past Bethany is an Ottoman khan, the Good Samaritan Inn (Khan Ahmar), which commemorates the Biblical story. The khan was once a prominent meeting place for travelers, who refreshed themselves and spent the night. A nomadic guardsman who lives on site gives tours of the place. Across the street from the inn stand the remains of the 5th-century St. Euthymius Church. All of this is part of Israel, and the government has given money for the inn's renovation.

Descending into the Wadi al-Rummaneh (valley of pome-granates), turn left to reach Wadi al-Qilt and the Monastery of St. George. Wadi al-Qilt is a long valley that originates in Ein Fawwar (south of the village of Anata) and empties into the Jordan River. It is fed by the springs of Ein Fara, Ein Fawwar, and Ein Qilt. When Herod needed water to supply his winter palace and garden in Jericho, the Romans built the first aqueduct from Ein Fawwar to Wadi al-Qilt. In contemporary times, under Jordanian rule, a new aqueduct was built along the same route. Because of the availability of water, visitors, pilgrims and would-be conquerors have used the valley as a route to Jerusalem, Damascus, and even far-away Baghdad.

During the Byzantine era monks and hermits lived in caves and shelters along this very route and ultimately built a *laura* (spiritual retreat where liturgy is taught). The *laura* was transformed into a monastery by John of Thebes (420 CE) who had the Monastery of St. George (Deir Mar Jiryis) built next to the caves used by the world-famous hermits, Prono, Elias, Einan, and Zenon. In the 6th century, St. George of Choziba gave the monastery his name. Reconstructed in 1179 under the patronage of the Byzantine Emperor Manuel Comnenus (1143–1180), the Arabic and Greek inscription above the old entrance attests to the strength of Arab Christendom.

The caves have two other famous legends attached to them. One is that Elijah hid here on the way to Sinai after he had slain the gods of Baal. He was being pursued by Jezebel, the Phoenician noblewoman and defender of the area's polytheistic beliefs and deities. The other legend involves St. Joachim, father of the Virgin Mary, who apparently was informed of his previously barren daughter's pregnancy while meditating in these caves.

The monastery remained a mecca for reclusive clergy until 1878 when reconstruction work took place again. Today the monastery contains 32 rooms for monks and 4 beds for visitors. What is said to be the skull of St. George, along with bones of at least 14 Christian martyrs are on display inside the church. The monastery contains three separate churches: the Church of the Holy Virgin, with a mosaic floor containing classical Byzantine motifs and wall adornments from the 19th and 20th century; the Church of St. John of Thebes and St. George Choziba, dedicated to the two earliest patron saints and with a mosaic floor dating back to the 5th–6th centuries; and the Church of St. Elias, which is built into stone, its sanctuary a cave used as a safe-haven and passage during times of persecution. A narrow tunnel leads to the summit of the mountain.

Sites

Ein al-Sultan (Spring of Elisha)
This important water source near the hill of Tel al-Sultan was undoubtedly one of the reasons the hunter-gatherer society first settled in the Jericho region. According to local lore, one of the kings of Jerusalem had his eyes poked out here by the Babylonians—thus the Arab name, "Sultan's eye." The Bible tells of the prophet Elisha

healing the polluted water of the spring at the request of people of Jericho. This spring still provides an important water source for the people of Jericho and their farmlands.

Sugar Mills
Jericho's sugar mills (Tawahin al-Sukkar) date back to the prosperous reign of the Umayyads. Later, the Crusaders restored them and exported Jericho's sugar to Europe.

Still visible are the remains of the aqueduct that brought water from Ein Duyuk to the mills and the pottery workshop. This site is important to understand the economic and social continuity of Jericho.

Synagogue
Not far from the Ein al-Sultan, in a small Arab house in a grove of trees, is a beautiful mosaic floor from a 5th- or 6th-century synagogue. It features a picture of candelabrum.

Tel Abu Alayiq (Herodian Winter Palace)
This elevated spot has been home to palaces during several historical periods. Potsherds dating from 4500 to 3100 BCE provide evidence of continual human habitation here. This part of Jericho appears to have been built after the natural disaster hit nearby Tel al-Sultan.

The Hellenistic era saw the construction of what are known as twin palaces. Johannes Hyrcanus (134–104 BCE) built the first; Alexander Jannaeus (103–67 BCE) built the larger of the two complexes. Swimming pools were central to both of the complexes. The domestic areas of both palaces included bathhouses, staircases, storerooms, and living rooms decorated with frescos.

The Roman era witnessed the building of three Herodian palaces between 33–25 BCE. The first, a large rectangular building, followed Roman building standards. The second, with its courtyard surrounded by rooms on three sides, departed from the Roman style (though it did have a Roman bathhouse, a stepped pool, and a caldarium). A large garden and two swimming pools surrounded the palace.

After Cleopatra's five-year rule had ended, Herod regained absolute rule in 31 BCE and used one of the palace pools to drown his brother-in-law and challenger Aristobulus III.

The third palace was built with hard mud brick made from clay mixed with sand, because it had become clear that the climate in Jericho was not suited for Rome's building materials. Only the traditional Roman baths were built in the Roman style. Many of the impressive remains, including decorated walls, pools, bathhouses, halls, and aqueducts, can still be seen today at this archaeological site.

Herod spent the end of his life at this palace. Before he died, he ordered the construction of a number of nearby fortresses, one of which, Kypros, was named in honor of his Edumite mother. This was later expanded and a palace built inside. The foundations of a round tower, a bathhouse, an aqueduct, and four water reservoirs remain on the site.

Tel al-Sultan

Tel al-Sultan is a mound northwest of the present city. In its heyday, in about 9000 BCE, archeologists believe that the city was heavily fortified and had some 2,000 inhabitants. A round tower from the pre-pottery Neolithic Period, tombs from the Chalcolithic Period, and walls from the Early and Middle Bronze Ages and later periods were also found here.

The fortress built at Tel al-Sultan stretched over six acres and had 20-foot walls. The public buildings had arched gates and courtyards and stone columns. Skulls of women had head dresses similar to the ones still worn by rural women in Palestine—and in fact, the Palestinian headdress is still known as "al-'usabh al-kan'aniyyah" (the Canaanite Turban). Tombs included household items such as weaving looms, clothes, bedding, mats, tables, chairs, plates, jugs, large copper basins, large water jars, pots, and clay ovens, not unlike those used less than a hundred years ago. Family tombs contained traces of food, cooked or grilled mutton in earthenware utensils, and the remains of cereals, pomegranates and raisins, next to the bodies.

Near Jericho

Most of the sites in "rural" Jericho are geographically very close.

Deir Hajla (Monastery of St. Gerasimus)

This monastery just outside the city of Jericho was founded in 455 CE by St. Gerasimus, who according to legend, befriended a lion that lived by his side until he died (whereupon the lion lay himself down next to the saint's grave and died himself). Although it is not always open, St. Gerasimus's grave and cave, in which he and the lion lived, can still be visited today. The monastery is marked on the Madaba map. Although reportedly inhabited by ten monks in the 8th century, a visitor allegedly found one lonely monk living in the ruins of the monastery in 1185. Toward the end of the 19th century, the monastery was renovated, but only one mosaic floor from the Byzantine era has survived the passage of time.

Deir al-Qaddis Yohanna al-Ma'madan (St. John the Baptist Monastery), or Qasr al-Yahud (Castle of the Jews)

The name of this site, located 10 kilometers (6 mi) southeast of Jericho is just one example of how complicated a name can get. This Greek Orthodox monastery, referred to locally as Qasr al-Yahud (Castle of the Jews), is believed to have been the site where the Israelites crossed the Jordan when invading Canaan. According to Christian tradition, John the Baptist baptized Jesus here. The monastery was built in the 4th century CE and has been destroyed and rebuilt more than once, most recently by the Greek Orthodox Church in 1882. The site contains the ruins of a Byzantine monastery and other Byzantine remains, a Crusader fortress and a church, and a contemporary church.

Deir Quruntul (Mount of Temptation and its monastery)

The Mount of Temptation is less than a stone's throw from the city of Jericho. From the monastery at the summit (accessible by foot or cable car), the entire Jericho district and the Dead Sea are visible.

The Greek Orthodox monastery derives its name from the Latin word *quarantena* (forty), after the Christian tradition of Jesus's 40-day fast in the wilderness here. The monks who lived here in the 4th century slept in caves in the cliff. The monastery was initially built during the Byzantine era (after a visit by Empress Helena) and by the 12th century two simple churches were built into the mountain, one inside the monastery and one on top of it. The latter fell into disuse in the 14th century; the former is the site where Jesus is believed to have fasted and refused to turn stones into bread.

The existing monastery was built through funding from the Russian Orthodox Church between 1875 and 1905, as the Russian empire was about to expire. Rasputin, the infamous advisor to the Emperor Nicholas and Empress Alexandra visited the monastery during his tour of the holy land.

Beside the monastery's Byzantine art treasures is a stone on which Jesus is believed to have sat during the Temptation. A large petrified footprint in the cave is allegedly that of Christ. It looks like a size 46.

Top: Monastery on the Mount of Temptation, where Christ prayed for 40 days
Bottom: The interior of the church on the Mount of Temptation, with monk in the background

Ein Duyuk

Ein Duyuk is a famous farming village and area first settled during the Roman era. It is interesting today because many still-existing houses were built according to the traditional architectural style of the Jericho valley. The mud-brick material and roofs of wooden beams and mud-covered reeds have been used for thousands of years. The first structures in the nearby refugee camps also used these building materials.

Na'aran is a site close to Ein Duyuk worth visiting. It contains the remains of both a 2nd-century Byzantine settlement and a 4th- or 5th-century synagogue with a beautiful mosaic floor (part of which is currently in the Rockefeller Museum in Jerusalem). Mosaics include commemorative inscriptions, flora and fauna inside geometrical designs, a zodiac, and Noah's ark.

Khirbet al-Auja al-Tahta

This Palestinian village 10 km north of Jericho is what remains of a Roman city built by Herod's son Archelaus. It was given to Salome, Herod's sister, who in turn bequeathed it to the wife of Emperor Augustus. Remains of buildings from the Byzantine and Arab Periods can be found in the village and its immediate surroundings. South of the village are remains of a monastery and a small chapel with a mosaic floor and an open channel water supply network. Shards and other remains indicate habitation in the Early Bronze Age and Iron Age.

Maqam Nabi Musa (Sanctuary of the Prophet Moses)

The sanctuary of Nabi Musa lies a kilometer south of the Jerusalem–Jericho road. According to Muslim tradition, it first became a site for pilgrims when the Crusaders barred Muslims from visiting and praying in Jerusalem. The sanctuary is built around a tomb said to be the burial site of Moses. Moses is not known to have entered Palestine during his lifetime, and most Christian and Jewish scholars believe he is buried near Mount Nebo in Jordan. But Palestinian lore has its own version of his burial site.

The Mamluk Sultan Baibars (1260–1277) supported the Palestinian version of history and promoted Muslim pilgrimage to the site. He had a mosque built to encase the venerated tomb in 1269. The Sultan frequently slept at the sanctuary while on his way to Karak, Jordan and Damascus. It remained a popular pilgrimage site throughout the Mamluk era. In the 1500s, the Ottomans added the mosque's current minaret. In the 1820s, the Ottomans began a popular festival at the site. During the Nabi Musa Festival, Palestinians from as far away as Haifa, Jaffa, Nablus, Hebron, and Jerusalem regularly partook in the celebration, sending delegations of dancers, poets, and artisans to represent their cities and villages.

In modern history, the site became a gathering place for the politically active and socially conscious. From here, activists broadcast anti-colonial and anti-Zionist opinions. A bit like Trafalgar square, it became a site for free speech and a podium for political dissent. As a result, the site was closed in 1937 by the British colonial government. The **festival of Nabi Musa** resurfaced after a 50-year ban in 1987, with 50,000 people in attendance. Every time there is political upheaval, the Israelis ban the festival in fear that it might once again become a stage for political dissent.

A rather large Muslim cemetery outside the walls of the sanctuary is dedicated to pilgrims and visitors who died at the sanctuary or people who requested that they be buried at the site. Of note are the graves of an Ottoman pilgrim of noble descent who was named after the Prophet's favorite wife Aisha and Hassan, the 19th-century guardian of the sanctuary. Hassan is the namesake of both the Prophet Muhammad's grandson and a shepherd boy, who according to Palestinian lore accompanied Moses on his journeys.

The upkeep of the sanctuary was guaranteed for several hundred years through a religious endowment, which pledged tax revenues for its maintenance. Sultan Baibars bequeathed the taxes of the agricultural land and villages of Turmus Aiya, al-Mazara'a, Khirbet Abu Falah, and Sur Baher for this purpose. Under the Ottomans, agricultural land and villages from the Nablus region and Ajlun in Transjordan were added to the *Waqf*, making it the largest single recipient of tax support in the whole country. According to the Ottoman records in 1875, some 10,000 pilgrims visited the site.

Today, a local Palestinian family lives at the sanctuary; they are happy to show visitors around.

Qasr Hisham (Hisham's Palace)
This most magnificent architectural site in the area was once an Umayyad winter retreat. Though the palace was commissioned by Caliph Hisham Ibn Abd al-Malik in the 8th century, it was actually his nephew, Walid Ibn Yazid, who oversaw the building, after he was banished from Damascus to Jericho for unseemly behavior. It was built as a royal retreat from the frugal and conservative Umayyad capital, where nude statues and frescos would undoubtedly have been frowned upon. In the Palestinian desert, the royals were free to enjoy their more liberal tastes in art and pleasure.

Mezze at Jericho's Garden Restaurants

Despite wars, the Occupation, and huge demographic shifts, Jericho has maintained a relaxed and unique charm. Perhaps it is the fertile soil and abundance of springs, which have fostered the cultivation of all sorts of vegetables and citrus fruits for centuries. Much of year, scorching heat keeps people indoors until dusk sets in, when agricultural activities can resume. But during its brief, mild winters, Jericho basks in its lush vegetation, lulled by the steady murmur of its water springs, and visitors arrive for a whiff of warm air during the dreary months from December to March. The visitors go to the colorful marketplace and enjoy lengthy repasts in Jericho's many garden restaurants.

The garden restaurants that have sprawled the slopes of Ramallah and the lowland of Jericho offer splendid spreads of Palestinian _mezze_— that assortment of salads and hot savory pastries and luscious dips best leisurely consumed over hours of nibbling and sampling, accompanied by a hubbly-bubbly, the water pipe traditionally called _nargila_.

A good selection of _mezze_ balances raw and cooked vegetables, grains and beans, the ubiquitous _kubbeh_ and hot savory pastries. Herbs— especially mint, parsley and thyme, and to a lesser degree rosemary and cilantro—are used profusely. Many grow wild, and some, like thyme and rosemary, grow in rocky, inhospitable areas, with little water to sustain them. _Tahini_ (sesame paste) is a basic ingredient for many dressings and adds a warm and slightly bitter flavor to the salads. Garlic and onion, another two essential components, are more or less used according to individual taste. Olive oil, an indispensable source of nourishment in a country that has witnessed long periods of penury, is used quite liberally. It moisturizes dry foods, such as _hummus_ (mashed chickpeas), and attenuates the sharpness of others, such as _mutabal_, which is based on grilled eggplants, or _harra'a_, a very spicy tomato mash.

Preparing raw salads is time consuming, as it requires a great deal of fine chopping of the tomatoes, cucumbers, onions, cabbages, greens, and bunches of parsley, mint, and cilantro. Eggplants and zucchini are fried or grilled and dressed with either a spicy tomato sauce (in Jericho, even spicier), or yogurt or _tahini_ dressing. Boiled potatoes, carrots, and beets chopped into fine cubes become vehicles for different herbs, onions, and garlic, with spectacular results. Many of the salads are served as dips: _hummus_; _baqdunsieh_, a parsley and tahini dip; and _mutabal_ are served smothered with olive oil and with plenty of hot _kmaj_ bread, or what is known in the West as pita bread. _Kubbeh_ is a mixture of meat and _burghul_ (cracked wheat) finely minced to a paste and shaped into hollow oblong balls, stuffed with a meat and onion mixture, deep fried, and served very hot. Pastries can be stuffed with cheese, meat, or greens, with spinach the most popular.

Jericho is a center for fresh produce

The palace consists of the palace, a mosque, and the bath. The main feature of the architectural design was the great courtyard with towers at its four corners. The site boasts elaborate stone friezes and mosaics, intricate plaster molds of half-nude dancers, partridges and floral patterns—all reminders of both the wealth and liberal attitudes of the Umayyad ruling class. Most of the nudes can be seen today in the Rockefeller Museum in Jerusalem.

The gate to the palace consists of a decorated domed ceiling, with niches along walls decorated with human and animal motifs. The palace itself is a two-square building with a central courtyard enclosed by four arcaded galleries. The galleries give access to the ground floor rooms, which were used by houseguests and people close to the caliph. The upper rooms were the private royal apartments.

The mosque, built for the caliph's family and guests, was accompanied by a rectangular swimming pool, which still survives (though its ceiling, held up by four pillars, does not).

Hisham's Palace has extensive remains, including the largest group of bathhouses ever discovered in the Arab and Islamic world. Sixteen pillars supported the hall through which one entered the mosque and the bath. Its walls were covered with marble-like plaster and decorated with geometric and floral designs set in exquisite mosaics. The floor of the hall contains the largest continuous ancient mosaic surface ever discovered.

The most famous remains of Qasr Hisham are that of a star-shaped window in a carved stone and a mosaic of the tree of life.

Qumran

Qumran, 20 kilometers (12.5 mi.) south of Jericho, is where the Arab shepherd boy from the Tama'ari tribe found the ancient Dead Sea Scrolls while he was searching for his lost goats. The boy's relative, a Bedouin shaykh, gave the scrolls to a Syriac priest, who gave them to an Armenian dealer in historic texts, who in turn sold them to an Israeli archeologist. Excavations began in 1947. The rest of the story remains murky.

Qumran is in the center of what was a farming community during the Iron Age (11th century BCE). Much later, the Essenes, a Judean group that shunned other Judean communities in Jerusalem and elsewhere (the Pharisees and Sadducees) as corrupt and unworthy settled in the caves of Qumran. They secluded themselves here in 150 BCE and wrote their histories, which were found on over 100,000 fragments. Although many books have been written about the contents of these so-called **Dead Sea Scrolls** (they are generally perceived to verify the Old Testament), lack of public access and the secrecy of translators and researchers have left their actual content a mystery. Today they are stored in the Israel Museum in Jerusalem, the Rockefeller Museum, and (to a lesser degree) in the Philadelphia Museum in Amman, Jordan.

Some clues about the scrolls maybe found through learning about the people who wrote them. Initially the Essenes lived in nearby caves before becoming more domesticated. Discoveries in the caves have indicated, though, that they continued to live in the caves even after urbanization. Purification pools carved into the caves also suggest that they continued to inhabit the caves. As critics of the pre-dominant Judean rulers, they may have been forced to hide—both themselves and their version of history—in these caves. They continued to live in Qumran until the Romans expelled them in 68 CE.

Refugee Camps

Aqabat Jaber Camp
Located 3 kilometers (1.8 mi) southwest of Jericho and just inside the Area A boundary (technically full

Development Projects

The Jericho Community Center (JCC) will include the following facilities when it is finished: a playing field and track, a horseriding club, a fitness center, offices, a café, and a winter camping site.

Although there is still no Palestinian independence, in 1998 the Committee for the Promotion of Tourism opened Independence Park and the Memorial Monument of Martyrs, in Ein al-Sultan refugee camp, north of Jericho on the Jericho-Nablus-Beisan Road. The garden has a lawn, a playground, a stone chessboard, seats, a fountain, and a café. The names of the martyrs of the Governorate of Jericho are inscribed on the monument.

Established in 1945, the Arab Development Society is the oldest continuously operating Palestinian non-governmental organization. Its prime objectives include raising the health and living standards of Arab rural communities, improving artisan and agro-industries, enhancing environmental health through forestation and commercial tree plantation, encouraging co-operatives and the provision of free agricultural and industrial training to orphans and destitute Arab youth.

PNA control), Aqabat Jaber sits at the base of the Jordan valley mountain plateau, near the Dead Sea. The camp was established in 1948 on 1.6 square kilometers (0.6 sq mi) of arid land belonging to the Jerusalem-based Husseini family. Prior to 1967, Aqabat Jaber camp was a holding ground for the largest single group of Palestinian refugees in the West Bank, with a population of at least 30,000 people (some estimates have put this figure as high as 60,000). After 1967, the great majority of the original refugee population fled the camp under fire and crossed the Jordan River to establish the largest Palestinian refugee camps in Jordan: Beka', Wihdat, and al-Nasr.

Today, Aqabat Jaber's 6,500 residents represent only a small percentage of its original size. The camp also includes a minority non-refugee population that moved into the camp and (illegally) constructed houses here. This history explains much of the camp's feel today. The large expanses upon which the camp was originally built, and the exodus of its residents in 1967, makes for a much more relaxed, less crowded setting than that of other camps. The first camp structures, which used local materials in traditional styles with mud-brick walls and thatched roofs, have been abandoned over the years in favor of concrete houses similar to many in Jericho itself. Many empty refugee shelters became hideouts for post-1967 PLO *fedayeen* (guerilla) groups, who snuck into Palestine across the Jordan river.

The original refugees of Aqabat Jaber came from a huge array of Palestinian cities and villages (possibly as many as 300), extending as far north as Haifa, and spreading down the coastal plain to the districts of Lydd, Ramleh, Jaffa, Gaza, and Hebron. Today, the majority of camp residents descend from 22 villages, among them Deir al-Dhibban, 'Ajjour, al-Mismiyya, Abbasiyyeh, Beit Jibrin, Tel al-Safi, Beit Dajan, Kufr 'Ana, and Yazour.

Residents of Aqabat Jaber are largely employed in agriculture, at the al-Karameh border crossing, or at the Mishor Adumim industrial settlement. In 1996, work began on a controversial PNA-led initiative to construct the Oasis Casino and a five-star hotel, just opposite the camp's main entrance. The casino was never popular among camp residents, and it was forced to close at the start of the al-Aqsa intifada. Opposition to the casino mainly stemmed from one of the camp's perennial problems: summer water shortages. Houses in the camp had been hooked up to water networks only in the mid-1980s (nearly 40 years after the camp began), and even then they were insufficient. This seemed unlikely to change after the casino announced plans to build a golf course.

Ein al-Sultan Camp

Just below the Mount of Temptation, 1 kilometer northwest of Jericho, Ein al-Sultan was established in 1948 on an 870-dunum plot of land belonging to the village of al-Diyouk. Ein al-Sultan was initially a holding ground of up to 30,000 refugees who originated from all corners of Palestine. After the Israeli occupation of the West Bank in 1967, Ein al-Sultan lost most of its residents when a massive second exodus took place. Officially termed "displaced persons," 200,000 Palestinians (many of them residents of the Jericho camps) fled to Jordan. Today Ein al-Sultan's population totals no more that 3,500 people; like Aqabat Jaber, it feels relatively spacious.

The current residents of Ein al-Sultan camp mostly come from villages in the Lydd, Ramleh, and Hebron regions. As a result of the 1967 War, many camp residents have relatives in the large Jordanian refugee camps of al-Wihdat, al-Beka and al-Nasser.

Ein al-Sultan camp was perhaps the last camp to receive electricity (1987) and a decent water network (2000). Before the water network was in place, the camp was infamous for its terrible water shortages. Residents were forced to go in the blistering Jordan Valley heat to a watering station open for a few hours a week—a challenge all the more difficult for the residents who lived in parts of the camp far from the watering station.

In 1994 Ein al-Sultan's relatively large tracts of land attracted the PNA, which used parts of the camp as a base for some members of the Palestine Liberation Army who returned from the diaspora. An abandoned school no longer used by the camp's residents was turned into a police station and army barracks, as were parts of the nearby Nu'eimeh refugee camp, which was completely abandoned in 1967. Between a third and a quarter of the camp's residents are now these returnees associated with the PNA.

Today most camp residents work as farm hands on Jordan Valley farms that grow grapes, banana, dates, and vegetables. A considerable part of the camp's work force is employed inside the Green Line or in Jewish settlements in the Jordan valley.

UNRWA operates a school, distinguished (together with the Aqabat Jaber refugee camp schools) for its co-ed classes. These schools allow the children of villagers and Bedouin from nearby Palestinian communities to attend as well.

A pilgrim at the
Church of the Holy Sepulcher

26.

Jerusalem (al-Quds)

Jerusalem is the residence of your father Abraham, the place of ascension of your prophet, the burial ground of the messengers, and the place of the descent of revelations. It is in the land where men will be resurrected and it is to the Holy Land, to which God has referred in his clear book. It is the farthest place of worship.

—Muhyi al-Din Ibn al-Zaki, October 9, 1187

Because of its centrality to the traditions of each of the three monotheistic faiths—Islam, Christianity, and Judaism—Jerusalem is often considered the holiest city in the world. But it is also a city where faith and science almost diametrically oppose one another. As home to so many sites central to what are believed to be historic events and miracles (for Muslims, Mohammed's ascension; for Jews, Abraham's sacrifice; for Christians, the crucifixion and resurrection), it is a city whose history is constantly being questioned, dug up, made up, and hotly disputed.

The Old City of Jerusalem, inhabited since about 4,000 BCE, is an intricate mosaic of cultures and traditions that have evolved over millennia. The first settlements were not permanent, but by about 3000 BCE, archeological evidence has established that the Canaanites, along with the Amorites and the Jebusites, built a city-like settlement. Many aspect of Canaanite culture and religion were later borrowed by both the Philistines and the Israelites.

Subsequently, Jerusalem was ruled by the Egyptians before the coming of the Philistines, Israelites, Persians, Romans, Byzantines, Arabs, Crusaders, Mamluks, and Ottoman Turks. The conquerors attempted to reshape the city to reflect their own religious and cultural

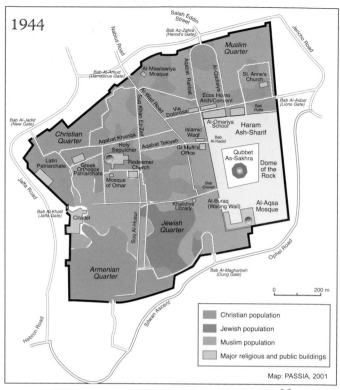

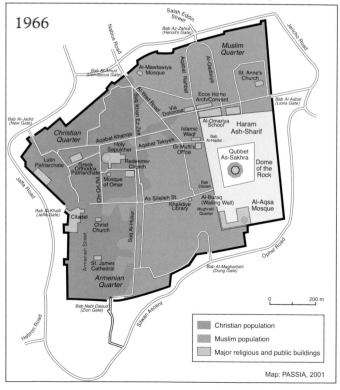

OLD CITY OF JERUSALEM, 1944 AND 1966

identities, claiming and rededi-cating or destroying the structures of the previous culture. Religious and political buildings served as symbols of power and domination. Today, Jerusalem contains within its walls the layers of this long history. In order to protect the city from further deterioration, Jerusalem was added to the World Heritage List in 1981.

Founders and Builders

Jerusalem existed at least as far back as the Bronze Age (4,000 BCE). Drawing on the fertility of the Wadi Farah, its founders, precursors of the Canaanites, built an initially small city on Jabal al-Dhuhur and called it Yara (and later Yara Shalem) after the Canaanite god of twilight. Over a thousand years later, a subgroup of the Canaanites known as the Jebusites ruled the city, which they called Jabus. The center of their city was called Zion, the Jebusite word for hill. Almost 2,000 years later, when King David ruled the city, he usurped the name Zion. There is dispute among scholars over whether David conquered the whole city or just the Jebusite city center.

Rulers of the city over the millennia were legion. The popular belief that one culture or civilization replaced another and evicted entire populations is almost entirely inaccurate. There were times when members of

The Position on Jerusalem

The Palestinian position on Jerusalem is straightforward. As part of the territory occupied in 1967, East Jerusalem is subject to UN Security Council Resolution 242: it is part of the territory over which the Palestinian state shall exercise sovereignty upon its establishment. The state of Palestine shall declare Jerusalem as its capital.

As stated in the Declaration of Principles on Interim Self-Government Arrangements, Jerusalem (and not merely East Jerusalem) is the subject of permanent status negotiations. All of Jerusalem should be an open city. Within Jerusalem, irrespective of the resolution of the question of sover-eignty, there should be no physical partition that would prevent the free circulation of persons within it.

As to sites of religious significance, most of which are located within the Old City in East Jerusalem, Palestine shall be committed to guaranteeing freedom of worship and access. It will take all possible measures to protect such sites and preserve their dignity.

The Palestinian position is based not only on the legal, religious, and historical rights of the Palestinian people, but also on their concrete needs and interests. Jerusalem is of strategic importance to Palestine and it is of sacred importance to Chris-tians and Muslims alike. It connects the northern region of the West Bank to the southern, and it is the hub of the main transportation network of the West Bank. Jerusalem is situated near the only airport in the West Bank. One-third of the West Bank's population resides within Jerusalem's daily commuting orbits. If a just and lasting peace is to be realized, Jerusalem, the vital center and future capital of Palestine, must be reconnected to Palestine and its residents—politically, geographically, and spiritually.

ethnic and religious groups were killed or evicted—during the Roman and Crusader periods, for example—but generally people stayed and communities continued to exist, if not always as equals, as neighbors.

Jerusalem today can be divided roughly as follows: the Old (walled) City, predominantly Arab East Jerusalem, predominantly Jewish West Jerusalem, the surrounding villages and refugee camps, and the illegal Jewish settlements built on land occupied after the 1967 war.

Visiting the Old City

The dominant Western and Israeli narrative separates the Old City of Jerusalem into four quarters, implying a neatly divided, heavily sectarian city with starkly differentiated communities. This is at the very least a simplification, if not a falsification, of the facts on the ground. The overwhelming majority of Jerusalemites are Palestinian; "subgroups" or communities, as defined by the groups themselves, are at least a dozen. Palestinian society was for generations largely integrationist, much like the United States. People of different ethnic and religious backgrounds met in Jerusalem, settled, and often within a generation, integrated. Some, like the Bukhara, Indian, and African community number in the hundreds; the Armenians are several thousand. These communities often consider themselves (and are considered by the majority) to be part of the greater Palestinian society. Thus, Christians as such are not a separate community. Most Christians are Arab Palestinians who belong to a range of denominations. The indigenous Jewish community, which was almost entirely Sephardic and spoke fluent Arabic and some Hebrew, is almost entirely gone, replaced by mostly Ashkenazi settlers who speak English, Yiddish, and Hebrew.

> ### The Aga Khan Award
>
> In 2004, the Old City of Jerusalem Revitalization Program, sponsored by the Palestinian Welfare Association, received the Aga Khan Award, one of architecture's greatest honors, for its approach to sustaining the life of a community that is continually threatened physically, socially, and economically. The ongoing project includes the restoration and rehabilitation of housing and the adaptive reuse of historic buildings and monuments.

Heavily armed, the Israeli army patrols Jerusalem, injecting an atmosphere of fear and intimidation to the souqs of the oriental bazaars and the spirit of the pious.

The entire Old City is wrapped by a 12-foot-high wall built in the

16th century during the reign of Suleiman the Magnificent. Of its eleven gates, seven are operational. The best way to see the Old City is to consult a map and begin a tour from one of the gates. We will begin with the frequently used Damascus Gate, and circle left.

Damascus Gate (Bab al-Amoud)

This gate, located next to a smaller one built by Hadrian, was so named because it points in the direction of the Syrian capital, an important reference point for many years. Also known as Bab al-Amoud (Gate of the Pillar) in Arabic, it is the largest of all the gates and the plaza around it the busiest. Entering the gate, what is known as the Christian quarter is on the right, and the Muslim quarter on the left. Souq Khan al-Zeit, the olive oil market, the liveliest part of the entire Old City, runs right through the middle. Halfway down the street at an intersection is the Via Dolorosa, the path of suffering.

Damascus Gate

Life in the Old City

New Gate (Bab al-Jadid)

The New Gate, in fact the most recent of the gates, is located on the northwestern segment of the wall. Leading directly into what is called the Christian quarter, it was built during the reign of Sultan Abed al-Hamid in 1887 in order to reduce traffic at the other gates. In the process, it connected the Christian community inside the wall with the newly emerging one outside the wall, in the western part of the city. The largest and most prominent Catholic landmark outside the gates of the Old City, **Notre Dame de France**, is across the street from the gate. A number of mainly Catholic institutions, including the Ecole des Freres and the Latin Patriarchate and Seminary, line both sides of the street.

Jaffa Gate (Bab al-Khalil)

Bab al-Khalil, also known as Jaffa Gate, the second largest of all the city's gates, is located at the western segment of the city wall. Originally built by King Herod in 40–44 CE, the gate was renovated in 1538 by Suleiman the Magnificent. In 1898, the actual gate was removed by the Ottoman Sultan Abed Al-Hamid II to allow his official guests to enter the city in carriages.

Entering the gate, the Armenian quarter is to the right and the Christian quarter to the left. In nearby Omar Bin al-Khattab Square stands the **Citadel**, or the **Tower of David** (its Israeli name). The tower is actually the minaret of an Ottoman-era mosque. This could very well be the site of the original Jebusite fortress, upon which David later built his own tower. Herod also built three towers here. Most of the Citadel's current architecture dates back to the Mamluk era.

Zion Gate (Bab al-Nabi Daoud)

This gate, located on the southwestern segment of the wall, leads directly into what is known as the Armenian quarter. According to inscriptions on the gate walls, the wall was renovated here in 1542. The gate is large and high compared to other gates and bears the scars of the 1948 war, when Jewish forces dynamited it with 70 kilograms of explosives.

Dung Gate (Bab al-Magharbeh)

The quickest way to get to what is known as the Jewish quarter is through Dung Gate. Probably first built by the early Ottomans, it led not only to the Western Wall but to the once prominent Moroccan/North African quarter, which the Israelis destroyed several days after the 1967 war. Today Dung Gate is the only entrance that leads directly into the new and enlarged Jewish quarter. Initially a small gate adjacent to city dumpsters, it was enlarged during Jordanian rule, because both Jaffa Gate and New Gate were closed for the duration of their two-decade rule.

During the Ottoman period, the gate was kept closed except for delivery of water from Silwan Spring. The gate was renovated and enlarged by the Jordanians after it was severely damaged during the 1948 war.

To the right of the gate (which is now equipped with electronic security devices), are the **Ophel Archeological Gardens**. In open-air exhibits of archeological and architectural finds from all eras of Jerusalem, the gardens include the remains of some previously unrecognized early Islamic edifices.

Lions' Gate or St. Stephen's Gate (Bab Sitna Mariam)
This closest gate to al-Aqsa Mosque leads directly into what is known as the Muslim quarter. Its many names have, of course, multiple origins. The most popular Palestinian name, Bab Sitna Mariam, refers to the route of the Virgin Mary. Israelis call it Lions' Gate for the two lions (the symbol of Baibars) above it. Western Christians generally call it St. Stephen's Gate, the name the Crusaders bestowed on it.

Herod's Gate (Bab al-Zahera)
The Arabic name of this small gate in the northern wall—Flowers Gate—is after the rosette panel above the arch. Built during the Fatimid period, this gate brings you straight into the middle of the Muslim quarter. Renovated by the Mamluks and then restored again in 1537, the gate was confused by some European pilgrims in the 16th century with another place associated with Herod Antipas. Their name has stuck.

Closed Gates
In addition to these seven gates, the Old City walls contain four sealed historic gates: the Golden Gate (also known as the Gate of Mercy, through which many believers think the Savior will re-enter Jerusalem), Single Gate (Bab al-Wahed), Triple Gate (Bab al-Muthallath), and Double Gate (Bab al-Muzdawage).

Muslim Quarter

The largest, most populated, and in many ways most lively part of Jerusalem, the Muslim Quarter has been largely ignored by Israeli and Western guides. It is accessed through Damascus Gate, which leads to both the Muslim and Christian quarters. The main arteries of the quarter are Souq Khan al-Zeit, which intersects with the Via Dolorosa, and al-Wadi Road, which leads to other major roads and the quarter's main sites, including the Dome of the Rock, the heart of Mamluk Jerusalem, and sites related to the city's Christian history, including the Church of St. Anne, the Convent of Flagellation, and the Ecco Homo.

While the Umayyads, the Abbasids, and Fatimids all built and added onto early Islamic shrines in the city, they appear not to have gone on building sprees, but instead contented themselves with the Haram al-Sharif (Noble Sanctuary) area and the Mosque of Omar. The bulk of Islamic architecture as it still exists in the Old City is actually a product of the post-Crusade era.

For an exhaustive history of this Mamluk era (1248–1517), the Jerusalem-born Mamluk historian Mujir al-din al-Ulaymi's (1456–1522) multi-volume encyclopedia is an excellent starting point. Mamluk Jerusalem thrived on Muslim pilgrimage. As if rediscovering their holy shrines, Muslims flocked in the tens of thousands to Jerusalem. Travellers from Morocco, India, Persia, and further afield came to the city to document every archway and every Islamic tomb. A new industry was built up around the needs of these pilgrims. Hostels, artisan quarters, way stations, postal stations, soup kitchens, and orphanages were established by the Mamluk rulers, along with schools, hospitals, and mausoleums. Buildings constructed in red, white, and black stone and arched entrances proliferated in the city and as far as Gaza on the coast.

One of the most impressive legacies of the Mamluks is the **Tankiziya School** (1328), opposite the women's hospice, Ribat al-Nisa. It was built during the rule of one of the great Muslim patrons of Jerusalem, Emir Tankiz al-Nasiri, the Mamluk governor of Damascus (1312–1340). The three-story school was alternately used as a courthouse, a residence, and a secondary school (under Jordanian rule), before it was confiscated by the Israeli army in 1967. Not far away is the **Tomb of Turkan Khatun**, a Mamluk noble woman who died in Jerusalem. Her tomb is visible from a street window, but entry into the chamber is difficult. Further down the street is the **Tomb of Baibars al-Jalik**, the Mamluk general who asked to be buried in Jerusalem after helping defeat the Mongols in Ain Jalout. And perhaps the most important 20th-century tomb in the city is just next to what was a Mamluk school, the **Madrasa al-Arghunia**: the **Tomb of Sharif Hussein of Mecca**, who led the Great Arab Revolt and is the great-great-grandfather of Jordan's King Abdullah II.

Several new markets were added to the city during the Mamluk period, the most prominent of which was **Souq al-Qattatin** (Cotton Market). The souk was built in 1336; its most recent renovations, begun in the 1970s, are still not complete. **Hamam al-Shifa**, one of the main Turkish baths in the Old City, is also under reconstruction. But one *hamam* that still shows how baths functioned long ago is nearby **Hamam al-Ain**, whose bathing rooms with heated floors can be still be visited.

Haram al-Sharif (Noble Sanctuary)

This compound encases the Dome of the Rock Mosque and al-Aqsa Mosque. It is Islam's holiest site in all of historic Palestine, and the third

Worshippers in a subterranean chamber, Dome of the Rock

holiest shrine after those in Mecca and Medina. Apart from the two famous mosques, scores of other monuments are encased in the sanctuary. Four gates lead visitors into the compound, although under strict Israeli military controls, non-Muslims may have difficulty entering.

The four gates to the sanctuary are, Bab al-Ghawanimeh, Bab al-Nazeer (Custodian Gate), Bab al-Silsileh (Chain Gate), and Bab al-Magharbeh (Morrocan Gate).

It is this whole area that fanatic Israelis want to destroy in order to "rebuild" a temple, which they claim once stood here. It has caused much bloodshed over the years and remains a major problem between Israelis and Palestinians and the larger Muslim world.

Africans in Palestine

From the time ambergris and frankincense were brought from Somalia and Ethiopia to Palestine, the peoples and cultures of Africa and Arabia have mingled. The African community in Jerusalem primarily traces its origin to Muslim pilgrims who came to Palestine mostly from Chad, Nigeria, and the western Sudan, beginning in the 15th century, though some notable pilgrims arrived several centuries earlier. A few African Palestinians had fathers and grandfathers who arrived as part of the Egyptian-led "Salvation Army," which tried to liberate the Palestinian areas held by Jews in 1948. After the defeat of that army and its retreat to Egypt, some Africans simply stayed in Palestine rather than return home. Men who came from Africa to Jerusalem often married local women, some of whom were of African descent themselves.

It is not certain when exactly the African quarter of Jerusalem was established, but eventually it grew up in the Muslim quarter, just beyond the large arch on Bab al-Majlis Street. Alaedin Street, off al-Wadi Road, is the main thoroughfare of the neighborhood, which lie just before al-Aqsa Mosque. By the beginning of the Ottoman era (1516), Africans were deemed important guards and caretakers of the mosque, and held keys to the holy site. Toward the end of the Ottoman rule, the African quarter itself was transformed into a prison for the rebels. The prison was infamous, with one section reserved for long-term incarceration and the other for executions.

After the British took over Palestine in 1918, the Ottoman prisons in the African quarter were closed and responsibility for the buildings returned to the *Waqf* authorities, which gave the buildings back to their African residents. Some of the Africans continued their traditions and worked as guards to the Muslim holy shrines and as bodyguards to the Mufti of Jerusalem until the Israeli occupation of the Old City in 1967.

Today seventy or eighty African-Palestinian families still live in apartments in the area. As for all non-Jewish residents in the Old City, building and expansion permits are hard to come by and thus the expansion of homes vertically and out into the once-open courtyard often happens secretly. Although Palestinian Africans are no longer allowed to guard the holy sites, having lost that battle to Israeli soldiers (who are often, ironically, Ethiopian Jews), few leave the city. Many of the quarter's residents are politically affiliated with secular leftist Palestinian factions.

Dome of the Rock (Qubbet as-Sakhra)

A magnificent mosque, built by Abed al-Malek Ibn Marwan in 691–692 CE on the site where the Prophet Mohammed is said to have risen to heaven in the nocturnal journey. The octagonal mosque has distinguished colorful tiling, a gilded roof, and a golden dome. In a box next to the rock, hairs from the Prophet Muhammad's beard are kept and shown once a year, during Ramadan.

Under the rock are two small shrines, one dedicated to Abraham and the other to Khader (St. George); beneath them is the Well of Souls, where spirits await the Day of Judgment in Muslim belief.

Most Africans in Jerusalem came as pilgrims from Chad, Senegal, and the Sudan centuries ago.

Al-Aqsa Mosque (Masjid al-Aqsa)

The construction on this architectural masterpiece began in 705 and was finished during the rule of Walid Ibn Abed al-Malik (709–715). It was rebuilt by the Abbasid al-Mansard after its destruction in 746 CE by an earthquake. The current structure dates to 1133. The mosque complex contains a museum and a library with copies of the Quran dating back to Ayyubite, Mamluk, and Ottoman times.

The Crusaders used the mosque as an armory, and the structures they built inside the complex are now used as the Women's Mosque and the Islamic Museum. Saladin had craftsmen brought from across the Islamic world to decorate and restore the al-Aqsa after defeating the Crusaders.

The mosque is distinguished by its porches, seven arches, domes, and seven fountains. The **Dome of Ascension** (Miraj) caps the point of the Prophet's ascension. Though it was probably originally built during the Umayyad era, the existing dome was built by the Ayyubites. The **Dome of the Prophet**, built during the late Ottoman Period

(1845), stands on eight marble columns. The eleven-columned **Dome of the Chain** stands in the middle of the compound.

Church of St. Anne

To the right of Damascus Gate is the Church of Saint Anne. According to tradition, Mary was born here, and the Crusader-built church commemorating her birthplace is, not surprisingly, one of the finest remnants of their rule. Small but fine in its minutest detail, a Byzantine church was built on top of an earlier structure. After the Crusades, the Mamluks turned into a school. Later, the Ottomans gave it to the French, for their support in the Crimean war. The existing structure is a mosaic of Byzantine, Crusader, Islamic, and French esthetics.

Christian Quarter

Moving to the west, stretched between Damascus and Jaffa Gates, lies what is known as the Christian Quarter. Note that shrines and churches exist all over the city—there are actually more in the Muslim Quarter than here. This area's highlights are the **Church of the Holy Sepulcher**, the Stations of the Cross along the **Via Dolorosa**, which is most easily accessed by entering **Souq Khan al-Zeit** and turning to the right when the two thoroughfares intersect. In Roman days, anyone condemned to death by crucifixion (and there were many) proceeded along this route carrying the cross on their backs, with a sign bearing their name and the charges against them. The tradition relating to Jesus' walk along the Via Dolorosa had its origin in Byzantine times, but then the procession began at Gethsemane and led to Golgotha. The present Via Dolorosa tradition evolved during Crusader rule. Whether or not the Stations of the Cross corresponds to historical fact is up for debate. Anglicans, for example, believe Jesus headed toward the Garden Tomb. **Souq Aftimos**, to the south of the Church of the Holy Sepulcher is a formerly Greek bazaar full of pilgrim paraphernalia. The **St. John the Baptist Church** is an 11th-century building run by the order of St. John's Hospitallers.

Church of the Holy Sepulcher (Kaneesat al-Qiyameh)

The Church of the Holy Sepulcher is the most historically significant church for Christians worldwide. It was first built in 325 CE after Empress Helena, mother of Emperor Constantine, identified it as the site of Golgotha, where Jesus was crucified and resurrected. Earlier a temple of Venus, built during the reign of Hadrian, had stood there. Like most of the venerable buildings in Palestine, it has been destroyed and rebuilt several times. Today, the basilica houses **six Christian denominations**. The Greek Orthodox, the Catholic, the Armenian Orthodox, the Coptic, the Syrian Orthodox (Jacobite), and the Ethiopian churches all share the premises. While the five big churches are housed in the main complex with chapels downstairs, the Ethiopians were sent to the roof when they lost in an 1808 fire their historic papers giving them permission to reside "inside" the church. Historically, the denominations have not been able to agree on sharing space or faith, so the Ottomans created a prayer schedule and handed the keys to the church over to two Muslim families. To this day, Jerusalem's Judeh and Nusseibeh families hold the keys to the holiest shrine in Christiandom and open its doors every morning and lock them every night.

At the entrance of the church is the **Stone of Unction of Anointing**, where Christ was either anointed or removed from the cross, depending on which denominational teaching one believes.

The Cavalry to the right of the Stone is where the skull of Adam supposedly rested. Today it is a Greek Orthodox. Chapel where Catholic Crusader kings are buried. To the left of the Stone is the rotunda, one of the few Byzantine structures still in place, where a tomb stands surrounded by 18 columns. The chamber itself is inside the Chapel of Angels, where the angels were said to tell of Christ's resurr-ection. A low doorway leads into the tiny Chapel of the Holy Sepulcher, home to the 14th station of the Cross.

The Roman Catholic Altar of Crucifixion and the Chapel of the Agony

Madaba Mosaic Map

In the late 19th century, during excavation and reconstruction of a Byzantine church in Madaba, Jordan, the oldest existing map of the Holy Land was found in a mosaic floor. Prominent in the mosaic, which has been dated to the middle of the 6th century CE, is a detailed map of Jerusalem as it appeared in 325-638 CE.

Running across the center of the Madaba Map of Jerusalem is the Cardo, the main street of Roman and Byzantine Jerusalem. At the north end of the Cardo is a gate and plaza constructed in the 2nd century by the Emperor Hadrian. The jewel of Byzantine Jerusalem was the Church of the Holy Sepulcher (called the Church of the Resurrection in the 4th century). Shown upside down on the map are the steps, a three-door entrance to a red-roofed basilica, and a separate domed structure.

of the Virgin are the centerpieces of the "Latin" part of the church.

The tiny Chapel of the Copts, known as St. Michael and the equally small Chapel of the Syrian (Jacobite) Church are almost in the middle of a large hall or square, dimly lit and filled with candles and incense. The former is the mother church to the largest Christian denomination in the Arab world, based mostly in Egypt and the Sudan. The Syrian Church has many followers in Syria and Iraq. The Greek Orthodox Church, cordoned off on the side, is where the Crusaders had their chapel.

At the eastern end of the Church is the Chapel of Helena and Crypt of the Cross, where Helena is said to have found Jesus' own cross (amid hundreds of crosses). All along the walls of the staircase, thousands of Crusaders and medieval pilgrims left their mark by etching their own crosses into the stone.

One has to ask to find the staircase leading up to the Ethiopian Chapel. Modest and small, it is central to the spiritual life of a denomination that has been in Jerusalem since the 4th century. An Ethiopian village-like community with mud huts dominates the roof of the entire church.

Ethiopians have set up their church on top of the Church of the Holy Sepulcher.

Church of the Redeemer

Prince Friederich Wilhelm had this Lutheran church (formerly the Church of St. Mary) constructed in 1869 upon the site of a decayed Crusader structure. The 178-step tower of the church leads to one of the best views of the city.

Mosque of Omar

Close to the Sepulcher is the Mosque of Omar. In order to keep the peace that he had brokered with the Christians, the Caliph refused to pray inside the Church of the Holy Sepulcher, instead choosing to pray outdoors nearby. Soon afterward (639) the foundation stones of this mosque were laid. The Crusaders turned the mosque into a garrison for the Knights of St. John. After Jerusalem was liberated by Saladin, a Moroccan family became the caretakers of the mosque.

Armenian Quarter

Jaffa Gate is the most direct way to access the part of the city where most of the Armenian community resides and where their churches and institutions are located. The Armenians, who embraced Christianity as their national religion in 301, constitute the oldest Christian nation in the world. Not surprisingly, they established the first quarter in Jerusalem. The Armenian Quarter encompasses about one-sixth of the area within Jerusalem's walls and is essentially a city within a city. It is dominated by the 5th-century **Saint James Cathedral** and monastery, one of the finest and oldest churches in the world.

In the early Christian period, thousands of Armenian monks lived in some 70 monasteries all over Palestine. Armenians also constituted a significant number of the early pilgrims, often coming in groups of 400 to 500 people at a time, a large number in the 5th and 6th century. They kept apart from other churches, and when the Caliph Omar conquered Jerusalem in 638 CE, he granted the Armenian patriarch a separate covenant safeguarding Armenian property and allowing freedom of worship.

With the improved security and infrastructure of early Muslim rule, the number of annual pilgrims swelled to 10,000 annually. Along with other Christian denominations and the Jews of Jerusalem, the Armenians generally enjoyed prosperity, until the Crusades. Then, most Orthodox communities were given the status of "secondary Christians," and the Armenians were similarly relegated to the margins. But the Armenian Catholic Church, born at this time, ensured the survival of the community in the quarter.

Inside the St. James Cathedral

Through donations and property leases the Armenians maintained continuity in the city throughout the 1,400 years of Muslim rule. The community grew constantly, as those who faced persecution in Armenia and elsewhere came to Jerusalem. Thousands of survivors of the Armenian genocide in what is now Turkey came to Jerusalem. Monasteries and pilgrim inns became a way station for the dispossessed. By 1922, two orphanages housing 700 Armenian orphans from Iraq and Turkey were established. The community grew overnight from 1,500 to 5,000 people.

Although the British were not inclined to welcome the refugees, the Armenians had the Arabs on their side. In 1922, an Arab chieftain known as Shaykh Breik gave the Armenian refugees land and they established the village of Athlit near Haifa. By 1925, 15,000 Armenians lived in Palestine, mainly in Haifa, Jaffa, Jerusalem, Bethlehem, and Gaza. Many came to Palestine from neighboring countries like Lebanon and Syria.

With their long tradition in Jerusalem in particular, it is not surprising that the Armenians have made many cultural contributions.

The first printing press in Jerusalem was opened by Armenians in 1833 and published more than 1,200 titles. With the training they received at this press, many Armenians started businesses in printing, typesetting, and bookbinding nearby. Armenians also specialized in ceramic tile-making, photography, and masonry. The first commercial photographic workshop in Jerusalem was started by an Armenian in 1885 and they continue to be among the most prominent photographers in the city to this day. Armenian ceramics were introduced to Palestine in 1919, when a group of Armenian artisans were hired to restore the tiles of the Dome of the Rock. During the 1920s, their tiles decorated the facades and interiors of many public buildings and institutions. They founded a big studio and factory on Nablus Road; at the height of their activity, they employed 20 painters. This studio, which was in operation for more than 75 years, inspired others to learn the craft. Today in Jerusalem there are five large pottery studios (see sidebar).

Popular lore has it that Armenians took a "neutral" position in the Palestinian–Israeli conflict, in part because after the 1948 war, out of a total of 10,000 residents left in the Old City, 6,000 were Armenians. But unlike the Arabs, who left the fighting to the soldiers, the Armenians civilians themselves fought for their territories. Forty civilians lost their lives and another 250 were wounded. Since 1967, the Armenian Patriarchate has lost several plots of land in Jerusalem through confiscation. Work on the Armenian Church on Mt. Zion has been delayed for 20 years due to denial of building permits.

Jerusalem Ceramics

Palestinian pottery was rejuvenated at the beginning of the 20th century when three Armenian artisan families from Kutahya, Turkey were asked to restore the tiles on the Dome of the Rock. In time their styles and designs became specific to Palestine, integrating as they did Byzantine, Roman, Crusader and Islamic themes. Connoisseurs can instantly recognize the work of each of the three Jerusalem schools of pottery (Ohannissian, Balian, and Karakashian) by the design and colors.

The Armenian-made tiles were used in both the interior and exterior of public buildings, overwhelmingly in the Armenian Quarter, but also in public and private buildings throughout the rest of the city and in other cities across Palestine. With the economic boom of the 1920s, many owners of urban villas in the greater Jerusalem area (including Bethlehem and Ramallah) commissioned Armenian artists to make both interior and exterior tiles to enhance the beauty of their homes.

In recent years, the craft has been passed on to non-Armenian Palestinians, many of whom are employed as potters, copyists, and assistants in the Armenian-run workshops. But today, most Palestinians, having learned that their homes can be confiscated, prefer portable valuables.

Crafting handmade ceramics in Jerusalem's Palestine Pottery Studio

The Armenian Quarter has lost property to the Jewish Quarter, which "claimed" 81 of the Armenian Quarter's 581 properties. In the late 1990s, when US President Clinton suggested that the Jewish and Armenian Quarters be allocated to Israeli rule, the Armenian community sent word to Yasir Arafat that they wanted to be attached to the Christian Quarter, which was proposed to come under Palestinian rule.

The Armenian Quarter—of which about two-thirds is taken up by the complex of the Monastery of St. James—is probably the only one that largely looks like it did when it was founded. The ceramic and pottery shops, the delicatessens and the pubs, and the Armenians' almost medieval sense of community make the quarter a unique and precious part of the mosaic that is old Jerusalem.

St. James Cathedral

Built in 444 CE and dedicated to Jesus' brother James, this cathedral is one of the most beautiful churches in the city. Rich in carpets, wooden and bronze engravings, paintings and golden lamps with Armenian ceramic eggs attached to them, the church is a most impressive house of worship. Its incense and music lend to the medieval atmosphere. It is best seen during the day, when the light accentuates the treasures adorning the church.

The original church was built in the 5th century, but most of what exists today is from later expansions and additions. The compound encompasses the residence of the patriarch, a hospice, living quarters for nuns and monks, a seminary, a library, a museum, a printing press, and two Armenian social clubs.

Mardigian Museum of Armenian Art and History

Thirty rooms, once living quarters for seminary students, house artifacts that trace Armenian history in Christianity, Jerusalem, Anatolia, the former Soviet Union, and Armenia itself. Built in 1843, the museum compound encases an old cemetery and several gardens. One display shows what the Armenian quarter looked like in Byzantine times while others exhibit beautiful jeweled crosses, embroidery and ceramic tiles from the 17th and 18th century.

The Convent of the Olive Tree, which lies within the Museum compound, is (according to Armenians) where Jesus was bound before he was placed on the cross. It is also known as the House of Annas, under whose authority Jesus was condemned to die.

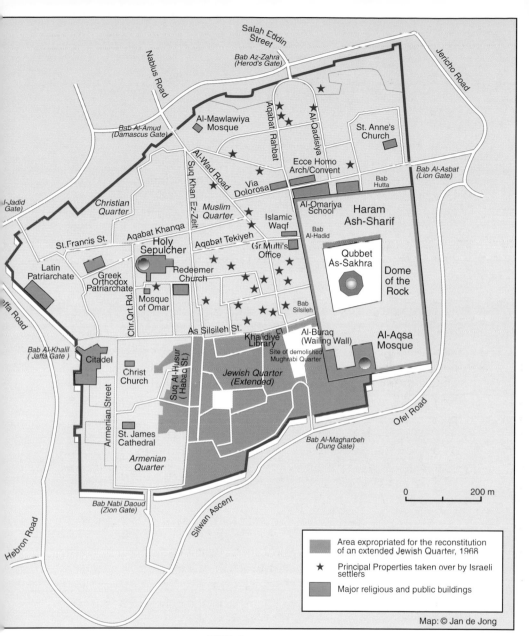

THE OLD CITY

Map: © Jan de Jong

Legend:
- Area expropriated for the reconstitution of an extended Jewish Quarter, 1968
- ★ Principal Properties taken over by Israeli settlers
- Major religious and public buildings

Yaácoubia Mosque

This small and not always accessible mosque occupies the site of a 12th-century Crusader structure that appears to have been built on top of a 5th-century tomb of a Persian Christian named James. When the Muslims turned it into a mosque they named it Yacoub al-Ajami Mosque (the Mosque of James the Persian).

Syrian Orthodox Church and Convent of St. Mark

The Convent of St. Mark is at the center of the Syrian Orthodox (Jacobite) community, which has been in Jerusalem for over a thousand years. According to Orthodox tradition, the **Last Supper** was eaten here, in the home of St. Mark's mother, Mary. The present-day church was built in the 12th century, presumably over an early structure identified by the Byzantines as a biblical site. The centerpiece in the churchyard is the stone basin in which, according to Orthodox tradition, Mary, the mother of Christ, was baptized. Experts believe that the portrait of the Virgin and Child above the basin said to have been painted by St. Luke, was probably actually painted in the early Byzantine era.

Jewish Quarter

Most easily accessed through Dung Gate, this part of the contemporary city includes areas where non-Jews lived historically. As with other parts of the city, the population was not strictly segregated until modern Israeli rule. The Jewish community of Jerusalem had two renaissance periods: in 700 BCE and after the expulsion of the Crusaders by Saladin. Jews were expelled twice from the city, once by the Romans after rebelling against them, and once by the Crusaders, for not sharing their faith.

Like much of Jerusalem, this quarter was damaged during the 1948 war. After the Israelis refused Arab-Christians the right to make pilgrimage to Nazareth, the Jordanian government denied Jews the same right in Jerusalem. After Israel's 1967 occupation of the city, this quarter was totally renovated and refurbished. As can happen with renovations, this area of the city seems sterile compared to the others: it lacks the medieval charisma much of the rest of the Old City has retained. Some 3,000 people live in this quarter.

The **Western, or Wailing, Wall**, is part of the edifice surrounding the al-Aqsa Mosque area. Jews believe that this wall is a remnant of the second Jewish temple. Archeologists tend to believe that it is part of a retaining wall built under Muslim rule. Whatever its origin, it is indubitably the greatest place of worship for Jews who come to Jerusalem to pray and lament at this site. Praying over the destruction of two of their temples in Jerusalem, worshippers insert written prayers into the cracks between the Herodian stones. The prayer area is divided into two unequal sections: the larger for men and the smaller for women. The large plaza around the Wall is where the Moroccan Quarter stood before the 1967 war.

Another way to get to the Jewish Quarter is through the Jewish

Moroccan Quarter

Harat al-Magharbeh was first constructed some 700 years ago and, on the eve of the 1967 war, was home to some 650 people. Then, in one of the starkest acts of dispossession, the entire neighborhood was demolished within a week after Israel occupied the Old City. Along with the more than 400 villages and communities destroyed in 1948, the wiping out of this quarter counts among the most notable transgressions against the Palestinians by Israel.

What is known today as the Western Wall Plaza was home to an old North African community of pilgrims, merchants, and artisans. Over the course of several centuries, Jewish, Christian, and Muslim Arabs from Palestine and elsewhere also took up residence in this quarter.

Several Jerusalem historians describe the Moroccan Quarter as dating from the time of the Ayyubites. Mujir al-Din relates that the son of Saladin, 'Afdal al-Din, endowed the entire quarter to the North Africans as a Waqf. As such, the area was to serve as a haven for new arrivals from North Africa, and from the 13th century until the last days of Jordanian rule in 1967, immigrants from the farthest corners of the Islamic world did come here, some making it their home.

This corner of the Old City was the site of a number of historically and culturally significant structures erected during the age of the Ayyubites and Mamluks. These included the Jami' al-Magharibeh near the Bab al-Magharbeh and the Zawiyya Fahriyya. During the later part of the 12th century, the Madrasa al-'Afdaliyya was built to serve the Maliki School of Jurisprudence. In the 13th century, the quarter came within meters of the Western Wall, which was used as a regular site of Jewish prayer after Suleiman the Magnificent (1520–1566) ordered that a space between the Moroccan Quarter and the Wall be cleared for that purpose.

Quarter Road, which contains the remains of several synagogues (Ramba and Hurva), built on the remains of Crusader churches. The remains of the Mamluk **Mosque of Sidi Omar** are also still visible. Across from the Sidi Omar minaret is the **Cardo**, which is what remains of "downtown" Aelia Capitalina and later Byzantine and Crusader Jerusalem. The replica of the Madaba Map (see page 310) shows what the city looked like during Byzantine times.

Sephardic Synagogues

Long before Jews from Eastern Europe came to Palestine in large numbers, Jerusalem's Jewish community was almost entirely Sephardic, so the city's most significant Jewish temples belong to this community. Built during Ottoman rule, these four synagogues are the center of Eastern Jewish life in Jerusalem: Rabbi Yohanna Ben Zakkai, Emtza, Stambouli, and Eliyahu HaNavi.

St. Mary of the Germans Church

This church stands near the Burnt House, which is said to be a 1st-century home burned during the destruction of the city in 70 CE. This Crusader-built church was part of a complex consisting of a hospital and a hospice run by German members of the Order of St. John.

East Jerusalem

Venturing outside of the Old City's walls, what is known as East Jerusalem is largely located around three thoroughfares: commercial Saladin Street, administrative Nablus Road, and service-oriented Zahra Street. A small area, largely accessible by foot, this constitutes the hub of what remains of Arab Jerusalem outside the city walls. Though it is extremely pinched by underfunding and Israeli control, East Jerusalem survives despite the occupation.

Administered from 1948 to 1967 by Jordan, with a Palestinian Mayor, most of area's shops and institutional buildings were established during that era, though the streets and neighborhoods had been largely established earlier, during late Ottoman and early British rule.

Shops on Saladin Street began appearing in about 1918, and the street remains the main shopping hub of the city. Clothing boutiques, electrical supply shops, snack bars, ice cream parlors, restaurants, and internet cafes dot the street, as do Arab jewelers and money changers.

During Jordanian rule, Nablus Road was the main thoroughfare from Jerusalem to Nablus but today Israeli municipal "development" has stopped the two-way traffic. Moving through heavy human traffic from Damascus Gate, the first impressive hallmark of Nablus Road is the **Schmidt School**, (also known as St. Paul's Hospice), which was established as a landmark by German Catholics during Europe's 19th-century rediscovery of Palestine. Built to house German pilgrims, it is still an efficiently run hospice, but serves mainly as a renowned girls' school, named after its first principal, Father Schmidt.

Just behind the school lies the **Garden Tomb**. It is part of **Skull Hill**, a rock-hewn tomb and a tranquil garden, first identified by the British General Gordon in the 19th century as the "real" Golgotha. Mainly Anglican-affiliated Protestant groups believe this to be the place of Jesus' crucifixion and burial. In fact, a burial site on Skull Hill was discovered in 1867 by the German researcher Conrad Schick. Since then, archeologists have dated the site to several hundred years before the birth of Christ. It remains a place of pilgrimage, however.

St. Etienne Monastery (St. Stephen's Monastery) lies just north of Skull Hill, also on Nablus Road. According to Christian tradition,

St. Stephen was the first martyr for his faith. The Byzantines built a tomb in his honor at the site where he was believed to have been stoned to death. The site was "resurrected" by the Dominican Order who bought the site and built the monastery in the 19th century. Tombs and bones dating back to biblical times have been uncovered. The **Ecole Biblique et Archeologique Francaise de Jerusalem** was established in 1891 on the monastery grounds.

Further up on Nablus Road is the **American Consulate of East Jerusalem**, just opposite of the **Palestinian Pottery Shop**. The shop and its adjacent factory have existed in one form or another since 1919 when Armenian artists and potters were brought in to repair the tiles on the Dome of the Rock. The rather large and extensive domed establishment is considered a pillar of the Palestinian artistic community in the city.

St. George's Cathedral, built in 1899, was an early British attempt to establish a foothold in what would, twenty years later, become their colony. The Anglican Cathedral serves the Arab-Anglican community as well as visitors; its hospice is one of the more quiet, reasonably priced, and pleasant inns in the city.

In contemporary times, **Orient House** served as the official Palestinian government residence in Jerusalem, where foreign dignitaries pay homage to Palestinian political rights in the city. But the building, which was closed several times during the al-Aqsa intifada, has a longer history. Built in 1897 by a leading member of the Palestinian Husseini family, it was a private home that hosted many foreign visitors before being converted into a hotel in the 1950s. The family loaned the house to the Jerusalemite community as a site where negotiators and politicians could meet toward the end of the 1980s.

Dar al-Tifl al-Arabi (House of the Arab Child) was first established in another of the Husseini family mansions. Set up under the auspices of the late Hind al-Husseini (the equivalent of a modern-day Muslim saint), this former family home was given to be a school for orphaned and underprivileged children. The converted home housed the orphans of the Deir Yassin massacre, and today it is one of the most prominent Arab educational institutions in the city. On the premises is the **Palestinian Arab Folklore Center**, a five-room museum dedicated to 19th- and 20th-century Palestinian traditions and folklore.

The ancient **Tomb of the Kings** at the corner of Nablus Road and Saladin Street is the site of the contemporary Arab Jerusalem Festival, organized by the Palestinian cultural organization, YABOUS. Though it is not entirely clear who was buried here, the consensus today seems to be that it was a leading Babylonian family, and not the kings of

In the garden of the American Colony Hotel, once an Arab home

Judah, as the French woman who bought the site in the 19th century thought. Her heirs gave the site to the French government. It is with the support of France that the Palestinian cultural festivals happen here.

The **American Colony Hotel** has actually very little to do with anything American. Once the Ottoman-era home of a very wealthy childless Palestinian, it was sold by heirs from his extended clan to American missionaries of Scandinavian decent. It was converted into a hotel, which is now under Swiss management with an almost entirely Arab staff. It is considered the most beautiful hotel in all of Palestine.

Almost adjacent to the Colony is the small and unobtrusive **Shaykh Jarrah Mosque** (built 1895), named after Saladin's physician.

Whether the mosque's tomb (dated 1201) still contains the remains of Hussam al-din al-Jarrahi is not certain. What is clear is that the lands bequeathed to him by Saladin still retain his name. It remains one of the more beautiful Jerusalem neighborhoods, and probably the most exclusive piece of real estate still belonging to Palestinians outside the Old City gates. From the beginning of the 20th century and through the 1930s, the landowning and feudal families of Jerusalem built magnificent homes and mansions here, some of which can still be seen today. Foreign missions, non-governmental organizations, and cultural institutions have set up in the quarters in this district, which also houses schools, hospitals, and some hotels.

Before getting to the Shaykh Jarrah neighborhood, just north of the Colony is the **Wadi Joz** (Valley of the Walnuts) area, which took shape between the 1948 and 1967 wars. This neighborhood is famous for its car repair shops and its lower-middle class housing for rural migrants and urban refugees from what was Arab West Jerusalem. Once an agricultural suburb of Jerusalem, it became an industrial zone during the tenure of the last Arab mayor of Jerusalem.

Land confiscation, mainly by the state of Israel, has created tension over the ownership of land that houses the **Hebrew University of Jerusalem**, the **Regency Hotel** and virtually all of the land designated "public" by the government. Public facilities, including water, telephones, and school services are hard to come by for Arab residents.

Sites East of Jerusalem

Augusta Victoria Hospital and Hospice
Commissioned by Kaiser Wilhelm and named in honor of his wife in 1910, this magnificent edifice was intended as a hospice for German

pilgrims. The British used it as their official residence. After 1948 it became a hospital mainly for Palestinian refugees registered by the United Nations. Both the hospital and hospice are fully operational; the World Lutheran Council runs the real estate (one of the best in the area).

Garden of Gethsemane and the Church of All Nations

The garden and caves where tradition has it Jesus prayed before being betrayed and arrested have been used as hiding places since Byzantine and Crusader times. Cisterns and an olive press are part of a subterranian complex that at times housed burial chambers.

The adjacent Church of All Nations is distinguished by its interior ceiling, which consists of twelve domes each containing beautiful mosaics. Also known as the Basilica of the Agony, it is situated at the foot of the Mount of Olives, the site of a Jewish cemetery in use since ancient times. The church was built in the early 1920s on the remains of a 5th-century Byzantine structure and a Crusader church. Designed by the Italian architect Antonio Barluzzi, the basilica features twelve cupolas, each representing one of the twelve sponsoring nations. The **Rock of the Agony**, where, according to Christian tradition, Jesus knelt to pray, is the central feature of the basilica. Much of the original Byzantine mosaic pavement has been preserved and the foundations of the Crusader church can be seen in the garden among the ancient olive trees.

Mount of Olives/Dominus Flevit Church

According to tradition, Jesus passed the Mount of Olives on his way to Jerusalem. The Byzantines built a church here. When construction on a new church began in 1954, a large cemetery was uncovered. The sarcophagi carry inscriptions in Hebrew, Aramaic, and Greek, with names like Zechariah, Jesus, Mary, and Lazarus.

Rockefeller Museum

Built opposite the walls of the Old City, this museum was established as a venue for the many archeological finds in Palestine in the first decades of the 20th century. In 1938, the American philanthropist John D. Rockefeller donated several million dollars to build, equip, and maintain a museum that would shed light on the history of the people of the "Holy Land" through archeological finds.

While the structure was inspired by Elizabethan and Jacobean buildings, it is the eastern features that are particularly striking: the inner arches, the doors made of Turkish walnut wood, the profusion of Armenian tiles, and the inner courtyard reminiscent of the 14th-century Islamic

In the Garden of Gethsemane

Alhambra in Spain. This beautiful inner courtyard is graced with stone engravings by the noted British artist Eric Gill that depict the peoples who lived in the country throughout the centuries: Egyptians, Canaanites, Phoenicians, Philistines, Israelites, Assyrians, Persians, Babylonians, Greeks, Romans, Arabs, Crusaders, Mamluks, and Ottoman Turks.

The finds here range from the prehistoric eras to the 1700s. Among its treasures are the **Dead Sea Scrolls**. After 1948, when much of Jerusalem came under Jordanian rule, an international council administered the museum briefly. Since 1968, the Rockefeller Museum has been an integral part of the Israel Museum. Still, it contains many, if not most, of the finds from Palestinian digs in the West Bank and Gaza.

Russian Church of St. Mary Magdalene

Commissioned in 1888 by Czar Alexander III in memory of his mother, the Empress Maria Alexandrona, the Church of St. Mary Magdalene is one of the country's most majestic churches. With its seven golden onion-shaped cupolas, it looks as if it could have been transplanted from Moscow.

Towns East of Jerusalem

Bethany (Eizariya)

Like many Palestinian villages close to the periphery of larger towns or cities, Bethany has lost much of its quaintness—not to mention agricultural land rich with fig, almond, olive, and carob—due to a lack of town planning, rapid expansion, and the general neglect under decades of occupation. Visitors at the beginning of the 20th century counted 40 homes in the village; today there is hardly enough room for everyone, even though most of Bethany's original inhabitants now live in Jordan, the US, and the Gulf countries. The proximity of Jerusalem and the expectation that the Palestinian central government might have its seat nearby has prompted quite a bit of real estate speculation. Many banks have set up branches in the village, which has now become a town of 4,000.

Beit Annia, as Bethany was once called, is believed to have been inhabited almost without interruption from the 6th century BCE to the 14th century CE. An excavation site lies just beyond the **House of Martha and Mary**, sisters to Lazarus. Though it cannot be substantiated that this was their house, it is nevertheless interesting as the oldest house in Bethany: a 2,000-year-old dwelling.

Although Bethany figures in the Bible, almost all of the town's inhabitants have been Muslim since the beginning of the 16th century. In order to accommodate the Muslim population, the Ottomans built **al-Ozir Mosque**, in honor of the town's patron saint, Lazarus. For almost 100 years after the mosque was built, Christians were also invited to worship in it. This practice was not, however, condoned by Europeans, who felt that separating the denominations was a better option.

Next to the mosque, a 1954 **Franciscan Church** marks the **Tomb of St. Lazarus** and its gardens feature remnants of the mosaic floor of the original 4th-century church. The Crusader Queen Melisande (1138) added an abbey complex and convent to the renovated church. If Crusader records are to be believed, the production of wheat and olive oil made the abbey one of the wealthiest in the kingdom. The famous Italian architect Antonio Barluzzi (1884–1960) considers this church one of his masterpieces.

West of the house said to belong to Mary and Martha stands the house of Simon the Leper, known locally as the **Tower of Lazarus** and run by the **Greek Orthodox Church**. That church, built in 1965 in honor of St. Lazarus, only opens during the Orthodox Feast of Lazarus in April of each year.

Silwan

Along with ancient Jerusalem, Silwan was once a Canaanite town. Located on the steep hills descending from the Old City, the town lived off the spring that was fed by the Birket al-Hamra. Little of its history in pre-biblical times is known, except that the community depended heavily on the water supplies, which the Israelites, under David, cut off in order to force the local residents to surrender. One monument from pre-biblical times can still be seen: the square **Tomb of the Pharaoh's Daughter**, dated sometime between the 9 and 7th centuries BCE. The water tunnels can be visited, as can tombs of biblical figures such as Absalom and Zechariah.

The Russian Church of
St. Mary Magdalene, Jerusalem

Al-Tur

Located on the Mount of Olives, al-Tur is believed to have been a Canaanite suburb of ancient Jerusalem. The **Chapel of Ascension**, which the Byzantines believed to be the site of Jesus' ascension, is located in a small compound known as the Elona Complex. First built around 350 CE, it was destroyed in 650, and later rebuilt by the Crusaders. Today the chapel is under Muslim protection. At various intervals, the chapel is used as a mosque and for Christian festivals. It is used as a house of prayer for Christian pilgrims at Easter, when they set up tents in the complex and conduct services throughout the week.

North of Jerusalem

On the small elevated hill above the Jerusalem–Ramallah road observe the rather ordinary housing complex of five-story buildings. Known as **French Hill**, it is the first illegal settlement built after the 1967 war.

The road becomes much bumpier past the next traffic light, which marks the beginning of post-1967 "extended" Jerusalem. Hundreds of archeological sites and thousands of finds spread out on both sides of the road. Some are in the middle of old village centers, some on isolated hills. A few selected sites are mentioned below.

Shu'fat is a Palestinian village that has become an Arab suburb of Jerusalem. It houses many Palestinian and international NGOs as well as several international missions. Built on the site of the Canaanite Dersophath, this village has been inhabited intermittently since 2000 BCE. It is believed to be the site of Nob. The old part of the village was largely built during the Ottoman era. Among the sites that can still be visited in the vicinity is **Tel al-Ful** (hill of beans), in the northern part of Shu'fat. It is a partially excavated ancient city and castle located on top of the ancient Canaanite village of Gibeh, which overlooked the Dead Sea and the hills of Moab.

Beit Hanina is located further down the same street. The Palestinian Medical Relief Services and UNICEF are among the agencies that have their headquarters here. This neighborhood, too, was once a village. The old town center is about a kilometer away from the main road. Beit Hanina contains four hamlets: Khirbet al-Byar, Khirbet al-Showmara, Khirbet Tlelia, and Khirbet al-Hazoor. These have the ruins of a military camp, rock-carved water cisterns and pools, ancient tombs, and a Roman road. Beit Hanina is known for the celebrities who once lived there, including the late King Hussein of Jordan, who had a weekend residence here prior to 1967. The village's most famous son is the Arab-banking scion Abdul Hameed Shoman, founder of the Arab Bank, which is still among the most powerful banking institutions in the Arab world. The **Sisters of Rosary School, al-Quds University Faculty of Arts, Saint Anthony's Coptic Church**, and the **Helen Keller School for the Blind** are all in Beit Hanina.

Pilgrims have been visiting the Canaanite village of **Mispha** and venerating it as the burial place of Samuel since the 6th century. The cloth-covered tomb in the cellar of **Mosque of Nabi Samuel** has become part of popular history. In 1099 the Crusaders caught their first sight of Jerusalem from here and so named this Mont de Joie (Mount Joy). In 1157 they built a church on the burial site believed to be Samuel's. In 1911 the church or its remains were incorporated into the mosque. From 1948–1967, the Jordanian legion headquarters were situated close to the mosque. After Israel occupied the West Bank, many of the homes in the village were destroyed. Now it is largely off limits to pilgrims who are not Jewish.

Al-Jib is the Canaanite Gibeon, a flourishing city in the days when Joshua, according to lore, stopped the sun from moving so that he could continue killing the Canaanites. Excavations just past the village turned up tombs and pottery from the Bronze Age, a massive city wall from the Iron Age, several buildings, a winery, a rock-cut pool 25 meters deep with an 11th- or 12th-century spiral staircase probably built by the Crusaders and a church from the same era. Yakut, writing in 1225, described al-Jib as a location with "two fortresses." Al-Jib, which is estimated to be 3,500 years old, was famous for its ancient water system and, in the 7th century BCE, its wine production. The Babylonians destroyed the town in 587, but the remains of the ancient town are still visible.

As with almost everything in Palestine, a story or a controversy surrounds every site. Today, the Israeli occupation and destruction of villages can almost overwhelm the rest of the history, as in the case of the destroyed Palestinian villages of **Qolonieh** and **Emmaus**. But these two villages, along with **Qubeiba** and **Abu Gosh** are mentioned as possible locations of the reappearance of Christ (after his death), in which it is said he will dine with his disciples, Simon and Cleophas.

Franciscans believe that Qubeiba is where Jesus appeared to Simon and Cleophas three days after he was buried. The **Franciscan Church** was built in the 12th century on the site of a Byzantine church, which in turn had been built on the house believed to belong to Cleophas, where Jesus shared bread with him. One of the church walls is said to be part of the 1st-century home. During Abbasid rule (750–1200) Arab clans began to settle in and around Qubeiba and built a caravanserai. The area has been continuously inhabited ever since. Most of the existing homes date back to the Ottoman era.

The village of Emmaus was turned into **Canada Park** after Zionist forces expelled its Arab residents in 1948. Largely paid for by members of the Canadian Jewish community, the park contains remains of the Byzantine city, several wine presses, a sophisticated Roman aqueduct system, a Crusader castle, and some other unusual Roman tombs. Other historical ruins of Emmaus are now the property of the monastery of Latrun.

The village was at least 2,000 years old, because it was known as a center of turmoil in the 1st century when the Romans rulers sold the village's inhabitants into slavery for not paying taxes. Identified by the Byzantine scholar, Julius Africans, as the place Christ dined with Simon and Cleophas, it was given the status of city by the emperor in 221 CE and renamed Nicopolis.

All residents of Emmaus, including the great Arab general, Abu

Ubaida Amer Ibn al-Jarrah, died of the plague during the early Islamic era. In 639 CE, a monument enshrining his grave was built by the Mamluks.

The largest of Emmaus's three monasteries was built by the Franciscans in the 7th century and renovated in 1901. Remnants of a 5th-century Byzantine church and a church built by the Templars in 1150–1170 within the Byzantine church are still visible. The Crusaders built a fortress in 1133 to guard the southern and eastern routes to Jerusalem.

Palestinian West Jerusalem

Before dying of heart failure, Faisal Husseini, the senior Palestinian representative from Jerusalem, reiterated in every meeting he had with Israeli negotiators that the Arab neighborhoods of West Jerusalem, most of which were confiscated from their owners, would have to be part of any negotiated peace agreement. As the peace process moved in reverse, discussion about these neighborhoods and Arab property across the Green Line effectively ceased. But the neighborhoods and landmark buildings that the Palestinians left remain. The neighborhoods Talbiya, Katamon, Abu Tor, Musrara, and Bak'a, built to the south of the city in the 1920s and 1930s, were comprised largely of the homes of affluent Palestinians, whose large gardens were filled with citrus, fig, palm, and cypress trees. Refined and eclectic architectural elements and modern designs intertwine in these mansions, where today Jewish Israelis live.

Musrara was the first Arab neighborhood to be built outside the city walls. Established toward the end of the 19th century, its residents were mostly upper-middle-class Muslims and Greek Orthodox Christians. As the Israelis drew their borders after the 1948 war, Musrara was divided into two, with about a third falling in the Arab sector.

The Israeli government confiscated all the homes in the part of Musrara that they occupied after the 1948 war. The owners were not allowed to return and their homes were "allocated" by the government to poor emigrants from rural Morocco. As Arab Jews, the Moroccans faced prejudice from the European-dominated Israeli government and the poor youths of the neighborhood founded a group called the Black Panthers. Musrara became the playground of the Panthers in the 1960s and 1970s and confrontations with the state were frequent. In recent decades many Moroccans have sold their homes and the neighborhood has been "gentrified," with real estate prices running into millions of dollars. None of the original owners, who still have their deeds, are able to reclaim their property or even to buy it back.

Thabor, a Swedish theological center, has a beautiful archeological garden in the heart of Musrara. Though it is not easily accessible to the public, it is well worth visiting. Israelis established the **Museum of the Seam** in the confiscated home of the Baramki family. The theme of the displays is the development of Jerusalem since 1948. Although the curators say the museum is designed to bring Arabs and Jews together from both sides of Jerusalem, the signs are only in Hebrew and English.

Notre Dame, built in 1887 as the papal residence in Jerusalem, comprises a church, monastery, and hotel—and Jerusalem's best French restaurant. Its size and an imposing view of the city reflects the importance of Jerusalem for the Vatican. A tug of war between the Vatican and the State of Israel over the complex is an open secret in Catholic and Israeli circles.

The neighborhood of **Mamilla** (Sanctuary of God) is directly west of the Old City. It first developed around a 13th-century Mamluk cemetery. Under the British Mandate, it became part of the "new" city center outside the walls. A post office, shops, and government bureaus all sprung up in Mamilla and neighboring Jaffa Street. Muslims, Armenians, Christian Arabs, and Jews all owned property here. The Israeli state desecrated the Muslim cemetery, leaving only a handful of graves and throwing the bones of the other former inhabitants into a now closed pit, in their making of **Independence Park**. As a single reminder of the Muslim past, the **Zawaiya Kubakiya**, under which the Mamluk Aidughi Kubaki was buried in 1289, still stands. Today Independence Park is a popular hangout for the Israeli gay community.

The **Palace Hotel** (1929), now the Israeli Ministry of Industry and Trade, was designed by Turkish architect Nahas Bey to be the showpiece of the Arab Muslim community that was establishing itself in West Jerusalem. It remains one of the most luxurious buildings in Jerusalem. Located at the bottom of what was Mamilla Road (now Agron Street), the building was adorned with engraved verses from the Quran and the entrance lobby, topped by an octagonal skylight, reached to the entire height of the building.

The **YMCA** was built between 1926 and 1933 by the American architect Arthur Loomis Harmon, who also built New York's Empire State Building. The hotel, restaurant, and sports facility center has one of the best views of this part of the city.

Terra Sancta on Keren Hayesod Street was designed by the Italian architect Antonio Berluzzi in 1924–27 to serve as a community center for Catholic youth. Later, with the opening of the YMCA, it became a vocational high school. This symmetrical building with its horizontal

lines between stories combines Italian Renaissance and neo-baroque elements. Prince Umberto of Italy came to Jerusalem in 1928 to dedicate the statue poised on the roof of the haloed Madonna, patron saint of Milan.

The 200-room, two-story **King David Hotel** was built by the Palestine Hotel Company in 1931 with pink sandstone from Bethlehem. It hosted such royalty as the Empress of Persia, Queen Mother Nazli of Egypt, and King Abdullah I of Jordan. The hotel afforded asylum to three royal heads of state who had to flee their countries: King Alfonso VIII of Spain, Emperor Haile Selassie of Ethiopia, and King George II of Greece, who set up his government-in-exile at the hotel in 1942. In the 1930s, the British government used it as its administrative and military center. In July 1946, the Jewish terrorist group Irgun, headed by Nobel Peace Prize winner Menachem Begin, placed a bomb in the kitchen, which killed 91 people and destroyed the southern wing. On May 4, 1948, the British flag was lowered, and the building became a Jewish stronghold.

Just south of Mamilla on the road to Bethlehem is the **Sultan's Pool**. The existing pool dates back to late Mamluk rule, when it was expanded and renovated by Sultan Zaher Barquq in 1399. It was renovated again by Suleiman the Magnificent in the early 1500s. Under Israeli rule it is called Merrill Hassenfeld Amphitheater and used for concerts and public events. The nearby 16th-century drinking fountain is all but forgotten across from the Israel Cinemateque.

Further along the road to Bethlehem is **St. Andrew's Church**. Built in 1930, it was used by the Scottish regiments of the British Army. Today it is used by Presbyterians who are members of the Diocese of the Episcopal Church in Jerusalem. A craft shop in the compound, **Sunbula**, promotes the work of Palestinian artisans, mostly village and refugee camp women.

Along the same street is what remains of the **Jerusalem Railway Station** (1892). Adjacent to the station is the former **Ottoman Travellers Inn**, which Israelis now use as a theater.

Talbiya (Komemiyut in Hebrew), just south of Mamilla, was once considered the most exclusive neighborhood in West Jerusalem and to some degree remains so today. Largely endowed by the Ottoman government to the Greek Orthodox Church, the land on which Talbiya was built was resold by the church to individual families and groups, as was the nearby Jewish neighborhood of Rahavia. The people who settled in Talbiya were predominantly Christians from

Former Palestinian homes in West Jerusalem

Bethlehem, Beit Jala, and Jerusalem. Wealthy Muslim families from Jerusalem were also major investors. Almost all the still existing homes of note were built between 1924 and 1937. Though there are no major historical sites, the grand mansions that once belonged to the Salamehs, Dajanis, and other wealthy, mostly merchant, families of the era, are still beautiful to see. What is now an international Christian mission at 10 Berner Street was the family home of the late Palestinian–American intellectual Edward W. Said.

The **Israeli Museum for Islamic Art** has a very interesting 17th- and 18th-century Islamic collection, which is worth looking at for those interested in Islamic art and artifacts. Palestine's Islamic artifacts, however, cannot be found here.

Baja's (Geulim in Hebrew) was the first of the new neighborhoods southwest of Jerusalem that developed during the late Ottoman period. Its inhabitants were mainly middle-class Muslims who had moved out of the Old City. They, too, were expelled and their property confiscated after 1948.

Katamon (Gonen in Hebrew) lies parallel to the Bethlehem route, also known as the road to Beit Safafa (Emeq Refaim in Hebrew). The road leads to both the neighborhood of Katamon, the former Greek Colony, and to what is now the "neighborhood" of **Beit Safafa**. The Greek Colony lies on the borders of the Katamon quarter in the vicinity of Rakhel Imenu Street. Initially established under the patronage of the Greek Orthodox Patriarch Eftimos in 1902 for Greek families accompanying the clergy, the property was later sold to both Christian and Muslim Arabs. Only foreigners were allowed to stay in the quarter after Israeli occupied it in 1948.

Distinguished by its red tiled roofs and well kept gardens, the **German Colony** was established in 1860, along with others in Haifa and Jaffa. Protestant German settlers from Wurtemberg were instrumental in upgrading the transportation industry in Palestine.

Al-Masqobia, the Russian compound built in 1858, was Moscow's headquarters in the Holy Land. Containing a church, a hospice, an administrative center, a school and a hospital, this compound was expropriated first by the British and later by the Israelis, who set up a police station and a detention center, with a reputation for torturing Palestinian prisoners.

To the south of Jerusalem lies **Abu Tor**, or al-Thori, which means "father of the bull"—a reference to a general in Saladin's army who used to ride a bull. It is a coveted residential neighborhood with one of the best views of Jerusalem, only a ten-minute walk from the Old

City. It is still inhabited mainly by Palestinians, but Israeli families have moved in.

Hidden among pines and cypresses on a 16-acre hilltop in a southern corner of the city is **Government House.** Inaugurated in 1930 by Sir Arthur Wauchope, the British high commissioner for Palestine, it served as the residence of a number of subsequent high commissioners. The unusual octagonal building is made of locally quarried stone and includes a fountain similar to those found in North African palaces. Other distinguishing features of the building are its domes, interior arches, crossed vaults and a monumental four-meter high ceramic fireplace of Armenian–Jerusalem tiles created by David Ohanessian. Today the building is the **UN Truce Supervisory Organization headquaters.**

Abu Gosh is an anomaly in the history of Jerusalem villages. It is one of the few villages that was allowed to exist, without its population being expelled or driven out by the Israelis. Located on the road to Tel Aviv, it was the home of the Abu Gosh clan, who extracted taxes from all travellers going and coming to Jerusalem during the Ottoman era. It is believed by Palestinians that the people of Abu Gosh "cut a deal" with the Zionist forces in order not to be expelled. Local lore has it that the Ark of the Covenant was kept in Abu Gosh before being taken to Jerusalem. The **Monastery of the Ark**, built in 1924, stands over the site of the house of Abinadab, where the Ark of the Covenant is believed to have been was kept. The large statue of Mary holding the baby Jesus can be seen for miles. The Crusaders confused Abu Gosh with Emmaus and built several churches here. The **Benedictine Monastery** rises above the ruins of a 1st-century Roman fort inscribed with the name of the Roman Tenth Legion.

Another beautiful Jerusalem village much praised in Palestinian lore is **Lifta.** Known by the Romans as Nephtoah, the Byzantines as Nephtho, and the Crusaders as Clepsta, today it is a Jewish neighborhood cleansed of its former inhabitants. The Israeli Knesset is partially built on Lifta land now known as Qiryat Ben Gurion (the village of Ben Gurion).

The Ottomans named the lands around the village of **Deir Yassin** "Khirbet Ayn al-Tut," because so many berries grew in its midst, but the village owes its name to a renowned local sage known as Shaykh Yassin. Neither the connection to the sage nor the berries did Deir Yassin much good when Israeli terror groups perpetrated a massacre in the village, killing more than 200 people, including at least 70 women and children. The name Deir Yassin has been synonymous with massacre since then. Many of the original Arab homes dotting the hill still exist, inhabited by Israelis. The orphans of the massacre were raised in the Dar al Tifl al-Arabi Orphanage in Jerusalem. The neighborhood of Deir Yassin now goes by the name of Giv'at Sha'ul.

Qastal was a tiny village with only 90 inhabitants, but what it lacked in physical size it evokes in emotion. Today no more than part of the Jerusalem–Tel Aviv highway corridor and part of an Israeli neighborhood known as Mevasseret Tziyyon, the village was the site of a famous battle between the Zionist forces and the Arab Liberation Army headed by Abdul Qadir al-Husseini, who was killed here.

Most of the 2,000 residents of **Malha** were expelled by Israeli forces in 1948. Today it is known as Ramat Danya and is the site of a large housing project and Jerusalem's biggest Israeli Mall, known as the Malha Kanyon. The main village mosque, the **Omar Ibn Khattab Mosque**, is still standing, but closed to worshippers. Many of the village's original houses still exist, with Israeli residents.

Before 1948, **Ein Karem** was known as the most beautiful of all the Jerusalem villages. Then, more than 3,000 villagers were forcibly evicted by Zionist forces, and the village, in its entirety, was repopulated by Moroccans Jews, most of whom have now sold their property to wealthy Israeli professionals seeking a relaxing life in a beautiful village. Although none of the original inhabitants were allowed to stay or return, just one Arab family from the ethnically cleansed village of Iqrit, northeast of Acre, was allowed to live in the village and work in the otherwise abandoned church dedicated to **John the Baptist**. Built in 1674 on Byzantine ruins by the Franciscans with the help of the Spanish monarchy, the Spanish-style church includes remnants of other periods, including a statue of Venus. The church contains the entrance to a natural cave, believed to be Grotto of Nativity of St. John. The village includes several churches and monasteries: the **Franciscan Monastery**, the **Convent of Saint Zechariah**, the **Church of the Lady of Sahyun** and her tombs, and the **Church of the Visitation**, built by the Byzantines to commemorate Mary's visit to Elizabeth. The existing structure, built in 1946 by Antonio Barluzzi, looks similar to the original two-story structure. The church is built around a grotto believed to date to Roman times. The village has two mosques. One, the smaller, **Mosque of Omar**, dates back to the 7th century, while the other, the **Mosque of Ein Karem** was built during Ottoman rule. Both are out of use, but still standing.

Top: Architectural details inside al-Aqsa Mosque
Bottom: Palestinian elders reading the Quran inside the mosque

Refugee Camps

Qalandia Camp

Qalandia camp, 11 kilometers (6.8 mi) north of Jerusalem, was established in 1949 on 90 acres of land belonging to residents of nearby Qalandia. The camp houses approximately 9,500 Palestinians, who originate mainly from Haifa (Sadoun), Lydd, Ramleh (Bir al-Mouien), Jerusalem (Sarees), and Hebron.

Qalandia's narrow streets twist up a rocky mountain, where the majority of the camp citizens reside. In the late 1950s, Qalandia became host to one of three UNRWA vocational training schools in the Palestinian refugee camp network. (The other two are located in Lebanon and Jordan). This facility has contributed to the presence of small industries within the camp, including car mechanics, aluminum workshops, furniture factories, and electronic repair shops.

The sound of heavy equipment can be heard coming from three visible stone quarries, which are operational 24 hours a day. Since Palestinian quarries are prevented from using dynamite by the Israeli occupation, Qalandia residents suffer sound and environmental pollution at an unprecedented level. North of the stone quarries looms the burgeoning Israeli settlement of Kohav Yakov, which is to be populated with ultra-Orthodox Jews. It is an important piece in the wide ring of Israeli settlements around Jerusalem.

Qalandia camp is one of the few West Bank camps to practice the Arab tradition of the *diwan,* a cultural phenomenon brought to the camp by refugees who came from Ashoukh, Bier Ma'in, and Saris. At sundown every day, the men of the camp meet in one of five *diwans* to discuss daily events, solve communal issues, and socialize.

After 1967, some Qalandia residents became second-time refugees in Jordan, while other new refugees came here. The newly displaced came from Deir Ayyoub, Beit Nuba, Emmaus, and the Gaza Strip.

Israel considers the area west of the Jerusalem–Ramallah road part of Jerusalem, which is part of the larger plan to illegally annex the territory acquired through the 1967 war. The land included for annexation included some Qalandia homes, whose residents subsequently received Jerusalem ID cards. The eastern part of the camp, on the other hand, received West Bank ID cards, which curtailed rights on travel, job opportunities, and health benefits.

The full repercussions of this invisible wall were not felt until the onset of PNA rule, when the section of the camp considered to be part of the West Bank became Area C, and the parts attached to Jerusalem

Children jump over the wall at Abu Dis

remained within the municipal boundaries of the city. In both cases, the residents had no forum through which their concerns could be met. They continue to receive little or no social services. As a result, the main Jerusalem–Ramallah road that divides the camp is in notoriously bad shape. Camp residents took it upon themselves to dig up parts of the road to act as speed-bumps, which were later replaced by "real" speed bumps.

Today, the Israeli occupation has erected one of the largest walls and checkpoints just south of the camp, intended to be the northern gateway from Ramallah to Jerusalem. As a result, long lines of cars seem to be perpetually piling up, all the way back to the entrance of the camp.

Shu'fat Camp

Shu'fat camp was established in 1965/1966 on 50 acres of land belonging to the village of Shu'fat. Established long after all other camps in the West Bank, it initially accommodated 3,300 refugees that had been living the Mu'askar camp located in the Old City, now within the Jewish Quarter. Mu'askar camp had been plagued by

East Jerusalem was occupied by Israel in 1967

unsanitary conditions and was closed down after the establishment of Shu'fat, which was able to provide more space for the refugees.

Shu'fat camp residents originate from 55 villages in the Jerusalem (Beit Thoul, al-Wallace, Malha, Katamon, Lifta), Jaffa, Lydd (al-Akbab), and Ramleh regions. Today Shu'fat camp is home to 15,000

Palestinian refugees. It is the only refugee camp that lies fully within the municipal boundaries of Israeli-occupied East Jerusalem. As such, the residents of Shu'fat camp suffer the double discrimination of being both refugees and Palestinians in a city Israel is constantly Judaizing.

Overcrowding is a major problem, especially with the inadequacy of the camp's basic infrastructure. UNRWA's technical/safety building regulations are completely ignored as more and more residents constructing three- and four-story shelters on foundations constructed to hold one or two stories. An already grave sewage problem has been compounded by the fact that the Jerusalem municipal slaughterhouse redirected its sewage in the direction of Shu'fat camp, resulting in frequent back-ups, especially in summer time. Strategically located on territory Israel desperately wants to complete the settlement ring that cuts off Jerusalem from the West Bank, Shu'fat camp is hemmed in by an ever-growing number of settlement units from the colonies of Rekhez Shu'fat, French Hill, Pisgat Zeev, Anatot Alanon, and Maaleh Adumim.

As part of its relief and social services efforts, UNRWA, in coordination with the camp committee, constructed and equipped a modern community center that provides a number of social and economic services to some 1,000 refugees, mainly the elderly, women and children.

PART FOUR

Southern Palestine

The pillar of the crying Jesus in the Church of the Nativity

27.

Bethlehem (Beit Lahem)

O Jesus Christ
when you roam
through the streets of Hebron
or down Bethlehem's lanes
in this night's cold,
and wander from Beit Ania
and Birzeit
envelope yourself
with your woolen cloak,
for the night is snowing,
the wind is screaming.

—"The Stranger," *Khalil al-Khoury, translated by*
Noel Abdulahad, 20th century

It is believed that some 500,000 years ago humans lived in the area of Wadi Khureitun, southeast of Bethlehem, when the area was lush and green and inhabited by very large animals. But written references to the city of Bethlehem appear much later, first in the al-Amarna letters, 1,400 years before the birth of Jesus Christ. In these letters, Bethlehem was referred to as Beit Ello (house of Ello), the Canaanite Wheat deity, and as a resting place for travellers going from Syria to Egypt.

It seems to have been a Canaanite town as early as 2000 BCE. The settlement was once known as Beit Lahama, perhaps in honor of the ancient fertility god Lahmothe. The site where today's Church of Nativity stands was where the Canaanites are believed to have worshipped this deity. In the Old Testament, Bethlehem was known as Ephrata. Assyrians and Persians came to live in the city and it was later Hellenized and Romanized during the various eras of rule.

According to Christian tradition, Jesus Christ was born in a cave in the east side of the city, toward the end of Herod's reign, circa 6 CE. During the reign of the Emperor Hadrian, probably around 130 CE, a temple venerating Adonis was constructed above the site where Jesus was apparently born. Hadrian had it built in memory of the recently deceased love of his life, Antinous. In Assyrian lore, Adonis is a male partner who dies and is reborn. Many Christians believed that Hadrian's love shrine signaled that he had knowingly built it over the birthplace of Christ in order to deter the new believers and followers of Christ from praying there.

By the time the Byzantine Empress Helena visited Palestine in 339 CE, it was already a site of secret Christian pilgrimage. She ordered the Church of Nativity built on the very site where the temple of Adonis stood. The mosaic floor and many columns of that era still exist.

Under the Byzantines, Bethlehem grew, along with Jerusalem, to become the holiest city in all of Christendom. Its residents virtually all converted and many newcomers who came for pilgrimage stayed to make the city of Christ's birth their home. In 388, St. Jerome settled in Bethlehem and translated the Bible into Latin, establishing the Vulgate, long the definitive version of the Bible in the Roman Catholic Church.

Though it is not known whether Byzantine or Canaanite, a protective wall surrounded the city and it appeared prominently on the Map of Madaba. In 529 CE much of the city and the church was damaged during the Samaritan Revolt, but the Emperor Justinian had the walls of the city and the church repaired and renovated in great splendor.

In 614, the Persians stormed through Palestine, laying waste to all signs of opposition. In the Church of the Nativity, however, they saw representations of the three magi, whom they identified as holy men from Persia, and in a sign of reverence to their ancestors, they left the church intact.

The Muslim Caliph Omar visited Bethlehem in 638 CE. For a while Muslims and the Christians prayed together in the Church of the Nativity. In future conflicts this fact protected the church as a venerated place for both religions. Today Muslim women still make fertility prayers to the Virgin Mary at the Grotto of the Nativity.

Top: Interior of the Church of the Nativity
Bottom: Muslim and Christian prayer in the Grotto of the Nativity

King Baldwin I had himself crowned in Bethlehem on Christmas Day 1100. Though the city was wrested from the Crusaders by Saladin in 1187, the Ayyubite Muslim ruler Sultan Malik al-Kamil agreed to Crusader rule over Bethlehem from 1229–1291.

During the Mamluk and Ottoman rule Bethlehem continued to have special status as a Christian city. Although they may have felt marginalized by their Muslim rulers, the people of Bethlehem had more religious autonomy than people elsewhere in the world, and proximity to Jerusalem meant easy access to ecclesiastical power.

At the beginning of the 19th century, Bethlehem increased its interaction with missionaries and benefited from their generosity. Cottage industries, such as making olive wood trinkets for pilgrims, found markets in Europe and North and South America. In 1915 at the World's Fair in San Francisco, Bethlehem artisans displayed their wares. Local masons who specialized in pink stone became famous and exported their goods and talent to Lebanon and Syria.

Early in the 20th century, Bethlehem merchant families began emigrating to Central, South, and to a lesser degree, North America in ever increasing numbers. Partly spurred on by trade and partly to avoid conscription into the Ottoman army, young men headed to Chile, Brazil, and Honduras to establish communities, which have flourished and grown tremendously throughout the century. Many Bethlehem families were Catholic and benefited from the network established by the church. Friars and fathers preaching and teaching at the town's many educational institutions provided language lessons and cultural preparations for emigration. The population of Bethlehem was just over 8,000 when the British took over Palestine. During the Mandate, Bethlehem witnessed an economic boom and many of its emigrants returned. The economic growth ground to a halt during World War II and ultimately went into reverse after 1948.

From 1948 until 1967, Bethlehem was part of the Jordanian-ruled West Bank. Local notables established close ties with the monarchy in Jordan, and the late King Hussein visited the town on several occasions. Along with the rest of the West Bank, Bethlehem was occupied by the Israeli military in June 1967 and came under direct Israeli military rule.

Bethlehem retains a slightly provincial character, despite a massive foreign presence in the town. Both the Christian and Muslim communities are considered conservative, and the two communities have generally lived together in harmony.

Between 1967 and 1993 Bethlehem did its best to steer clear of confrontation with the military occupiers, although its otherwise conservative youth did become politicized and often supported the PFLP and the PPP. The refugees, many of whom live inside the town, were often supporters of Fatah and, more recently, Hamas. The town's long-time mayor, Elias Freij, managed to accommodate the Israeli occupation authorities, the PLO, and the government of Jordan—no small feat.

During both the first intifada and the al-Aqsa intifada, the students at the Bethlehem university played an important role in involving the town's youth in the resistance. While most of the young men involved in political activities in Bethlehem tended to be from the refugee camps, many of the town's local boys and girls were active in providing healthcare, help to needy families, and advocating an end to the occupation.

It was in the al-Aqsa intifada that Bethlehem became most visible when a stand-off between the Israeli army and armed activists inside the Church of Nativity turned into a nightly internationally televised saga for more than a month. Although technically under PNA rule, Bethlehem remains an occupied city, which the Israeli army invades at will, arresting and assassinating political activists.

It is second only to Jerusalem in the number of historical religious sites in the country and so it remains a major destination for pilgrimage and veneration. With the beginning of Palestinian "self-rule" in 1995, Bethlehem became a centerpiece for efforts to revive cultural tourism and religious pilgrimage to Christian and Muslim holy sites. The Bethlehem 2000 Project was established to prepare the town and nearby Palestinian-ruled villages, towns, and cities for the new millennium in hope of better times.

Visiting Bethlehem

The road to Bethlehem from Jerusalem was once simple, but today it is like traveling to another country. With walls and Israeli military checkpoints in place, the city of Christ's birth has been turned into a military fortress. Along the route, parts of Arab West Jerusalem can still be seen. **Sultan's Pools**, the **Scottish Church**, **the British-built railway station**, the **German Hospice**, the **Monastery of the Poor Clares**, **Allenby Barracks**, the Jewish colony of **Talpioth**, and the formerly Arab neighborhood of **al-Baqa'a** line up along the route like a welcoming committee.

Before the military checkpoint lies **Bir al-Qadismu** (from Kathisma, meaning "place of rest" in Greek). Palestinian lore has it that this is the Well of the Magi, where the three Magi saw the star guiding them from the East.

Bethlehem Culinary Traditions

South of Bethlehem is the garden of Palestine. With traditional agricultural villages like Artas, Battir, Khader, and Aroub—to mention just a few—sprawling over the countryside, Bethlehem does not lack fresh produce. By long tradition, quite a number of village women used to bring in their seasonal hand-picked vegetables and fruits to sell them in the Bethlehem marketplace or to private clients they maintained all year round, year after year. This network of women has unfortunately dwindled in the last two decades, mainly due to the confiscation of thousands of acres of orchards and agricultural land by Israel to make way for the settlements that continue to grow.

Though it is certainly true that the cuisine of the Bethlehem area has evolved more dramatically than that of other Palestinian cities—partly due to its proximity to Jerusalem, but because in its own right, Bethlehem has been exposed to outside influences, particularly Western, for two centuries—mainstream cooking remains quite traditional. Though it is quite possible to be served fine French, Italian, or Mexican dishes in some Bethlehem homes, the fact is that large contingencies of southern villagers have moved here, keeping a village culture in the midst of the town.

Culinary traditions have persisted. One particular heart-warming dish merits special mention: *yakhni kusaa b'laban*, zucchini stew, served with rice. When zucchini, grown organically, the traditional way, is in season in mid-summer, it is a choice vegetable, for vegetarians and meat-eaters alike. Zucchinis are delicious lightly fried and seasoned with an herb sauce or garlic dressing.

Stews are popular in everyday cooking, because a relatively small amount of meat can go a long way in feeding a large family, and their mix of grain, vegetable, and meat provides a range of nutrients. Since dry weather dominates most of the year in Bethlehem, stews supply the extra liquid people need to avoid dehydration.

Stews are traditionally cooked with choice juicy cuts of lamb: from the middle neck and shoulder, the shank, the loin, or around the rib. The meat is left to cook until it is very tender and further cooking is required after adding the trimmed vegetables. But the good news for vegetarians is that what gives the stew its particularly Palestinian flavor is the spices: pepper and allspice, of course; and a hint of nutmeg, cinnamon, cloves, cumin, coriander, and cardamom. Always buy spices whole (as grains, sticks, or roots) and in limited quantities to guarantee optimum flavor. Keep in tightly closed containers away from any source of light or heat.

Zucchini Stew

3 pounds lamb, cut in chunks
6 tablespoons olive oil
2 teaspoons salt
1 teaspoon pepper
¾ teaspoon allspice
dash each of nutmeg, cinnamon, cloves, cumin, coriander and cardamom
3 pounds zucchini
3 garlic cloves, crushed
4 cups *laban* (sour yogurt)
4 teaspoons cornstarch
2 teaspoons tomato concentrate
2 teaspoons dried, crushed mint leaves

1. Brown the meat in 3 tablespoons of oil in a large pan over high heat. Add the salt and spices and turn over the chunks until they are evenly browned. Add enough hot water to cover the meat. Bring to a boil, and then let simmer for 60–70 minutes.

2. While the meat is cooking, wash and dry the zucchini and cut them across. Add 1 tablespoon of oil to a deep frying pan and stir-fry the marrows and the crushed garlic over medium heat for a few minutes; cover the pan and let them cook in their juice for five minutes. After making sure the meat is done, add the zucchini to it.

3. In the pan you used for the zucchini, add the *laban*, the cornstarch dissolved in 4 tablespoons of water, and the tomato concentrate. Bring to boil while stirring the mixture gently. Then add to the stew. Taste and adjust the salt and pepper. Add the crushed mint leaves to the pot and simmer for five minutes more. Serve immediately in a deep bowl accompanied with vermicelli rice.

Nearby **Mar Elias** (Convent of St. Elias) is variously ascribed to be the site of patronage of the Egyptian patriarch of Jerusalem, St. Elias (494), the resting place for the Prophet Elijah, and a mausoleum for the Greek Bishop Elias of Bethlehem (1345). It was and remains a site of pilgrimage for barren women, the sick, and the crippled. Before heading to Bethlehem the patriarchs of Jerusalem still stop at Mar Elias on Christmas day to meet with local notables. Once a prime spot for panoramic views of Jerusalem and Bethlehem, today the most visible site is Har Homa (Jabal Abu Ghneim in Arabic), one of the ugliest illegal Israeli settlements built in the post-Oslo era. Opposite the monastery is a stone seat dedicated to pre-Raphaelite painter William Holman Hunt, to mark where he painted his major religious works during his sojourn in Palestine.

Just before the Bethlehem checkpoint is **Tantour**, a former hospice and chapel built by the Knights of Malta that is now Palestine's most important ecumenical institute of dialogue promoting understanding between the monotheistic faiths.

Past the Israeli military checkpoint on the righthand side the Israeli-built separation wall is in full view, as is the fortress-like **Tomb of Rachel**. An important symbol to grieving mothers, Muslims venerate the biblical matriarch, whose male children were killed at Herod's orders. Women have come to her tomb to pray for health and fertility since time immemorial. Initially built by the Byzantines, the existing tomb was built by the Ottomans. In 1841 a British Jewish philanthropist had the domed roof restored and reportedly made "special" arrangements for Jews at the site. Although the **Tomb and Mosque of Bilal Ibn Rabah** and a tribal cemetery of the Ta'amre Bedouin tribe share the property with the matriarchal tomb, they are off-limits to Muslims by order of the Israeli military. (Until 1977 the site had been under the protection of the Islamic Wafq and accessible to all.)

Today local residents must receive Israeli military permits to leave their neighborhood. The fortress-like walls around the entire neighborhood were built in the 1990s after the Oslo Peace Agreement was signed.

Bethehem City Quarters

The history of Bethlehem's people is best found in the city quarters, rather than religious sanctuaries. Almost all of the city quarters revolve around the recently renovated (1998–1999) **Manger Square**. Adjacent to the main plaza with the **Church of Nativity**, the **Church** of **St. Catherine**, the **Mosque of Omar**, and the **Bethlehem Peace Center**, it is the cultural hub of the town and the site of Christmas Eve festivities every year.

Harat al-Najajreh, the oldest of the town's quarters, is west of Manger Square. Local lore has it that the residents are descendants of the Arab Ghassanite tribe, who were among the first communities in the world to convert to Christianity. The Ghassanites lived in the entire region from the northern Levant in Syria to the Yemeni mountains in the south, with their base in the Yemeni region of Najran.

Harat al-Farahiyeh is located on **Star Street**, northwest of Manger Square. For centuries, this street was the main shopping street in town. Still every year church patriarchs take a procession from Jerusalem to Bethlehem along it. The quarter itself was named after a Patriarch named Farah (joy in Arabic), who was a descendent of the first Christian Arabs. His family migrated from the Wadi Musa area in what is contemporary Jordan and settled in Bethlehem after performing pilgrimage. It is not certain if they came in the Byzantine or the Muslim-Arab era.

With the coming of the Crusaders, a third quarter was established north of Manger Square. **Harat al-Tarajmeh** (quarter of translators) was founded by the families formed when the mostly French, Italian, and Spanish men working as translators for the Franciscan friars married Arab women.

During the 400-year Ottoman era three additional tribes established town quarters. One tribe, who came from the village of Antar (meaning brave) near Herodium, established **Harat al-Qanatre**, just south of the Church of Nativity. Their neighbors, a tribe from Tekoa, established **Harat al-Qawawse**. **Harat al-Hraizat** was established north of Manger Square by a tribe from Um Tuba, a village just south of Jerusalem.

After making an alliance with the tribes of Bethlehem not to pay taxes to the Ottomans in 1780, clans from the village of Fagur, close to Solomon's Pools, established their own city quarter on a hill west of the city. Their Harat al-Fawagreh was the last historic Bethlehem quarter to be established, and the first of the town's Muslim quarters.

Religious Sites in Bethlehem City

Christmas Church

Built in 1886 by Lutheran Pastor Ludwig Schneller and funded by Empress Augusta Victoria, the Christmas Church was the first major Protestant Church in Bethlehem. Kaiser William II visited it during his historic 1898 visit to Palestine. The Church was established to serve the congregation that became active in Bethlehem after the Ottomans liberalized and allowed for missionary activities in 1854.

Church of the Nativity

This most important site is in the center of Bethlehem, built upon the cave where Mary is said to have given birth to Jesus. The present church is basically the structure that was commissioned by Empress Helena in the 4th century, with a basilica that looks like earlier structures borrowed from pre-Christian Roman mausoleums. The church is the shape of a cross, 170 feet long and 80 feet wide. It contains the three convents: to the northeast, Armenian; to the northeast, Franciscan; to the southeast, Greek Orthodox. The compound also includes the Church of Saint Catherine, the medieval Cloister of Saint Jerome, as well as the network of monastic caves, and most importantly, the Grotto of the Nativity.

A narrow passage leads into the original narthex, and two side entrances under the main altar lead to the Grotto of the Nativity. The rectangular grotto (about 35 by 10 ft) has two entrances to the Holy Manger. A silver star with the Latin inscription, "Here Jesus Christ Was Born of the Virgin Mary," marks the hallowed spot.

One of the two entrances to the grotto has 44 columns, 18 feet high, dividing the basilica into five aisles. The paintings on the columns are from the Justinian period; the mosaics on the upper side walls from the Crusader period. Under the various wooden trap doors are parts of the original mosaic floor. The church today dates mostly to the time of Justinian, except for the church entrance, which was downsized to keep out invaders on horseback. Also, the Crusaders expanded the compound, redid the roof, and had the walls decorated with mosaics by Greek artisans.

At the center of the roofed churchyard is a floor made of heavy flagstones that were discovered a few feet down. These evidently belonged to the outer court or to a street leading to the inner court (atrium) of the church. During the reconstruction of the church, under Justinian in the 6th century, the floor was raised.

Today, the church ceiling and roof have fallen into dangerous disrepair. A disagreement between the different denominations housed in the church led to a standstill until they asked the PNA to take charge of the church's renovation. In the midst of the al-Aqsa intifada, repairs were put off until the political situation allows the PNA to make the necessary arrangements to repair the roof.

Near the church is the Milk Grotto, a hollowed-out grotto of soft white rock. It is called Magharet al-Saayideh (grotto of the lady) in Arabic, in honor of the Virgin Mary. Tradition has it that Mary nursed her baby here, and a few drops of milk fell on the floor, turning the rocks white. Used as a fertility temply in pre-Christian times, today it is still a sanctuary venerated by Christians and Muslims. The building of the church here was commissioned by St. Paula sometime in the latter part of the 4th century. The Franciscans have been the caretakers of the site since 1347 and renovated it in 1872.

Greek Catholic Church
This church is the hub of the Greek Catholic community, many of whom originally belonged to the Greek Orthodox denomination. They preserve Eastern liturgy and language. The view of Bethlehem from the church's main tower is breathtaking.

Mosque of Omar
This mosque commemorates the 638 CE visit to Bethlehem by Omar al-Khattab, the Caliph of Islam. According to lore he prayed where the mosque now stands. The existing mosque was built in 1860 on lands donated by the Greek Orthodox Church and renovated in 1954, during Jordanian rule. The increase in the Muslim population here following the 1948 Nakba made it necessary to enlarge the mosque, which is the only Muslim shrine of worship in Old Bethlehem.

Silesian Church & Convent
The Silesian complex includes a church, orphanage, and technical school, all built between 1872 and 1892 by an Italian priest, Anton Balloni. Father Balloni came to Bethlehem to help orphans after a terrible epidemic of cholera. He raised funds to establish an orphanage by selling the city's handcrafts (made mainly from olive wood) in Italy.

Syriac Orthodox Church (Church of the Virgin)
The Syriac Orthodox Church was built in 1955 as part of a complex that is the spiritual home of the Syriacs, a Christian people originally from southern Turkey and northern Iraq. Many Syriacs came to Palestine as pilgrims and refugees in the 1800s and stayed, keeping their own language and liturgy, and living in their own quarter of the city, the Hosh or Harat Syriac.

Other City Sites

Bethlehem Peace Center

This center opened as part of the Palestinian millennium celebrations on July 1, 2000. Mainly a cultural center with the aim of promoting peace, democracy, religious tolerance, and diversity, it hosts art and book exhibits, theater productions, and movie screenings, as well as a variety of cultural seminars and courses all year round.

City Market

In 1929 this popular market was moved from Manger Square to this old marketplace. Merchants, farmers, and artisans come from all parts of the Bethlehem and Hebron districts to sell their goods here.

Dar Mansour

The Mansour house, with its mix of eastern and western elements, is a good example of the turn-of-the-century building style popular in Bethlehem. The Mansour family rents the building to the PNA to house the Center for Cultural Heritage Preservation. The government of France financed the renovation of the 1912 building as part of the millennium restoration of Bethlehem.

Dar Talamas

Dar Talamas (House of Talamas or "Viewpoint") was built in the second half of the 19th century. This family home is a typical example of traditional Bethlehem architecture. Its big room opens to the valley and offers a remarkable view.

International Center of Bethlehem (Dar al-Nadwa)

Dar al-Nadwa was founded by the Lutheran Church under the leadership of Pastor Ludwig Schneller in 1886. This cultural and educational center has become a cornerstone of dialogue, education, and understanding in the Bethlehem community.

Jacir Palace (Intercontinental Hotel)

Originally a mansion built in 1910 for Suleiman Jacir, a wealthy Bethlehem merchant, the building has since been a school, the ballot center for the first Palestinian elections in 1996, and now a hotel. The frescoes have been well-kept and the tiles of the original mansion restored. A portrait of Suleiman Jacir in Turkish headdress and caftan greets visitors in the lobby of this hotel, which is second only to the American Colony in Jerusalem, as the most beautiful in Palestine.

Madbasseh Square

Madbasseh Square, one of the most colorful produce markets in Bethlehem, was once known for its grape molasses mill. Grapes have been a major crop in Palestine since pre-Biblical times.

Old Bethlehem Home Museum

This museum in the restored and renovated Bethlehem Women's Union pays homage to the cultural heritage of the women of Bethlehem and to a quickly dying way of life. The museum, furnished primarily through the donations of belongings of Bethlehem families, shows how homes in 19th-century Bethlehem were furnished and decorated.

Quos al-Abid

During the reign of Ibrahim Pasha in the 18th century, migrants from the Sudan came to Bethlehem and settled close to this gate, which was rebuilt at the time and renamed Gate of the Africans.

Jacir Palace

Old Bethlehem Home Museum

Quos al-Zarara (Old Gate)

Old Gate is the main gate to Bethlehem from Jerusalem. Tradition has it that Mary and Joseph entered Bethlehem through this gate. Its name refers to the belief that it existed in pre-Christian or even Canaanite times. The remains of the existing gate were built during the reign of Emperor Justinian and renovated during the days of Suleiman the Magnificent.

Beit Sahour

Nearby Beit Sahour is highlighted on the traditional tourist itinerary as the home of the Shepherds' Fields, where the angels are said to have visited the shepherds to foretell the birth of Jesus. Few visitors are aware that there was life in Beit Sahour long before biblical times, as far back as the Bronze Age. And today, Beit Sahour is a hub for both high-tech and revolutionary Palestine.

The town's long history of education has brought back many of its skilled youth, a high percentage of whom sensibly studied computer science, and has also made the town a leftist stronghold. During the first intifada, the people of Beit Sahour made a landmark move when they collectively refused to pay taxes to the Israeli occupation forces under the banner of "no taxation without representation." In both the first and second uprising, the town suffered many casualties. But since tourism to Palestine began, Beit Sahour has always been on the itinerary.

Bir al-Sydah (Well of Mary)

This well is believed to have been dug by Jacob, son of Isaac and grandson of Abraham. Mary is said to have drawn water at this well on her way to Egypt. The water apparently rose on its own accord when she asked to drink. Since then, it has been said to be the site of many miracles, including the occasional sighting of the Virgin Mary. Christians and many Muslims pray for miracles here.

Catholic Church

The "Latin" Church, as it is known to locals, was built in 1859 during the opening up of Palestinians to the west, and to missionaries in particular. Although they are a minority among Christians in Beit Sahour, the Catholic community is active and well funded. An impressive ivory altar, which depicts various scenes from the Annunciation to the arrival of the Holy Family in Egypt, was crafted by local artisans. The church runs a secondary school and a scouts group.

Catholic Shepherds' Field

Excavations made in the 19th century indicate that a 5th-century church once stood in this field. In the 1950s, further excavations revealed a vast agricultural establishment, with olive presses, cisterns, silos, grottos, and a unique ritual bath, which is believed to have been used for baptisms or similar rituals as far back as the 2nd century.

Franciscans built a chapel here designed by Antonio Barluzzi and decorated with paintings and scenes from the early life of Jesus Christ. A natural grotto with an altar inside is encased within the church. Pilgrims from all over the world celebrate Christmas at this site.

Greek Orthodox Church

Up to the end of the 19th century, prayer service was often held outdoors next to the Greek Orthodox Shepherds' Field, but eventually, yearnings for comfort won out, and local parishioners raised money to build a church in 1895. The church features 19th-century icons and recent work by Greek artists.

Greek Orthodox Shepherds' Field

Located in a valley of ancient olive trees is a subterranean church known as Deir al-Ra'wat (convent of the shepherds). The site is revered as the spot where an angel appeared to bewildered shepherds, saying "Glory to God in the Highest, and on earth, peace among men." The tombs of three of these shepherds are still visible in the west side of the

Intifada Street, Beit Jala

cave church. Only the crypt of the church remains. On Christmas day, local clergy, the community's faithful, and pilgrims pray at the cave.

Omar al-Khattab Mosque

The Ottomans built the original mosque and an adjacent schoolroom to accommodate the community of semi-nomadic Muslims who had settled in Beit Sahour at the beginning of the Ottoman era. In 1953, the building was expanded. Now the Islamic Society runs a school, nursery, and cultural center adjacent to the mosque.

Beit Jala

The other major town near Bethlehem (2 km to the north), Beit Jala has been known as home to St. Nicholas since the early Christian era. Its name, which means "grass carpet" in Aramaic, certainly dates far back. In the 1940s, Beit Jala was also known across the Arab world as a beautiful summer resort amid green mountains. It is famous for its olive oil, vineyards, and apricots, as well as its master stonemasons.

But life for this Christian, mostly Greek Orthodox community became very difficult after the 1967 Israeli occupation, and nearly impossible after a serious land grab by Israeli settlers stripped local citizens of their agricultural lands. Often the site of conventions for international Christian groups, the town has been trying to ward off the growth of at least three illegal Israeli settlements on its lands: Gilo, Har Gilo, and Giv'at Hamatos. Israelis have also constructed two tunnels and settler bypass roads on the town's confiscated land. To give a sense of the scale of these settlements, Gilo, the oldest of them (est. 1970) has 30,000 occupants. The more recent Giv'at Hamatos (1992) was built on about 85 acres belonging to the Orthodox Church in Beit Jala. The Israeli government plans to expand this colony to 350 acres and build an additional 3,600 housing units on it.

Church of St. Nicholas

The most impressive religious site in Beit Jala is the Church of St. Nicholas, which was built for the Greek Orthodox community in 1925. It was built on the remains of a Byzantine church, which in turn was built over the cave where St. Nicholas is believed to have lived during his stay in Palestine.

St. Nicholas was a 5th-century archbishop from Anatolia who lived in the Beit Jala cave in order to worship and be near the Church of Nativity. Inside the cave is an icon of St. Nicholas and an oil lamp whose flame is never extinguished.

Nicholas is the patron saint of Beit Jala, and his feast day is celebrated every year on December 19 with a grand carnival in the town. His fame, of course, has gone far afield, as the contemporary Western Santa Claus. A northern European celebration of St. Nicholas features leaving gifts in polished shoes by house doors on December 6.

Monastery of Cremisan

The Cremisan monastery and winery can be reached by a long winding road from Beit Jala. The route gives a good bird's-eye view of Palestine's political landscape: on the left are Palestinian houses and on the right, the Israeli settlement of Gilo.

For some three dozen theological students from around the world who study at the monastery, it is an island of tranquility. The main 19th-century building has stone floors and high-arched ceilings and houses a library and high school. The buildings are adorned with framed photographs of Pope John Paul II and Don Bosco, founder of the Silesian order, which runs the monastery.

The **wine cellar** and adjoining shop, a few hundred meters beyond the monastery, welcomes guests and offers wine-tasting. They make a modest 700,000 liters of wine a year from local grapes.

Near Bethlehem

Church and Convent of Our Lady of the Garden (Monastery of Hortus Conclusus)

This convent and chapel was built with the support of Monsignor Soler, the Archbishop of Montevideo, Uruguay, in 1901. With support from the Vatican, the convent was staffed by Italian nuns from South America who opened a clinic, a primary school, and an orphanage. At the end of the century it became a base for American evangelists. In close proximity to the church are the remains of a Crusader church, a Roman palace, several Roman mills, Roman channels, an Arab fortress, Byzantine floors, Islamic ruins, and a spring.

Herodion/Herodium

Strategic fortress, place of refuge, Herodion rises 750 meter above sea level. Believed by Josephus to be the burial site of Herod the Edumite, this fortress was used as a stronghold by the Jews after his death. Built in about 30 CE, on a hilltop 6 kilometers southeast of Bethlehem, Herodion dominates the countryside and overlooks the Dead Sea. It must have been a lavish place in its day, this city of round walls and fortress enclosing apartments, baths, and gardens. The ruins of a large pool and extensive administrative buildings are at the foot of the hill. Byzantine remains indicate it was inhabited and used as a Christian place of worship in the 5th and 6th centuries.

Al-Khader (St. George)

Al-Khader is a little town 3 kilometers south of Bethlehem, surrounded by vineyards, fig and olive trees, and is important as a major pilgrimage site for local Christians and Muslims, who trek to the Greek Orthodox monastery of St. George to ask for protection and safety. The Church of St. George was built in 1600 over the 3rd-century house belonging to the family of St. George. The existing church, along with its convent, was built in 1912.

St. George is probably the most popular saint in Palestine. Known for his defense of a maiden sacrificed to a vicious dragon, he is seen as a protector of the weak. At a time when Christianity was still very much a secret religion, he is said to have openly made the sign of the cross before slaying the beast. In Christian and Muslim homes across the country the symbol of St. George on his horse challenging the dragon is carved over entrances.

According to legend, St. George brought the slain dragon back to his hometown, Lydd, and showed the townspeople the corpse, whereupon they all converted to Christianity and were baptized that day by St. George himself.

It was probably after the Crusaders came to Palestine in the 12th century that the cult of St. George came to Britain. St. George became the patron saint of England thereafter. The Feast of St. George is celebrated every year on May 5th.

Mar Saba Monastery (St. Saba)

The most famous monastery in the country is located 12 kilometers east of Bethlehem. Founded by St. Saba (439–532), the present monastery consists of the original carved section and another part constructed in 482 CE, where St. Saba himself lived until he died at the age of 94.

The monastery contains the tomb of St. John and a cave full of the skulls of monks who were killed during the Persian invasion in 614. It reached its golden age during the late Abbasid and Fatimid period (8th and 9th century), and even during the Crusades continued to be inhabited by Greek Orthodox monks. In 1840 the Russian Orthodox Church helped to renovate parts of the monastery. In 1965, St. Saba's body, which had been interred in Venice for centuries, was returned to the monastic grounds.

St. Saba was, like his teacher Theodosius, from Cappadocia. At the age of 18, he had entered the Passarion monastery in Jerusalem. Eventually he went to St. Theodosius, where he studied for seventeen years. In 478, he went to live in a grotto in neighboring Wadi Nar (Valley of Fire) and in 483 he founded this hermitic community known as the *laura*.

Note that women are barred from visiting all but two of the monastery's towers, the Women's Tower (1605) and the Tower of St. Simon (1612).

St. Theodosius Monastery

Founded in 476, the monastery is located east of the village of Ubeidiyya and its white-walled cave marks the burial site of St. Theodosius. Tradition has it that the wise men rested in this cave after receiving a warning from God in a dream that they should stay away from Herod.

St. Theodosius was born in 414 in Cappadocia (part of Hellenistic Anatolia) and came to Palestine in 450. He initially joined a community of monks in the Tower of David before he attached himself in 455 to the monastery founded by Hikelias at Kanthisma, on the road to Bethlehem. He went to live in the famous grotto of the wise men and had the monastery built there. It was one of the largest of such hermitic institutions; at the height of its popularity, the monastery was home to 400 monks. St. Theodosius died in 529 at the age of 105.

In 1863 the French Orientalist, Guerin describes St. Theodosius Monastery, but calls it Deir Ibn Ubeid. It was occupied for several generations by the nomadic Anatolian tribe of al-Ubeid, which went on to establish the village of Ubeidiyya. In 1877 the German scholar Conrad Schick gave an exact plan of the site so that by the time the Greeks came in 1879, they could reclaim it and clear the crypt and turn it into a chapel. The present church was completed in 1952 on the remains of the Byzantine church.

Solomon's Pools

Hidden among very tall pine trees in a small valley 4 kilometers (2.5 mi) south of Bethlehem, Solomon's Pools consist of three huge rectangular reservoirs of stone and masonry that can hold 160,000 cubic meters (or 42 million gallons) of water. Although tradition attributes these to King Solomon, the pools almost certainly date from the time of Herod, and may have been built during the rule of Pontius Pilate. In the past, the reservoirs collected spring and rainwater and pumped it to Bethlehem and Jerusalem. **Qalat al-Burak**, an Ottoman fortress built in the 17th century, protected the pools.

A 12th-century Arab traveler documented the existence of 2 pools, which he called the Pools of al-Marji' (Return). Here, according to a legend, the brothers of Joseph are thought to have returned after they dropped him in the well. The third pool is believed to have been built by a Mamluk Sultan in 1460.

Late in the Ottoman era, water from these pools reached Jerusalem through a four-inch clay pipe laid in 1902. The pools were renovated in the 1920s by British Mandate authorities, who also installed a pumping station to increase the efficiency of water transportation to the nearby communities. Supplying water to East Jerusalem from the pools ceased after the Israeli occupation of the West Bank in 1967. Today, the pools are in a dilapidated state, though the neighboring village of Artas (from the Latin "Hortus," paradise) still uses them, despite heavy pollution. In the 16th century, Suleiman the Magnificent had exempted the town's population from taxation in return for their guarding and upkeep of the pools.

Wadi Khureitun

Scholars believe that people lived in the caves here and used fire 500,000 to 120,000 years ago. Three caves have been identified as historically important—Um Qatfa, Erq al-Ahmar and Um Qala'—but many other caves here contain signs of life from as long ago as 8,000 to 120,000 years ago. Evidence shows that this area, which is 2 kilometers southeast of Herodian, was also once inhabited by very large animals.

But the area's current name is of relatively recent origin. "Khureitun" honors the 4th-century hermit, St. Chariton, who lived here in what is known as the Hanging Cave of St. Chariton. There used to be monastery here that went out of use in the 12th century.

Refugee Camps

Aida Camp

This camp was established in 1950 on 16 acres of land between Bethlehem and Beit Jala. Its name originates from a popular coffee shop of the same name located nearby. Eventually the coffee shop was sold to the nearby Franciscan church, so many of the younger generation mistakenly think the camp's name comes from the church.

The camp's 4,000 residents came from seventeen destroyed Palestinian villages, largely from the Western Jerusalem (Beit Natif, Deiraban, Ras Abu Ammar, Allar, Malha) and Western Hebron (Beit Jibrin, Ajjour) regions. After the 1967 occupation, virtually all the camp's residents were within a half-hour's drive of their former homes, but none were permitted to return.

The middle-sized of the three Bethlehem refugee camps, Aida shares its services with nearby, smaller Beit Jibrin. UNRWA runs one co-educational school on a double shift (morning and evening classes) and emergency food supplies and health services are provided by the UNRWA health center at a facility located at the main Bethlehem junction Bab al-Zkak.

Due to Aida's proximity to the Israeli military fortress at Rachel's Tomb, the camp has historically suffered from living literally at gun point, particularly during the al-Aqsa intifada, where there were times when Apache helicopters attacked the camp with rocket and machine-gun fire, destroying several buildings. Yet all refugee camps are supposed to be entitled to international protection. Additionally, Israel has recently determined to build the southern portion of the Wall on land directly adjacent to Aida's northern neighborhoods. One side of a main street is likely to be demolished so that the Wall can be constructed.

Beit Jibrin/Azzeh Camp

This very cramped camp is wedged between the fork of Bethlehem's two main roads, Manger Square Road and the

Hebron–Jerusalem Road. The camp is also known as Azzeh camp, after the Azzeh family from the destroyed village of Beit Jibrin, who compose about 60 percent of its residents. With 1,800 residents, this is one of the smallest officially recognized Palestinian refugee camps.

Like most camps, Beit Jibrin generally failed to benefit from any services provided by ruling authorities. This was particularly striking for the Bethlehem camps, as residents witnessed, but did not partake in, the short-lived economic boom that the city underwent during the "peace process" years. This, together with other social, economic, and political discrepancies makes the Bethlehem camp–city relationship particularly tense.

Inadvertently, an archeological site is located beneath the camp. On the western side, on an empty lot where the camp children seem to be perpetually playing soccer, are the remains of an Ottoman-built aqueduct that used to bring water from Solomon's Wells to Jerusalem. Archeology lovers used to regularly visit the site, though most seemed oblivious to the refugee camp.

In 1995, the Israeli occupation army redeployment resulted in the border between Palestinian and Israeli control being drawn very close to the northern entrance to the camp, with the camp itself falling under PNA control. This meant that popular demonstrations in Bethlehem always resulted in the camp being in the thick of confrontations. This was exacerbated with the onset of the al-Aqsa intifada, when the camp's central location made it a target for shelling by the Israeli army, who frequently lobbed anti-personnel shells and shot high caliber bullets at the camp from the nearby Israeli military compound and the distant Israeli settlement of Gilo.

Dheisheh Camp

Dheisheh spreads along the rolling slopes of the southern West Bank, 2 kilometers south of Bethlehem. Established in 1949 on 108 acres of land within the municipal boundaries of Bethlehem, Dheisheh is now home to approximately 11,000 refugees and their descendants. They originate from approximately 45 villages in the West Jerusalem (Zakariyeh, Beit I'tab, Ras Abu Ammar, Jrash, al-Walajeh) and Western Hebron (Beit Itab, Beit Jibrin) districts.

Dheisheh is a camp that prides itself on a long tradition of alternative approaches to the national struggle, particularly its activism around the issue of the Palestinian right of return. During the first intifada, Dheisheh was considered to be at the vanguard of popular resistance. A large monument in the shape of the map of

Olive harvest in the fields of Bethlehem

Palestine stands near the entrance to the camp in commemoration of those from Dheisheh who have been killed in the pursuit of Palestinian rights and freedom. Some were killed even before the 1967 occupation. Lively and sometimes artistic graffiti adorns the walls, some of which was composed for a March 2000 visit Pope John Paul II made to the camp.

A local community center known as **Ibda'** has gained international recognition for several of its activities, including an international folkloric dance troupe, the world's only hostel in a refugee camp, a large internet cafe, a community-run restaurant, and an assortment of grassroots initiatives involving much of the camp's population (though largely focusing on children and women) in the fields of art, skills-training, cultural exchange, sports, and community health.

In 1995, the camp residents established a camp committee, which organized a "telethon" under the sponsorship of a popular Palestinian Legislative Council member, collecting pledges to buy 600 tons of asphalt and $20,000 for resurfacing the camp's roads and alleys. Along many of these alleyways, markings in Hebrew from the first intifada are still visible, evidence of the Israeli army's pursuit of Dheisheh's stone-throwing youth through the camp's labyrinthine alleys and streets.

28.

Hebron (al-Khalil)

Its Equal For Beauty Does Not Exist Elsewhere, Nor Can Any Fruits Be Finer....

—al-Maqdisi, 985 CE

Just 36 kilometers south of Jerusalem, Hebron is in many ways Palestine's southern capital. It lies in the most elevated area in the country (1,000 m/3,040 ft above sea level), stretching between two ranges of hills in the northern upper reaches of Wadi Hebron. The fertile soil, abundant rainfall, mild temperatures, and the skilled farming techniques of its inhabitants have made Hebron one of the most flourishing in the country—this is, after all, the biblical land of milk and honey. Throughout the ages, the Hebronites were regarded as the best viticulturists in the Near East. In the 10th century CE, al-Maqdisi wrote about the export of grapes, grape syrup, and raisins to Egypt and other countries in the region.

Hebron is as rich in history as its land is fertile. The Canaanites are believed to have inhabited the Hebron area since 4000 BCE, before settling in Hebron, Halhoul, Carmel, and Jabal al-Rumeideh when they became a sedentary society about 1,000 years later. This makes Hebron, along with Jericho, one of the oldest settled communities in the world.

The Arba, a prominent Anakite–Canaanite tribe, lived in the hills that stretch from Hebron to Jerusalem, and the city was called Arbo'a. Some historians believe, however, that the name, which meant four in Canaanite, did not come from the name of the tribe, but was a reference to the four Canaanite tribes that resided in the area. Still others claim the name refers to the four mountains surrounding the city.

Ceiling in the Mosque of Abraham

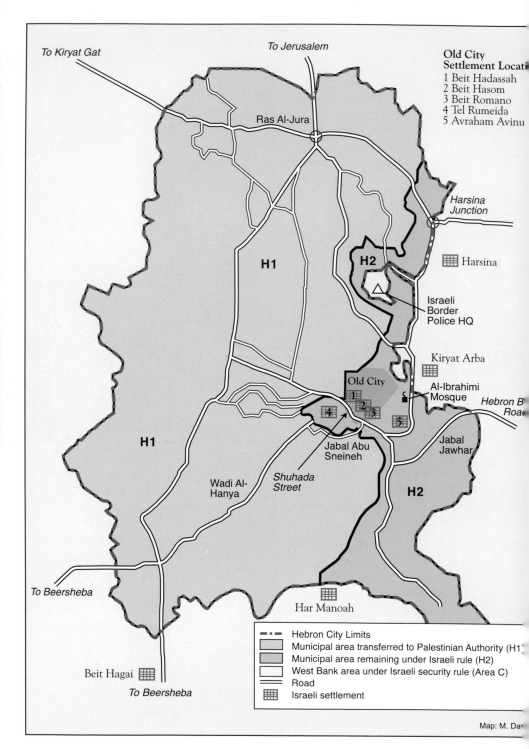

HEBRON 2001

Recent excavations have uncovered a 20-foot-wide section of the wall that enclosed the first fortified city at Tel Abu Rumeideh. It was built between 3300–2200 BCE. Built of stones weighing as much as a ton and a half each, the wall is preserved to a height of 10 feet. It is estimated that it originally stood 15 to 20 feet high. Beside it are the remains of fortifications dating to 2200–1550 BCE, which would have existed when Abraham came to the city in 1900 BCE. Tel Abu Rumeideh, just west of today's old city, is actually the Canaanite and Bronze Age Hebron; when people migrated, they usually went up the street and no further. When Hebron (the recent city) was built up during the Roman era, people simply went from Tel Abu Rumeideh to the adjacent metropolis.

According to monotheistic tradition, Hebron is the city where the prophet Abraham and some of his family, including Sara, Isaac, Rebecca, Jacob, and Leah were buried. Muslim lore has it that Adam and Eve are also buried here. The burial tombs are what made Hebron a holy city for Muslims and Jews alike. Its Arabic name, Ibrahim al-Khalil al-Rahman, means city of Abraham, the Friend of the Merciful. "The Merciful" is one of the 99 names of God in the Quran.

Abraham

Most Muslims consider Hebron the fourth holiest site in Islam (after Mecca, Medina, and Jerusalem). As the final resting place of the forefather of the prophets, the Holy Cave (al-Ghar al-Sharif) is a venerated site of pilgrimage. Abraham fathered many children: with Hagar, an Egyptian, his first-born, Ismail; with Sarah, Isaac; with Ketura, Zimran, Jokshan, Medan, Midian, Ishbak, and Shuah. The ethnic and religious origins of Ketura are uncertain, as is the fate of Abraham's female offspring.

Tradition holds that Ismail and his six half-brothers from Ketura are the forefathers of the Arab nation, and Isaac the father of the Jews.

Hebron and Tradition

The Tel al-Amarna letters indicate that in the mid-14th century BCE much of Canaan was ruled by a local leader, Shuwardata, a member or an ally of the local Anak-Canaanite clan. According to the Bible, the spies that Moses sent on a reconnaissance mission to Canaan reported that the locals were so large, they felt themselves to be "grasshoppers" by comparison. According to Old Testament tradition, an invasion followed 38 years of wandering in the desert and "Joshua and all Israel with him went up from Eglon to Hebron and attacked it. They took the city and put it to the sword, together with its king, its villages, and everyone in it. They left no survivors" (Joshua 10:36–37). Later, in about 1000 BCE, David made Hebron his capital for seven years before moving to Jerusalem.

During their rule (587 BCE) the Babylonians exiled all inhabitants from the city. In 134 BCE, Jews led by John Hyrcanus destroyed the city. Herod, who ruled in 37–34 BCE rebuilt the town, sealed the Cave of Machpelah, and erected the wall that still surrounds it. Though there is no mention of the city in the life of Jesus, there was clearly wealth in the city in those days, for in 68 CE the city was raided by both Jewish rebels and Roman legions. By 70 CE the Romans had expelled all the monotheists from the city. By the 4th century, the Christian chronicler Eusebius characterized Hebron as no more than a "large village."

The Roman Emperor Justinian (527–565 CE) felt Hebron was an important Christian site. He had a church built over the Cave of Machpelah, incorporating the Herodian structure. Much of what he built was destroyed in 614 during the last war between Byzantium and Persia. Hebron remained a destination for pilgrims venerating Abraham.

Islam's First Endowment

Under Muslim rule (635 CE), Hebron again became a major center of pilgrimage. Tradition holds that the Prophet Muhammad visited Abraham's grave during his night flight to heaven, paying respect to his forefather.

According to Muslim sources, the Prophet gave Hebron to his friend and companion, Tamim al-Dari. He and his family were among the first converts to Islam in Palestine. The Tamimi clan still has thousands of members in Hebron and throughout the Arab world. This gift to the clan, the first charitable endowment in Islam, was recognized throughout the ages, even by the British in 1927.

In keeping with the practices of Abraham, hospitality—in any case, a central virtue in Arab and Muslim culture—thrived. Muslims set up soup kitchens, offering lentil soup, olives and bread to visitors. In 985 CE, al-Maqdisi reported being a recipient of this hospitality: "[I]n all Islam, I know of no charity or almsgiving that is better regulated than this one; for those who travel and are hungry may eat here of good food." He also mentions that a prince of Khurazan and the ruler of Ghurjistan had left large donations to assure the upkeep of the site and its guesthouse.

In 1047, Nasir Khusrau reports that the many villages surrounding Hebron provide generously from their revenues for "pious purposes" associated with the city. He describes the interior decorations of Herbron's main sanctuary as including the finest carpets and most beautiful brocades—a strong contrast to the current state of affairs.

During Crusader rule (1099), most Muslims and Jews (who had maintained their synagogue and right to worship throughout Muslim rule) were expelled. Godfrey de Bouillon bestowed Hebron to Gerhard d'Avennes. The mosque was turned into a church and called St. Abraham's Castle. In 1167 it became the seat of a Latin Bishop.

In 1172, the Persian chronicler Ali of Herat visited Hebron while it was under Crusader rule. He recounts that a guard at the sanctuary reported that King Baldwin II had discovered the bodies of Abraham, Isaac, and Jacob. According to Ali's account, the king ordered that they be provided with new burial garments and had their burial chambers closed up.

Mamluk Rule

In 1187 the troops of Saladin expelled Hebron's European overlords, and Muslims and Jews were allowed to return to the city. His Ayyubite successors made improvements and restorations to the damaged mosque. Saladin himself had new pillars for the sanctuary made in Askalan.

In many ways Mamluk rule (1187–1517) brought a new "Golden Age" to Hebron. The new rulers bequeathed many riches on Hebron. By 1318 the city center had been restored, the grand mosque refurbished, and an additional mosque built. Known as the **Djaouliya Mosque**, it remains an architectural masterpiece of the era.

The Mamluks also built a shrine to mark the **Tomb of Joseph** inside the Haram complex. In the western corner of the complex another small mosque was built exclusively for women. Inside this mosque is a venerated stone with a footprint believed to be the first footprint of Adam after he left the Garden of Eden. This footprint perpetuates Muslim lore that Adam and Eve spent their lives in Hebron and that they are buried underneath the burial chamber of Abraham.

In a 1333 account of the city, the Jews of Hebron were engaged in a prosperous trade in cotton, which they themselves wove and spun, and glasswork. Some scholars maintain that Venetian merchants introduced the art of blue glasswork to Hebron.

In the 16th century Andalusian Muslims fleeing the massacres in Spain settled in Hebron, as did their Jewish compatriots. **Al-Andalus Mall** and the **Cordoba School** are cultural remnants of that exodus.

The work of the Mamluks was augmented by the patronage of the Ottomans (1517–1917). Under the reign of Suleiman, who made endowments to Muslim holy cities his favorite form of contribution to the people of his faith, city planning was introduced and relatively advanced infrastructural additions implemented.

Hebron Culinary Tradition

Guests are treated like royalty in any Hebron home, whether wealthy or modest. They are often honored with the traditional *mansaf*, still usually served by the woman of the house, who, in her colorful *dushdash* (house dress) disappears as soon as the traditional brass tray, piled high with rice and meat, is laid on the table. The patriarch does not partake of the food, but instead hovers over his guests to make sure that their every need and whim is instantly gratified. Although western tableware is commonly available, it is much more satisfying to go local, dipping your right hand to pick up a mouthful of rice or a morsel of meat and keeping your left hand still behind your back , as required by table etiquette. While alcohol is conspicuously absent, any type of soft drink available on the market is sure to be served.

    Mansaf is a ceremonial dish of lamb and rice that holds the place of honor at every celebration. Its origins go back to the Bedouins of Transjordan. Though Palestinians everywhere have adopted it wholeheartedly, it is Hebron that claims the specialty.

    One of the main features of *mansaf* is *laban jmeed*, which is made from sheep's milk churned to extract the butter. The buttermilk, or *laban mkheed*, is processed for year-round storage. After being left to drip through cheesecloth for a few days, the resulting paste is kneaded with salt, cumin, and a hint of *curcuma* (turmeric), a bittersweet spice with a musky flavor and a distinctive bright yellow color. The paste is then shaped into balls, left to dry on wooden boards, and finally stored in cloth bags in a cool, dark place. Individual balls of *laban jmeed*, as it is called in its new state, are diluted as needed for sauces that are noted for their pungent flavor. Commercial plain yogurt can be substituted for it in a pinch.

    Another important ingredient is *samneh*, clarified butter made from sheep's milk. *Samneh* is boiled with cracked wheat, nutmeg, and *curcuma*, and then strained. It is one of those ingredients that cannot simply be bought: it must be obtained through a network of contacts among the nomadic Bedouins who breed the sheep and make the butter.

    Finally, the Palestinian way of cooking rice is highly recommended: it allows all the water to be absorbed in the cooking process, trapping all the nutrients in the rice.

Mansaf

Mansaf

A few clumps of *laban jmeed* or 3 cups plain yogurt
3 pounds lamb, cut into large chunks
1 whole onion, peeled
2 teaspoons salt
1 teaspoon freshly ground pepper
½ teaspoon allspice
1 small cinnamon stick
4 tablespoons *samneh* or clarified butter
2½ cups round-grain rice
3 grains of cardamom
½ teaspoon saffron flowers or turmeric
3 cloves garlic
handful of corn flour
⅛ cup pinenuts and almonds, for garnish
tannūr or pita bread

1. If you are using *laban jmeed*, soak a few clumps (about 7 ounces/200 grams) for 24 hours with enough water to make 3 cups of thick laban. Use a food processor once it has dissolved, to give the *laban* a smooth, creamy texture.

2. Put the meat, onion and spices into a pot with ample water to cover. Bring to boil, then cook covered until the meat is tender, about one hour. When the meat is done, keep it hot while you cook the rice. You can use some of the broth to cook the rice, but first set aside 1 to 1½ cups for the sauce.

3. To cook the rice, heat 3 tablespoons samneh or butter in a medium-sized cooking pot and add the rice and cardamom. Stir until the rice is coated. Then add the saffron, diluted in two teaspoons of hot water, and stir again. Measure 4 cups of liquid, using as much broth as is available and hot water, and add to the rice. Bring to a boil and adjust the seasoning. Cover and cook over medium heat until most of the liquid is absorbed. Reduce the heat to very low and cook for another five minutes before turning off the heat.

4. Prepare the sauce while the rice is cooking. Melt 1 tablespoon *samneh* in a medium-sized pan over low heat; add three whole garlic cloves, taking care not to burn them. Add the *laban* and the reserved broth—how much depends on how creamy you want the sauce—and cook for 20 minutes over very low heat. If you are using yogurt, mix corn flour in the yogurt and add the hot broth a small quantity at a time to avoid any clumping. With the yogurt, you need only simmer for 5 minutes. Turn off the heat, salt and pepper to taste.

5. To serve: Spread the hot bread on a large round tray and spoon over it at least one cup of the hot sauce. Pile up the rice and spoon sauce over it, too. Arrange the meat atop the rice, and scatter fried almonds and pinenuts on top. Pour the remainder of the sauce into small individual bowls on the side. Serves at least six.

Ottoman Rule

Under the Ottomans, commerce flourished, and by the beginning of the 19th century Hebron was the biggest producer and exporter of glassware in all of Palestine. But though urban Hebronites were merchants, the rural clans were mostly involved in agriculture.

Popular history has it that in 1834 the troops of Ibrahim Pasha plundered and destroyed much of Hebron in response to the lack of a suitable welcome. Many people were killed and hundreds were forcibly conscripted into the Egyptian army. On the heels of this massacre, a 1837 earthquake destroyed portions of the city. By the time the Ottomans returned, the local rulers saw no reason to pay taxes to the Ottoman vassals in Jerusalem. By 1846 the Ottomans allowed their troops to plunder the city in order to quash this rebellion.

Hebron remained an important pilgrimage site, especially for Muslims and Jews, but it also became a mercantile center for an increasing number of Europeans who came to buy glass and silver jewelry.

By this time the Jewish community in Hebron had begun differentiating themselves from other Hebronites. They were no longer regular Ottoman subjects but rather fell under British or Austrian protection. Nevertheless, until the beginning of the 20th century they continued to play their traditional role in the city, where the majority worked as peddlers selling Hebron goods to communities around Palestine.

In the early 20th century, hundreds of Hasidim from Poland came to Hebron. By 1925 their numbers swelled with an influx of Russian Jews. Emotions ran high all over Palestine as talk of the establishment of Jewish state spread like wildfire after the 1917 Balfour Declaration. The relative peace and harmony that had existed for generations between the two communities came to an end. In 1929 armed Jews killed Muslim worshippers in Jerusalem. Shortly afterwards an angry mob attacked Jews in Hebron in one of the saddest moments of Jewish–Muslim relations in the city. Jewish families left Hebron, settling in Jerusalem and Haifa. Some 31 families returned to Hebron but in 1936 the British colonial government forced them to leave, saying they feared further violence.

Jordanian Rule

Following the creation of the State of Israel in 1948, the Jordanian Arab Legion took control of Hebron and administered it until 1967. An agreement by which Jews would be allowed to worship in Hebron and Jerusalem, which were under Jordanian control, in exchange for the right of Arab Christians to worship in Israeli-controlled Nazareth

A view of the Mosque of Abraham

broke down after Israel refused to honor the agreement.

Jordanian rule was particularly welcomed by Hebronites, who see themselves as "friends of the Prophet Muhammad." The Hashemite rulers of Jordan are descendents of the Prophet members of the same legendary Arab Qais clan, to which most Hebronites also belong. Even under Palestinian self-rule, many shops and homes still have pictures of the late King Hussein of Jordan on their walls as a sign of allegiance and association.

Israeli Occupation

Hebron came under full Israeli control after the 1967 war. On the eastern perimeters of the city the Israeli government established Qiryat Arba (named after the Canaanite Hebron), arguably the most militant Jewish settlements in the West Bank

Hebronites played a leading role during the first intifada. Hundreds of the city's young were martyred, thousands wounded, and close to 100,000 from the Hebron district imprisoned for their role in the resistance.

While Palestinians and Israelis were negotiating an Israeli withdrawal from the city in 1994, an American-Jewish physician, Baruch

Goldstein, walked into the mosque during dawn prayers on February 25 and opened machine-gun fire into the backs of kneeling worshippers, killing 29 Palestinians and wounding dozens more. After this, the mosque complex was divided into two units, one for Jews and one for Muslims. The Djaouliya Mosque fell into the Jewish section of the complex; it is now off-limits to Muslims except during religious holidays.

On January 17, 1997, Hebron was the last Arab city in the West Bank to watch Israeli troops leave. Yasir Arafat received a hero's welcome as he entered the Hebron almost at the same moment the occupation forces withdrew. But actually only 80 percent of Hebron was handed over to Palestinian rule. The area under PNA rule is known as area H1 and the rest as H2. Israel maintains a iron military grip over area H2, the entire market area in the heart of the Old City. Palestinian civil institutions are theoretically allowed to operate under tight restrictions imposed by the Israeli military administration, but in fact are frequently kept from functioning normally due to "security" considerations. Near area H2, 400 armed Jewish settlers have placed themselves in direct confrontation with approximately 15,000 to 20,000 Palestinian civilians. Al-Shuhada Street (Martyr's Street) runs through H2 and connects the western to the eastern part of the city. A rotating force of several thousand Israeli soldiers tightly controls the traffic on this street, where three of Hebron's four Israeli settlements are located. This has led to the suffocation of the economic activity along the street, which was once the hub of the city's economic life. Because of the punitive measures imposed on the city by the Israeli occupation forces, the Qasba (old city) is no longer among the most densely populated areas of the city. The PNA has made continuous efforts to renovate and redevelop the center of Hebron. For example, the Hebron Rehabilitation Committee, set up in the former home of the Dweik family, restores, renovates, and revitalizes Old City homes and buildings dating back to Ottoman and Mamluk times with the help of funding from foreign donors and the technical support from the UNDP. But they work against heavy odds: at the beginning of the al-Aqsa intifada, Hebron was put under curfew and large parts of the city were re-occupied by the Israeli army. The main street leading into Hebron through Halhoul was closed off with mounds of dirt and trenches.

Today, the city of Hebron is home to 120,000 Palestinians, 400 Jewish settlers, and 3 Russian priests, the custodians of the Russian church. The district of Hebron is home to some 400,000, which makes it the second most populated Palestinian district after Gaza.

Visiting Hebron

Several Palestinian companies offer tours of the Hebron, Jerusalem, and Bethlehem area. Walking tours through the Old City, visits with craftsmen who make Hebron glass and Palestinian pottery, and hikes through the countryside for visits with villagers allow tourists and visitors to enjoy the multifaceted beauty of Hebron.

Quaint Arabic coffee and teahouses beckon at every street corner of the city. Here visitors can enjoy a variety of hot drinks and tasty falafel or *shawirma* sandwiches and have interesting conversations with the city elders, many of whom speak English. The market, or souk, with its arched walls and maze of alleys is definitely worth exploring. The shops and stalls sell everything from pottery, olive wood, blown glass, and a wide array of aromatic spices and dried fruits.

Hebron is a city where mercantile cunning and conservative social mores have flourished for centuries. Observant and traditional, Hebronites are known for their generosity and hospitality. Since most Hebronites are observant Muslims, large families are the norm, as is a sense of family loyalty and cooperation. Most Hebronites live as extended families, and these families are affiliated to larger clans. Many of these clans, known as the "Hebron families," trace their origins back either to tribes from the Arabian Peninsula who came to Palestine with the spread of Islam, or to Kurdish clans that came with Saladin, or to Crusaders who settled in the region.

There are two main hotels in Hebron: the **Al-Mizan Regency Hotel**, a four-star establishment with some 70 rooms, half a dozen suites, and a Turkish bath, and the three-star **Hebron Tourist Hotel**.

Hebron City

The city is divided into four sectors, which lie in pairs on either side of a valley. Historically gates to each quarter could be closed when necessary.

Among the main quarters of the Old City are Haret al-Shaykh, built around the Mosque of Shaykh Ali al-Bakka (1269–1270); Haret al-Akrad, founded by the Kurds who fought alongside Saladin; Haret al-'Akkabi, founded by the water-skin makers; Haret al-Qazzazin, the glassblowers' quarter, where these artisans worked for centuries before the large stores along the Halhoul–Hebron route sold Hebron Glass; Haret Qaytun, the cotton makers' quarter and Haret al-Haram is the quarter of the Haram al-Ibrahimi Mosque.

Haram al-Khalil

The most important site is the Haram al-Khalil, which stands in the

Fresh juices are a Hebron specialty

same place a Byzantine church built by Justinian once stood. The place remained in ruins until after the Muslim conquest in 637, when a mosque was built inside the edifice. Restorations and additions to both the outer and inner structure of the Haram were commissioned by the Umayyads, Abbasids, Fatimids, Ayyubites, Mamluks, and Ottomans. The Haram includes minarets, domes, arches, doors, marble columns, side mosques, richly decorated cenotaphs covered with decorated tapestries, inscriptions. One of the mosque's most famous pieces of handwork is the sumptuously carved pulpit, made in 1091 for the Mashhad al-Hussein in Askalan, and brought to Hebron in 1191 by Saladin.

The entrance to the sanctuary is separate for Muslims and Jews, as is true of life in general here. The Muslim entrance is the long Mamluk

stairway outside the north wall of the edifice, which leads into the
Djaouliya Mosque. A small door cut into the southern Herodian wall
provides access to the largest prayer hall. Pass through a metal detector
and enter the **Al-Is'hazyya** (Grand Mosque). The interior retains the
gothic arches of the Crusader church.

Here are the "tombs" of Rebecca (left) and Isaac (right), last
renovated in the 14th century. Between the cenotaphs, at the end of
the room against the wall, is the famous pulpit; beside it, to the left, is
a *mihrab* of multi-colored marble and fine mosaics.

Around the other side of the complex, a monumental stairway
leads up to the synagogue through a square building revered by
Muslims as containing the remains of Jacob's son Joseph. Before the
sanctuary was divided, it served as the women's mosque. Joseph's
cenotaph is largely ignored by Jews, who believe his remains were
brought from Egypt to Nablus. Just inside the Jewish section are the
9th-century tombs of Abraham and Sarah, and the 14th-century
tombs of Jacob and Leah.

Note: No visits during prayer times except for visibly devout
Muslims. Muslims must enter through Muslim gate and Jews through
Jewish gate. Those belonging to neither faith must prove it and can
then enter through either.

Archeological Museum
Located next to an old bath house, known as **Hamam Abuna
Ibrahim**, this museum contains a small collection of archeological
findings from the Canaanite to the Islamic period.

Haram al-Rameh/Ramet al-Khalil (Oak of Abraham)
About 3 kilometers north of the Old City is this spot known in
biblical tradition as **Mamre**. Offerings and sacrifices were first practiced
by the Canaanites. Herod erected an imposing enclosure to mark the
spot where Abraham and his family are believed to have lived. He built
a large complex with statutes to Edumite deities, such as the god Quos.
When Hebron was destroyed by Vespasian, Mamre briefly became a
commercial center. Today the site is somewhat neglected and
encroached upon by the expansion of the city. Except for the ruins of the
excavated Byzantine church, nothing is left of the site.

Reference to the site first appeared in the writings of Josephus,
who named the Abraham Oak as the place where Abraham pitched
his tent. According to biblical tradition, this is where three angels told
Abraham that his barren wife Sarah would give birth to a son.

Christian tradition also identifies this as a resting place of Joseph and Mary on their way back from Egypt.

Hadrian destroyed and rebuilt the site and dedicated the temple he built to pagan deities.

When the Emperor Constantine's mother-in-law, Eutropia, came to Mamre as a pilgrim she was so shocked to find pagan worship flourishing she had Constantine destroy the deities, and the temple was transformed into a basilica. It can still be seen on the Madaba map. The basilica was the earliest of its kind and although destroyed, it was rebuilt and large quantities of Roman Byzantine pottery have been recovered, including hundreds of coins.

Excavations begun in the 1920s indicate that there were at least four successive eras in which construction took place here: Herodian, Hadrian, Constantine, and Arab.

Masqobia

This alternative site to Mamre, 2 kilometers west of the city center, is venerated by followers of the Russian Orthodox church. A monastery built in 1871 stands close to a dead oak tree, which some believe is where Abraham pitched his tent. Access is through the western entrance.

Near Hebron

Bani Na'im

Bani Na'im (6 km east of Hebron) is not a popular tourist site, but tradition has it that the Prophet himself gave this village to two brothers. Muslims believe that a rather insignificant looking tomb is the final resting place of the biblical Lot. Adjacent **Nabi Yaqin** is where Abraham is said to have viewed the destruction of Sodom and Gomorrah.

Beit Jibrin

Beit Jibrin (House of the Giants) and is one of two famous Throne Villages in Hebron district. Most of the Throne Villages became prominent during the Ottoman era, but Beit Jibrin's history goes back to antiquity. It was first mentioned in Latin sources by Josephus Flavius as Betogabra, a village in the heart of Edumea, linking it to the Negev, Petra, and Herod. In 200 CE, the Roman Emperor Septimus Severus granted the town a large tract of land and gave it the status of Roman colony. In the 4th century its population converted to Christianity and the village became a bishopric.

The first caliph, Abu Bakr al-Siddiq (d. 634 CE) buried the Prophet's companion Tamim al-Dari, known locally as Abu Ruqayya, in Beit Jibrin.

Al-Maqdisi wrote in 985 that Beit Jibrin was the center for the towns and villages in the surrounding countryside. The Crusaders mistook it for Bir es-Saba, built a castle in 1137 and called it Beth Giblin. Saladin destroyed the castle and built a mosque. Under Mamluk rule, Beit Jibrin was the central postal station between Gaza and Karak in Transjordan.

A local mystic, Muhammad ibn Nabhan al-Jibrini (d. 1343), turned the town into a mecca for mystics and after his death it became a center of pilgrimage.

During the British Mandate, archaeologists working on the site south of the village known as Tel Sandahanna recovered mosaic floors from two churches dating to the 4th and 6th centuries, as well as remnants of formerly inhabited dwellings, Phoenician burial caves, and pigeon towers.

In May 1948 many inhabitants of Jaffa driven out by the Israeli army found refuge in the Beit Jibrin area. But the village was not

Rooftops of the Old City, Hebron

spared. The *New York Times* reported on October 20 the same year that "Beit Jibrin was added to the usual targets of the Israeli air force for the first time last night"; it was "pummeled" over the next few days. The village inhabitants sought shelter elsewhere, and when the fighting ceased they were prevented from going home. The Israeli settlement of Beit Guvrin was established on village lands the next year.

Today all that remains of the original village is a mosque, an unidentified shrine, probably the Tomb of Tamim al-Dari, and a number of houses. Some are occupied by Israelis, and others remain empty. One two-story stone house has been converted into an Israeli restaurant and outdoor cafe, bearing the Arab name "al-Bustan" (garden).

The people of Beit Jibrin, who live in refugee camps and more than two dozen countries have a website to keep in touch with each other and keep the memory of their village alive. They can be contacted at www.palestineremembered.com/Hebron/Bayt-Jibrin.

Beit Ummar

This is one of the most scenic villages on the way to Hebron. Home to Khirbet Kufin, it contains remains of a two large dressed-stone Roman structures that were found along with an underground vaulted Byzantine structure. Nearby **Deir Asha'ar** has remnants of a Byzantine church, a mosaic floor, an olive press, and the **Maqam al-Nabi Matta** (Tomb of the Prophet Matta), the father of Jonah, whom Muslims revere as a prophet.

Beit Zur

Also called Khirbet al-Tubeiqa, Beit Zur (6 kilometers north of Hebron) is the site of the ancient Canaanite city of Bethsour. According to the Bible, it was taken by the tribes of Judah and became a frontier town between the Hebrews and the Edumites. **Ein Edirwa/Diroueh** (spring of the peak) is near the ruins of Beit Zur. According to Christian tradition, this is where St. Philip baptized a eunuch of Queen Candace of Ethiopia and thus helped found the Church of Ethiopia. The spot also has ruins of a Roman way station, burial caves, and a Byzantine Church.

Al-Dhahriya

Al-Dhahriya was named in honor of the 13th-century Mamluk Sultan Baibars al-Daher. The village is interesting for its traditional Bedouin and village market life, the liveliest in the country. Market day is Wednesday.

Durra

Durra is a Throne Village 8 kilometers southwest of Hebron. Archeologists have found here evidence of human habitation as early as the Iron Age and extensive relics from the Roman and Byzantine periods and the Middle Ages. According to Arab tradition, Noah is buried here. Tradition has it that John Hyrcanus enslaved the inhabitants of Durra, forcing them to convert to Judaism or face death.

Halhoul

On the way to Hebron, travellers traditionally pass through this mid-sized town. It is home to the **Mosque of Nabi Yunis** (prophet Jonah), built by the Mamluks in 1226. The town is known for its luscious grapes, which are made into a sweet chewy paste called *melban*.

Samu

Samu, built on the ruins of a Canaanite town, was used by the Romans (and later Saladin, the Mamluks, and the Turks) as a caravan station on the road to Jordan. It is now close to the Green Line between the West Bank and Israel. Excavations in 1983 exposed a 7th-century mosque, which was renovated by Saladin and is still in use.

Tel Abu Rumeideh

Tel Abu Rumeideh, in northwestern Hebron (the oldest part of the city), is believed by some to be the site of Canaanite Hebron. On this hill are the remains of an ancient wall and the Monastery of the 40 Martyrs. Recently, archeologists discovered 40 clay jugs estimated to be 4,000 years old here.

Tel Beit Mirsim

Tel Beit Mirsim, site of a typical Canaanite city, is located on the fringe of fertile hills. The site is believed to have been inhabited around 3000 BCE. Around 1540 BCE, Beit Mirsim was abandoned after a number of Canaanite cities suffered severe destruction at the hands of the Egyptians. It was repopulated later by the Philistines, who lived here at least until the end of the 10th century BCE. It was destroyed in the 6th century BCE by the Babylonians.

Refugee Camps

Arroub Camp

Arroub Camp is 15 kilometers (9.3 mi) south of Bethlehem on the main Hebron–Jerusalem road, enmeshed with Gush Etzion, an Israeli settlement that is heavily fortified by the army. The army has made a military garrison out of several houses it occupies at the entrance of the camp, closed off the main road with dirt barricades, and set-up a checkpoint on the main road. Caught in complete Israeli occupation (Area C), Arroub camp has a sense of total isolation and vulnerability to the whims of the Israeli army and the militant settlers that drive past on the main North–South artery of the West Bank.

Established in 1950, Arroub's population today is estimated to be 7,000 people, originating from 33 Palestinian villages in the Gaza, Hebron, and Ramleh regions.

Arroub's population has invested its energies in education. The camp boasts 12 residents with doctorates, 25 with master's degrees, and over 600 with bachelor's degrees. These statistics are significant given that the populations of most Palestinian refugee camps traditionally serve as concentrations of cheap, unorganized labor for Israeli construction and industry. Only 25 percent of Arroub's residents fit into this category.

Despite its founding near 15 fresh water springs, Arroub faces a severe water shortage, as well as frequent blackouts, and a rudimentary sewage system. The bottom third of the camp, roughly a kilometer in length, has been known to go 70 days in summertime without water. The entire camp is "serviced" by a 2-inch water pipeline, and the water simply runs out by the time it reaches the last section of the camp. Camp residents have been forced to spend large percentages of their household income just to purchase water.

At the very end of the camp's main street lie the stone ruins of a Roman pool, which until 1917 was used as a water source for Jerusalem. It is now being refurbished by the Palestinian Ministry of Antiquities, presumably as a tourist site. Ironically, the pool (now just collecting waste water) was part of the great historic water system that once included Solomon's Pools to the north and the Roman aqueduct beneath Beit Jibrin Camp.

Across from the entrance to the camp are two small colleges (one technical, the other agricultural) administered by the PNA.

Hand-blown Hebron glass

Fawwar Camp

Established in 1949, Fawwar is home to refugees from 18 villages in the Hebron and Bir es-Saba (Negev) districts. As is the case with many of the southern refugee camps, many refugees are within walking distance of their original properties.

Like Arroub, Fawwar is isolated—it sits in the midst of agricultural fields with an Israeli military base only half a kilometer away, also under full Israeli control (Area C). The closest Palestinian village is Durra, a good five kilometers away. In recent years the camp has suffered 24-hour curfews, army tanks at its entrances, and the cutting off of the main access roads. Though most of the camp's men used to work as laborers inside the Green Line, Israeli closure policies, especially during the al-Aqsa intifada, have brought extreme economic depression to the already impoverished refugee population.

Fawwar boasts an active camp community, which arose out the need for the community to address its own needs, given its extended isolation. In the mid-1970s, Fawwar residents put together their collective money and talents to provide electricity: a service that runs efficiently to this day. Likewise, a child and youth center was established in 1995 to meet the educational, social, and cultural needs of the camp's children. The initiative was able to construct a library with over 7,000 children's books, servicing not only the camp, but also the surrounding Hebron villages and communities. In 1996 UNRWA constructed and equipped a new boys' school (868 pupils) with contributions from the European Union, to complement the pre-existing girls' school (595 pupils).

The destroyed remains of Isdud

29.

Isdud (Ashdod)

The Great City of Syria

—Herodotus, 5th century BCE

The few remnants of what was once the town of Isdud are hardly visible to a passerby. Four kilometers from the sea, Isdud was one of the five most important Philistine cities in antiquity, and a vibrant Palestinian town of over 5,000 in 1948. Now, there are only dirt mounds and a few ruins overgrown with shrubs and weeds. From the roadside, it hardly seems possible that Isdud was a historic town of note, almost continuously inhabited from 1700 BCE until 1948 CE.

The 3,700-year-old town was a strategic city in antiquity that stood on the main route from Palestine to Egypt. Believed to have been built in the Middle Bronze Age by the Canaanites on the acropolis of the present mound, it was known for its weight standard and its harbor, from which it exported its textiles and traded in dyes. Its main trading partner was neighboring Egypt.

In about 1300 BCE, the city appears to have been completely laid to waste. At the time, towns were destroyed either by invaders or by the local population who burned their own homes rather than allow the invaders to have them. Shortly after Isdud's destruction, the Philistines arrived. They appear to have used the remains of the Canaanite buildings. They rebuilt the city and settled it, expanding its borders beyond the acropolis for the first time. The size of the town went from an area of approximately 20 acres to at least 90 in a few years. According to the Old Testament version of history, the Philistines captured the Ark of the Covenant and took it to their main sanctuary, the Temple of Dagon in Isdud.

One of the most culturally revealing archeological finds—the result of seven seasons of digs—was a figurine of a seated woman that forms part of a throne. Archeologists and biblical scholars, who had worked together to prove biblical claims, had asserted that the Philistines worshipped only male deities. The unearthing of Ashdoda put an end to this claim once and for all. She was, apparently, one of several Philistine female goddesses. The goddesses were found toward the bottom of some 23 layers of civilization. The ancient fortified city was known as Ashdod Yam to the Israelites, Azotos Páralios to the Greeks, and Castellum Beroart to the Crusaders.

Close to the highest point of the mound archeologists unearthed an 11th-century BCE burial site of a single male skeleton. A heavy dagger with an iron blade lay next to him and within a short distance of the man's skeleton was the burial chamber of a horse.

Other finds indicate that by the end of the 11th century a vast shift in lifestyle, art, and religion began. Pottery shapes and images began to change, the deities became almost entirely male, and the musical instruments reverted to Canaanite types rather than Philistine.

One of the most significant Isdud finds to date is a group of figurines, five in all, which probably represented the orchestra at the court of the local ruler. They included statues of double flutes, cymbals, a tambourine, and a lyre.

Assyrian sources indicate that the city witnessed a renaissance for about 200 years, with substantial trade and mercantile activity from the 10th to 8th centuries BCE. But the Philistines were not to live in peace and prosperity: the city was destroyed again, this time by Uzziah, the king of Judah. Uzziah's 8th-century war to control the trade routes pitted him against the king of Israel as well as against the Philistines.

By 712 BCE the Assyrians made Isdud a tributary under Sargon II. Archeological finds in the late 1960s indicated that hundreds, if not thousands, of people were massacred during that conquest of the city. Mass graves containing dismembered bodies were uncovered at the time on the lowest part of the Mount of Isdud. Although Isdud became an Assyrian vassal state, it rebelled in no time. In 713 BCE, Azuri, the king of Isdud, refused to pay tributaries. Sargon then sent his armies to enslave the local population and settle the cities with people he had picked up as booty on the way. Archeological finds indicate that the Philistine population of Isdud was sent into exile and replaced by another, who simply moved into their homes.

Subsequently another ruler of Isdud, King Mitini, revitalized the city and with a largely new population, paid taxes to the Assyrian treasury. The Egyptians took the Assyrians to task and besieged the coastal city for 29 years. According to Herodotus, "Azotos [as Isdud was later called] held out against a siege longer than any city of which I have heard." But it was the Babylonians who finally brought Isdud to its knees. The city, exhausted and depopulated, shrank to a small town on the acropolis, while an adjacent city, Ashdod, more Persian and Hellenistic in character, was built further north by the sea.

During the Persian period in the 5th century BCE, many Judeans married into Isdud families and were condemned by their governor, Nehemiah. After Alexander's conquest of Gaza, Isdud became known as Azotos. Finds from that period indicate that it again grew to be a city of some significance. Recent archeological finds indicate that the deities of the Philistines survived an overlay of Hellenistic culture that Alexander introduced.

In Byzantine times it was the site of a bishopric. The evangelist Philip came to the town after baptizing the eunuch of Queen Candance of Ethiopia. Isdud's first bishop was Sylvanus (323 CE), who according to church records actively participated in the bitter theological debates in the 5th century at the Council of Chalcedon. Sixth-century Isdud can be seen on the map of Madaba.

During the Arab-Muslim era Isdud became predominantly Muslim. During the Mamluk period it became one of the main postal stops from Gaza to the rest of the country and Syria. After the Middle Ages it provided the main stopover for travellers going from Gaza to Jaffa, and its inhabitants protected the route to Ramleh. Today's remnants of the Mamluk caravanserai to the south of the village are believed to date back to the days of Baibars. By the beginning of the 19th century it was already in disuse and local villagers were dismantling it, using its stones for building houses in the village.

During the Ottoman period Isdud was part of the administrative district of Gaza. In 1596, records show that the population of 413 harvested wheat, barely, and sesame, and tended goats and beehives.

Most homes in Isdud were built of mud brick, in the architectural style of the southern Palestinian coast. The town was filled with palm and fig trees, which provided staples for both the local and surrounding populations.

One of the town's two mosques was built during the era of Baibars, while the other was built during the Ottoman era. In 1929 the Mosque of Sidi Amer was reported to have been supported by "ancient" columns of white marble.

20th and 21st Centuries

In 1948 Isdud was a quiet Palestinian town with some 5000 inhabitants. Local lore has it that the three shrines in the town were erected in memory of Salman al-Farisi, a companion of the Prophet Muhammad, an Egyptian clergyman Shaykh al-Matbuli, and an otherwise unattributed Ahmad Abu al-Iqbal.

Isdud was on the front lines between Israeli and Egyptian forces, which sent its 6th Battalion to Isdud in May 1948. Some fierce fighting took place around Isdud in early June, but the town did not fall to Israeli forces until October, when the townspeople fled after a three-night air bombardment. The 300 people who stayed and surrendered to the Israelis with white flags were expelled.

The 5,000 inhabitants of Isdud went to the Gaza strip in their entirety; most of them live in the Shati and Jabalia refugee camps to this day. Many of their children and grandchildren were active in the first and second Palestinian uprising. Many Palestinians laborers work at the port in Ashdod and elsewhere in the city. Under existing trade agreements much of the imports and exports coming to Palestinian self-rule areas must go through Ashdod or one of the other Israeli coastal cities. Isdud, in the meantime, is known to Israelis as the archeological site Tell Ashdod.

Near Isdud

Ashdod

Founded in 1956, this modern Israeli city is 7 kilometers north-northwest of the ancient city ruins. An archeological museum on 15 Hasheyatim Street contains a few of the artifacts found in Isdud. The artificial port, enclosed by breakwaters, is southern Israel's only outlet to the Mediterranean; much of the country's citrus crop is exported through Ashdod. There are large synthetic-textile plants and a number of other industries. In addition, Ashdod has a petroleum refinery and one of Israel's major power plants. It has a population of 80,000.

Ad-Halom Bridge

This bridge was built toward the end of the Ottoman era on the remains of an older Roman bridge. It passes over the Lachish River (Wadi Suchrir) at the southern entrance of modern Ashdod. The small concrete tower served as an observation point and military post for the British west of the bridge. To the south, an obelisk symbolizes peace between Egypt and Israel. The monument honors the Egyptian soldiers who fought and died in defense of the Palestinians in this region.

Cactus often grows from the rubble of destroyed villages

Minet al-Kala'a (Port Castle)

Built by the Fatimids in the 10th century, the former Port Castle is a rectangular fortress (60 by 40 m/197 by 131 ft) with a guard tower at each corner. The towers were enclosed by a high wall. Two huge gates in the wall gave access to the stronghold. It is southeast of Isdud's ruins, close to Ashdod.

Isdud was home to 5,000 Palestinians

Yibna

Known as Jabneel in the Bible, Yahve to the Philistines, Iamnia or Gabinius to the Romans, and Yavne to the modern Israelis, this town has been inhabited continuously for 3,000 years.

Though it appears to have been a secondary town to the Philistines, in Hellenistic times Yibna was a regional administrative center. The Hasmonians eventually destroyed it, but the Romans had the town and its port rebuilt. At the time the port superseded that of

Jaffa in importance and the Judeans took refuge here in CE 70. Muslims from nearby Ramleh also settled there and by 985 a beautiful mosque was built adjacent to the tomb of Abu Hureira, one of the Prophet Muhammad's companions.

The Fatimids ruled the town when Crusaders claimed a stake in Yibna, expelling all Muslims and building a strategic outpost. The town was already back in Mamluk hands by the time they defeated the Mongols and Baibars had the grand mosque renovated to mark the long-awaited victory. At the start of Ottoman rule the population was just under 1,000, but by the early 17th century that number had more than tripled.

By the time the Israelis invaded Yibna it had a settled population of 5,500 and some 1,500 nomads. Five hundred of its residents were schoolchildren and most of these, their children and grandchildren now live as refugees in the Gaza Strip. Eight Israeli settlements were built on Yibna's land by the 1960s.

Some 4 kilometers northwest of the town is Israel's first atomic research reactor. Today the "old" Yibna is a ghost town. Less than half a dozen houses of the village are occupied, mostly by Jewish families, one still by Arabs. The dilapidated mosque, over 1,000 years old, is falling apart. The Tomb of Rabbi Gamliel was super-imposed on the tomb of Abu Hureira.

30.

Askalan & Majdal

Majdal is too busy to pay us any mind, and the vegetable market is full of people and peddlers, and the sycamore tree is blessed and bears fruit several times a year, and the beautiful day isn't necessarily followed by another that is lean....

—*"Hunger," Ghareeb Asqalani, 20th century*

Legend has it that Askalan was the home of the first temple ever built in honor of the mermaid Derketo, the Canaanite fish divinity. The Philistines later adopted Derketo and gave her a Greek name, Atargatis.

The Canaanites built the oldest and largest seaport known in the country (2000–1550 BCE) in Askalan to serve a thriving metropolis that stretched over more than 150 acres. The oldest arched city gate in the world still stands two stories high by the sea.

According to the inscriptions on the temple walls at Karnak, Ramses II ruled Askalan before it became the commercial center of the Philistine Pentapolis (1200 to 586 BCE). Until the Babylonian period it remained a staunchly Philistine city damned in Old Testament narratives. It was the last of the Philistine cities burned down by the Babylonian armies, who destroyed all 50 of its look-out towers in 604.

For much of the Persian era, Askalan was part of the Phoenician territory of Tyre. It became fully Hellenized under Alexander and defended itself against Maccabean and Hasmonian rule by becoming a protectorate of Rome. It was the birthplace of Herod the Edumite who endowed it with spectacular public monuments. Eusebius claimed that in his time, there were still wells in Askalan that had been used by the

A date palm amongst the ruins of Askalan, now an Israeli park

MUNICIPALITY OF MAJDAL

Prophet Abraham. According to Palestinian tradition, a well used by Abraham is still located in the Roman amphitheater.

Askalan prospered under the Romans, Byzantines, and Muslim Arabs, who under the rule of Abdul Malik (685) built a magnificent Umayyad Mosque. Arab travellers marveled Askalan's splendor. "The city is spacious, opulent, healthy and well fortified," wrote Al-Maqdisi in 985.

It faced its first era of discontent with the coming of the Crusaders, who killed 10,000 Muslims during the first of their many campaigns to conquer the city. It was the last Muslim city to fall to the Europeans. Perhaps because of its coveted status, Baibars himself had it destroyed for good in 1270 to avoid another battle with the Crusaders. He founded the city of Majdal nearby.

The UN partition plan allotted Majdal to the Arab State in Palestine but it was taken by the Israelis as booty in the 1948 war and never returned.

Majdal

Majdal was founded in the 14th century during the rule of Baibars, who put an end to the wars over Askalan by destroying it and starting fresh with this inland city. Majdal served as a substitute for the people of Askalan. It was famous for producing cloth and clothing: its advanced weaving industry served much of southern Palestine, including Gaza and the Negev.

About 75 years ago Majdal was described as a "thriving town of some 8,000 souls, pleasantly surrounded by orchards and a well-stocked bazaar, with several small factories, which wove cotton materials." Today the city center is called "downtown" and the main attraction of Arab Majdal, the area around the mosque, has been turned into a flea market. The mosque itself has been turned into a museum, in which a few archeological finds from the city are housed. An interesting selection of photographs from the 1930s and early 1940s shows life in Arab Majdal, which was clearly very different from what it is today.

Majdal had 11,000 homes when it was bombed by the Israelis in July 1948. By the time the military campaign was over, only 1,500 people were left in the city. They were herded into three city districts and by 1951 they had been evicted through a series of military and

Top: Photographs of Majdal housed in the town mosque, now used as an Israeli museum
Bottom: View to the sea in a gap in the ancient wall of Askalan

administrative security measures. Most of the refugees and their descendents live in the Gaza Strip refugee camps to this day. Majdal itself is a quarter in the Israeli city of Ashqelon.

Modern Ashqelon, a popular seaside resort, adjoins the site of ancient Askalan. Industries in the town manufacture agricultural products, wristwatches, and plastics. The town was settled by Jewish immigrants from Iraq, Morocco, and Yemen after 1948. Since 1990, it has been settled mostly by Russian émigrés, very few of whom are religious Jews. Thus you will find shops open on Saturdays and several restaurants serving pork.

Visiting Askalan

Most of the remains of the Canaanite and Philistine city of Askalan make up an archeological park in the southwestern part of the modern city. There are remains of the Philistine port and winery, Roman ramparts, Byzantine and Crusader churches, and an open-air amphitheater, which Israelis use for cultural festivals and performances.

Among the many archeological finds are a Canaanite silver calf icon, massive ramparts, a Philistine winery and bazaar, a dog cemetery, and Egyptian bones.

An arc of earthworks 2 kilometers (1.2 mi) long and in places 40 meters (131 ft) high encloses ancient settlements that span 6,000 years, from the Chalcolithic to the Mamluk periods. Fortifications included the largest mud-brick towers that still exist and a rampart protecting the seaport. At the time of the Philistine settlement, zoologists believe a dramatic shift in the domestication of species took place: pigs and cattle replaced sheep and goats. This shift appears to have taken place along the coast, but not further inland.

In addition to producing distinct Mycenaean pottery, the textile industry appears to have been a very intrinsic part of both the cultural and economic fabric of Askalan, so much so that the fabric industry still existed, albeit in a different form, in Majdal in 1947.

Among the latest archeological discoveries is the so-called "City of the Dead," which includes a cluster of sixteen Canaanite burial chambers. According to the experts, children were given full burial rights and were adorned with Egyptian scarabs and other magical charms around their necks.

Near Askalan and Majdal

Askalan and Majdal are themselves located 16 kilometers (10 mi) north of Gaza and 63 kilometers (40 mi) south of Jaffa.

Hamama (Tel Mishqafa)

Hamama, a large village before its destruction in 1948, is located less than 10 kilometers from Askalan. It was inhabited as early as the 5th century BCE and was the site of a major battle between the Crusaders and Muslims in 1099. It was home to several Muslim scholars during the Mamluk era and the village lands contained two archeological sites, Khirbet Khawr Bayk and Shaykh Awad, both believed to date back to the 13th century BCE.

During the air bombardment of Isdud, Hamama became a temporary home to hundreds of refugees, only to be emptied in subsequent military expeditions by the Israeli army. Most of the people of Hamama live in Gaza camps to this day. There are only gravestones where the village once stood.

Jura

Also known as Jurat Askalan, this village is located some 3 kilometers (1.8 mi) northwest of Askalan, and just 1 kilometer from the sea. It was known to the Romans as Jagur. Its seaside location made it a summer resort for the people of Majdal, and an annual spring festival gave the village a further reputation of celebration. Its distinguished fishing industry provided many of inland towns and cities with seafood.

In 1948, the village was the victim of the same air bombardments that helped empty Majdal. Today the village land in its entirety has been built on by the Ashqelon municipality and is part of the Israeli city. Apparently only one of the community's over 400 homes still exists, and most of Jura's refugees live in Gaza. Its most famous former resident is Shaykh Ahmad Yassin, the wheelchaired leader of the Islamic Resistance Movement, Hamas, who was assassinated by Israel while leaving prayer at a mosque in 2004.

31.

Ekron

The temple which he built, 'kyš (Achish, Ikausu) son of Padi, son of Yśd, son of Ada, son of Ya'ir, ruler of Ekron, for Ptgyh his lady. May she bless him, and protect him, and prolong his days, and bless his land.

—Inscription found on a stone in Ekron, Babylonian period, circa 600 BCE

Built over the ruins of what was probably a Canaanite metropolis, Philistine Ekron became an important part of Philistine economic domination of the coast. Archeological excavations conducted at the site between 1981 and 1996 by Israeli archeologicsts provided unprecedented information about the history and culture of the Philistine city during the 600 years of its existence, from the 12th to the 7th century BCE. It is believed to have been the greatest olive oil producing center of the ancient world during Philistine rule.

According to the Bible, Ekron was destroyed at the beginning of the 10th century BCE. The city was rebuilt by its inhabitants on a smaller scale, with its confines limited to the main mount. As elsewhere in the Philistine world, a gradual assimilation began with the local population as well as the Phoenicians and other local cultures.

By 712 BCE Sargon II, King of Assyria, had conquered Ekron. The siege of the city was immortalized in relief-carved stone slabs on the walls of his unused palace in Dur-Sharrukin (modern Khorsabad, Iraq). Rebuilt with the help of the Assyrians, who also settled in the city, Ekron enjoyed relative peace and prosperity for the next 100 years. The city was carefully planned and divided into residential quarters, with separate quarters for the rulers and the elite and for industry and trade. Toward the end of the Assyrian era, it had expanded to some 85 acres, making it one of the largest cities of the era.

Ekron's mainstays were olive oil production, textile weaving, and trade. Only a few of the city's known 115 oil installations have been excavated thus far. It is estimated that during this period the city produced up to 700 tons of oil per year. The excavated installations indicate that factory buildings consisted of three rooms: one for crushing and pressing olives, one for oil separation and storage, and one for textile production. For four months a year the factories were used for olive oil production, and the other eight months for making textiles.

In 603 BCE Nebuchadnezzar destroyed the city. Archeological finds suggest that the residents of Ekron hid their valuables as the Babylonian army approached the city, for hoards were found under the debris of the destroyed houses: silver jewelry, precious stones, cut pieces of silver, and the silver currency of that period.

In the fourth century CE Eusebius described Ekron as a village. But it appears to have been abandoned from the seventh to the fourteenth centuries CE. During the Ottoman era it was part of the village lands of Jilya, an Arab village of small to medium size. It belonged to the governorate of Gaza. The visible surface remains of ancient Ekron were known in Arabic as Khirbat al-Muqanna and lay approximately one kilometer from the center of Jilya.

Today Ekron is known as Tel Mikne or Khirbat al-Muqanna. It is very much an invisible place, overgrown with weeds and largely anonymous. An inscribed stone tablet on permanent display at the Israel Museum, is a testimonial to the rich past of this now lonely hill. The inscriptions make reference to Philistine kings Ysd, Ada, and Ya'ir, and Ikausu.

Tel Mikne can be reached from Kibbutz Revadim, off Route 3, near the Re'em and Nachshon junction. Here exists the only museum dedicated to the Philistines. (Tel 972-8-858-8762; Fax 972-8-858-8913; ekron_mu@revadim.org.il)

Philistine oil lamp

32.

Gaza (Ghazza)

... a city so rich in trees as to be like a cloth of brocade spread out on the sand.

— Dimashki, 1300

Once known as Philistia, Palestine's coastline served as a nexus between Asia and Africa where travellers, pilgrims, and merchants of the ancient world met. Coveted since the time of the Pharaohs, the beautiful coast and pleasant climate attracted artisans, merchants, desert mystics, philosophers, lawmakers, and conquerors alike. Spices, fruits, and wines were among the coast's main produce and exports. For most of the last 5,000 years it has been inhabited by an amalgamation of Arab and Mediterranean peoples.

Today the cities of ancient Philistia, which included Askalan and Isdud as well as Ekron, are no longer united under one political umbrella. Some 400,000 people live in Gaza City, and the rest of the 1.45 million people who reside in the "Strip" live in three main cities, nine major villages, and eight refugee camps. Divided by the sword and ruled by the politics of separation, this Philistine coast is controlled mainly by modern Israel.

In August 2005 the last vestiges of Israeli rule, a military presence of some 12,000 soldiers and 6,000 settlers, unilaterally withdrew from Gaza. Thus 40 percent of Gaza has been repatriated, and constitutes the largest land area and population under Palestinian rule.

But the beaches of the Mediterranean are as seductive as they always were and the cuisine of the seafarers of the Philistine Coast is still sumptuous. A few remains of Mamluk and Ottoman architecture allow glimpses of the long history of human civilization here. And the

Moonrise over Abu Jihad's Mosque

past is still being dug up, literally, making the region's history ever more accessible.

Early History

The Canaanites are believed to have given Gaza its name, which means strength. The Egyptians called it "Gazzat" (prized city). The Persians under Cambyses (539 BCE) are believed to have called it "treasure," and the Arabs often refer to it as Gazzat Hashim, in honor of Hashim, the Prophet Muhammad's great-grandfather, who is buried here.

During an archeological excavation in 1998 and 1999 in Wadi Gaza (about 6 km south of the city), a joint Palestinian–French dig began unearthing a walled city, Tel al-Sakn, which dated back to 3200 BCE. The city was apparently abandoned around 2000 BCE when its inhabitants moved to Gaza's ancient capital, Tell el-Ajjoul (2000–1200 BCE). Archeologists called it Tel al-Sakn (mound of habitation) because it has so many layers of human settlement. The city was clearly a Canaanite city under heavy Egyptian influence at its early stages, and later became a more "pure" Canaanite city. The inhabitants of Wadi Gaza (Gaza Valley), were fishers, hunters and cereal cultivators and were also knowledgeable in Bronze and Iron production.

Gaza was the focal point of the ancient route that led from Pharaonic Egypt to the Fertile Crescent and back. The Egyptian Pharaohs controlled much of Gaza from 1538–1484 BCE until the Philistines arrived (c. 1200 BCE). Among other finds, archeologists uncovered evidence that around 1500 BCE massive caravans of camels and horses refueled and rested in Gaza.

The Philistines inherited the coast from the Canaanites, absorbing their customs and ways and making them their own. Gaza was one of five main cities known as the Pentapolis (along with Askalan, Isdud, Ekron, and Gath/Tel al-Safi) built up by the seafaring Philistines along the coast of Canaan. An Aegean people, the Philistines' settlement in the country marked the most extensive integration of a non-Semitic people.

Along with new bloodlines, the Philistines brought highly decorative and elaborate art, mercantile skills, new burial customs, and an advanced knowledge of metalworking and warfare. Despite the opposition to their presence in Canaan they stayed and integrated. Philistine history, to its detriment, was long interpreted through Old Testament texts. Archeological finds during the last two centuries, however, have changed the way most scholars now interpret the Philistines and their accomplishments.

Walking home from school, Deir al-Balah

The Hellenistic Era

Alexander the Macedonian put an end to Philistine affluence when he occupied Gaza in October of 332 BCE after a two-month siege. As he had done in Tyre, he sold Gaza's inhabitants, mostly ethnic Arabs, as well as Persians and Greeks opposed to his rule, into slavery.

An unknown number of his 40,000 Macedonian and Greek soldiers stayed in Gaza, while inhabitants of surrounding towns and villages were brought in to re-populate the city. Alexander sent home ten ships of war plunder. One of his favorite teachers, Leonidas, received a consignment of eighteen tons of frankincense and myrrh from the Gaza markets as a gift.

Both the city and its once Arabized population became Hellenized. Alexander's successors in Egypt, the Ptolemies, ruled from 301–198 BCE. Ministry of finance records show that Gazans sold wheat, olive oil, wine, fish, dry fruits, frankincense, and slaves and that they imported dyes, aromatic essence, ginger, pepper, balsam, vermilion, specially processed woolen cloth, precious woods, silk, brocade, and medical drugs. In 198 BCE the Seleucids (who had

Byzantine flooring, Gaza

succeeded Alexander's rule in Syria) defeated the Ptolemies and
became the rulers of Palestine. These two parallel dynasties established
Hellenistic culture and what amounted to Greek rule in the entire
Near East. Greeks, in large numbers, migrated to Palestine, Syria,

Mesopotamia, and Egypt. They made up the elite ruling circles while the native Arabs and migrant Persians made up the working classes.

At this time Gaza had eight main temples, the most important of which was dedicated to Marne (or Marneion), the supreme god of the city, who was considered the equivalent of the Cretan-born Zeus. The main city square was adorned with a marble statue of Aphrodite. There were also temples dedicated to Venus, Apollo, Tyche, Helios (Sun), Kore, Proserpine, and Hierion.

The Seleucids' control of Gaza eventually waned and Judeans under the Hasmonaean dynasty tried to wrest control of the city in 140 BCE. It did not come under Judean rule until Alexander Jannaeus destroyed large parts of Gaza in 96 BCE after a one-year battle. Josephus wrote in his journal that Gazans burned their properties and committed suicide rather than fall under the rule of Jannaeus.

One colonizer was replaced by another in 64 BCE when the Romans, under Augustus, took Gaza from the Hasmonaens.

Christianity

On the eve of Jesus' birth in Bethlehem, Gaza was a center for pagan deities and Hellenistic culture and would remain so until the 4th century. Gazans had their household gods, street corner idols, and special rituals associated with birth, harvest, marriage, rain, and death. The upper classes and intellectuals paid homage to the Greek deities. Coins with a replica of Marna were still being minted during the reign of Emperor Caracalla (198–217 CE).

Olympian games were introduced in 130 CE and held in Gaza to honor the visiting Emperor Hadrian. Until the 4th century CE, these games, which comprised both athletic and oratorical competitions, were the most important in the entire Levant.

Many social historians have attributed Gaza's late acceptance of Christianity to its relatively wealthy and urbanized population. A religion that catered to the downtrodden and poor was not that attractive at the time on the Philistine coast.

It could very well be that on his way to Egypt, Mark sowed the seeds of the new religion to members of the peripheral society around the port of Maioumas. For it was at this harbor that the first Christian faithful of Gaza were born. By the time that the undeclared Christian, Philip the Arab (243–248), ruled the Roman Empire, much of the population of Maioumas had already converted. Diocletian (284–305) and other Roman emperors however, continued persecutions and the Gazan Bishop Sylvanus was put to death. Christianity continued to be practiced underground until the rule of Constantine.

The almost 400-year battle between the devotees of pagan gods and the forces of Christianity was often fierce and bloody. Halarion, a leading figure on the side of Christianity, was the Gazan founder of monastic life in Palestine. Near his birthplace of Tabatha, also known as **Um al-Tuut** (Nuseirat), he built a monastery, which was later destroyed by Julian the Apostate (361-363).

The Christian era began for Gazans in 402 when the Byzantine Emperor Arcadius instructed his troops to burn the holiest shrine in Gaza, the Temple of Marna. Many local people fled in horror as they watched their temple burn, and many buried or hid their own deities to save them from the Christian authorities.

In the place of the Temple of Marna, a church named Eudoxia, in honor of the empress, was built under the auspices of the Antioch-based architect Rufinus. Close by stands the **Church of St. Porphyry** (the Greek Orthodox Church), which opened its doors to worshippers on Easter in 407. The existing church has the tomb of St. Porphyry encased in it, and a Christian cemetery still stands adjacent to the church.

At this time, wine exports accounted for much of Gaza's revenue. Gaza jars that were used to export the wine have been found across Europe and the Near East. As a result of sophisticated irrigation and water channeling techniques introduced by the Nabateans (200 CE) in southern Palestine, the Negev became a main center of pressing and storing wine that was exported through the harbor of Gaza and on to Egypt and Europe.

In the early Christian era (484–550) Gaza was home to some of the most important thinkers and scholars in the region. Procopius of Gaza (500 CE) was a leading figure in the rhetorical world in his age.

Mamluk lion

Dorotheos of Gaza, probably a student of Procopius, is considered to be the most historically significant of Gaza's Christian monks.

At about this time, pilgrims began to visit the Holy Land. Churches added hostels, and Gazans made souvenirs of dried earth with clay stamps and inscriptions. Gaza was second only to Jerusalem in size by 527. By the time the prophet Muhammad was born (c. 570 CE), Christianity was prominent in the coastal region. But perhaps the Byzantines never went beyond the conversion of the upper and ruling classes, who conversed in Greek. For when Islam came in 637, Gazans were among the first to pledge their allegiance to the new religion. Islam came to them in Arabic, a Semitic language akin to their own Aramaic.

Al-Shafi'i, the Lawmaker

It was the Imam Muhammad Ibn Idris al-Shafi'i, born in 767 CE, who placed Gaza on the map of the Islamic world forever. A native Gazan who descended from the noble Quraish tribe of the Hijaz, al-Shafi'i went to the city of Medina as a youth to study jurisprudence under the famous jurist and teacher Malik Ibn Annus. From there he went on to attend universities in Baghdad and Cairo. Upon completing the study of the existing legal systems in Islam, he formulated his own vision of Islamic jurisprudence. Deciding for a middle ground, which combined the liberal Baghdad and the conservative Medina schools, he founded the Shafi'i School of Jurisprudence, which remains one of the five main legal schools of Islam, along with the Hanafi, Malki, Hanbali, and Jaffari.

The Shafi'i school has some 180 million adherents and is predominant in Palestine, southern Egypt, East Africa, western and southern Arabia, as well as India and the East Indies. Al-Shafi'i died in Cairo in 820. A ruler of the Ayyubite dynasty built a tomb over his grave, which lies at the foot of al-Muqqatam, Cairo, and is still a site for pilgrimage.

The Calling of Islam

Merchants from the Arabian Peninsula, Africa, and Egypt had traded in and traveled to Gaza for centuries, using it as a base for their business ventures in the Levant and as far afield as Iraq, Persia, and India. Among these merchants was an Arabian named Hashim Ibn Abd Manaf who lived in the middle of the 6th century. Hashim died in Gaza before his great-grandson, Muhammad, became the Prophet of Islam. Out of respect for the Prophet Muhammad, Hashim's grave became a shrine, venerated by visitors to this day.

Many of the Arabians who would become the Prophet Mohammed's companions had visited Gaza as traders before the birth of Islam. Omar Bin al-Khattab, later credited with the Islamization of Palestine, was one such friend. Many mosques and public service buildings are still named in his honor. The **Mosque of Omar** in Gaza is one such house of prayer. But unlike others of its kind, it has a Gaza-specific narrative. In 614, shortly before the advent of Islam, the wars between Byzantium and the Persians led to the almost total destruction of the Church of Eudoxia. Since it was seen as the center for religious veneration, converted Gazans pushed to have a mosque built at the site. Remains of the church are thus still visible in parts of this mosque.

Despite the adoption of Islam by much of the population, Byzantine traditions prevailed until the Baghdad-based Abbasids established their rule in 750. The Abbasids built watchtowers that were precursors to lighthouses along the coast at Maioumas-Gaza, Askalan, Isdud, Yubna, and Jaffa. By the early 10th century, a specifically Islamic/Arab character was in place.

Before the Storm

In the 9th and 10th centuries Palestine made vast contributions to the coffers of the caliphs in Damascus and Baghdad, in the form of gold coins, olive oil, and raisins.

By the middle of the 11th century the existing regional powers were all in decline, and vulnerable to nomadic Seljuk Turks, who had come from central Asia to conquer the region. By 1071, they had control of Syria and Palestine. Their mercenary soldiers in Gaza demanded payment in the form of land; thus feudalism was introduced in Gaza.

Byzantium saw the Seljuks as a threat to the heart of Christendom, so the Christian empires of Europe prepared for a crusade that would wrest Jerusalem from the nomadic Muslims who had conquered it. Unlike the Arabs, the Seljuk Turks allegedly restricted access of pilgrims to the Christian holy sites. When Jerusalem fell to Crusader swords in July of 1099, Gaza City was controlled by soldiers loyal to the Fatimid dynasty in Cairo. Launching attacks against the Crusaders in Jerusalem from Gaza, the military held out in Gaza, while many families fled to the countryside after hearing about the massacres in Jerusalem.

By 1149 the Fatimid forces had withdrawn from Gaza, but had established an independent rule in Askalan. King Baldwin III, now King of Jerusalem, bet on victory against them. He had handed over control of the largely abandoned city of Gaza to the Templar Knights. Under Crusader rule, Gaza became more of a garrison town than a flourishing mercantile capital. Defensive forts were built in Gaza and Darum (Deir al-Balah) in preparation for an attack on Askalan. Manned by a large fighting force that consisted of the Templar Knights and the Knights Hospitallier from Jerusalem, Baldwin fought for several months before destroying the large fortress that was Askalan. From 1149–1170, the Crusaders ruled the Philistine coast.

A church was built on the site of the Mosque of Omar. (It is not clear that the Crusaders destroyed the mosque, but someone did.) Today, some of the 12th-century architecture is still visible in the structure, which has been reconverted to a mosque.

In 1169 Saladin was sent as a representative of the Seljuk, Nur al-Din, to the court of the Fatimids in Cairo. Within a short time the aging and tired Fatimids were replaced by the Kurdish forces of Saladin. Upon Nur al-Din's death, Saladin brought Damascus and Cairo under his rule and planned the defeat of the Crusaders.

In the summer of 1170 an earthquake put a temporary end to the fighting between the Crusaders and Ayyubite forces, but nevertheless, by

Icon with Arabic bible, Church of Porphyrus, Gaza

the end of the year parts of Saladin's army entered Palestine through Darum, now Deir al-Balah. Until well into the following century a tug-of-war prevailed between the Crusaders and the Cairo-based Muslim forces. Not until the slave-soldiers known as Mamluks overthrew the Ayyubites from within the palace walls did the Muslim forces achieve a final victory over the Crusader forces.

Mamluk Period

One of the most significant improvements under the Mamluks (1250–1517 CE) was the development of a postal system, of which Gaza became a central hub. The threat of a Mongol invasion led the Mamluk Sultan Baibars to set up this efficient communications network. Traversed by mounted messengers with colored sashes, regular mail routes were introduced from Cairo to Gaza via Rafah, al-Salqa (north of Khan Younes), al-Darum (Deir al-Balah), Malkas, Beit Jibrin (and from there to the Transjordanian city of Karak), Beit Hanoun, Beit Daras, Qatra, Lydd, 'Oja, Tira, Qatoun, Fahmah and Jenin (and from there to Damascus). The Mamluks built roads and bridges, and postal stations and khans for the messengers all along the route. They also reintroduced the pigeon mail service, for which towers were built. This postal system and its infrastructure was perhaps the greatest achievement of the Mamluk reign.

In 1348 Gaza, along with all the cities of the Nile Delta, was devastated by the plague. The city managed to recover, however, and the economic prosperity of Gaza was unequalled by any other city in the country during the Mamluk reign. This abundance was reflected in the produce available at the daily market: barley, wheat, grape leaves, grapes, olives, raspberries, lemons, figs, sweet melons, pomegranates, and dates.

Ottoman Gaza

The Mamluks had been based in nearby Cairo, so Gaza's proximity to the seat of power had given it influence and wealth. When the Ottomans in far-off Istanbul became masters of the region, Gaza was a distant dominion without much consequence. Although it continued to be patronized for its religious and historical importance, it tended to benefit as an afterthought, only once Jerusalem and Hebron were accorded first rights.

Urban planners were hard at work during this period, however. The Old City was divided into quarters: Shuja'ia, Burgilia, Zeitoun, Daraj, Tuffah, Khuder, and Bani Amr. Some industries developed, too:

by the second half of the 18th century, four large soap factories had
made this industry one of the most profitable. Gaza also produced the
coveted "Rosenthal" pottery, for daily kitchen and household use.
These exports, and also hand-woven carpet, went mostly to Egypt.

But though some industries developed, overall social and
economic conditions deteriorated. The Ottoman lords and their local
vassals inherited the feudal ways the Seljuks had introduced. Thus the
population did not own much of its own property, and taxation was so
high that Gazans were only slightly better off than serfs in the Russian
hinterland. As a result, trade slowed and the once prosperous
mercantile class became largely extinct.

By the end of the 18th century some Western ideas and concepts
touched the shores of Gaza. Although Napoleon came to conquer, he
left behind the seeds of European enlightenment, which eventually led
to nationalism and class-consciousness, if not to secularism. But the
manifestation of these concepts was still far in the future.

It was the Albanian ruler of Egypt, Muhammad Ali, and his
dynasty that brought change to Gaza. By the 1850s, Gaza was the
second largest city in Palestine. Its prime geographic location and the
know-how of its inhabitants had given it prominent economic
standing. Although largely rural, it was becoming increasingly
urbanized. Gaza City boasted a reported 50 mosques, one for every 200
men, a sign of increasing wealth and piety. Handicrafts and trade were
second only to agriculture as a source of income, and Egypt was, as
always, the main trading partner.

British Mandate

On February 27, 1917 an expedition of British and Commonwealth
forces marched into Khan Younes. They fought a joint
Turkish–German force for some 8 months before they took Gaza City
in November. The Turks and Germans had built a defensive wall to
keep the Brits and their allies at bay. Archibald Murray led the British
assault with some 44,000 troops, almost the same number of soldiers
that Alexander had brought to Gaza more than 2,000 years before.
And as with Alexander's army, the invading forces suffered heavy
losses: some 4,000 Allied troops lost their lives in Gaza. The British
war cemeteries in Northern Gaza and in al-Zaweideh (close to
Nuseirat) are an awesome site, well worth a visit.

The destruction that both the retreating and approaching armies
wreaked on Gaza was horrendous. The pre-war population of Gaza was
42,000 and after the war it was only 17,000. Merciless bombings on

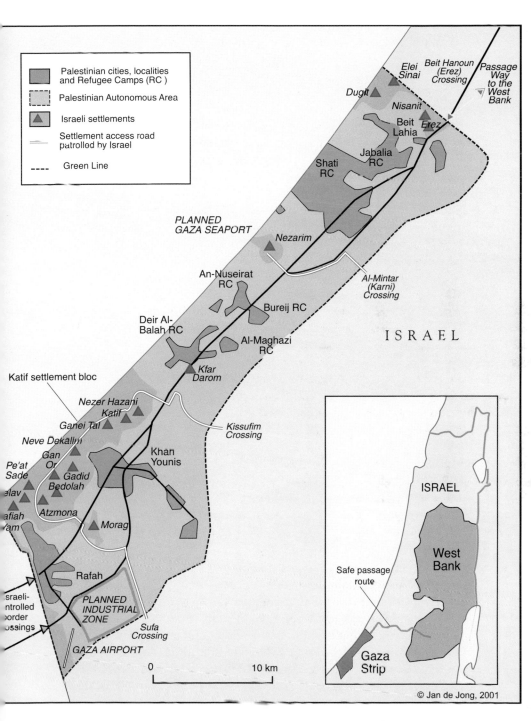

GAZA STRIP. INCLUDING ISRAELI SETTLMENTS, 1967–2005
The Israeli settlements shown above were evacuated in August 2005

Hassan, a fisherboy in Gaza

the one hand and scorching of the land on the other was how the opposing sides dealt with a city not their own. The people of Gaza bore the brunt of the war between two empires. As a result, for the next three decades, Gazans were among the most ardent opponents of British rule and also its collusion with the Zionists.

By 1929 events were coming to a head: an increasing number of known Zionists were buying land and talking about statehood; three Gaza youths were killed by British soldiers; reports of mass arrest and torture were widespread; Jewish settlers living in southern Palestine

had reportedly received arms. In September 1929, Gazans voted to rid themselves of part of their feudal heritage. The city's main street was rather pointedly changed from Jamal Pasha Street (an Ottoman feudal governor) to that of the Libyan independence hero and martyr, Omar Mukhtar, who had been killed that year by Italian colonialists. In the same spirit today, most Arab capital cities have a street named after the famous Gazan child martyr Muhammad al-Durra, who was killed by the Israelis in 2000.

Gazans were among the most observant supporters of the 1936 National Strike, which lasted 6 months. Local activists cut telephone lines to disturb the communications of the British army. After the death of two British soldiers, Gazans were subjected to long curfews and the homes of families of activists were blown up, as a precursor to the collective punishment later practiced by the Israeli occupiers. Education, too, was curtailed. Public schools run or overseen by the British did not extend beyond 7th grade. Only the wealthy, most of whom worked with the British, could afford to send their children to private schools, where they were steeped in Western culture.

By 1945 Gaza City had a population of 18,000. The majority (95 percent) were Muslim; the minority Christians belonged to the Orthodox, Latin, and Protestant communities. Most people worked in agriculture, trade, or handicrafts. When the United Nations voted to separate Palestine into two countries in 1947 almost all the main cities of the ancient Philistines and the Sea Peoples, were slotted to be part of the Arab state, including Gaza, Askalan, Isdud, Jaffa, and Acre.

But the well-armed Jewish militias broke beyond the UN-sanctioned lines and occupied 78 percent of Palestine. Askalan, Isdud, Jaffa, and Acre were taken and made part of the Israeli state. Only Gaza remained under Arab rule. By May 14, 1948, the creation of the state of

Israel was declared by the Zionist forces. Through October of that year tens of thousands of people were herded out of their communities. Entire villages were dynamited to assure that no one could return to live there. All along the coast north of Gaza people walked southward in one of the most famous exoduses in the 20th century.

Hundreds of thousands of refugees from Askalan, Isdud, Majdal, and other areas along the coast found refuge on the sand dunes and under the trees in Gaza. Initially, the Egyptian army distributed tents and the Quakers and the Red Cross followed with rations. The refugees brought with them stories of destruction, the keys and deeds to their homes, and their traditions and crafts. The refugees from the Askalan-Majdal region brought their beautiful clothes and weaving talents with them. The colors of the cloth they weave—shades of dark blue, purple, and red—are the colors of Gaza's Canaanite, Philistine, and Phoenician heritage. The Gazan refugees, as those elsewhere, are indeed the key to understanding Palestine's past, present, and future.

Egyptian Rule (1948–1967)

Of the some 800,000 Palestinians who became refugees, 200,000 ended up in Gaza.

On September 22, 1948 an all-Palestine government was assembled, and independence declared in Gaza. But the attempt at independence failed. Amid continued fighting between Israelis and Egyptians, the Palestinians had no choice but to choose sides. The Egyptians, unlike the British or the Turks, were not thought of as occupiers or even foreigners, but as neighboring rulers.

And for most of the 1950s and 1960s, the Egyptian leader Jamal Abdul Nasser kept the Israelis at bay. Yet the Palestinians were not as fully embraced as they might have hoped initially. Egypt issued the Palestinians "identity cards," but did not make them Egyptian nationals. Palestinians and Egyptians intermarried, but Palestinians did not have any political rights and were especially scrutinized by Cairo's intelligence services.

Palestinian refugees, wanting to return to their homes, which were now in Israel, frequently tried to cross the border, sometimes bearing arms. This created "reprisals" by the Israeli army. After he had taken power, President Nasser came to Gaza personally in 1955 to assure the local population that Egypt would do what it could to protect people from Israeli attacks. After a series of attacks by Israel, the Palestinians, who were for the most part unarmed, took to the streets demanding that Egypt arm them. The Egyptian government responded at first by arresting Palestinian political leaders, and later by establishing military units with Palestinian volunteers. Ultimately Gaza was enveloped in the Suez Crisis, when Egypt nationalized its own canal only to see Britain, France, and Israel go to war in protest.

In October 1956, the Israelis brutally overran Gaza, despite formidable resistance at Khan Younes. A Palestinian battalion fought the Israeli tanks and aircraft with rifles. Ultimately the Egyptians returned to Gaza, but with UN forces deployed along the border between the Israelis and the Arabs. In 1958 an executive council, headed by Haidar Abdul Shafi, was established in Gaza. Some 33 years later, Abdul Shafi spoke on behalf of the Palestinians at the Madrid Peace Conference. He spoke of how Gazans had come to realize in the late 1950s that Egypt was not really a "brother" nation; they could count on no one but themselves to defend their rights and their land. It was the beginning of political and military self-determination.

Israeli Occupation

The Israeli occupation began in June 1967. During the first three decades of the occupation, archeologists, many of whom were Israeli, made amazing discoveries, all of which were carried off to Israeli museums where most Palestinians still cannot see them.

Israel turned other parts of Gaza into a trash heap. The Israeli state quite literally dumped its residuals along the road to Gaza, creating an unbelievable stench. With the Beit Hanoun/Erez checkpoint, they redefined the borders of the Gaza Strip, unilaterally confiscating hundreds of acres of Gazan land.

The first intifada began in Gaza on December 9, 1987 in the Jabalia refugee camp. Over the next seven years, some 1,600 Palestinians died and thousands were injured. The conflict was mainly driven by Palestinian youth with stones. Their opponents were the world's fourth strongest army.

Partial Autonomy

Gaza City became the first headquarters for the post-Oslo Palestinian government soon after Yasir Arafat arrived in Rafah in June 1994, ending nearly 30 years of exile. Immense development projects to up-grade the life of the Strip's 1.45 million people began within six months of Arafat's arrival. International donors helped train civil servants, a police force, and bureaucrats for the jobs necessary to make self-rule effective. Symbols of sovereignty were built and created—an airport, a seaport, a duty-free zone, postage stamps. The airport, designed by a Moroccan architect, is

Martyrdom in Gaza

Palestine is like no other place in the world: the posters plastered all over walls, monuments, and lampposts are likely to be in memory of a martyr rather than a campaign ad for a politician. With so many having died in the struggle for independence, martyrdom has become similar to the iconoclastic culture of saints in medieval Europe. Instead of wooden icons painted in gold, the colored photo poster serves as a symbol of the martyr's memory. Some families have even established web pages in memory of their beloved martyrs.

Palestinians, Israelis, and others have published over half a dozen books in English about the first intifada. One book documenting the lives of the first hundred martyrs of the al-Aqsa intifada is available at the Ramallah-based Sakakini Cultural Center.

The most famous of Gaza's contemporary martyrs, is the child Muhammad al-Durra, who was filmed by an AFP cameraman as he was shot to death while huddling in his father's arms in October 2000. In the Arab world the 12-year-old child martyr from Breij camp became a symbol of the Palestinian struggle. The Arab League, with its 22 countries, voted to name a street in every Arab capital in honor of Muhammad al-Durra.

Historically Gaza has been a site of martyrs, not only of contemporary Palestinians, but also of many who professed to be different. Among the early Christian martyrs were Bishop Sylvanus, killed in 285; William of Castellamare was also martyred for his faith in 1364. A former hospice of the Franciscan friars, St. Anthony's, still pays homage to these Christian martyrs.

particularly functional and beautiful.

Within only a couple years, political assassinations of many Palestinians and one Israeli politician had created a hardened atmosphere, and the Oslo honeymoon was over. A right-wing Jew assassinated Israeli Prime Minister Yitzhak Rabin. Implementation of the accords was delayed and the sticking points became further sources of aggravation.

After the September 29 massacre of Palestinians at the al-Aqsa mosque, Gazans joined other Palestinians in the West Bank and inside Israel in protest and in acts of defiance against the Israeli occupation. The settlements and Israeli military posts were thorns in the sides of every Palestinian and they became targets of their contempt. Every government institution in Gaza was bombed into oblivion over the coming two years, ten percent of Palestinian-controlled land was reoccupied or "cleared" of its trees, and large areas were closed for months, threatening parts of the population with starvation.

There is general consensus in Gaza that armed resistance and acts of violence against Israelis, soldiers and civilians, brought about the end of the occupation of 40% of Gazan territory. Gaza's coastline was free again as of August 2005.

Visiting the Gaza Strip

The Strip, just 40 kilometers long and 10 kilometers wide (25 by 6.2 mi), with a total land area of some

360 square kilometers (224 sq mi) is one of the most densely populated spots on earth. It is home to some 1.3 million Palestinians, more than half of whom are registered refugees. They live on 60 percent of the land, while some 3,000–4,000 Israeli settlers and their army occupy the other 40 percent of the strip.

The August 2005 unilateral Israeli withdrawal from the Gaza Strip was the second step in the self-determination process that the Palestinians had been struggling for. It left most, if not all, of Gaza's territory under Palestinian sovereignty, though the entry points at all but the Rafah–Egyptian border remain under Israeli control. The sea coast was still controlled by Israelis as was the airspace over Gaza.

For travellers from the West Bank or Jerusalem, the Israeli Erez checkpoint, built on land belonging to the Palestinian town of Beit Hanoun, remained the only point of entry. Controlled by a colossal military infrastructure, the Israelis reserved the right to allow or deny entry of Palestinians and non-Palestinians into and out of the Gaza Strip at this "border."

There is no public transport on the Palestinian side of the Gaza–Israel crossing point, but taxis, costing less than $10 a ride will take travelers to Gaza City where group transport known as "service" and buses can take them to other locations in the Strip. Driving in, the town of Beit Hanoun is on the left and Beit Lahya and Jabalia are on the right. Large warehouses owned by Israeli firms stand at the entrance. They employ Palestinians, but have the status of "off-shore" businesses.

Most of Gaza's seashore, occupied for 38 years, stands ripe for developers who plan to build housing projects, tourist villages, and agricultural havens.

Beit Lahya

Beit Lahya, 7 kilometers north of the old city of Gaza, was a Roman garrison town that came into its own during the Byzantine era when it was known as Bethelea. Then, as now, its sweet water nourished delicious fruits and beautiful gardens. It once looked like a forest, with many apple, fig, peach, and orange trees. In fact, it was the main supplier of apples in 19th-century Palestine. Even today, those "Grade A Strawberries" marked "Made in Israel" are actually Beit Lahya strawberries, grown and packaged here.

The town has two main mosques. The western part of town, al-Seifa, is considered a bourgeois suburb; it sits on the hill overlooking the sea. The **Tel al-Thahab** (Golden Mound) is in this part of town. Gold coins, pottery, and marble pieces, mostly from the Roman,

Byzantine, and Mamluk eras were discovered by archeologists at this site, which is now hardly visible.

Beit Hanoun

Beit Hanoun is located to the left as one enters the Gaza Strip. Beit Hanoun lands are cultivated with grape vines, and fig, apple, orange, and almond trees.

In 1239 a famous battle between Muslims and Crusaders was fought nearby on a hill known as al-Nasr (the victory). The town's one historic mosque, which dates back to the Ayyubites, commemorates this historic event. Unfortunately nothing is left of the original **al-Nasr Mosque**, apart from the southern portico with its beautiful roof with fan vaults and a shallow dome in the center. A tribute in Arabic script known as Naskhi, commemorating the battle, is engraved on a plate inside the mosque.

Beit Hanoun was also an important part of the postal route during the Mamluk era; its horsemen were known for riding to Jenin and Damascus. According to folklore, a number of Beit Hanoun families come from the Houran region of what is today southern Syria. Many of the families trace their family lineage to Kurdish dynasties in Egypt, and many have clan affiliations with Bedouins from the Wadi Mousa area and the tribes of al-Howeitat and al-Adwan in southern Jordan.

Jabalia

Local tradition holds that Jabalia was established as a garrison town for soldiers when a Mamluk governor, Sinjer Alamudin al-Jawli, acquired the land in and around the area and built a mosque. The soldiers, many of who were Turkmen from mountainous areas in the Caucasus, settled around the mosque built.

After Palestinian workers accidentally stumbled on some mosaics while working on new roads in 1996, the Palestinian Department of Antiquities declared the area a national heritage site. They discovered a cemetery dating back to the Roman and Byzantine periods, and a large **Byzantine complex**, consisting of a church, courtyards, and both domestic and public rooms was subsequently discovered. The oldest inscription dates to 444 CE, but the complex is believed to be even older. The incredible mosaic floors are made of marble, basalt, glass, and pottery showing human figures, wild animals, birds, plants, trees, and Greek scripts. The cemetery stands on a hill of rough sand about 48 meters (158 ft) above sea level. Different kinds of tombs were found containing skeletons, jewels, glass, pottery, metals, and decorated stones. The area has been largely covered up with sand to protect it from the elements and Israeli invasions. The UNDP has set aside money to sponsor an archeological park, which would allow the sites to be labeled and protected while being visually accessible to visitors, educators, and tourists.

Visiting Gaza City

"Life" in Gaza city takes place mostly in the Shuja'ia and Daraj quarters. The most famous 20th century Gazan poet, Mu'een Bseiso, immortalized his memories of these city quarters in the *Palestinian Notebooks* when he wrote

> In the Mosque of Sit Ruqayya, in the Shuja'ia, I used to jump over the backs of the men as they prostrated themselves in prayer. 'Bring him to me,' the imam of the mosque would say...

Al-Daraj Quarter

The Mosque of Omar is an integral part of the al-Daraj district and counts as the largest and best known mosque in the city. Of its five entrances only one is Ayoubite, while the others were added by the Mamluks and Ottomans.

In 1917 the Mosque was largely destroyed during a British bombardment. The Supreme Islamic Council had the destroyed parts rebuilt. The mosque houses the largest library in the city, with some 20,000 volumes. It is said to have been established in the 13th century as a gift from the Mamluk Sultan Baibars.

In July 2002, al-Daraj was again attacked from the air, when an Israeli F-16 fighter jet bombed the home of a Daraj resident claimed to be a terrorist. Fifteen people, mostly women and children, were killed and more than a hundred wounded.

The city's barrel-vaulted **Kaisaria** (gold market) lies just south of the mosque. Built in the 1470s, it was a large market for valuable goods during the reign of Sultan Qaytbay (1468–96). Mamluk architecture is evident throughout the khan, which is one of the oldest examples of a vaulted market in the country. Here gold can still be bought and currency exchanged.

The existing **Mosque of Sayyed Hashim** was built in 1850, on the orders of the Ottoman Sultan Abdul Majeed. Some of the exquisite, very old materials used in the mosque's construction were taken from mosques and other buildings destroyed by Napoleon. The original Ottoman minaret was rebuilt in 1903, along with the north and west

The Mosque of Hashim commemorates Prophet Muhammad's great-grandfather

aisles. The **Mausoleum of Sayyed Hashim** is in the northwest corner of the mosque. A mosque and hostel have been located at this site since at least the 12th century. The mosque had a *madrasa* and was a center for religious learning in the 19th and parts of the 20th century. The mosque was named to honor Prophet Muhammad's great-grandfather, Hashim, a prominent Arab trader who died in Gaza before the advent of Islam. Hashim is allegedly buried in a cave inside the city walls. The mosque was frequented by visiting traders from Egypt, Arabia and Morocco.

The **Mosque of Shaykh Zechariah**, on al-Wahda Street in the same neighborhood, was named in honor of a cleric from the city of Palmyra who died in Gaza in 1057. The only existing part of the original mosque is the minaret. The existing mosque does not use any of the original foundation stones, though one preserved stone indicates that the original mosque was built around 1400. The plaque refers to the Kingdom of Gaza, a term last used in that era. A textile factory now exists on one side of the mosque.

The **Mosque and Tomb of Shaykh Khalil** is also on al-Wahda Street. Shaykh Khalil Ibn Shabib (d. 1348) was buried in the court of the mosque compound, close to the western wall of the mosque. The engraving on the tomb indicates that the mosque was renovated and partly rebuilt at the beginning of the Ottoman Era in 1548. Most of the mosque was destroyed to create space for the construction of al-Wahda Street (one of Gaza's main streets) during the Egyptian administration, but the Gaza Waqf restored what was left of the mosque in 1993.

A little further down the street is the **al-Ahmediya Shrine**, established in the 14th century by a local ruler for the followers of al-Sayyed Ahmed al-Bedawi, a Muslim cleric whose adherents had built the shrine in honor of his memory. Al-Bedawi (the Bedouin) had a habit of covering his face to shield it from the scorching sun, making him a "veiled man." He established a Sufi order known as al-Ahmediya. He died in Tanta, Egypt in 1276. The dome is one of the largest surviving Mamluk domes in the country. The prayer area is surrounded by three vaulted iwans and has a beautiful marble fountain. Within the southern quarters of the al-Ahmediya is the marble and limestone **Tomb of Qutlu Khatum**, a Mamluk noblewoman who died in 1332. Her father, Bahadur al-Jukandar, was known as the Emir of Forty, (prince of 40 Mamluk soldiers). He lived in Damascus and had a close relationship with the Emir Turuntay, who had the al-Ahmediya Shrine built. The polo sticks engraved one each side of the tomb indicated her father's position at the Royal Court.

Still on al-Wahda Street, stands **Qasr al-Basha** (al-Radwan Castle), also known as Napoleon's Fort. Local lore has it that in the 13th century when the Mamluk Sultan Baibars was still a soldier fighting the Crusaders and Mongols in Syria, he came through Gaza several times, and apparently found female companionship here. Later when he had become Sultan in Cairo, he is said to have built this grand home for his Gazan wife and children. The symbol of the Sultan Baibars (two lions facing each other) still dominates the building. Note the geometrical patterns and domes, fan and cross vaults symbolic for the Mamluk architecture of the Bahri period.

The castle was turned into a 17th-century fortress by al-Radwans, a family of Ottoman vassals, making it an equivalent of a governor's mansion. During this era the castle was outfitted for defense with arrow slits and narrow openings that expanded for the flexible use of cannons. According to local lore, Napoleon spent three nights there during his siege of Acre in 1799, which is the only reason it is sometimes called Napoleon's Fort.

During the British colonial period it was used as a police station. During the Egyptian rule it became the Princess Ferial School for Girls. After the royals were deposed in Cairo, it was renamed al-Zahra Secondary School for Girls. Under contemporary Palestinian rule, the UNDP was asked to help build a more modern girls' school and Qasr al-Basha was then turned into a museum, which is expected to house Neolithic, Pharoanic, Phoenician, Hellenistic, Persian, Roman, and Byzantine artifacts.

Next to the castle is the **Sultan Abdul Hamid Fountain** (Sabeel), built in the 16th century by the son of a local notable, Behram Bin Mustafa Basha. Because of the stress on cleanliness and washing before prayer, both small and large fountains are a common sight in Islamic cities. Charitable donations in the form of fountains were both

Al-Radwan Castle, also known as Qasr al-Basha

relatively inexpensive and quite visible. There were about 200 such fountains built in Gaza during the reign of the Ottomans. The fountain was renovated for a second time during the reign of Sultan Abdul Hamid II in 1900 and renamed in tribute to him.

Shuja'ia Quarter

Off the Shuja'ia market is the second largest Muslim shrine in Gaza city, the **Mosque of Ibn Othman**, named after the nobleman from Nablus who commissioned the building of the mosque. He died in Mecca in 1402. Inside the mosque is the tomb of a venerated Mamluk Governor of Gaza, Yalkhja, (d. 1446) who served at the court of the first Burji Mamluk Sultan, al-Zaher Barquq (1382 CE). The mosque has retained most of its architectural details. Standing lower than street level, the mosque consists of four vaulted iwans supported by stone piers.

Another beautiful shrine is the **Mahkama Mosque**, originally part of the school built in 1455 CE by the governing Mamluk Prince Bardabak al-Dawadar. Although the western façade of the mosque has been virtually destroyed, the minaret remains intact and is a good example of the Burji–Mamluk architecture. The school has several washing places and a courtyard. During Ottoman times it was used as a courthouse, and then the British used it as a school once again.

Al-Sayida (Lady) Ruqayya Shrine, also known as the Sayida Ruqayya Mosque, is also located in the al-Shuja'ia quarter. The "lady" was the wife of an Ottoman governor who is believed to have built the mosque in memory of her namesake, Ruqayya, the oldest daughter of the Prophet Muhammad. It is one of two Muslim religious shrines in Gaza dedicated to a woman.

The other is **al-Jummaiza al-Salha** (The Holy Sycamore Tree), at Tel al-Mintar considered a sanctuary because the Virgin Mary is believed to have rested here on her way to Egypt. Since the tree protected her and Joseph from harm, a popular cult developed during the Ottoman era around the tree. Mothers would bless their sons under the tree before they went off to war, asking that the good omen of the tree protect their boys from harm.

It is worth noting that women in contemporary Gaza play a very important role. Of the five women elected in the first Palestinian Parliamentary elections in 1996, three were from Gaza: Intisar al-Wazir, Rawiya Shawa, and Jamila Saydam.

Tuffah Quarter

The **Mosque of Ibn Marwan**, on Jaffa Street in the Tuffah quarter, was built in the late 13th or early 14th century. It houses the tomb of Shaykh Ali bin Marwan, a spiritualist from Morocco who settled in Gaza and died here in 1316. The old cemetery at the foot of the eastern cliff of the old city of Gaza was also named after him. The mosque stands on six marble columns that form the base for nine domes. An inscription on the gate to the minaret indicates that a certain Muhammad Ibn Abdullah dedicated a new minaret, iwan, and storage rooms to the mosque compound in the 14th century. The governor of Gaza, Emir Yahya, had the mosque renovated in December 1802, as indicated by the marble plaque on the western gate.

The **Mosque of al-Aybaki**, a 13th-century shrine in honor of a Muslim clergyman, Shaykh Abdullah al-Aybaki, is also located in Tuffah quarter. The shaykh was a relative and supporter of Izzedin 'Aybaki, the first Mamluk Sultan.

Zeitoun Quarter (Olive Quarter)

As the name makes clear, all the city's olive oil production once took place here. In the southeastern part of the city, it can be reached by going off Omar Mukhtar Street.

The small **Mosque of Kateb al-Wilayia**, built in 1334, is one of several highlights of the quarter. Additions were made during the Ottoman reign and it was renamed to honor the chief scribe at the court of Sultan Murad III in 1587 after he visited Gaza. The northern arcade carries a fragment of a marble panel with a Mamluk foundation inscription mentioning a mosque built near the Sea Gate (Bab-al-Bahr), one of the gates of Gaza that now exists only in historical documents.

The **Orthodox Church of Porphyrus** lies adjacent to the mosque. Erected in honor of the Byzantine patron saint of Gaza (whose body is buried on church grounds), who effectively helped impose Christianity on the city. The church was renovated and changed in the 12th century. In the vicinity of the church, where many homes have small crosses etched into stone above their house doors, live members of the small Christian community. The **Catholic Church**, established by an Austrian monk named Herr Gatt in 1879, is also in the al-Zeitoun quarter. It still serves Gaza's small Catholic community.

The newly renovated **al-Samara Public Bath** (Turkish bath house) is within walking distance of both the Orthodox Church and Kateb al-Wilayia Mosque. Although Gaza once had five large bathhouses, only this one remains operational. Built in the Mamluk era, it was in a debilitated state for decades before the PNA stepped in and the UNDP as well as the Islamic University began work on restoration and renovation. The Palestinian Ministry of Tourism and Antiquities declared it a Gaza Heritage Site.

Other Neighborhoods and Sites in Gaza City

Al-Bilakhya Harbor

Al-Bilakhya Harbor (Port of Anthedon) is the place from which Alexander the Macedonian is believed to have mounted the siege of Gaza in 332 BCE. The port was in use between the 8th and 1st centuries BCE. Today the mud-brick walls around the port are only partially visible; most run underneath nearby Shati Camp. The port was abandoned during Roman times

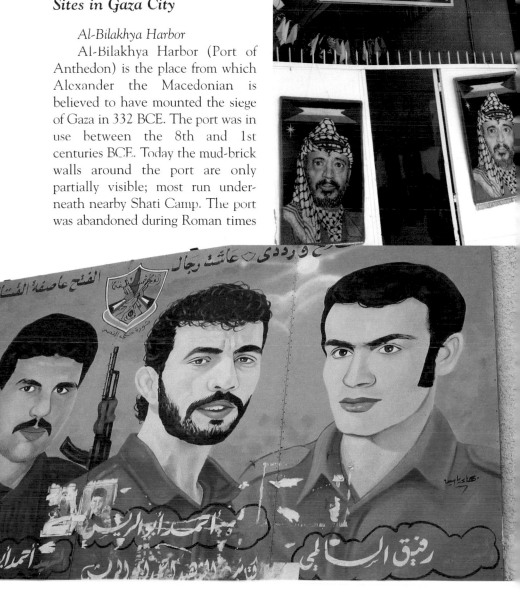

Top: The PLO flag shop sells flags, buttons, and other political souvenirs
Bottom: Portrait of intifada martyrs

and another, Maimoumas, was built to the south of it. Nearby remnants of a Roman temple at Bilakhya have come to light recently.

Port of Maimoumas
In 331 CE, the Roman Emperor Constantine gave the port the status of a city and named it "Constantania" to honor his sister and to mark the inhabitants' conversion and allegiance to Christianity. Julian the Apostate made the Port City a tributary. After his rule the city regained its independence as well as its original name, Maimoumas. During the Islamic era the port was called Tida. During the al-Aqsa intifada, the nascent Gaza port rebuilt by the PNA was bombed. Its remains, as well as the ruins of the ancient ports, are still visible.

Nasr
Next to Remal and just northwest of al-Daraj lies the new neighborhood of Hay al-Nasr, usually called simply Nasr. This neighborhood was established in 1957 during Egyptian rule to house the families of soldiers or martyrs who had given their lives in the war against Israel.

Remal
Remal was a sandy outskirt of Gaza City until a road built in the 1920s linked it to the town center. In the 1930s, British authorities built the city's main prison here. During Egyptian rule, government employees were given subsidized housing in this quarter. Subsequently cinemas, hotels, private schools, and two-story villas sprung up in the neighborhood, making it upper-middle-class by definition. After self-rule came to Gaza, the Palestinian Legislature established its head-quarters in Remal.

Sabra
The Sabra neighborhood was built up during the British mandate period. Its most important site is the **Municipal Park**, which was established in the 1930s south of Omar Mukhtar Street.

Shaykh Ajleen
Southwest of Gaza City, this sanctuary by the sea is named in honor of a Muslim cleric who, along with his brothers Radwan and al-Batahi, is counted among Gaza's "holy men" or saints. In 1966, the Egyptian Department of Antiquities discovered Byzantine mosaics here. They turned out to be part of the floor of a church built in 509 CE.

The most visible site in this district today is the **Khalil al-Wazir Mosque**, which commemorates the Palestinian leader who was killed by an Israeli assassination squad in Tunisia in 1988.

Shaykh Radwan

Local legend has it that this neighborhood was named after a local religious figure who some say was the brother of Shaykh Ajleen and al-Batahi and thus a descendent of Omar al-Khattab, the Muslim general who conquered Palestine. In 1973, Israel attempted to resettle residents of Shati Camp in this neighborhood. Fearing that they would lose their "right of return," many refugees refused to move. When their camp shacks were destroyed, however, they were forced to move. Today some 22,000 former residents of al-Shati call Shaykh Radwan home.

Tell el-Ajjoul

Tell el-Ajjoul, just south of Gaza City, is believed to be the center of the ancient Canaanite Gaza. The location was apparently abandoned because of a malaria outbreak sometime in the 12th century BCE. The discovery of two large cemeteries and the contents of the graves and tombs found indicate that Tell el-Ajjoul must have been a major city around 2000–1200 BCE.

During archeological excavations begun in 1930 under the British archeologist Flinders Petrie, several important aspects of life in the Canaanite era came to light. The city apparently had a wall 0.75 meters (2.5 ft) wide and 15 meters (50 ft) high. Horsemen were found buried with their horses and metal weapons in a 150-meter-long (500-ft-long) tunnel. The remains of five temple-like structures were also found. The structure of one of the temples resembles Egyptian burial grounds and contains the remains of an Egyptian family (1580–1350 BCE), entombed and mummified. Other temples have been dated to the 16th, 15th, and 12th centuries BCE. Clay and copper pots, golden bracelets, earrings, wooden beds, cork pillows, and other personal belongings were buried with the families in the tombs, indicating that like the Egyptians, Gazans believed in the afterlife. Remnants from the Philistine era include the remains of at least one palatial structure. Pottery from the classical era was also found. Remains from the Byzantine era were found, showing that the Tell was still in use then. According to Mamluk historian Ibn Iyas, visiting Mamluk Sultans held public meetings in audience halls on the outskirts of the hill. Southwest of Tell el-Ajjoul is **Khirbet Um 'Itout**, once the site of the Roman town of Thabatha.

Tel al-Mintar

Tel al-Mintar (guarding place), just east of Gaza, is the most elevated spot around. The hill, which is 85 meters (279 ft) above sea level, was used as a look-out point.

The **Mosque of Mintar** was named after the man who guarded the hill, Shaykh Ali al-Mintar. But the hill is considered a site of festive pilgrimage because the **Tomb of Shaykh Muhammad al-Batahi**, one of the three sons of Shaykh Arkoub Zein Hamada, is here.

According to local folklore, Joseph and Mary rested here under the shade of the Holy Sycamore Tree on their return from Egypt. Gazans celebrate "al-Mintar Season" season every spring.

Tel al-Sakn

Located 5 kilometers south of Gaza city, Tel al-Sakn was discovered by accident in 1998. It is the only Early Bronze Age (3300–2200 BCE) site thus far excavated in the Gaza Strip. It is the site of ancient Gaza and a precursor of nearby Tell Ajoul. It covers an area of five hectares and has become the showpiece of the Palestinian Department of Antiquities, which has garnered the support of the French archeological community as well as the UNDP. Excavations have revealed remnants of 4th millennia BCE Egyptian and 3rd millennia Canaanite rule and promise revelations about the history and customs of ancient Palestine.

Tel an-Naqid or Tel as-Sanam

An unexcavated temple to the Hellenic deity Serapis was located here. Today only a few potsherds and marble pieces are left. Serapis was worshiped throughout the Hellenic Mediterranean. Some say he was the Egyptian god Osir-Hapi and others the Greek Osirapis, god of sun and enlightenment.

Near Gaza City

Deir al-Balah (Convent of the Dates)

In a 1946 traveler's guide to the Holy Land, Deir al-Balah is described as a small town of 1,000, with the remains of a medieval fort built by Richard the Lionheart in 1192. Some 13 kilometers (8 mi) south of Gaza City, Deir al-Balah today is mainly known as a refugee camp. Little do people suspect that this sandy coastal town was a city of considerable wealth in the late Bronze Age.

In the early 1970s, while Gaza was still fully under Israeli occupation, archeologist Trude Dothan and a field team working under her direction began to unearth significant burial sites here. The discovery of anthropoid coffins linked Deir al-Balah to the Amarna Letters of the mid-14th century BCE. The large clay coffins, which resembled those of Egyptian mummies, held pottery and fine jewelry. Several bone and gold scarabs had the name Tuthmosis III (1450 BCE) inscribed into them. It is still not known if these were the coffins of local rulers buried in Egyptian burial rites, or Egyptian rulers buried in Gaza. The former is more likely.

Evidence of papyrus archives, indicating a highly literate leadership in Deir al-Balah, was discovered in the remains of a 60-square-foot citadel built in the late 14th century BCE. Next to this enormous structure was an artisan's compound, where evidence indicates Deir al-Balah residents could obtain all the craft services required for the elaborate funeral rites.

An immense find of Philistine pottery was also discovered on the beaches and sands. It is clear from these massive finds, which are mostly housed in Israeli museums, that the Philistines adapted quickly after their arrival to the Canaanite and Egyptian habits of the land where they settled.

Located just south of Deir al-Balah is the **Mosque of al-Khader** (St. George), which is believed to have been a Crusader monastery. It is located below street level and reached from the courtyard of an adjacent mosque now in ruins. Today Deir al Balah is struggling to rebuild itself. It is one of five governorates in the Gaza Strip with a population of over 200,000, the vast majority of which are refugees.

Khan Younes

In 1866, a European traveler found the market in Khan Younes plentiful, and the town streets "wide and clean," and "laid out with surprising care and accuracy." The city today, which still has the same **14th-century khan** at its center, has a population of 170,000. Several old gates stand apart, as if alone, signs of a grander past.

Khan Younes, the second largest city in the Strip, is about 4 kilometers from the sea (the **Shari al-Bahir** is a lovely walk to a beautiful beach when things are calm) and some 25 kilometers (15.5 mi) from Gaza City. It can be accessed by taxi from Palestine Square in Gaza or from the center of Deir al-Balah, just 7 kilometers away.

The khan for which the city is named was built during the reign of Sultan Barquq by the Mamluk official Younes Norozi al-Dawadar. The khan, which borders the town square, was used as a garrison for Ottoman soldiers guarding pilgrims on their journey from Jerusalem to Mecca. The weekly market near the khan is a fascinating picture of traditional life.

Gazan Culinary Traditions

The prosperity Gaza once witnessed is long since gone and much of its population, a third of which is refugee from other parts of Palestine, lives below subsistence level, barely making ends meet. A discussion of traditional food practices cannot but reflect a standard that only few Gazans can maintain presently—though it is true that religious feasts are still observed, in spite of economic hardships.

The daily fare of Gaza consists of fried vegetables, *hummus* (chickpea dip), *ful* (broad beans cooked to a purée and seasoned with onions and hot peppers), and lentils. Meat is a luxury that few can afford, and then only occasionally. During the feast of *al-Adha* (the Muslim feast of the Sacrifice), tradition calls for the slaughtering of a lamb, with one third to be eaten by the family, another third by friends and neighbors, the last third given away to the poor. This practice has guaranteed the survival of such dishes as *kidreh* and *mansaf*, which are based on rice and lamb and are also typical of other regions of Palestine.

Summakieh, a typically Gazan food for *Eid al-Adha*, gets its name from sumac, a red spice with a slightly acid yet warm tang. This elaborate stew involves boiling big chunks of lamb meat and adding them to a mixture of fried onions, garlic, and Swiss chard. A large quantity of sumac seeds is then boiled and strained and the liquid added to the stew. Finally, a small amount of *tahini* (sesame paste) is added to give consistency to this highly relished dish, which is delicious even reheated.

The Gaza Strip enjoys a long stretch of coastal land and its long fishing tradition has always brought fish and shellfish to the Gazan table. True to their Mediterranean identity, Gazans love salted fish. If fish was once salted to preserve it, now it is salted because of tradition. Gazans have not particularly developed special dishes for certain kinds of fish, a practice suggesting affluence and easy living; instead, the different varieties are used interchangeably, depending on the catch. Whether the fish is baked, grilled, or fried, it is the sauce (always highly spicy!) that makes the dish.

Gaza is home to celebrated red peppers

Dakka (Gazan hot sauce)

2 garlic cloves
salt
2 hot peppers
4-5 tomatoes, finely chopped
lemon juice and olive oil, to taste

1. Using a pestle and mortar, crush the garlic cloves with half a teaspoon of salt.

2. Chop two hot peppers, being sure to discard the seeds (they irritate the stomach), and add them to the garlic, crushing the mixture to a paste.

3. Fold this paste into the chopped tomatoes, adding lemon juice and olive oil to taste. Add more salt, or another hot pepper, to taste!

Rafah

Located on the southernmost tip of Gaza, Rafah is much more than the sandy border city that serves as the gateway to Egypt. It is believed to have been a Canaanite settlement, though excavations have been hindered due to its "sensitive location" and "other priorities." The town was given its name by the Greeks and the Romans who called it "Raphia." Here, Mark Antony married Cleopatra and Ptolemy IV fought against Antiochus in 217 CE, in another struggle between paganism and Christianity.

Most of the 170,000 people who live in Rafah today are refugees, but before 1948 a small population prospered here in the trade and transportation-oriented businesses that still dominate the city. Carnations are among the city's major exports.

When Egypt signed a peace agreement with Israel in 1979, Rafah was divided into two, with half becoming Egyptian and half remaining Palestinian under Israeli occupation. This was not changed until August 2005, when the Israeli army finally withdrew from Rafah, allowing for thousands of families to be reunited despite the continued presence of a border.

During the al-Aqsa intifada, the Israeli army carried out merciless attacks against the citizens of Rafah. Air and land bombardments, house demolitions, and assassinations brought Rafah into the headlines around the world. International solidarity movements camped out among civilians in an attempt to stop the carnage. A young American, Rachel Corrie, was crushed by an Israeli bulldozer when she tried to prevent it from destroying the home of refugees. Rafah is trying to rebuild after the Israeli withdrawal.

Tel Ruqeish

A large, flourishing Phoenician settlement with massive defensive walls and a cemetery once stood here. Remains of burial chambers dating from the late Iron Age to the Persian period (538–332 BCE) were found in the cemetery.

Refugee Camps

Jabalia Camp

Jabalia is the northernmost refugee camp in the Gaza Strip, about 2 kilometers north of Gaza City. The neighboring village of Jabalia has in many ways been dwarfed by the sheer size of the refugee camp, whose population of over 100,000 makes it the largest camp within the borders of historic Palestine.

The residents of Jabalia camp come overwhelmingly (90 percent) from the towns and villages that belong to the historical boundaries of the Gaza district, but now exist within the Green Line, including 'Abdes, Barqa, Bashiyyeh, al-Battaneh (East and West), Beit Affa, Beit Daras, Beit Jarjeh, Beit Jiseir, Beit Teimeh, Breir, Damireh, Deir Isneid, al-Falloujeh, Hamama, Hatta, Hirbiwyeh, Hleiqat, Howj, al-Ihsas, Iraq al-Manshiyyeh, Iraq Suweidan, Isdud, al-Jiyyeh, Joulis, Karatiyeh, Kofakha, Kowkabeh, al-Majdal, al-Mihraqa, al-Mismiyya (Small and Large), Na'liyeh, Nahzeh, Najad, Qastina, Qatra, Ras al-Kheimeh, al-Sawafir (West and East), Simsim, and Tel al-Turmus.

As in the case of at least half of the Palestinian refugees, the expulsion and exile of many of Jabalia's residents from their original villages began when their villages were attacked by Zionist militias during the period between the declaration of the UN Partition Plan in November 1947 and the end of the British Mandate (May 1948). In Gaza, two massacres in the fairly large villages of al-Breir and Beit Darras elicited a wave of panic throughout the surrounding area. Waves of refugees began flocking in the direction of what is now the Gaza Strip. In other cases, such as in al-Majdal, the villagers were made refugees in the early 1950s, well after the declaration of the State of Israel, as a result of dispossessing governmental policies.

The early days of Jabalia camp were marked by great suffering. The high numbers of refugees that swelled the Gaza Strip were a great strain upon the humanitarian resources of the international aid agencies (first the Quakers and the Red Cross, and later UNRWA) trying to care for them.

The camp was organized into 13 separate, lettered blocks. This initial camp division meant little to camp residents: entire villages instead remained together, exiled within the camp, the names of the villages eventually became the names of areas of the camp; the refugees from the village of Simsim lived in Jabalia's Harat al-Simsim, and so forth. Approximately 60 percent of Jabalia still retains this kind of basic village identification, though in recent years, the sheer lack of space, has broken down this system.

Since the mid-1950s, Jabalia residents have been vocal advocates of the Palestinian right to return. This has made the camp home to a rich and diverse political life, with representatives of the Communist Party, the Arab Nationalist Movement, the Islamic Brotherhood, and other groups vying for followers. The camp was attacked several times in the mid-1950s by elite Israeli militias to stop the Palestinians from attempting to return to their original properties inside the Green Line (in most cases, short distances away).

After the June War of 1967, Jabalia was at the forefront of resistance activity. Between 1967 and 1972, the camp was known as a hotbed for the Popular Front for the Liberation of Palestine (PFLP), largely because of the presence of Mohammed al-Aswad, a resident of the camp called "Guevara Gaza." Local saying had it that "Israel ruled Gaza by day, but Guevara Gaza ruled by night." Al-Aswad led a popular rebellion that spread through much of the Gaza Strip. Though he was eventually killed by the Israeli army in 1970, the uprising left an undeniable impression on Jabalia's youth. Given this history, it comes as no surprise that the first Palestinian intifada began in here in December 1987.

Jabalia's basic infrastructure has always been weak, and remains so to this day. The first attempt to install a working sewage system came only in 1992. Until January 2001, the main roads of the camp were nothing more than dirt roads, which become infamously muddy throughout the rainy season. UNRWA runs 24 schools (18 elementary and 6 preparatory) with 26,000 pupils enrolled. UNRWA also runs a health care center in the camp that employs 70 workers and sees on average 22,300 patients per month.

Many of the refugee shelters in the camp are the original structures constructed in the 1950s. No less than 3,400 families (15,200 individuals) were characterized before the al-Aqsa intifada as "special hardship" cases. Throughout the course of the current intifada, this figure has increased dramatically, with 86 percent of the residents of the entire Gaza Strip living off less than US $2 per day.

Shati (Beach) Camp

Established in 1951 on 187 acres of sandy coastline in northern Gaza City, the camp is known simply as Shati. The 75,000 plus residents of the camp make it arguably one of the most densely populated places in the world. The original 23,000 refugees who first came to the camp originate from villages and cities in the Lydd, Jaffa, and Negev regions, including Askalan, Beit Dras, Deir Isneid, al-Falloujeh, Hamama, Isdud, al-Jiyyeh, al-Joreh, and Karathiych.

The camp can be roughly divided into three sections: the western portion, which spans the shoreline and is largely populated with refugees who originate from other seaside villages and cities; the eastern portion, known locally as Camp al-Majadleh, whose residents, originally from the town of al-Majdal, suffered an extended process of expulsion between the years 1948–1952 and brought with them a small local fabric industry; and finally, the northern or new section of the camp, which is largely inhabited by refugee populations who were

initially settled in the southern camps of Rafah and Khan Younes, but who moved to here in the early and mid-1950s.

Beach camp used to be infamous for the suffering it endured in times of bad weather. Older camp residents recall difficult winters, in which they battled flood waters and rain from washing away and destroying the encampment. UNRWA later replaced the tents with mud brick shelters in the early 1950s, and with cement block shelters with asbestos roofs in the 1960s. Though the main camp streets were paved in 2000, with a basic storm drainage water system, Beach camp's alleyways and side roads can still resemble a swamp in the rainy season.

In 1971, Israeli occupation authorities demolished more than 2,000

Gaza as seen from the Mediterranean

refugee shelters inside Beach camp to create "security roads." This policy of Ariel Sharon's has been implemented throughout the Gaza Strip refugee camps, most visibly here and in Jabalia, and Khan Younes.

Shati residents have suffered the closures as elsewhere, with their livelihoods very often curtailed. Some refugees have work in small workshops and sewing factories or are owners of small shops in the camp's marketplace; a sizeable number of families fish for a livelihood; others work in Gaza City itself. It should be noted that many camp residents participate in and receive services from Gaza City neighborhoods. But it's not easy being near the city, either: construction of the port in Gaza City has changed the flow of tides, bringing the sea right up to the Shati's first row of houses.

Nuseirat Camp

Nuseirat camp, considered to be the capital of Gaza's midsection, is located 8 kilometers south of Gaza City. Established soon after the Nakba, the camp's initial 16,000 refugees primarily originated from Abu Zrief, Bataneh (East and West), Beit Daras, Hamama, Isdud, Joulis, al-Joureh, Kowkabeh, Lydd, al-Mughar, Qatra, Qattaneh, Sarafand, Sawafir, Yafa, Zarnouqa, and the Negev. The camp is named after a local Bedouin tribe Ashirat al-Nuseirat and is built on land owned by the Abu Medein and Abu Mehadi families. It is now the largest of the camps in the middle Gaza Strip, with a population of 63,000 and vibrant grassroots community organizations that offset its geographical isolation.

Nuseirat's agriculturally rich setting serves as the bread-basket for much of the Gaza Strip's produce. (A public market is held on Mondays.) It also has historically served as a military headquarters for the regimes that have attempted to rule over the Gaza Strip region. In fact, many of the original refugees who first established the camp were initially housed in a former British military prison known as the Kallaboush, a structure which still stands today.

UNRWA initially divided the camp into ten different lettered sections. Since 1967, these forms of division have overlapped with the Israeli occupation's division of the camp, into over 40 numbered sections. This has lent itself to the current confusing situation (especially for outsiders) in which local residents routinely interchange numbers and letters when describing a certain section of the camp. Today, the poorest section of the camp is known as "new camp," or Block J, home to the last refugees.

Like the other Gaza camps, Nuseirat lacks a complete sewage network and waste water flows in open channels along roads and pathways, as well as through agricultural lands toward Wadi Gaza. Camp resident complaints are many, ranging from the lack of a hospital in the immediate area (residents are dependent upon Gaza or Khan Younes hospitals, which are equally far and sometimes difficult to reach because of the Israeli closure policies), to shortage of classrooms (UNRWA operates 13 schools here, but only 3 are run in single shifts), to polluted water and daily blackouts—not to mention the continued denial of their political-national rights.

Breij Camp
Breij camp was established in 1949 on 132 acres in the center of the Gaza Strip. The camp originally housed 13,000 refugees, some of whom were put up in abandoned British army barracks. Others remained in tents for several years, until UNRWA constructed the cement block shelters in the 1950s.

There is little that distinguishes Breij camp from the other three refugee camps—Deir al-Balah, al-Mughazi, and Nuseirat—in Gaza's midsection. Most of its residents live in typical crowded refugee shelters, most of them covered with asbestos sheeting. A part of the camp still has no sewage system and as a result sewage runs in open drains that accumulate in Wadi Gaza to the north. The once-beautiful wadi is now completely polluted and full of mosquitoes, both of which pose serious health hazards.

Today Breij is the home to about 30,000 people. UNRWA operates seven schools in the camp (5 elementary and 2 preparatory), with about 9,000 students. Prior to the closure of the Gaza Strip, most of the refugees worked as laborers inside Israel or in local agriculture. Some refugees run their own shops and workshops. A public market every Thursday attracts traders from all over the Gaza Strip.

Mughazi Camp
Mughazi camp is situated in the agriculturally dominant midsection of the Gaza Strip, just south of Breij camp. Its lush setting of orange groves and fields brings welcome fresh air to the city congestion of the northern camps, or the more desert-like feeling of the southern Strip. Mughazi camp was established in 1949 on 140 acres that belonged to Hajj Freih al-Masdar and the community of Zawcideh. Mughazi became home to 9,000 refugees forced out of their homes in central southern Palestine, from al-Bataneh, Beit Daras, al-Falloujeh, Karatiyeh, Lydd, Majdal, al-Mansoura, al-Mismiyya, Negev, Qastina, al-Qataneh (East and West), Ramleh, Tel al-Safi, Tel al-Turmus, Wad al-Hanin, al-Wafir (East and West), Yafa, and Yazour. Today Mughazi's population stands at around 22,000 refugees, the second smallest Gaza camp.

Mughazi has a relaxed feel to it because of its relatively lower population density and its agricultural setting. Still, 75 percent of the shelters have asbestos roofing, and the camp is yet to enjoy an operating sewage system.

The origin of the camp's name is ambiguous. The Ottoman-era grave of a well-known and respected woman of the same name is located near the camp's boundaries. But another root of its name may be the Arabic *"mughaza"* (military invasion). Indeed, many invasions have taken place here. The camp is near the main artery road that leads to Gaza (given an invasion from the north) or to Egypt (in the case of an invasion from the south). Indeed the entire midsection of Gaza has often held military garrisons, the remains of which are still evident today in Nuseirat camp's Kallaboush barracks, or in the British military cemetery from the Mandate years in Mughazi itself.

The Israelis continued with the divide and rule policies by parceling up the Gaza Strip into north, center and south through the establishment of settlements. These essentially colonial outposts were used as an excuse for their military basis. Some settlements, such as Nizarim, were inhabited by 8 families. Thousands of militant settlers (mostly youth), many of them armed and dangerous, descended on the Gaza Strip to make the August 2005 withdrawal look like a large scale human tragedy rather than the exit of a colonial army and its profiteers.

Prior to the closure of the Gaza Strip, most of the camp's residents worked as laborers in Israel or locally in agriculture. Every Sunday, a public market offers the products of local workshops and bountiful agricultural produce.

Deir al-Balah

Deir al-Balah camp is the smallest camp in the Gaza Strip, home to fewer than 20,000 refugees. It covers 40 acres by the sea, west of the town of Deir el-Balah. Like the rest of the residents of the Gaza Strip, the refugees who reside in Deir al-Balah camp originate from villages in central and southern pre-1948 Palestine. The camp originally housed 9,000 refugees in tents, which were later replaced by mud brick shelters, and then in the early 1960s by the current cement-block structures.

Deir al-Balah camp has a reputation as a serene camp—at least compared to the others. In fact, it is sometimes mockingly called "Kfar Shalom" ("peace village" in Hebrew) by some Palestinians who take jabs at the town for not engaging sufficiently in the resistance to the Israeli occupation. This characterization, however, fails to take into context Deir al-Balah's setting: both town and refugee camp are quite small and relatively isolated from other Palestinian towns and camps. Once lush and fertile, much of Deir al Balah land was occupied for 38 years by two Israeli settler colonies. The infamous Abu Holi junction, an Israeli invention, which divided the Gaza Strip into north and south, and was located on Deir al Balah land, has now been dismembered, and the Abu Holi clan is reclaiming its tribal properties.

The British Military Cemetery has graves from WWI and WWII

Throughout the course of this intifada, Deir al-Balah has had thousands of acres of its land bulldozed.

Most Deir al-Balah camp residents worked as laborers in Israel before this intifada, but were prevented from doing so early on. A minority of residents work as local farm laborers, though this profession is also increasingly coming under attack, not only because of Israel's attacks—with their routine of bulldozing crops, ripping up water networks, destroying greenhouses, and preventing of crops getting to markets—but also because of the incredible urban construction boom that is rapidly taking up agricultural land throughout the Gaza Strip. Farming is becoming increasingly untenable.

Deir al-Balah camp had no sewage system until 1998, when UNRWA completed the construction of the system with financial assistance from Japan. UNRWA also runs a total of eight schools in the camp (6 elementary and 2 preparatory) for about 8,000 pupils.

Visitors should try to visit the camp on a Tuesday, when a large public market is held.

Khan Younes Camp

Khan Younes camp is two kilometers from the sea in the southern portion of the Gaza Strip, north of the border city of Rafah. Established in 1949 slightly west of the city of the same name, the camp is largely indistinguishable from its city surroundings, which has historically acted as a major commercial center for the Egyptian–Asian trade route. Its original 35,000 residents have now swelled to 65,000 people, the majority of whom come from the villages in the Gaza–Jaffa coastal strip as well as from villages and Bedouin communities in the Negev. An additional 85,000 original refugees and their descendants live outside the Khan Younes camp boundaries, though most have remained within the Gaza Strip.

The camp's official boundaries are demarcated within 140 acres of sandy land. Largely due to its peripheral status, Khan Younes camp, together with Rafah camp, is among the poorest and most underdeveloped of the refugee camps in the country. Even before the al-Aqsa intifada began, almost one in four families within the camp received "special hardship" assistance—meaning they were directly dependant upon UNRWA handouts for survival. Most of the shelters, as elsewhere, are cement brick with asbestos roofs. There is no sewage system in the camp. The camp is divided into 13 blocks, some of which are in low-lying areas that flood in the winter. All shelters are supplied with water from municipal and private wells though the quality is poor, and electricity blackouts a daily phenomenon. UNRWA operates 18 schools (14 elementary and 4 preparatory) for 18,200 pupils, but only 4 schools run in single shifts.

The westernmost block of the camp, "Block I," had the unfortunate status of being extremely close to the Israeli settlement block of Gush Qatif, which was composed of eleven Jewish-only colonies. This proximity meant that during times of political strife, the camp was in the thick of Israeli shelling. During the al-Aqsa intifada, the destruction wrought upon Khan Younes camp is comparable only to that suffered by its southern sister camp of Rafah. More than 90 residents (a third children) were killed and 200 refugee shelters completely destroyed. Throughout the course of the al-Aqsa intifada, the Israeli army conducted several full-scale invasions of the camp, constructed a kilometer-long, 10-meter high cement wall to separate the camp boundaries from the settlement, and tested new forms of incapacitating gas, hospitalizing over 120 people with its first trial usage.

Perhaps because of its peripheral geographical position, and its subsequent marginal service provision, Khan Younes has an unruly image: it is viewed as ungovernable. In the early years of the camp, a special unit known as the Soudani was used as a crack-force to "police" (usually through use of force) dissent among the refugee population. During the 1987 intifada, both Khan Younes and Rafah were the unprecedented centers of the most violent oppression from Israeli collective punishment measures, registering the highest number of injuries from live ammunition in all Palestine (about 5 percent of the population).

Khan Younes (camp and city) also have a tragic unknown history that few people (even Palestinians outside of Gaza) know about. In 1956, Israeli troops who attacked Egypt and occupied the Sinai throughout the course of that war, passed through Khan Younes, which put up a fight for six days. Then, throughout the first two weeks of November 1956, Israelis went door-to-door in many neighborhoods in central Khan Younes and in the camp, collecting men and summarily executing them. No less than 500 Palestinians were killed during this massacre, making it the largest single massacre of Palestinians at the hands of Israel to take place within the borders of historic Palestine. At least 1,000 Egyptian troops were also massacred in Khan Younes and buried in mass graves. Though this massacre has etched itself indelibly into the collective consciousness of residents of Khan Younes, it has never been officially acknowledged by Israel, and it failed to receive international attention as a result of the attention being paid to the events of the 1956 War as a whole.

Before the al-Aqsa intifada began, most of Khan Younes' residents worked as laborers in Israel or locally in agriculture and fishing. After the uprising began in September 2000, the closure has largely prevented Gazans from reaching their work within the Green Line. Also, the Khan Younes district has witnessed great destruction of agricultural land by the Israeli occupation, in addition to the severe curtailing of the waters within which fisherman can cast their nets.

Rafah Camp

Rafah camp is Palestine's southernmost camp, located on the Egyptian border. The camp was established in 1949 to house 41,000 refugees; at the time, it was the largest and most concentrated population of refugees in the Gaza Strip. Today, Rafah's population is over 90,000. Several thousand residents have, however, moved from the camp to a housing project in nearby Tel al-Sultan. Today the camp is almost indistinguishable from the adjacent town of the same name.

In 1956, Rafah camp was the scene of a massacre in which at least 120 residents (according to a UNRWA reports) were killed. Israeli troops using loudspeakers called upon the men of the camp to congregate in a school after occupying the town. Though it is not entirely clear what then took place, most Palestinians were killed on their way to the school, and others in their homes. The events in Rafah, like similar events in Khan Younes, are scarcely known to the outside world.

After the Israeli occupation of Sinai and Gaza in 1967, an extension to Rafah camp was built on former Egyptian territory for some 5,000 refugees whose shelters had been demolished by the Israelis when they were widening their infamous "security roads." This area became known as Canada camp, after the Canadian Contingent to the United Nations Emergency Force (UNEF), which was based in the area after 1956. After Israel and Egypt signed a peace treaty in 1979, Israel returned the Sinai to Egypt, drawing the international boundary directly through Rafah camp. Some 5,000 persons were left on the Egyptian side with families often split and forced to communicate with one another by shouting across the international border. Although outside of UNRWA's area of operations, the Agency continued to provide services to the refugees in Canada camp until the refugees were finally fully repatriated in 2000. The majority of families were housed in the Tel al-Sultan housing project. Canada, in its capacity as the gavel holder of the Refugee Working Group, and the Kuwaiti Fund for Arab Economic Development, contributed funds for this repatriation.

Rafah Camp's sewage system covers the needs of 80 percent of the camp and about 60 percent of the town of Rafah. UNRWA carried out a feasibility study for a new sewage network in 1994, which is now underway, with funding provided to Rafah Municipality by the European Commission.

Rafah was the scene of some of the most severe destruction throughout the course of the al-Aqsa intifada. As of November 2003, the Israeli army had destroyed no fewer than 750 homes in Rafah, making some 7,000 people homeless. Residents of the camp who reside near the Egyptian border lived a life of constant fear that their houses would be the next target of demolition as Israel routinely and determinately shaved off row after row of refugee shelter with massive armored bulldozers. Israeli General Yom-Tov Samia, former commander of the IDF's Southern Command, even explicitly elaborated Israel's intentions for localized ethnic cleansing campaign

Commuting to work, Gaza City

on Israel Radio, saying that the army "must raze all the houses within a strip of 300–400 meters in width [from the Egyptian border.]" No less than 20,000 Palestinian families reside in this area.

Additionally at least 150 residents, many of whom were children, have been killed and several thousand injured in this program. At least 2,000 homes have been damaged by gunfire and 65 workshops and stores have been destroyed. Some 750 acres of agricultural land, once rich with citrus, olive, fruits, vegetables, almonds, wheat, and hay have been razed. Rafah has been the most consistently volatile and dangerous place in Palestine throughout the course of the al-Aqsa intifada.

33.

Neğev (an-Naqab)

This is the well which Abraham, peace be on him, dug and built up.

—Yakut, Muslim Geographer, 1220

Often perceived to be the Palestinian Desert, the Negev, or the lands of Bir es-Saba (seven wells) is one of the most unexpected spots of beauty and outposts of civilization in the country. Inhabited by tribes from the Arabian Peninsula since antiquity, this large tract of land, more than a third of historic Palestine, is nestled into the intricate topography of the triangle that encompasses the Dead Sea/Wadi Araba, the Gazan Mediterranean, the Egyptian Sinai and the Red Sea. The Negev, an immense land mass of rugged mountains, arid highlands, and geological treasures, has been inhabited since prehistoric times. Nabateans, Romans, and Byzantines built magnificent cities and made the desert bloom millennia before Israel was created.

The Negev of this century, however, is no longer home to its age-old inhabitants, most of whom have been sent into exile. Today's tenants are a mix of peoples from Russia, Morocco, and Ethiopia, along with the Israeli prime minister himself, Ariel Sharon.

Some History

Though nomadic life existed in the Negev as far back as 4000 BCE, it was 2000 years later that cities and urban civilizations were established by a combination of Canaanite, Amalkite, and Edomite groups. The Pharaonic Egyptians, ever influential, appear to have spearheaded copper mining and smelting efforts in both the Negev and Sinai by 1400–1300 BCE. Suitable weather patterns and technical know-how helped build a decentralized network of towns and cities that were,

Window of closed-down mosque in Bir es-Saba

above all, involved in trade. Jews too lived in small settlements (1020–928) in the areas close to Bir es-Saba and later, further afield.

Later, in the 9th century BCE, the development and expansion of mining centers from Edom (modern Jordan) to the Negev coincided with the rise of the Assyrian Empire. Assyrians frequently crossed the Negev for trade and pilgrimage. Bir es-Saba, the region's capital, was an essential hub of both passage and trade in the 8th century BCE. Nearby Tel Jemmeh was an administrative center for the Assyrians, who first tried to conquer, and later settled for appeasing the tribal confederations of the area.

The peoples of the Negev have almost exclusively been pastoral nomadic groups of Arab stock. But during the so-called Assyrian peace, copper mining and wealth from vast trade with Arabia increased the nomads' propensity to settle, and the seeds of urbanization were sown.

The arrival of the Nabateans in the 4th century BCE was a turning point for the Negev. An indigenous Semitic people, the Nabateans controlled the trade and spice route between their capital in Petra (Jordan) and the Gazan seaports and developed irrigation systems that supported the establishment of no less than five urban centers (Oboda, Mamphis, Sobata, Elusa, and Nessana). Remains of the caravanserais they built can still be seen along the route from Bir es-Saba and Gaza. Their own currency has been found all along this route, as have the red and orange potsherds that are a trademark of their civilization.

The Nabateans remained in full control of southern Palestine until the Romans annexed their empire in 106 CE. Despite new trade routes and a realignment of the political and military order, the population remained tribal (both Arabian and Nabatean) and thus independent of Rome. Their beliefs were animistic and pagan and provided them with the necessary means to run a cohesive society.

Byzantine rule in the 4th century brought conversions to Christianity and a changed society. Six agriculturally wealthy cities were established in the Negev. Over 300 years of Byzantine rule, the population exploded, mostly because of agricultural expansion and emigration. Power struggles and corruption in the empire lent a helping hand to the Muslim armies, who had no trouble conquering an area whose indigenous population was also Arab. The people of Negev embraced Islam with relative ease.

Little is known of the next thousand years, mainly because the Negev was completely reclaimed by nomadic tribes who kept away from conflict and significant trade. What we know of their life and interaction with other nomadic Arab tribes, mainly in the area of Wadi Musa and Petra in Jordan, comes from oral histories and folktale.

It was not until late in their rule that the Ottomans rediscovered the strategic value of this "desert," and the Negev reappeared in written history. The Ottomans established an administrative center for southern Palestine in Bir es-Saba, renovating caravanserais and building schools, a railway track, and a station. The region's nearly hundred tribal chiefs were invited and brought into the fold, becoming "leaders" of Southern Ottoman Palestine.

In 1917 Bir es-Saba was the first city to be taken by British forces, who turned the Negev into a policing center with closed military zones.

The Peel Commission Partition Plan of 1937, a precursor to the UN partition plan, recommended that the Negev remain under Palestinian rule, since it was exclusively Arab. Jewish merchants from Gaza had been involved in trade with Bir es-Saba traders, but otherwise the area had no Jewish community. In response to the Peel Plan, Zionist planners established Jewish settlements throughout the Negev and in 1947 the UN decided to allot the entire part of southern Palestine, with the exception of the city of Bir es-Saba and Gaza, to the proposed Jewish state. The so called Negev Brigade, an Israeli military unit, took Bir es-Saba by force in October 1948 and made it a part of Israel, de facto if not de jure.

Nabateans

Based in Petra in what is now modern Jordan, the Nabateans turned from being nomads to becoming civilization builders in Palestine some 400 years before the birth of Christ. After migrating to Palestine in two different waves some 300 years apart, they developed irrigation techniques that allowed them to turn the desert green. They developed an agriculture based on hillside terracing. To capture flood waters, they constructed dams in the valleys; to collect rain water, they cut cisterns in the rock. Modern Israelis grudgingly attribute their own success in reforesting the desert to some techniques established by their indigenous predecessors.

Nabateans began their migration into the Negev before the 4th century BCE but by 106 CE, Nabatean influence in the Negev began to wane. They intermarried with other Arab tribal groupings who gained predominance and flourished under Roman and later Byzantine rule and eventually amalgamated with the Arab tribes that came to the Negev with the spread of Islam.

Many of the Arab tribes in the Negev today believe they are descendents of the Nabateans. Oral histories are the encyclopedias of the nomads; each tribe knows its origin according to the folk narrative of the Negev.

Palestinians of the Negev

Known as Arab es-Saba (literally the Arabs of Bir es-Saba), the Palestinian population of the Negev was estimated at 90,000 in 1946. Belonging to 96 different tribal groups, they were mostly pastoral and had begun trading in livestock, predominantly with Gaza, since the beginning of the 20th century. By the time the Israelis had entrenched themselves in this area in 1953, there were only 11,000 Palestinians left. The population had been driven out to refugee camps in Gaza, the Sinai, and the West Bank. Some natives of Negev were "relocated" by the Israelis in Lydd and Ramleh. Like all Arab population centers that remained in what became the Jewish state, the Negev became a military zone until 1966. The Palestinians of the Negev were given an Israeli ID card, which stated that they were "Bedouin" rather than Arab, Druze, or any other non-Jewish identity. Like other racist regimes, the state of Israel administratively divided people on the basis of their ethnic, religious, and in this case lifestyle, identities.

With 90 percent of their land confiscated, the remaining Palestinians of the Negev were regrouped into 19 tribal confederations. Many of the tribal leaders were co-opted by the Israeli government, which promised municipal services to the now forcibly settled communities, in return for "co-operating" with the state authorities. Thus many young Negev Palestinians were drafted into the army with the promise of running water and electricity for their communities in return.

The Israeli occupation of the Negev had profound consequences for the Palestinians that stayed. While the Palestinians of the Negev speak Arabic at home, they often speak Hebrew in public and although they live next to Jewish Israelis, they always live in separate neighborhoods. Some Palestinian collaborators, predominantly from Gaza, have been resettled in the Negev, but are social rejects forced to live in separate neighborhoods.

Although the Israeli army has often placed Arabs from the Negev, who serve in the army, at some of the most dangerous military "checkpoints," they have denied them mechanisms for economic upward mobility. The Palestinians of the Negev continue to make up the poorest sector in Israel. Some 50 percent of Negev's Arabs, estimated at around 140,000, live below the poverty line.

Israel has established four "development" towns (Rahat, Tel-Sheva, Aro'er, Segev-Shalom) specifically for the Palestinians of the Negev but denied them the option of living elsewhere, in or around Jewish-dominated urban centers. Not wanting to be treated like

Bedouins and the Unrecognized Villages

Israel's first prime minister, David Ben Gurion, wrote to his son eleven years before the birth of the Jewish state: "Negev land is reserved for Jewish citizens whenever and wherever they want. We must expel the Arabs and take their place." Moshe Dayan, commander of the Israeli forces in the 1967 war and the country's most renowned military hero, gave voice to a common wish when he predicted in 1963 that "this phenomenon of the Bedouin will disappear." In April 2003, Ariel Sharon's government approved a five-year plan, with a budget of more than $200 million, as a "real attempt to deal with problems faced by [the Bedouin] sector, as well as the land issue."

The Palestinian's main lobbying group, the Regional Council for the Unrecognized Villages, has worked relentlessly to have a member on the Southern Regional Planning Committee, which oversees planning issues in the Negev. Thus far not one Bedouin or Arab-Palestinian representative has been appointed, despite the fact that they make up a quarter of the Negev's citizens.

The five-year plan is a coordinated policy of using force to transfer all the Arabs from their "scattered" villages into three new reservation-like development towns. While geographically based on three formerly unrecognized villages, this Israeli plan would allow the area's Arabs to live on only 2 percent of their land. In the meantime, work on fourteen new Jewish settlements in the Negev began in 2003. The new construction will mark the first time in 25 years that the World Zionist Organization has financed settlement-building in Israel "proper" rather than the West Bank and Gaza Strip. While the Arabs will not be able to legally establish housing units or communities on their historical areas and villages, the Jewish settlements will.

Denying the Arabs the right to live freely in their ancestral homelands is a policy of Israeli governments, past and present. The Negev, with its intricate topography, is considered difficult to infiltrate and an ideal setting for military bases. Israel's nuclear reactor is located near the Negev town of Dimona, as is its implicitly acknowledged nuclear arsenal.

Native Americans on a reservation, half the Palestinians of the Negev (about 60,000) have independently established "unrecognized" hamlets and villages. Without state recognition, these areas receive no municipal services and depend on electric generators and natural wells for their most essential needs and are constantly under threat of being destroyed by the state. Today Rahat is the largest of the relocation towns built for the Arabs and houses 38,000 people.

The Israelis

The Israelis of the Negev generally belong to the poorer groups of society. Moroccan, Ethiopian, and Russian immigrants and their children live in Jewish (although many of the Russians are not actually Jewish) development towns. Almost all speak their native language as well as Hebrew. They largely vote for the Likud or émigré parties and are still not quite integrated into mainstream Israeli society. Ben Gurion University in Bir es-Saba, with its high academic standards and good research, is the only real cultural accomplishment of the Israelis in the Negev. Among a faculty of several hundred are three Arabs. Today, only 1,400 Arabs still live in the city.

Visiting Bir es-Saba

Bedouin Thursday Market

The Thursday market in Bir es-Saba has been an attraction for visitors for centuries. Colorful woven carpets, silver jewelry, and copper pots can be bought at good prices. Social interaction of the still nomadic parts of the Arab community can also be glanced. It stands to the north of Ottoman Bridge.

Governor's Mansion/Museum

The Governors Mansion house was built in 1906 by the Ottoman government as part of its effort to create a regional government in southern Palestine. The two-story building housed a reception hall on the ground floor and living quarters on the second floor, with separate entrances for each floor.

In 1938 the building became a girls' school, which remained in use until 1948. In 1949 the Israelis established their own municipality and used the Governor's Mansion as their headquarters. Today the building is part of what is known as the Negev Museum, which houses permanent and temporary Israeli exhibits.

Mosque of Bir es-Saba

Also built around 1906 to accompany the Governor's Mansion, this late Ottoman mosque is no longer a house of worship. After the 1948 war, Israelis used it to incarcerate Arab prisoners.

Although the Muslims of Bir es-Saba have no other mosque available to them, and petitioned the courts to re-open it, Israel has ruled out its use for worship. The state has said it wants to use the shrine as an archeological museum. The official justification for not

Bedouin children study math using fruit boxes for desks

allowing the only mosque in the city to be used for prayer, is that its minaret overlooks an Israeli military site, and thus poses a threat to the security of the state.

Muslim Cemetery

There are many more dead Palestinian Arabs in Bir es-Saba than there are living ones. The Muslim cemetery is perhaps the last testimonial to the urban population that once lived in this city. Today, the city's Muslims are buried in the development towns set up for them by the state, since the Muslim cemetery has not been given permission to expand.

Ottoman School

In accordance with the new plans for Ottoman Negev, the government in Istanbul built a boys' boarding school in 1913. During World War I it was converted into a military hospital to treat Ottoman troops. After Bir es-Saba was captured by the Israelis, the military first used it as an encampment and later for office space. Today it stands abandoned and empty and is not open to the public.

Palestinian Homes

Across the street from the Governor's Mansion is the 1930s home of the former district ruler and known Jerusalem historian Aref al-Aref. An Israeli company now uses it as office space. It is the only building in Bir es-Saba that has a plaque on the door identifying it as part of the town's Arab history. It is well kept.

The home of the former mayor of Bir es-Saba under British rule, Shaykh Abu Medein, has been turned into a fast food restaurant and drug store. Above are the offices of the Regional Council for Palestinian Bedouin Unrecognized Villages of the Negev. This NGO is the largest Arab institution of its kind in the district. They host solidarity groups and give tours of Arab communities and arrange for volunteers from within the community and abroad to work in local communities.

Russian Cemetery

The large-scale Russian emigration, encouraged specifically by the Israeli Likud party, is evident at the nearby Russian cemetery. Latin and Orthodox crosses abound, indicative of the non-Jewish identity of those who are playing an ever increasing role in displacing Palestinians from their homeland.

Train Station

This is the famous German- and Ottoman-built railway popularized by Lawrence of Arabia. Completed in 1915, it led to Damascus in the north and Nitzana, on the Egyptian border, in the south.

The railway was only operational for two years before the British occupied the country. They in turn connected the line to train lines leading directly to Egypt. In 1948 the station was briefly used by the Egyptian army. Today it stands abandoned among modern high rises, waiting to be torn down.

World War I Cemetery

For war buffs, it may be of interest that Bir es-Saba hosts the largest foreign troop cemetery in the country. In all 1,239 allied soldiers are buried here, many of them from Australia, New Zealand, Wales, and elsewhere in the Commonwealth. While reasonably well kept, its sister graveyard in Gaza is better maintained.

Top: An abandoned Ottoman-era public building in Bir es-Saba
Bottom: The abandoned railway station, the Hijazy

Near Bir es-Saba

Abraham's Well

To the south of the city is a well allegedly built by the biblical Abraham. The existing well dates to the 12th century, while the current technical equipment to draw the water was probably constructed by the Ottomans.

Arad

A fortified Canaanite city built sometime between 2950–2650 BCE, Arad was a relatively large (25 acre) agricultural metropolis with a population of 2,500 at the peak of its glory. The establishment of this large outpost was a feat in its day. Its agricultural land, which produced wheat, barley and beans, was irrigated through the construction of dams in the valleys.

Archeological finds include two twin temples, dedicated to what appear to be a mixture of Canaanite and Mesopotamian deities, among them Tammus, who represented both the season of fertility and death. Baptismal basins (probably for ceremonial immersions) and altar stones (perhaps for ritual offerings) were also central to their temples of prayer and worship.

The city appears to have been abandoned around 2,500 BCE for reasons that are not certain; climate changes are most probably the cause.

A series of outposts established by Hebrews, Persians, Greeks, and Romans were built here after 1250 BCE. The Arab Muslims built a fortress and caravanserai to serve traders and pilgrims who came through the area.

Isbeita

Isbeita was founded 40 kilometers (25 mi) southwest of Bir es-Saba in the 1st century CE by the Nabateans. The names of the Nabatean King Aretas IV and the sun-god Dushrat were found on several stones uncovered by archeologists. Most of Isbeita's visible remains are from the Byzantine period, during which it was notable for its many churches and its rain harnessing systems.

The so-called **Southern Church** is the earliest Christian shrine in the Negev. What remains of the local governor's house, in the Central Church is one of the few buildings from this era that has a second floor. The 40-room **Northern Church** was built in 517, with a system of courtyards and a mosaic floor. A baptistery lies south of the church complex.

A cemetery, which contains several gravestones with the names of monks and priests, dating between 612 and 679, also lies close to the church. It was largely destroyed in an earthquake in the 5th century. Subsequently the Muslim Arabs built a mosque right next to the churches, but Isbeita appears to have been abandoned at some point during the 9th or 10th century.

Kurnub (Mamshit)
Located some 40 kilometers (25 mi) east of Bir es-Saba, Kurnub was founded by the Nabateans in the 1st century CE. It was a major center for trade and commerce, but declined when the Romans turned it into a garrison city. It did, however, flourish under the Byzantines. Among the visible remains are a Nabatean horse stable, two Byzantine churches, and mosaic floors. Mamshit appears on the map of Madaba.

Oboda
Established as a caravan center and later developed into a Nabatean city, Oboda was named after the Nabatean King, Oboda I, and was a popular stop for travelers, traders, and merchants. It was especially famous for its good race horses. Archeologists have found retaining walls, the temple court, the staircase tower, as well as the remains of a small temple identified with the deified king.

Subsequently the Romans established a military outpost on what remained of the Nabatean city in the middle of the 3rd century. On the acropolis in 267 CE, a temple to Zeus was erected, though it was later dismantled and its stones used in Byzantine buildings. Remains from this era include a well preserved tower, a patrician villa, and a burial cave. At the time Romans forced local nomadic groups to become sedentary.

During Byzantine rule Oboda again became a center for Arab caravan trade and parallel to this development agricultural growth boomed. All remnants of Nabatean and Roman structures were destroyed or built over. Archeologists have called it Oboda's last era of glory. Inscriptions, including a cross and an appeal to St. Theodorus, patron of the city, to protect it against the evil eye can still be seen. Byzantine remains include the two churches constructed within what was the Nabatean sacred compound, a cave dwelling, a burial cave, and a bath house.

Tel Bir es-Saba
An early civilization that worshipped female fertility gods and used stone and flint for tools and weapons, sheltered in subterranean dwellings in several agricultural hamlets on both sides of the Bir es-

Boys in a village next to Rahat

Saba valley during the 4th millennia BCE. Consisting of a string of extended families and clans engaged in agriculture and domestication of animals, these communities protected themselves from severe temperatures by living beneath the earth. Finds indicate that while they carved their own deities out of ivory and other precious materials, they probably imported the material itself.

Tel Jemmeh
A town covering about 12 acres, and home to human settlements from the 18th through the 3rd centuries BCE, Tel Jemmeh offered archeologists 46 feet of accumulated debris once they started digging.

Tel Jemmeh is outside the borders of what is today the Gaza Strip and within the administrative area of the Negev. An ancient fortification dating back to 1450–1200 BCE can still be seen. Extensive pottery remains with Aegean and specifically Cypriot motifs, clearly identifying a Philistine settlement, were unearthed. Today they can be seen in the Israel Museum in Jerusalem.

In the 7th century, Tel Jemmeh was an Assyrian administrative and trade center where Yemeni merchants brought frankincense and myrrh. Southern Arabians had a significant cultural and political impact on the region at the time and many settled in and around Tel Jemmeh.

During the rule of the Nabateans, Tel Jemmeh is believed to have been the largest grain center in the country, home to as many as twelve granaries, the largest of which held up to 132 tons of wheat. During the reign of the Ptolomies in Egypt, it was a storage center for grain and oil collected as taxes. Tel Jemmeh was distinguished by its use of mud architecture and vaulted roofs.

Umayyad Town

The gold rich Wadi Tawahin, 4 kilometers (2.5 mi) north of Eilat, was an industrial site established by the Arabs during the Umayyad period (7th–8th centuries). Nearby in Ein Evrona, in the areas of Wadi Araba, a few kilometers north of Eilat, remains of what was clearly a wealthy farmstead of the early Arab period (7th–9th centuries) was unearthed. In what was clearly a successful early Arab endeavor to make the desert green, the inhabitants of this settlement dug a well into the aquifer at the foot of the mountains and from it dug a network of shafts with connecting tunnels. Eventually the water flowed into an open ditch to irrigate the fields.

Valley of the Ancient Copper Mines (Timna)

Located some 30 kilometers (19 mi) north of the Gulf of Aqaba and the Israeli city of Eilat is the Timna valley. It became a copper mining center during the reign of the Pharaohs of the 14th–12th centuries BCE. An Egyptian temple (1318–1304 BCE), dedicated to Hathor, Egyptian goddess of mining, was excavated at the foot of the valley.

Appendix I: Travel Information

I. Organizations & Institutions

Tourism Organizations

Palestinian Tourism and Antiquities
Bethlehem: 02-2741581-3
Gaza: 08-2824866/9461
Ramallah: 02-2988433
www.visit-palestine.com; www.visit-palestine.ps

Regional Departments of Tourism & Antiquities
Bethlehem: 02-277-0750/1,
    02-274-1581/3
Gaza City: 08-282-9719
Hebron: 02-2227630, 02-222-9633
Jenin: 04-2438381
Jericho: 02-2324011, 02-232-2935
Nablus: 09-238-5244, 09-238-5045
Qalqilia: 09-294-3143
Ramallah: 02-295-56060,
    02-295-9561
Salfit: 09-251-5971
Tulkarem: 09-267-9701

Higher Council for the Arab Tourism Industry
Jerusalem: 02-6281805,
    hcat-pal@palnet.com

Research Centers

Arij (Applied Research Institute)
Tel: 02-274-1889/70535,
pmaster@arij.org, **www.arij.org**

Arab Institute for Research and Transfer of Technology
Tel: 02-2954223, kassaf@planet.edu

Bisan Center for Research and Development
Tel: 02-240-7837/9,
bisanrd@palnet.com, **www.bisan.org**

CPRS (Center for Palestine Research & Studies)
Tel: 09-238-0383/1619,
cprs@zaytona.com,
www.cprspalestine.org

Ecole Biblique et Archaeologique Francaise
Tel: 02-626-4468,
ebaf@netvision.net.il,
www.ebaf.op.org

HDIP (Health, Development, Information & Policy Institute)
Tel: 02-298-5372, hdip@hdip.org,
www.hdip.org

PASSIA (Palestinian Academic Society for the Study of International Affairs)
Tel: 02-626-4426, passia@palnet.org,
www.passia.org

Institute of Jerusalem Studies
Tel: 02-295-0767,
Ips-quds@palnet.com,
www.jqf-jerusalem.org

Cultural Organizations

For information on current cultural events, see the monthly *This Week in Palestine*:
www.thisweekinpalestine.com

Bethlehem

Anat Palestinian Folk & Craft Center: 02-2772024, Fax: 02-2772024

Artas Folklore Center: 02-2767467, Fax: 02-2760533, artas_fc@ yahoo.com

Bethlehem Academy of Music: 02-2777141, Fax: 02-2777142

Bethlehem Peace Center: 02-2766677, Fax: 02-2741057, info@peacenter.org

Cardinal House: 02-2764778, Fax: 02-2764778, cardinal_house@yahoo.com

Center for Cultural Heritage Preservation: 02-2766244, Fax: 02-2766241, info@bethlehem2000.org

Higher Institute of Music: 02-2740441, Fax: 02-2740441, highiom@hotmail.com

Inad Centre for Theatre: 02-2766263, inad38@yahoo.com

International Center of Bethlehem–Dar Annadwa, 02-2770047, Fax: 02-2770048, annadwa@palnet.edu

al-Liqa' Center for Religious & Heritage Studies in the Holy Land: 02-2741639, Fax: 02-2741639

National Conservatory of Music: 02-2745989, Fax: 02-2770048

Palestinian Group for the Revival of Popular Heritage: 02-2747945, Fax: 02-2747945

Palestinian Heritage Center: 02-2742381, Fax: 02-2742642, sacar@palnet.edu

Sabreen Association for Artistic Development: 02-2750091, Fax: 02-2750092, info-bidayat@sabreen.com

Turathuna (Heritage Centre): 02-2741241, Fax: 02-2744440, pdaoud@bethlehem.edu

Gaza

al-Qattan Centre for the Child: 08-2839929, Fax: 08-2839949 reem@qcc.qattanfoundation.org

Arts & Crafts Village: 08-2846405, Fax: 08-2846405, artvlg@palnet.com

Ashtar for Culture & Arts: 08-2833569, Fax: 08-2833569, atlas9@palnet.com

Atfaluna Society for Deaf Children Craft Shop: 08-2828495, www.atfaluna.net

British Council: 08-2825574/282594, Fax: 08-2820512

Culture & Light Centre: 08-2865896, Fax: 08-2865896, ifarah@palnet.com

Culture & Free Thought Association: 08-2851299, Fax: 08-2851299

French Cultural Center: 08-2867883, Fax: 08-2828811, ccfgaza@palnet.net

Gaza Theatre: 08-2824860, Fax: 08-2824870

Holst Cultural Centre: 08-2810476, Fax: 08-2808896, mcrcg@palnet.com

Rashad Shawwa Cultural Center: 08-2864599, Fax: 08-2868965 shawacentre@hotmail.com

Science & Culture Center: 08-2810476, Fax: 08-2808896

Theatre Day Productions: 08-2836766, Fax: 08-2836766, tdpgaza@palnet.com

Hebron

Association d'Echanges Culturels Hebron-France: 02-2224811, Fax: 02-2224811

Beit Ula Cultural Center:

02-2211019, Fax: 02-6288448
British Council Info-Point (Hebron
    University): 02-2220995,
    Fax: 02-2229303
Palestinian Child Arts Center:
    02-2224813, Fax: 02-2220855,
    pcac@hotmail.com

Jericho

Jericho Community Center:
    02-2325007, Fax: 02-2325007
Jericho Culture & Art Center: 02-
    2321047, Fax: 02-2321047
Jericho Equestrian Club: 02-2325007,
    Fax: 02-2325007
Municipality Theatre: 02-2322417,
    Fax: 02-2322604

Jerusalem

British Council: 02-6282545,
    Fax: 02-6283021,
    britain.jerusalem@fco.gov
French Cultural Centre:
    02-6282451/6262236,
    Fax: 02-6284324,
    ccfjeru@consulfrance-jerusalem.org
Gallery Anadiel: 02-6282811,
    Fax: 02-6282811
Goethe Institute: 02-5610627,
    Fax: 02-5618431
Hakawati Theatre Company:
    02-5854513, Fax: 02-5854513,
    tdp@palnet.com
Issaf Nashashibi Center: 02-5813233,
    Fax: 02-5818232,
    decc@palnet.edu
al-Jawal Theatre Group: 02-6280655
Jerusalem Centre for Arabic Music:
    02-6274774
al-Kasaba Theatre: 02-6264052,
    Fax: 02-6276310
al-Ma'mal Foundation for
    Contemporary Art: 02-6283457,
    Fax: 02-6272312
National Conservatory of Music:
    02-6271711, Fax: 02-6271710,
    info@ncm.birzeit.edu
Palestinian National Theater:

02-6280957, Fax: 02-6276293,
    pnt@palnet.com
Palestinian PEN Center: 02-6262970,
    Fax: 02-6280103
al-Ruwah Theatre Group:
    02-6274041, Fax: 02-6274041
Sabreen Association for Artistic
    Development: 02-5321393,
    Fax: 02-5321394,
    sabreen@netvision.net.il
Sanabel Culture & Arts Theatre:
    02-6714338
Spanish Cooperation: 02-6286098,
    Fax: 02-6286099,
    cooperac@netvision.net.il
Turkish Cultural Centre: 02-5400592,
    Fax: 02-5400563,
    kudustur@netvision.net.il
al-Urmawi Centre for Mashreq
    Music: 02-2342005,
    Fax: 02-5660578,
    info@urmawi.org
al-Wasiti Art Center: 02-5822859,
    Fax: 02-5817853
Yabous Productions: 02-6261045,
    Fax: 02-6261372,
    info@yabous.org

Nablus

British Council Info-Point (al-Najah
    University): 09-2375950,
    Fax: 09-2375950
Cultural Center for Child
    Development: 09-2386899,
    Fax: 09-2397518,
    nutaleb@hotmail.com
French Cultural Center:
    09-2385914, Fax: 09-2387593,
    ccfnaplouse@hotmail.com
Palestinian Scientific Society:
    09-2942111, Fax: 09-2942111
al-Yasmin–Assalah Center:
    09-2386723, Fax: 09-2384568

Ramallah

Amideast: 02-2408023,
    Fax: 02-2408017,
    westbank-gaza@amideast.org

A. M. Qattan Foundation:
02-2960544, Fax: 02-2984886,
info@qattanfoundation.org
Ashtar for Theatre Production:
02-2980037, Fax: 02-2960326,
ashtar@p-ol.com
Baladna Cultural Center:
02-2958435, Fax: 02-2958435
British Council: 02-2963293,
Fax: 02-2963297
al-Kasaba Theatre and
Cinematheque: 02-2965292/3,
Fax: 02-2965294,
info@alkasaba.org
al-Rahhalah Theatre: 02-2988091,
alrahhalah@hotmail.com
First Ramallah Group: 02-2952706,
Fax: 02-2980583
French Cultural Center: 02-2987727,
Fax: 02-2987728,
ccframa@p-ol.com
Goethe Institute: 02-2981922,
Fax: 02-2981923,
info@ramallah.goethe.org
Greek Cultural Center:
02-2981736/2980546,
Fax: 02-2981736/2980546,
makdonia@palnet.com
Karmel Cultural Foundation:
02-2987375, Fax: 02-2987374
In'ash Al-Usra Society Center For
Heritage & Folklore Studies,
02-2401123, Fax: 02-2401544
Khalil Sakakini Cultural Center:
02-2987374, Fax: 02-2987375
Manar Cultural Center:
02-2957937, Fax: 02-2987598
National Conservatory of Music:
02-2959070, Fax: 02-2959071
Palestinian Association for Cultural
Exchange: 02-2958825,
Fax: 02-2986854
Palestinian Network of Art Centers:
02-2407939, network@p-ol.com
Popular Art Center: 02-2403891,
Fax: 02-2402851,
pac@palnet.com
Ramallah Cultural Palace:

02-2984704,
director@ramallahcultural
palace.org
RIWAQ: Center for Architectural
Conservation: 02-2406887,
Fax: 02-2406986,
riwaq@palnet.com

Museums

Bethlehem
al-Bad Museum for Olive Oil
Production: 02-2741581
Baituna al Talhami Museum:
02-2742589, Fax: 02-2742431
Bethlehem Folklore Museum:
02-2742589
Bethlehem Peace Center Museum:
02-2766677, Fax: 02-2741057
Crib of Nativity Museum:
02-2760876, Fax: 02-2760877,
crib@p-ol.com
International Museum of Nativity:
02-2747825
Natural History Museum:
02-2774373,
wildlife@palnet.com
Palestinian Ethnographic Museum:
02-2767467, Fax: 02-2760533,
artas_fc@yahoo.com
Palestinian Heritage Center:
02-2742381, Fax: 02-2742642,
sacar@palnet.com

Hebron
Hebron Museum: 02-2228122,
Fax: 02-2228293

Jerusalem
Armenian Museum: 02-6282331,
Fax: 02-6264362
Dar al-Tifl Museum: 02-6272477,
Fax: 02-6273477
Islamic Museum: 02-6283313,
Fax: 02-6285561

Nablus
al-Kassaba Museum, Thafer al-Masri
Foundation: 09-2384126

Ramallah
Museum of Palestinian Popular
Heritage/Inash el Usra':
02-2402876, Fax: 02-2401544
Palestinian Archeological Museum:
02-298200

II. WHERE TO STAY
& WHERE TO EAT

Hotels

Bethlehem
Abraham Herberge (Beit Jala):
02-2742613, Fax: 2744966,
shihadeh@luthchurch.com
Alexander Hotel: 02-2770780,
Fax: 02-2770782
Andalus Hotel: 02-2741348,
Fax: 02-2765674
Beit al-Baraka Youth Hostel:
02-2229288, Fax: 02-2229288
Bethlehem Hotel: 02-2770702,
Fax: 02-2770706,
bhotel@p-ol.com
Bethlehem Inn: 02-2742423,
Fax: 02-2742424
Bethlehem Palace Hotel:
02-2742798, Fax: 02-2741562
Bethlehem Star Hotel:
02-2743249/2770285,
Fax: 02-2741494,
htstar@hally.net
Casanova Hospice: 02-2743981,
Fax: 02-2743540
Everest Hotel (Beit Jala):
02-2742604, Fax: 02-2741278
Golden Park Resort & Hotel
(Beit Sahour): 02-2774414
Grand Hotel: 02-2741602/1440,
Fax: 02-2741604,
khalid9933@hotmail.com

Inter-Continental Hotel (Jacir
Palace): 02-2766777,
Fax: 02-2766770
Lutheran Guesthouse "Abu Gubran":
02-277 0047
Nativity Hotel: 02-2770650,
Fax: 02-2744083,
nativity@nativity-hotel.com
Paradise Hotel: 02-2744542/4543,
Fax: 02-2744544,
paradise@p-ol.com
Saint Antonio Hotel: 02-2744308,
Fax: 02-2770524
Saint Vincent Guest House:
02-2760967/8, Fax: 02-2760970,
svincent@p-ol.com
Santa Maria Hotel: 02-2767374/5/6,
Fax: 02-2770063,
smaria@p-ol.com
Shepherd Hotel: 02-2740656,
Fax: 02-2744888,
info@shepherdhotel.com
St. Nicholas Hotel: 02-2743040/1/2,
Fax: 02-2743043
Talita Kumi Guest House:
02-2741247, Fax: 02-2741847
al-Zaytouna Guest House:
02-2742016, Fax: 02-2742016

Gaza
Adam Hotel: 08-2823521/19,
Fax: 08-2823521/19
al-Amal Hotel: 08-2861832
Beach Hotel: 08-2825492,
082848433, Fax: 08-2825492,
082848433
Cliff Hotel: 08-2823450,
Fax: 08-2820742
Commodore Gaza Hotel:
08-2834400, Fax: 08-2822623,
hotel@commodorgaza.com
al-Deira: 08-2838100/200/300,
Fax: 08-2838400,
ADEIRA@P-I-S.com
Gaza International Hotel:
08-2830001/2/3/4,
Fax: 08-2830005
al-Hilal Al-Ahmar Hotel:

08-2054261, Fax: 08-2054261
Hotel Sea Breeze: 08-2830277,
08-2842654, Fax: 08-2824231
Marna House: 08-2822624,
Fax: 08-2823322
Palestine Hotel: 08-2823355,
Fax: 08-2860056
al-Quds International Hotel:
08-2826223/63487/5118,
Fax: 08-2826223/63487/5118
Summerland Tourist Village:
08-2847171, Fax: 08-2864008
Zahrat Al-Madain: 08-2826801

Hebron

Beit Abouna Ibrahim (Family Inn):
02-2224811, Fax: 02-2224811,
lownp@palnet.com
Hebron Tourist Hotel: 02-2226760,
Fax: 02-2226760
Regency Hotel: 02-2257389/98,
Fax: 02-2257388,
regency@palnet.com

Jericho

Deir Hijleh Monastery: 02-9943038
Hisham Palace Hotel: 02-2322414,
Fax: 02-2323109
Inter-Continental Hotel:
02-2311200, Fax: 02-2311222
Jericho Resort Village: 02-2321255,
Fax: 02-2322189,
marketing@jericho-resort.com
Jerusalem Hotel: 02-2322444, Fax:
02-9923109
Tel Sultan Tourist Center:
02-2321590, Fax: 02-2321598,
info@jericho-cablecar.com

Jerusalem

Addar Hotel: 02-6263111/
02-6260791, www.addar-hotel.com
Alcazar Hotel: 02-6281111,
Fax: 02-6287360,
admin@jrscazar.com
Ambassador Hotel: 02-5412222,
Fax: 02-5828202,

amb@netvision.net.il
American Colony Hotel:
02-6279777, Fax: 02-5828202,
reserv@amcol.co.il
Capitol Hotel: 02-6282561/2562,
Fax: 02-6264352
Capitolina Hotel: 02-6286888,
Fax: 02-6276301,
capitol@east-jerusalem-ymca.org
Christmas Hotel: 02-6282588,
Fax: 02-6264417
Commodore Hotel: 02-6271414,
Fax: 02-6284701
Gloria Hotel: 02-6282431,
Fax: 02-6282401:
gloriahl@netvision.net.il
Golden Walls Hotel: 02-6272416,
Fax: 02-6264658,
info@goldenwalls.com
Holy Land Hotel: 02-6272888/
6284841, Fax: 02-6280265
Jerusalem Claridge Hotel: 02-2347137,
Fax: 02-2347139,
claridge@palnet.com
Jerusalem Hotel: 02-6283282,
Fax: 02-6283282,
raed@jrshotel.com
Jerusalem Meridian Hotel:
02-6285212, Fax: 02-6285214
Jerusalem Panorama Hotel:
02-6272277, Fax: 02-6273699,
panaroma@trendline.com.il
Knights Palace Guesthouse:
02-6282537, Fax: 02-6282401,
kp@actcom.co.il
Lawrence Hotel: 02-6264208,
Fax: 02-6271285,
karine@actcom.co.il
Metropol Hotel: 02-6282507,
Fax: 02-6285134
Mount of Olives Hotel: 02-6284877,
Fax: 02-6264427,
info@mtolives.coml
Mount Scopus Hotel: 02-5828891,
Fax: 02-5828825,
mtscopus@netvision.net.il
New Imperial Hotel: 02-6272000,
Fax: 02-6271530

New Metropole Hotel: 02-6283846,
    Fax: 02-6277485
New Regent Hotel: 02-6284540,
    Fax: 02-6264023,
    atictour@palnet.com
New Swedish Hostel: 02-6277855,
    Fax: 02-6264124,
    swedishhost@yahoo.com
Notre Dame Guesthouse: 02-6271995
Palace Hotel: 02-6271126,
    Fax: 02-6271649
Petra Hostel and Hotel: 02-6286618
Pilgrims Inn Hotel: 02-6272416,
    info@goldenwalls.com
Rivoli Hotel: 02-6284871,
    Fax: 02-6274879
Savoy Hotel: 02-6283366,
    Fax: 02-6288040
Seven Arches Hotel: 02-6267777,
    Fax: 02-6271319,
    svnarch@trendline.co.il
St. George Hotel: 02-6277232/6277323,
    Fax: 02-6282575,
    stgeorge1@bezeqint.net
St. George's Pilgrim Guest House:
    02-6283302, Fax: 02-6282253,
    sghostel@netvision.net.il
Strand Hotel: 02-6280279,
    Fax: 02-6284826
Victoria Hotel: 02-6274466,
    Fax: 02-6274171
YWCA Hotel: 02-6282593,
    Fax: 02-6284654, ywca@pl.org
al-Zahra Hotel: 02-6282447,
    Fax: 02-6283960,
    azzahrahotel@shabaka.net

Nablus

Asia Hotel: 09-2386220,
    Fax: 09-2386220
Chrystal Motel: 09-2333281,
    Fax: 09-2333281
al-Qaser Hotel: 09-2385444,
    Fax: 09-2385944,
    alqasr@netvision.net.il
al-Yasmeen Hotel: 09-2333555,
    Fax: 09-2333666,
    yasmeen@palnet.com

Ramallah

al-A'in Hotel: 02-2400683,
    Fax: 02-2405925
Best Eastern Hotel: 02-2960450,
    Fax: 02-2958452,
    besteastern@jrol.com
al-Bireh Tourist Hotel: 02-2400803,
    Fax: 02-2400803
City Inn Palace Hotel: 02-2408080,
    Fax: 02-2408091
First Ramallah Group: 02-2952706,
    Fax: 02-2980583
Gemzo Suites (Furnished Flats)
    02-2409532, Fax: 02-2409727,
    gemzo@Palnet.com
Grand Park Hotel: 02-2986194,
    Fax: 02-2956950,
    info@grandpark.com
al-Hajal Hotel: 02-2987858,
    Fax: 02-2987858
Merryland Hotel: 02-2987176,
    Fax: 02-2987074
al-Murouj Pension (Jifna):
    02-2957881, Fax: 02-2957881
Pension Miami: 02-2956808,
    Fax: 02-2956808
Plaza Hotel: 02-2982020
Ramallah Hotel: 02-2953544,
    Fax: 02-2955029
Rocky Hotel: 02-2964470:
    022961871, Fax: 02-2961871
Royal Court Suite Hotel:
    02-2964040, Fax: 02-2964047
al-Wihdah Hotel: 02-2980412,
    Fax: 02-2980412

Restaurants

Bethlehem

Abu Eli: 02-6263344
Abu Shanab Restaurant: 02-2742985
Andalos: 02-2743519
Central: 02-2741378
Checkers Restaurant: 02-2766338
Dar Jdoudnah Coffeeshop:
    02-2743212
Diwan: 02-2770333, 02-2770329

Dolphin: 02-2743432
Golden Roof: 02-2743224
al-Makan Bar & Cigar Bar: Jacir
    Palace Hotel: 02-2766777,
    Fax: 02-2766754
Mariachi (Grand Hotel): 02-2741440
RadioNet Cafe (Beit Sahour):
    02-2774883, Fax: 02-2774882
Shepherds Valley Village: 02-27773875
Tachi Chinese: 02-2744382

Gaza

Abu Nuwas: 08-2845211
Alladin: 08-2823355
al-Andalus: 08-2821272
al-Baidar: 08-2861321
Cyber Internet Café: 08-2844704
al-Deira: 08-2838100/200
al-Diwanea Tourist: 08-2825062
Fisher Tourist: 08-2834779
Granada: 08-2822165
La Mirage: 08-2865128
Lido: 08-2864198
Lotus: 08-2842431
Love Boat: 08-2861353
al-Marsa: 08-2863599
Matouq: 08-2826245
Mika Cafeteria: 08-2866040
al-Molouke: 08-2868397
al-Nawras Tourist Resort: 08-2833033
Palm Beach: 08-2860142
Pizza Inn: 08-2840415
al-Salam: 08-2822705
Salam Beach: 08-2844964
al-Sammak: 08-2864385
al-Sammak Ghornata: 08-2840107
al-Sayad: 08-2834779
Sea Breeze: 08-2830277
Summerland Village: 08-2453441
White Tent: 08-2860380

Jericho

al-Amara: 02-2323500
Green Valley Park: 02-2322349
Jabal Quruntul: 02-2322614,
    Fax: 02-2322593
Jericho Tent: 02-2323820
al-Nafoura Restaurant (Jericho Resort

Village): 02-2321255,
    Fax: 2322189
Old Jericho Tent: 02-2323820
al-Rabiyah Park & Restaurant:
    02-2324060, 055-5338295
al-Rawda: 02-2322555
Samhouri: 02-2323252
Seven Trees: 02-2322781
Sultan Restaurant: 02-2324025

Jerusalem

Abu-Shanab Pizza: 02-6260752
Arabesque (American Colony
    Hotel): 02-6279777,
    Fax: 02-6279779
Armenian Tavern (Old City):
    02-6273854
Askidinya: 02-5324590
Border Line Café: 02-5328342
Café Europe: 02-6284313
Café Imperial: 02-6282261,
    Fax: 02-6271530
al-Diwan & Antonio's (Ambassador
    Hotel): 02-5412213/ 5412222,
    Fax: 02-5828202
al-Dorada Coffee Shop & Internet
    Café: 02-6260993
Four Seasons Restaurants:
    02-6286061, Fax: 02-6286097
Gate Café: 02-6274282
Kan Zaman (Jerusalem Hotel):
    02-6271356
Lotus and Olive Garden (Jerusalem
    Meridian Hotel): 02-6285212
Mocca Café (Beit Hanina):
    02-5836821
Moon Light Pizza: 02-6275277
Nafoura: 02-6260034
Notre Dame: La Rotisserie:
    02-6279114, Fax: 02-6271995
Papa Andreas: 02-6284433
Pasha's: 02-5825162, 02-5328342
Patio (Christmas Hotel): 02-6282588
Patisserie Suisse: 02-6284377
Philadelphia: 02-6289770
Pizza House: 02-6273970
Popular Arab: 02-5833226
al-Quds al-Arabi: 02-6273963

al-Shuleh Grill: 02-6273768
Sizzling Restaurant and Bar:
    02-6263344
Victoria Restaurant: 02-6283051
al-Zahra: 02-6282447
Zeit ou Zaater: 02-6569889

Nablus
al-Mankal: 09-2675362
Rozana: 09-2385676
Salim Afandi: 09-2371332
Zeit Ou Zaater (al-Yasmeen Hotel):
    09-2383164

Ramallah
Addar (Bir Zeit): 02-2810274
Angelo's: 02-2956408
al-Aseel: 022980456
Baladna Ice Cream: 02-295 6721
al-Bardauni's: 02-2951410
Benny's: 02-2960937
Caesar's (Grand Park Hotel):
    02-2986194
Café Mocha Rena: 02-2981460
Café Olé: 02-2984135
Casablanca: 02-2987658
Champs: 02-2987188
Chinese House Restaurant:
    02-2964081
Cliff House (Rocky Hotel):
    02-2964470
Darna: 02-2950590
Ein al-Marj (Bir Zeit): 02-2810220/1
Elite Coffee House: 02-2965169
Fawanees: 02-2987046
K5M Caterers: 02-2956813
Kings: 02-2964040
La Strada: 02-2965968
La Terrace: 02-2987701
al-Mattal: 02-2986529
Mr. Pizza: 02-2403016
Muntaza Restaurant: 02-2956835
New Flamingo's: 02-2966128
Osama's Pizza: 02-2953270
Pizza Inn: 02-2981181/2
Plaza Restaurant & Park: 02-2956020
Pollo-Loco (Mexican): 02-2981984
Pronto Resto-Café (Italian)

02-2987312
Rukab's Ice Cream: 02-2956467
Saba Sandwiches: 02-2960116
Samer: 02-2405338
Sangria's: 02-2956808
Season (Bir Zeit): 02-2950058
Skippy's: 02-2950058
Stones: 02-2966038
Tabash (Jifna): 02-2810932
Taboun: 02-2980505
Orthodox Club: 02-2956520
Urjuwan: 02-2987783/4
Vatche's Garden Restaurant:
    02-2965966
Zarour Barbeque: 02-2956767;
    02-2964480
Ziryab: 02-2959093

III. GETTING AROUND

General Information

Border Crossing Information
Allenby Bridge: 02-9943358/
    3702/483
Sheikh Hussein/Bisan Bridge:
    06-6586422
Erez: 08-2458790
Rafah: 08-6713683-7

Gaza International Airport
Tel: 08-2134119/4129,
    08-2134279/89/99,
    gaza-int@hally.net
    www.gaza-airport.org

Palestine Airways
Tel: 08-282-9526-8,
    www.palairlines.com

Jerusalem Tourist Transportation
Kawasmi Tourist Travel Ltd:
    02-6284769, 02-6284710
Mahfouz Tourist Travel: 02-6282212,
    02-6284015
Mount of Olives: 02-6271122

Car Rentals

Bethlehem
Murad: 02-2747092
Orabi: 050-372687
Petra: 050-511105

Gaza
Imad: 08-2864000
Palestine: 08-2823841
Yafa: 08-2825127

Hebron
Holy Land: 02-2220811

Jericho
Orabi: 050-405095
Petra/Allenby Bridge Branch:
    02-9400494/02-9400493

Jerusalem
Abdo Tourist: 02-6281866
Auto-Nation: 02-5851666 & 050-
    414449
Good Luck: 02-5327126
Dallah Al-Baraka: 02-6564150
Green Peace: 02-5859756
Orabi -02-5853101
Petra: 02-5820716

Nablus
Orabi: 09-2383383

Ramallah
Good Luck: 02-2342160
Mena: 02-2965744
Orabi: 02-2403521
Shkoukany: 02-2954764
Shorouq: 02-2986154
Twins: 02-2964688

Taxis

Bethlehem
Asha'b: 02-2742309
Beit Jala: 02-2742629

Gaza
Azhar: 08-2868858
Midan Filastin: 08-2865242
al-Nasser: 08-2861844/2867845

Hebron
al-Asdiqa': 02-2229436
al-Badawi: 02-2228545
al-Itihad: 02-2228750
al-Khalil: 02-2228276
Maydan al-Quds: 02-2253320
al-Najah: 02-2228996
al-Nissreen: 02-2228346
al-Sha'b: 02-2228726

Jericho
Taxi (Petra): 02-2322525

Jerusalem
Abdo Tourist Taxi: 02-6281866
Aqsa Taxi: 02-6273003
Beit Hanina Taxi: 02-5855777
al-Eman Taxi & Limo Service:
    02-5834599 Fax: 02-5835877
Holy Land Taxi: 02-5855555
Imperial Taxi: 02-6282504
Itihad Taxi: 02-6286941
Jaber Taxi: 02-5855566
Jerusalem of Gold Tourism Taxi:
    02-6737025/6 & 050-259186
Khaled al-Tahan Taxi: 02-5855777
Mount of Olives Taxi: 02-6272777
Nijmah Taxi: 02-6276699
Panorama Taxi: 02-6281116
Rashid Taxi: 02-6282220
al-Sha'ab Taxi: 02-6724908
Ummeh Taxi: 02-2340378

Nablus
al-Ittimad: 09-2371439
al-Madina: 09-2373501

Ramallah

Amer Alam Airport Transfer:
02-2953675
al-Bireh: 02-2402956
Hinnawi Taxi: 02-2956302,
02-2956186
al-Itihad: 02-2955887
Omaya: 02-2956120
Petra 2: 02-2953915
al-Salam: 02-2955805
Shamma' Taxi Co.: 02-2960957
al-Wafa: 02-2955444

Travel Agencies

Bethlehem

Alternative Tourism Group:
02-2772151, Fax: 02-2772211,
atg@p-ol.com
Angels Tours and Travels:
02-2775813, Fax: 02-2775814,
angels@p-ol.com
Crown Tours & Travel Co. Ltd:
02-2740911, Fax: 02-2740910,
crowntt@p-ol.com
Gloria Tours & Travel: 02-274 0835,
Fax: 02-274 3021,
gloria@p-ol.com
Golden Gate Tours & Travel:
02-2766044, Fax: 02-2766045,
ggtours@palnet.com
Guiding Star Ltd: 02-2765970,
Fax: 02-2765971,
info@guidingstar2.com
Kukali Travel & Tours: 02-2773047,
Fax: 02-2772034,
kukali@p-ol.com
Lama Tours International:
02-2743717, Fax: 02-2743747,
litco@p-ol.com
Millennium Transportation:
02-6767727, Fax: 02-6767727
Mousallam International Tours,
02-2770054, Fax: 02-2770054:
mitours@palnet.com
Nativity Travel: 02-2742966,
Fax: 02-2744546

Sky Lark Tours and Travel:
02-2742886, Fax: 02-2764962,
skylark@palnet.com
Terra Santa Tourist Company:
02-2770249, Fax: 02-2770250

Gaza

Halabi Tours and Travel Co.:
08-2823704, Fax: 08-2866075,
halabitours@E-mail.com
Maxim Tours: 07-2824415,
Fax: 07-2867596
al-Muntazah Travel Agency:
08-2827919, Fax: 08-2824923
National Tourist Office: 07-2860616,
Fax: 07-2860682,
shurafa@mtcgaza.com
Time Travel Ltd.: 08-2836775,
Fax: 08-2836855,
timetravel@marna.com

Hebron

al-Amir Tours: 02-2212065,
Fax: 02-2212065,
alamiredu@yahoo.com
Alkiram Tourism: 02-2256501/2,
Fax: 02-2256504,
alkiram@hebronet.com
al-Salam Travel and Tours Co.:
02-2215574, Fax: 02-2233747

Jenin

Asia Travel Agency: 04-2438056,
Fax: 04-2438057

Jerusalem

Abdo Tourist & Travel: 02-6281865,
Fax: 026272973,
abdotours@hotmail.com
Albina Tours: 02-6283397,
Fax: 02-6281215,
albina@netvision.net.il
Arab Tourist Agency (ATA):
02-6277442, Fax: 02-6284366,
jack@a.t.a.wslmail.com
Aswar Tourism Services: 02-6282183,
Fax: 02-6282189,

hai_mou_t_s@yahoo.com
Atic Tours & Travel Ltd.:
    02-6286159, Fax: 02-6264023,
    atictour@palnet.com
Awad & Co. Tourist Agency:
    02-6284021, Fax: 02-6287990,
    admin@awad.tours.com
Aweidah Bros. Co.: 02-6282365,
    Fax: 02-6282366,
    aweidah@netvision.net.il
Ayoub Caravan Tours: 02-6284361,
    Fax: 02-6285804,
    caravan@palnet.com
Bible Land Tours: 02-6271169,
    Fax: 02-6272218,
    links@palnet.com
Blessed Land Tours: 02-6286592,
    Fax: 02-6285812,
    blt@blessedland.com
Carawan Tours & Travel:
    02-2447495, Fax: 02-2349826
Daher Travel: 02-6283235,
    Fax: 02-6271574,
    dahert@netvision.net.il
Dajani Palestine Tours: 02-6264768,
    Fax: 02-6276927,
    dajani@netvision.net.il
Dakkak Tours Agency: 02-6282525,
    Fax: 02-6282526,
    dakkak@netmedia.net.il
4M Travel Agency: 02-6271414,
    Fax: 02-6284701
Gates of Jerusalem Travel Agency:
    02-2344365, Fax: 02-2343835 -
    gates@alqudsnet.com
George Garabedian Company:
    02-6283398, Fax: 02-6287896,
    ggc@ggc-jer.com
Guiding Star Ltd: 02-6273150,
    Fax: 02-6273147,
    mark@guidingstar2.com
J. Sylvia Tours: 02-6281146,
    Fax: 02-6288277,
    sylviatours@yahoo.com
Jiro Tours: 02-6273766,
    Fax: 02-6281020,
    jiro@netvision.net.il
Jordan Tourist Agency: 02-6274389,

Fax: 02-6275037,
    Jordanta@netvision.net.il
Jordan Travel Agency: 02-6284052,
    Fax: 02-6287621
KIM's Tourist & Travel Agency:
    2-6279725, Fax: 02-6274626,
    kim@shabaka.net
Lawrence Tours & Travel:
    02-6284867, Fax: 02-6271285,
    info@lawrence-tours.com
Mt. of Olives Tours Ltd: 02-6271122,
    Fax: 02-6285551,
    moot@netvision.net.il
Nawas Tourist Agency Ltd.:
    02-6282491, Fax: 02-6285755
Near East Tourist Agency (NET):
    02-6282515, Fax: 02-6282415,
    operations@netours.com
New Holy Land Tours: 02-532 3232,
    Fax: 02-532 3292,
    info@holylandtours.biz
O.S. Hotel Services: 02-6289260,
    Fax: 02-6264979,
    oshtls@jrol.com
Overseas Travel Bureau: 02-6287090,
    Fax: 02-6284442,
    otb@netvision.net.il
Pioneer Links Travel & Tourism
    Bureau: 02-6261963,
    Fax: 02-6284714
Safieh Tours & Travel: 02-6264447,
    Fax: 02-6284430
Samara Tourist & Travel Agency:
    02-6276133, Fax: 02-6271956,
    samto@palnet.com
Shepherds Tours & Travel:
    02-6284121, Fax: 02-6280251,
    shepherd@baraka.org
Shweiki Tours Ltd: 02-6736711,
    Fax: 02 6736966
Sindbad Travel Tourist Agency:
    02-6272165, Fax: 02-6272169,
    sindbad1@bezeqint.net
Siniora Star Tours: 02-6286373,
    Fax: 02-6289078,
    travel@siniora.net
Tony Tours Ltd: 02-6288844,
    Fax: 02-6288013,

tonytour@aelia.com
United Travel Ltd: 02-6271247,
    Fax: 02-6283753,
    unidas@palnet.com
Universal Tourist Agency:
    02-6284383, Fax: 02-6264448,
    uta@palnet.com
Zatarah Tourist & Travel Agency:
    02-6272725, Fax: 02-6289873,
    zaatarah@jrol.com

Nablus

Dream Travel & Tourism:
    09-2335056, Fax: 09-2372069
Holiday International: 09-2389159,
    Fax: 09-2840630
Yaish International Tours: 09-2381410,
    Fax: 09-2381437,
    yaishtrl@palnet.com

Ramallah

Adventure Tourism & Travel:
    02-2407705, Fax: 02-2408273,
    info@paladventure.com
Amani Tours: 02-2987013,
    Fax: 02-2987013,
    amanitr@p-ol.com
Anwar Travel Agency: 02-2956388,
    Fax: 02-2956517,
    alaa@palnet.com
Arab Office for Travel & Tourism:
    02-2956640, Fax: 02-2951331
al-Asmar Travel Agency:
    02-2954140, 2965775,
    Fax: 02-2954140, 2965775,
    asmar@p-ol.com
Atlas Tours & Travel: 02-2952180,
    Fax: 02-2986395
al-Awdah Tourism & Travel:
    02-2952597, Fax: 02-2952989
Darwish Travel Agency: 02-2956221,
    Fax: 02-2957940
Golden Globe Tours: 02-2965111,
    Fax: 02-2965110,
    gg-tours@palnet.com
Issis & Co.: 02-2956250,
    Fax: 02-2954305

Jordan River Tourist & Travel
    Agency: 02-2980523,
    Fax: 02-2980524
Kashou' Travel Agency: 02-2955229,
    Fax: 02 2953107,
    mkashou@palnet.com
Pioneer Links Travel & Tourism
    Bureau: 02-2407859,
    Fax: 02-2407860
    pioneer@pioneer-links.com
Raha Tours and Travel: 02-2961780,
    Fax: 02-2961782,
    raha@palnet.com
Ramallah Travel Agency:
    02-2953692, Fax: 02-2955029,
    admin@kaoud.org
Reem Travel Agency: 02-2953871,
    Fax: 02-2953871
Royal Tours: 02-296 6350/1,
    Fax: 02-296 6635,
    royaltours@palnet.com
Salah Tours: 02-2959931,
    Fax: 02-2987206
Shbat & Abdul Nur: 02-2956267,
    Fax: 02-2957246
Skyway Tourist Agency: 02-2965090

Appendix II: Resources on Refugees

This collection of contacts is intended as a portal to the world of organizations related to Palestinian refugees—international, national, and non-governmental. By no means a comprehensive list of all those involved in this field, it aims rather to provide a starting point from which information and other contacts can be gathered.

UNRWA
All inquiries related to the official role of UNRWA should be addressed here. UNRWA is sensitive about information related to it and to Palestinian refugee camps and has thus established a well centralized chain of command to deal with inquiries. **www.unrwa.org**

West Bank: 02-589-0408; Fax: 02-532-2842,
    Media and Communications Officer: Sami Msha'sha', wbpio@unrwa.org
Gaza Strip: 08-677-7488, Fax: 08-677-7219
    Public Information Officer: Jamal Hamad, Gazapio@unrwa.org
Aida Camp: Ibrahim Ghatasheh (Abu Wisam), 02-274-3167
Al-Am'ari Camp: Heidar Eideh, 02-248-6907/8
Aqabat Jaber Camp: Yousef al-Ajjouri, 02-232-2411
Arroub Camp: Issa Abu Khairan (Abu Ramiz), 02-252-2289
Askar Camp: Ibrahim Saleh (Abu Qays), 09-232-7036 or 02-238-8036
Balata Camp: Taysir Dawoud (Abu 'Asem), 09-238-8038
Beit Jibrin Camp: Ibrahim Ghatasheh (Abu Wisam), 02-274-3167,
    (cell 05-025-3020)
Dheisheh Camp: Hussein Shahin, 02-274-2445
Ein Camp (Camp #1): Jamal Mousa, 09-238-8107
Ein al-Sultan Camp: Yousef al-Ajjouri, 02-232-2411
Far'a Camp: Yousef Subouh (Abu Feisal), 09-257-8850
Fawwar Camp: Yousef Halcyqawi (Abu Iyad), 02-228-2663
Jalazone Camp: Mahmoud Radwan Adarbeh, 02-281-0874
Jenin Camp: Ahmed Qassem Obeid, 04-250-1113
Nur Shams Camp: Jamal Buqileh, 09-269-1116
Qalandia Camp: Khalil al-Sous, Tel: 02-585-7827
Shu'fat Camp: Jamal Mohammed Awad, 02-581-5926
Tulkarem Camp: Mohammed Abu Haykal, 09-267-1106

UN Committee on the Exercise of the Inalienable Rights of the Palestinian People
This committee was established to recommend to the UN General Assembly a program of implementation designed to enable the Palestinian people to exercise their inalienable rights, including that of their right to return to their homes and properties.
Visit **www.un.org/Depts/dpa/qpalnew/committee.htm**

UN Division for Palestinian Rights

Provides services for the Committee on the Exercise of the Inalienable Rights of the Palestinian People, including preparing studies and publications relating to the question of Palestine and Palestinian rights. Visit **www.un.org/Depts/dpa/qpalnew/dpr.htm**

Official Palestinian Organizations and Bodies

PLO Department for Refugee Affairs

Contact: Daoud Barakat, 050-464-273, barakat@planet.com

Palestinian Legislative Council (PLC)

Contact: Jamil Shati, 0599-205-121

Non-Governmental Organizations

Badil Resource Center for Palestinian Residency and Refugee Rights

By far the most organized and active resource center on Palestinian refugees, BADIL has also published a series of informational briefs that are considered vanguard material on the subject matter.
P.O. Box 728, Bethlehem
Tel/Fax: 02-274-7346; Tel: 02-277-7086, info@badil.org, **www.badil.org**

Union of Youth Activity Centers (UYAC)

This is the headquarters of a collection of local youth centers found in all camps. The youth centers were originally established with the help of UNRWA but are now entirely run and administered locally. The headquarters coordinates various activities, collects information on the refugee population, and is in constant contact with their grassroots branches.

West Bank Headquarters, Qalandia Refugee Camp
Contact: Wajih Atallah (Abu Marmar)
Tel: 02-583-5731, 050-537-793
Gaza Headquarters, Jabalia Refugee Camp, Contact: Jamal Abu Habal
(Abu Nidal), 08-287-4151, 0599-740-961

Union of Women Activity Centers (UWAC)

Women's Activity Centers are located in all UNRWA-registered camps, to try to provide income-generating projects for refugee women. The headquarters is located in al-Am'ari camp.
Contact: Rifa't Abu Rish, 02-298-1970, 0599-735-759

National Society for the Internally Displaced

The central organization located within the Green Line dedicated to protecting

the rights of Palestinian refugees who are citizens of Israel (known as the internally displaced) and who comprise one quarter of the entire population of Palestinian citizens of Israel (approximately 250,000).
Contact: Suleiman Fahmawi, 04-632-3294, 050-267679

Web Resources

Across Borders
A creative internet project established in 1999 to link Palestinian refugee camps on the web.
www.acrossborders.org

Al-Awda Right of Return Coalition
A non-partisan, international association of activists and organizational representatives lobbying for the Palestinian refugee right of return. Al-Awda is Arabic for "return."
www.al-awda.org

Center for International Studies (FAFO)
A project for the Refugee Working Group established during the peace process that provides research reports and resource bibliographies on Palestinian refugees.
www.fafo.no/IsesWeb/Engelsk/Mainpage

Council for Palestinian Restitution and Repatriation (CPRR)
A non-profit, non-partisan organization established to help Palestinians achieve the right of return.
www.rightofreturn.org

Palestine Remembered
Extensive information about Palestinian refugee villages and lands, including background information, photos, maps, and a discussion forum. English and Arabic.
www.palestineremembered.com

Palestinian Diaspora and Refugee Center (SHAML)
A Ramallah-based NGO dedicated to studying and promoting the rights of Palestinian refugees.
www.shaml.org

Palestinian Refugee Research Net (PRRN)
Extensive listing of research projects, research papers, documents, and internet resources on Palestinian refugees.
www.prrn.org

Palestinian Return Center
A forum for monitoring issues pertaining to the Palestinian diaspora and promoting the right of return.
www.prc.org.uk

Community Organizations in Refugee Camps

Balata Camp
Committee for the Defense of Palestinian Refugee Rights
Established in 1994, together with the Yafa Cultural Center, the Committee aims to promote refugee rights both by providing advocacy and services (computer training, library facilities, and cultural events).
Tel: 09-238-5930

Yafa Cultural Center
YCC is a cultural organization dedicated to the development of skills necessary for the evolution of civil society, which the Center views to be crucial to the realization of an independent Palestinian future based on human rights and democracy.
Balata Camp, Nablus, P.O. Box 1683, West Bank; Contact: Tayseer Nasrallah; 09-233-3553, yafacult@haly.net

Beach Camp
Youth Activities Center
A youth activities center (rebuilt in 1994) offering athletic, social and cultural programs.
Contact: Ali Husseinien; 08-282-2082

Beit Jibrin Camp
Beit Jibrin Cultural Center
Run by a vibrant activist community and many of the camp's youth, this center presents an impressive array of activities for an organization its size.
Contact: Ala al-Azzeh; 054 78-96-741

Breij Camp
Note that Breij shares many organizations and services with neighboring Nuseirat Camp.

Society for the Rehabilitation and Development of Palestinian Homes
Contact: Basima al-Tartouri; 08-253-1960, 08-255-2011

Deir al-Balah Camp
Camp Service Center
08-253-0898

Deir al-Balah Social and Cultural Center
Contact: Imad Abu Ra'nouneh; 08-253-0898

Dheisheh Camp

Ibda' Cultural Center for the Development of Children's Skills and International Cultural Exchange
Contact: Ziad Abbas; 277-6444, 0547-698-215, ibdaa@hotmail.com
www.dheisheh-ibdaa.net

Jabalia Camp

Jabalia Community Service Center
Jabalia's largest social, cultural, and sporting activity center, providing a wide array of activities and services to the Jabalia community, including 15 different sports, a library, computer lab, and community outreach programs.
Contact: Jamal Abu Hbiel; 05974961

Khan Younes Camp

Camp Service Center
Contact: Jamal Ahmed; 08-205-0205, 08-205-1989

Builders of the Future Center
Offers sports, cultural and social programs.
Contact: Maha al-Ra'i; 08-206-6030

Mughazi Camp

Camp Service Center
08-255-7966

Palestine Cultural Center
Contact: Nasser; 08-255-6744

Nuseirat Camp

Refugee Popular Services Committee
Contact: Sherif Ghandeel; 08-255-7744

Rafah Camp

Sanabel/Rafah Educational Enhancement Center
Contact: Darwish Abu Sharkh; 08-213-6779

Rafah Community Center
This community center runs handicraft workshops, literacy programs

Appendix III: UN Agencies

UHCHR – United Nations Office of
the High Commissioner for Human
Rights
Tel: 02-2965534
Fax: 02-2989470
E-mail: ohchr.wb@undp.org
Ramallah

OCHA – United Nations Office for
Humanitarian Affairs
Tel: 02-5829962
Fax: 02-5825841
E-mail: ochaopt@un.org
East Jerusalem

UNDP/PAPP – United Nations
Development Program/Program of
Assistance to the Palestinian People
Tel: 02-6268200
Fax: 02-6268222
E-mail: registry.papp@undp.org,
www.papp.undp.org
East Jerusalem

UNVP – United Nations Volunteer
Program
Tel: 02-6268000
Fax: 02-6268222
E-mail: diana.nammour@undp.org,
www.unv-pal.org/first.asp
East Jerusalem

UNESCO – United Nations
Educational, Scientific and Cultural
Organization
Tel: 02-2959740
Fax: 02- 2959741
E-mail: c.farina@unesco.org
Ramallah

UNFPA – United Nations Population
Fund
Tel: 02-5817167
Fax: 02-5817382

E-mail: unfpa.ps@undp.org,
www.unfpa.ps
East Jerusalem

UNICEF – United Nations
Children's Fund
Tel: 02-5830013
Fax: 02- 5830806
E-mail: Jerusalem@unicef.org,
www.unicef.org
Shu'fat, Jerusalem

UNSCO – UN Special Coordinator
in the Occupied Territories
Tel: 08- 2843555
Fax: 08-2820966
E-mail: UNSCO-Media@un.org
Gaza City

UNTSO – UN Truce Supervision
Organization
Tel: 02 - 5687200
Fax: 02- 5687400
East Jerusalem

WFP – World Food Program
Tel: 02- 5401340
Fax: 02-5401453
E-mail: jean-luc.siblot@wfp.org
East Jerusalem

WHO – World Health Organization
Tel: 02-5400595
Fax: 025810193
E-mail: info@who-health.org
East Jerusalem

ILO – International Labor
Organization
Tel: 02-6260212
Fax: 02-6276746
E-mail: khaled.doudine@undp.org,
www.ilo.org
East Jerusalem

Appendix IV: Index of Places

Qalqilia, 95, 97, 98, 196, 205–209
    zoo, 37, 206–207
Qannir, 192
al-Qasbah Museum (Nablus), 217
Qastal, 342
Qasr al-Basha (Gaza), 3, 435–436
Qasr Hisham, see Hisham's Palace
Qasr al-Shaykh (Kur), 198
Qasr al-Yahud, see Deir al-Qaddis
    Yahanna al-Ma'madan
Qastina, 446, 451
Qatoun, 423
Qatra, 446, 450
Qattaneh, 450, 451
Qolonieh, 335
Qubeiba, 335
al-Quds, see Jerusalem
Qumran, 298–299
Quos al-Abid (Bethlehem), 363
Quos al-Zarara (Bethlehem), 364
Quarter of the Knights (Acre), see
    Underground Crusader city

R

Radwan Baths, see al-Wazir Bathhouse
al-Radwan Castle, see Qasr al-Basha
Rafah, 10, 423, 445
Rafah (refugee camp), 448, 454,
    455–457
Rafat, 278
Rafidia (Nablus), 211
Rahat, 462–463
Railway Museum (Haifa), 123
al-Ramal Mosque (Acre), 108, 111
Ramallah, 3, 4, 62, 64, 69, 71, 92–93,
    95, 99, 104, 265–281
Ramallah Cultural Palace, 270
Ramet al-Khalil, see Haram al-Rameh
Ramleh, 10, 37, 104, 200, 237,
    251–257, 259, 269, 279, 280,
    301, 344, 346, 392, 451, 462
Ras Karkar, 278
Ras al-Kheimeh, 446
Ras Shamra (Syria),
Red Mosque (Safad), 144
al-Rehaniyeh, 192
Remal (Gaza), 440
Rihaniya, 145

Rockefeller Museum (Jerusalem),
    330–331
Roman cemetery (Nablus), 211
Roman theater (Caesarea), 137
Russian Church of St. Mary
    Magdalene (Jerusalem), 331
Russian cemetery (Bir es-Saba), 466

S

Sabarin, 280
Sabastiya, 7, 221–222
Sabbarreen, 192
Sabil Subakh (Lydd), 262
Sabra (Gaza), 440
Sadoun Janzeh, 279
Safad, 3, 12, 13, 16, 139–145, 147
Saffuriya, 177, 179
St. Andrew's Church (Acre), 110
St. Andrew's Church (Jerusalem), 339
St. Etienne's Monastery (Jerusalem), 326
St. George's Cathedral (Jerusalem), 327
St. Gabriel's Church (Haifa), 122
St. George's Church (Acre), 110
St. James Cathedral (Jerusalem), 318,
    322
St. John's Church (Acre), 110
St. John the Baptist Church
    (Jerusalem), 315
St. John the Baptist Monastery, see
    Deir al-Qaddis Yahanna al-
    Ma'madan
St. Joseph's Church (Haifa), 122
St. Louis French Hospital, 248
St. Mary's Church (Acre), 110
St. Mary of the Germans Church
    (Jerusalem), 326
St. Peter's Monestery (Jaffa), 245
St. Stephen's Gate, see Lions' Gate
St. Theodosius Monastery
    (Bethlehem), 369–370
Sakhnin, 179, 181
Sakiyeh, 280
al-Saksak Mosque, 245
Salfit, 222
al-Salqa, 423
al-Samara Public Bath (Gaza), 438–439
Samu, 391
Sanur, 189